Religion and Politics in America

ARELIGION AND POLITICS IN A
MERICA

Faith, Culture, and Strategic Choices

FOURTH EDITION

ROBERT BOOTH FOWLER
University of Wisconsin–Madison

LAURA R. OLSON
Clemson University

ALLEN D. HERTZKE
University of Oklahoma

KEVIN R. DEN DULK
Grand Valley State University

WESTVIEW
PRESS

A MEMBER OF THE PERSEUS BOOKS GROUP

Find us on the World Wide Web at www.westviewpress.com.

Every effort has been made to secure required permissions to use all images,
maps, and other art included in this volume.

Westview Press books are available at special discounts for bulk purchases in
the United States by corporations, institutions, and other organizations. For
more information, please contact the Special Markets Department at the
Perseus Books Group, 2300 Chestnut Street, Suite 200, Philadelphia, PA
19103, or call (800) 810-4145, ext. 5000, or e-mail
special.markets@perseusbooks.com.

Library of Congress Cataloging-in-Publication Data
Religion and politics in America : faith, culture, and strategic choices /
Robert Booth Fowler ... [et al.]. — 4th ed.
     p. cm.
   Includes bibliographical references and index.
   ISBN 978-0-8133-4436-2 (alk. paper)
   1. Religion and politics—United States. 2. United States—Religion. 3.
United States—Politics and government. I. Fowler, Robert Booth, 1940–
   BL2525.F677 2010
   322'.10973—dc22
                              2009047220

10 9 8 7 6 5 4 3 2 1

To our students

CONTENTS

LIST OF ILLUSTRATIONS

TABLES

FIGURES

BOXES

PREFACE

Religion and politics and the dynamic interactions between them are visible every-where in the United States—and they are the focus of this book. We see the contin-uing presence of the conservative religious movement and its concerns with abortion, homosexuality, sex education, and family breakdown—as well as its in-creasing interest in human rights, the environment, and poverty. We also see the assertiveness of the Roman Catholic Church, which allies itself with evangelical Protestants on abortion and educational choice and with mainline Protestants on foreign policy and social welfare issues. We note the enduring legacy of African American churches in American politics, as well as the increasing political relevance of Latino religious expressions. We continue to observe vigorous lobbying efforts by progressive religious groups, both Protestant and Catholic. We consider the prominent role of Jewish groups in American politics, especially regarding support for Israel and the continuing efforts of the United States's growing Muslim popu-lation to gain political influence. We watch the persistent flood of cases in the Amer-ican judicial system, especially cases brought by religious minority groups. Everywhere one looks, religion and politics appear to be intertwined in American public life.

The aim of this book is to understand the politics of religion in the United States and to appreciate the strategic choices that politicians and religious participants make when they participate in politics. We try to make sense of how religion and politics come together in the voting booth, Congress and the state legislatures, the executive branch, the courts, the interest group system, and the larger culture of the United States. The subject is large and complex, and it features fascinating and often contradictory currents. It is a topic of tremendous importance because we believe one can understand American politics and society today only with an appreciation of religion's role in them.

We have worked hard to make this book accessible. Although we take account of what many political scientists, historians, and other scholars have said about religion and politics, our goal through four editions has been to produce a readable and informative text, not a scholarly tome. We have thoroughly updated the content from the third edition here to reflect current trends and important changes in the relationship between religion and politics. One of the challenges we have faced in preparing this edition relates to the very nature of American religion—its real and ever-growing pluralism, its diverse regional and ethnic bases, and its tendency to change rapidly. These characteristics preclude the possibility of any single definition of religion. Moreover, we are not especially attracted to elaborate philosophical or linguistic attempts to define such a changing and fluid concept as religion. Rather, we define religion phenomenologically. That is, we discuss the politics of religion in the United States with the understanding that what the culture generally treats as religion (or as a religion), we do too—from Protestantism in all of its varieties, to Judaism, Roman Catholicism, Islam, the LDS Church, and innumerable other faiths. Despite the great religious diversity of American culture, religion is ordinarily assumed to involve the acknowledgment and worship of a transcendent god or gods, spirit, or force. Usually it is more specific than the alternate definition, which would suggest that any general system of meaning is a religion.

We endeavor to strike a balance between providing enough information and cluttering the narrative with endless nuance. Historical background, we believe, is an essential part of this context, so we devote an entire chapter to historical roots, in addition to providing historical details elsewhere in the text. As we present the big picture, we may oversimplify at times or give short shrift to some subjects. For example, there are plenty of complexities today in the relationship between evangelical Protestants and Roman Catholics, and we discuss many of them in various chapters. But the most significant development may be their emerging cooperation—a fact that can be appreciated only if one understands the deep historical antipathy between these two groups.

Our book also depicts the arena of struggle and strategic calculation, of the clashing ideals and necessary compromise that mark all of politics, a concept we define as conflict and agreement in public life. We shift back and forth between describing practical politics, religious traditions, and theology. We try to illuminate religious politics as it operates in government, among clashing interest groups, and in American voting behavior. At the same time, we explore the nature of citizens' faiths and the personal values that have so much effect on their political beliefs and behaviors. Only by doing both tasks may the dynamics of religion in American politics today be appreciated.

Chapter 1 of this book begins with a thematic interpretation of religion and politics in American history. We avoid presenting a merely chronological review because we are more interested in broad themes that resonate with current issues. We move to the contemporary scene in Chapter 2, where we describe the status of religion in America today. Here we examine the religious affiliations of the American people, their religious practices, and the theological and political outlooks of major Christian religious traditions in America—evangelical Protestantism, mainline Protestantism, and Catholicism. In Chapter 3 we turn to the politics of Judaism; Islam; the LDS Church; and other, smaller religious traditions in the United States. Not only do such traditions highlight important themes in religion and politics, they sometimes have a tangible impact on politics in the United States. In the next three chapters we turn to practical politics: voting and party politics in Chapter 4, lobbying in Chapter 5, and political elites in Chapter 6. Chapter 7, which is new to the fourth edition, examines the intersection of religion and political culture, and especially the role that religion plays in fostering the values and norms of American democracy.

This brings us to the legal and constitutional arenas, which are the subject of Chapters 8 and 9. Here we consider clashing views about the meaning of the First Amendment's provision for religious free exercise and its prohibition of official religious establishment. We explore crucial court cases that have defined church-state law and indelibly shaped the way religion and government interact; we also examine various legal interest groups involved in the relevant legal battles both within and outside of the courtroom. We then explore several important topics that merit focused treatment, including Latino and African American religion in Chapter 10 and gender, religion, and politics in Chapter 11. Finally, in Chapter 12 we discuss several broad theories that attempt to explain religious politics in America today. Looking at the big picture helps us to understand the fascinating, ever-changing world of politics and religion in America.

Several individuals helped immeasurably in the preparation of this book. We would like to thank Toby Wahl, our editor at Westview, for his advice and patience. John Green of the University of Akron and the Pew Forum on Religion & Public Life shared voting data from the University of Akron's 2008 National Survey of

Religion and Politics. Corwin Smidt of Calvin College shared data from the Paul B. Henry Institute's 2008 National Survey on Religion and Public Life. The Pew Forum on Religion & Public Life proved an invaluable source of information, data, and support. We also benefited from the excellent research assistance of Cohen Simpson at Clemson University. To all, we are very grateful.

1

RELIGION AND POLITICAL CULTURE IN AMERICA: THE HISTORICAL LEGACY

It would be very difficult to understand American politics today without knowing something about American religion. And it would be equally difficult to understand either politics or religion without a sense of history, a sense of how the interplay among religion, politics, and culture has shaped the story of the United States. Since colonial days, religion has played a profound role in molding American culture, directly and indirectly, in ways that no one at the time of the founding could ever have imagined or predicted. In order to sort out the complex history of the relationships among religion, politics, and culture, we have organized this chapter around four themes: the Puritan temper, pluralism, the evangelical dimension, and populism.

THE PURITAN TEMPER

The United States was born of religious zeal. Its colonization coincided with, and was fueled by, vast upheavals in Europe that had been unleashed by the Protestant Reformation. None of these was as important as the Puritan revolution, which shook England and inspired many to emigrate to the New World. Today the term *puritanical* connotes a narrow-minded, self-righteous rejection of anything pleasurable. But the Puritan legacy is something quite different. The Puritans bequeathed to Americans strong civic institutions, a sense of national mission, and a reformist impulse that continues to shape American society and political culture.

The Puritans earned their name from their desire to "purify" the Church of England and, more broadly, society itself in the late 1500s and early 1600s. Inspired by Calvinist Reformed theology, Puritans reacted vehemently against what they saw as laxity and corruption in Christian churches. Infused with a sense of moral urgency, Puritans threatened established political and religious elites, and they often suffered persecution as a result of their agitation. But if the encrusted Old World of Europe resisted renovation, the American colonies offered a fresh start. Thus the Puritans (along with other religious dissenters) found their way to the American seaboard in the early 1600s.[1]

Although the American colonies were characterized by religious diversity from the beginning, the Puritans brought with them such a powerful vision that they exercised a disproportionate influence for a century and a half before the Revolutionary War. Many people at the time, regardless of their denominational affiliation, embraced the central tenets of Puritanism, and several of the leading colonial intellectuals were Puritan ministers.[2]

To the Puritans, the new land was not just a place where they could freely exercise their religion. It was literally the New Israel, the Promised Land on which the faithful could build a holy commonwealth unencumbered by Old World corruption. The Puritans called their mission an "Errand in the Wilderness" and saw it as divinely ordained. In the celebrated Puritan phrase, America was to be "a city upon a hill," a light to all nations. This sense of the New World's providential destiny continues to fascinate, mystify, and not infrequently horrify people in other countries. From the "manifest destiny" of westward expansion, to Abraham Lincoln's determination to preserve the Union, to Woodrow Wilson's quest to "make the world safe for democracy," to John Kennedy's Peace Corps, to George W. Bush's "war on terror," Americans have continued the Puritan legacy by acting on a sense of special mission and destiny. Understanding this legacy is especially important now that the United States strives to define its global responsibilities in a complex world—often in the face of resistance from other countries.

Puritan doctrine also helped to nurture self-government in the new land.[3] Puritans articulated a "covenant theology" that was a blatant rejection of the long-standing "divine right of kings" doctrine. As the Puritans saw it, political leaders did not derive their authority directly from God; instead, Puritans favored a model of government based on a community's covenant with God. Puritan churches were autonomous, self-governing parishes. This "congregational" tradition gave rise to a parallel political preference for community self-governance.

To be sure, the Puritan conception of democracy was hardly today's understanding of democracy. Only the religious "elect," or church members, were allowed to participate. People could become church members only by persuading church leaders that they were most likely predestined for salvation; this status was understood to be enjoyed by only a small percentage of the population. But even if the Puritan colonies were more theocracies than democracies, they fostered a form of self-government from the start. Christian colonists had become outraged by 1775 as England and its established church continued to assert authority over the colonies. By then, the colonists had governed themselves for more than a century, and their religious doctrine, they believed, justified their action.[4]

The Puritan emphasis on all humans' tendency to sin also affected American politics, though scholars disagree on the extent. Certainly the Puritans' skeptical view of human nature contributed to the American fear of concentrated governmental power. If political leaders are as tempted by sin as other human beings, then precautions against abuse must be built into the system. Thus some scholars see evidence of the residual cultural influence of Puritan doctrine in James Madison's concern about diffusing and checking power in the U.S. Constitution. Others note that early Americans largely avoided romantic and utopian thinking of the sort that led to the excesses of the French Revolution. A deeply ingrained understanding of sin thus tempered the early American practice of popular democracy.[5]

In addition, throughout the nation's history, many Americans have based their social practices on the Puritan understanding of the need to restrain individual sin for the good of the community. As the French observer Alexis de Tocqueville noted in the 1830s, the majority of Americans shared the Puritan conviction that "freedom" did not mean license to do anything one pleased, but rather the ability to do those things that are good and right. Tocqueville found Americans remarkably faithful to this ideal in their organization of churches, schools, communities, and families. Powerful socialization forces restrained human impulses deemed destructive to the community.[6] Thus morally intrusive laws and practices that may seem suffocating today were actually viewed as helpful in early America, as they would liberate the individual from "slavery to sin."[7]

And many Americans continue to share these views. When popular radio commentator and psychologist James Dobson argues that Satan uses human appetites, greed, and lust to destroy us, he is echoing the basic Puritan understanding of the world. So is the Rev. Jesse Jackson when he argues that the moral laws contained in the Ten Commandments protect the individual from self-destructive behavior and are thus "liberating."[8]

Puritans emphasized the community's central role in nurturing and restraining the individual. This aspect of their outlook is receiving renewed attention today. The Puritans and their heirs could be harsh, but their focus on community meant that people were not isolated. Women were not abandoned if they became widows; orphans were cared for; people did not suffer from rootlessness. Religious mores and strong communities restrained the atomizing tendencies unleashed by modern political freedom. Even today most Americans continue to align themselves at least nominally with religious groups, even if their attendance is sporadic, in part just because they perceive vestiges of this sense of community in congregations.[9]

Finally, Puritanism bequeathed to the nation a mighty store of moral zeal that often did not recognize that shades of gray are needed in a political system whose lifeblood is compromise. Critics note how Puritan clergy moved with equal stridency from depicting the French as anti-Christian during the French and Indian War to viewing the British in similar terms only a decade later during the American Revolution.[10] More sympathetic voices note that politics sometimes cries out for an infusion of religious conviction and fervor. Where would the nation be, they ask, without the uncompromising fervor of the abolitionists in the nineteenth century or the reformist energies of suffragists?

Whether for good or ill, we see evidence of this zeal among religionists across the political spectrum today. When today's religious leaders prophesy against the evils of society and equate their political struggles with God's cause, they are exemplifying the American Puritan tradition.

RELIGIOUS FREEDOM AND PLURALISM

Important though the Puritan legacy was and is, the reality of religious pluralism played an equally powerful role in shaping the nation's history. The roots of the dominant characteristic of American religion today—its almost bewildering multiplicity of religions, denominations, theologies, and organizational styles—may be traced to early colonial patterns. Moreover, the American break with the 1,500-year European tradition of maintaining a state-established church, as well as the eventual constitutional protection for religious freedom, combined to allow religious pluralism to flourish in the New World. And no one in any way planned this confluence of events.

Most colonies installed official state churches. The New England colonies formally designated the Congregational (Puritan) Church as their official faith; Maryland was officially a Catholic colony; most southern colonies established the Anglican Church (the Church of England, which later became known as the Episcopal Church in the United States). This commonplace practice of establishing an official faith meant citizens had to pay a tax to support the colonial church and had to be married by a government-supported clergyperson.[11]

Despite the existence of these established churches, members of other religious groups, including Jews, Quakers, Baptists, and many more, all found more room to practice their faiths in the New World than they had in Europe. If one found Massachusetts too suffocating, there was always Rhode Island, home to a host of dissenters, or New York, which had received numerous Jewish settlers by the late seventeenth century. Then there were the middle colonies—especially Pennsylvania, where religious freedom was official policy from the start—which modeled religious tolerance for the rest of the new nation. And there was always the seemingly endless wilderness, which became a haven to religious nonconformists and visionaries. So Catholics settled in Maryland and tolerated Protestants; Quakers settled in Pennsylvania and tolerated Lutherans; Baptists agitated for their own freedom in a number of colonies. The idea of a society in which each faith tolerated all others in order to enjoy its own freedom took root.[12]

Religious tolerance was strengthened in the late eighteenth century when the Constitution and the Bill of Rights were drafted and adopted, officially founding the United States. The framers of the U.S. Constitution faced an enormous challenge: knitting together thirteen colonies with different cultures, religions, economies, and climates. The solutions were born of necessity and compromise, as we can see in the language of the religion clauses of the First Amendment, which are clearly an attempt to address the complexities of religious pluralism: "Congress shall make no law respecting an establishment of religion, or prohibiting the free exercise thereof." The federal government will not be allowed to favor one religion over all others, nor will it have the power to limit the practice of any particular religion.

Then as now, the idea of religious freedom meant different things to different people. Some of the framers, such as Benjamin Franklin, Thomas Jefferson, and James Madison, hoped to reduce clergy's interference with politics, which to them represented a vestige of the corrupt and oppressive European world. Others were Enlightenment deists who believed in a God who had set the universe on course with natural laws and then left it alone. They saw a chance to create an enduring United States free of the intense religious squabbles that infected the Old World.

Jefferson, a religious skeptic who wrote his own version of the New Testament in which he did not affirm Christ as God, authored the Virginia Statute of Religious Freedom (a precursor to the First Amendment). Madison shared Jefferson's belief that leaving individual conscience unfettered by the state would be the best guide in religion and morality. He therefore joined Jefferson's effort to disestablish the state church in Virginia.

But this is not the full story. Fervent Baptists, along with other religious dissenters, strongly supported constitutional protection of religious freedom and an end to state support for Virginia's established church. Persecuted by Anglican authorities in the southern colonies and Puritan leaders in New England, Baptists remembered the times when they had been jailed for seeking marriages outside the established church or for refusing to pay the church tax. As a result they were natural allies of separationists such as Jefferson and Madison.

Even for those Christians who initially favored state-established churches, the sheer necessity of protecting their own faiths ultimately led them to support religious freedom. Given the religious pluralism already present in the thirteen colonies, no one could ensure that any particular church would be the one established by the new national government. All believers wanted freedom for themselves, but they concluded that the "only way to get it for themselves was to grant it to all others."[13]

The bold national experiment in religious freedom, as embodied in the First Amendment, did set the stage for an end to established churches in the states. Even though the language of the Religion Clauses was understood to prohibit only establishment by the *federal* government, the national model eventually swept through the states, which took it upon themselves to end the practice. Massachusetts was the last state to do away with its official faith, disestablishing the Congregational Church in 1833.[14]

This ideal of church-state separation and religious freedom is deeply ingrained in American culture today. It is also one of the central contributions of the United States to the world. To understand the uniqueness of the American experiment, it is necessary only to observe that from the time of the Emperor Constantine in the fourth century to the founding of the colonies in the seventeenth century, European practice and doctrine always had been to establish an official religion by law. So embedded is this practice in Europe that government support for religion continues to this day even though most European countries are largely secular. On the other hand, from the start the United States never had a state-established national religion, which has had the somewhat ironic effect of allowing religion to flourish.

By the nineteenth century in the United States, state governments continued to help organized religion in a few ways, but religious institutions were mostly on their own. Cut off from the paternalistic hand of government and largely freed from persecution, churches became voluntary associations, dependent almost entirely upon the continued support of their members for survival. And contrary to what some expected, churches thrived. Indeed, in the wake of disestablishment, remarkable religious growth and innovation occurred in the nineteenth century, spurred by those faith traditions—especially the Baptist and Methodist varieties of Christianity—that adapted best to the rapidly changing conditions of life on the frontier. Unsupported by the state and facing all the challenges of westward expansion, "volunteerist churches" sprang up as circuit-riding ministers traveled west to preach the gospel.

A new kind of entrepreneurial climate fostered the emergence of a multiplicity of worship styles and faith interpretations. If you did not like the local minister or if you held unorthodox views, you could always join a new congregation or form your own. Such freedom was unheard of in Europe, and (to a lesser extent) even on the east coast of the United States. Churches blossomed and new faith traditions sprouted as religious entrepreneurs competed with one another for the loyalty of the faithful. Religious practice, in turn, adapted endlessly to changing economic and social circumstances as Americans pressed westward. The peculiar vitality of American religion that we observe today (in contrast to the relatively moribund state churches of Europe) owes its origin to this unique blend of religious freedom, evangelical fervor, and frontier life.

The fruit of this nineteenth-century pioneer religious culture was a proliferation of religious experiments, from utopian communities to the practice of transcendentalism. Another development was the rise of millennial sects. Convinced they could divine the coming of the End Times prophesied in scripture, charismatic leaders of the nineteenth century forged new denominations and contributed to the eschatological theology of modern fundamentalism. A host of movements and sects today trace their lineage to this era. The immense popularity of the Left Behind series of novels and related media (including movies, music, and even a video game), which focus on the End Times, is an indication of the continuing appeal of millennial religion in America today.[15]

This God-intoxicated culture also produced religious movements in the nineteenth century that the Protestant-dominated society viewed as threats. The most important of these was the Church of Jesus Christ of Latter-day Saints (LDS Church), whose adherents are called Mormons. Its story illustrates the limits of tolerance and how religious clashes in America sometimes took violent turns. The Mormon story also illustrates how the American experience can give rise to a popular new faith, one with worldwide membership that is continuing to grow rapidly in the twenty-first century.

Mormons trace their origins to the vision of Joseph Smith Jr. of Palmyra, New York, who claimed to have found sacred tablets describing how the lost tribe of Israel migrated to the New World. A farmer's son with limited formal education, Smith published his translations of the sacred tablets in 1830, thereby writing what became known as the Book of Mormon, which Mormons take to be an additional testament of Jesus Christ. Within a few years of the book's publication, Smith's following became a serious new movement within Christianity.[16]

But the new religious movement Smith fashioned, which was fervent, disciplined, and situated outside of the mainstream with its practice of polygamy, aroused the enmity of neighbors. Smith's followers were chased successively out of New York, Ohio, Missouri, and Illinois. Smith himself fled a near war in Missouri (where the governor issued an extermination order against Mormons); after founding the city of Nauvoo, Illinois, he was arrested by the Illinois state militia. Before Smith could stand trial, a lynch mob stormed the jail in Carthage, Illinois, and killed him. Smith's successor, Brigham Young, then led the faithful across the Rocky Mountains to safety in the Salt Lake Valley, where he founded what amounted to a theocratic nation.[17]

The safe haven was short lived, however, because the territory of Utah came under United States control in 1848, following the Mexican War. To Protestant society the Mormon practice of polygamy (which was grounded in their interpretation of faith) was repugnant, and politicians responded aggressively. President James Buchanan ordered troops to besiege Salt Lake City in 1857, and Congress followed suit by passing a series of laws outlawing polygamy in the territories. Penalties included the confiscation of church property and the loss of citizenship privileges. These actions, which the U.S. Supreme Court deliberated in its 1879 decision in *Reynolds* v. *United States*, ultimately succeeded in forcing Mormons to conform to the marital norms of mainstream American society. LDS Church leaders issued a declaration late in the nineteenth century against plural marriages and pledged loyalty to the laws of the United States. Only then could Utah be admitted to the Union, which officially happened in 1896.[18]

In addition to homegrown pluralism, of course, immigration also fueled religious diversity and continues to do so. By far the most important legacy of the nineteenth century was the dramatic expansion of the Roman Catholic population in the United States. From the mid-1800s on, successive waves of immigrants from Catholic countries such as Ireland, Italy, and Poland poured into the United States. This phenomenon produced a long-enduring cultural divide in American history—the Catholic-Protestant split—which shaped partisan political loyalties for over a century and a half. Indeed, one cannot understand the significance of John F. Kennedy's election to the presidency in 1960 or of current political alliances between Catholics and evangelical Protestants without appreciating how much the divide between Protestants and Catholics once shaped American political history.

The first large wave of Roman Catholics arrived in the 1840s and 1850s, as Irish immigrants settled in American cities and built a vigorous and public Catholic Church. A second group came from Germany in the second half of the nineteenth century. A third came at the turn of the century, this time from southern, central, and eastern Europe. As the American Catholic presence grew, some political issues took on overtones reflecting religious division. Temperance was in part a Protestant attempt to discipline Catholic drinkers; campaigns against corrupt big-city party machines also were partly a reaction against the political power of Catholic immigrants and their descendants. Even before the Civil War there were occasional Catholic-Protestant skirmishes. Civil War draft riots in New York, in which Irish Catholics protested military conscription, reflected their resistance to the evangelical Protestant tendency to view the Civil War as a holy crusade.

Political parties, which were much stronger in the late nineteenth century than they are today, naturally channeled this cultural combat, especially in the North. There, Protestant voters were disproportionately Republican, whereas most Catholics became loyal Democrats. Some vestiges of this division linger to this day. As we will see in Chapter 4, white Protestants as a group are still more Republican than are Catholics.

One of the most graphic examples of the Catholic-Protestant split concerned education. Although church and state institutions were constitutionally separated in nineteenth-century America, Protestant domination of society produced an unofficial, cultural Protestant establishment. Public schools frequently used texts—from the Protestant King James Bible to the McGuffey Readers—that promoted Protestant values. Catholics developed their own parochial school system and, where they were strong enough, pushed for state aid for it. Protestants fought against such efforts.

After the Civil War, Catholics intensified their effort to secure public support for their church-run schools. Protestant fealty to the Republican Party produced its response: the Blaine Amendment, an attempt by the Republican administration of

Ulysses S. Grant to amend the U.S. Constitution to prohibit any state governmental aid to parochial schools. Introduced in the House of Representatives by James G. Blaine of Maine in 1875, the amendment became a symbol of anti-Catholic sentiment among the Protestant majority (Blaine, a Republican, became associated with the charge that the Democrats were the party of "Rum, Romanism, and Rebellion"). The proposed constitutional amendment passed the House but fell short of the two-thirds vote needed in the Senate. Republican platforms from 1876 to 1892, however, continued to call for an end to government aid to sectarian schools.

These kinds of battles continued to be fought at the state level. Many states passed a version of the Blaine Amendment in their own constitutions, but state-level restriction of parochial education did not end there. In the 1920s, for example, Catholics had to take their case all the way to the U.S. Supreme Court when the State of Oregon decreed that all children had to attend public schools—in effect making parochial systems illegal. Catholics won, and the Oregon law was overturned.[19] With that victory, however, the battle shifted once again to state public support, which remains a major constitutional issue today.

THE EVANGELICAL DIMENSION

Intimately linked with both the Puritan heritage and the American experiment in religious freedom is the strong evangelical dimension of American religion. We mean "evangelical dimension" in two senses. First, we mean the branch of Protestantism that is deeply committed to the Bible as the only authoritative source of God's revelation and stresses the adult conversion ("born-again") experience and vigorous evangelizing (seeking converts).

Second, the evangelical dimension also refers to the fact that all major churches, to some extent, had to adopt evangelizing strategies to survive in the American religious marketplace. Because evangelical Protestants have been assertive about seeking converts, evangelical Protestantism has become the paradigm of successful religious growth in America. But whether Protestant or Catholic, Mormon or Muslim, any faith must spread the word—that is, evangelize—to thrive. And given the close link between culture and politics, this sense of evangelicalism often produces political fallout.

These two senses of the evangelical dimension are strongly related. In a major study of religious growth and decline from the revolutionary era to today, Roger Finke and Rodney Stark contend that there is a consistent pattern in which disestablishment, religious freedom, and the frontier have combined to produce a "religious marketplace."[20] In this marketplace, religious faiths thrive or decline on the basis of how well they serve the needs of existing and potential members. And contrary to what we might expect, the faiths that thrive are often those that are most conservative, most evangelical, and most in tension with the broader culture.[21]

Finke and Stark's study supports what others have argued: Sometimes the intensity of the religious experience offered by a particular faith tradition wanes over time; this is usually due to the fact that members become comfortable and worldly. Clergy contribute to this decline in intensity when they grow complacent and accommodating. As a result the religious message becomes watered down, and the church[22] itself becomes unable to convey a powerful message about the meaning of life. People yearning for such meaning will therefore leave and seek out other religious settings. And there is ample evidence that the United States today is a nation of seekers; in fact many people who do not profess any particular faith attend religious services anyway in search of answers to life's questions.[23] As Dean Kelley notes, the "business of religion is meaning," and many evangelical faiths convey that they really mean what they preach with their often-demanding style. Churches that do not convey such conviction cannot expect to flourish.[24] Religious communities must distinguish themselves by conveying clear, consistent, and meaningful messages.

In American history we do observe this pattern of rising sects and the decline of once-dominant churches. For example, Puritan sects of the seventeenth century, which were otherworldly and severe, eventually were transformed into the comfortable Congregational churches of the eighteenth century. When they became more comfortable, these churches lost a good share of their members to the new evangelical congregations born of revivals in the 1730s and 1740s. As these churches in turn became comfortable with the world and less distinct from the mainstream culture, upstart Methodist and Baptist congregations, which had grown dramatically since the founding era, eclipsed them. The cycle continued: As Methodism became the home of an increasingly settled membership and its ministers grew less strict about enforcing traditional rules in the late nineteenth century, a fervent Holiness religious movement drew away a significant portion of its membership (Box 1.1).

This market dynamic occurs because many people turn to religion in part because they seek something distinct and different from what can be found in the broader culture. When churches become too accommodating and worldly, they offer a less unique experience and therefore cease to address this need. Some measure of sect-like tension with the world, along with an evangelical zeal, is a key to continued church success.[25]

The great religious movements in American history have often stimulated significant political upheaval. Consider several major examples of political fallout from Protestant evangelical revivalism, beginning in the eighteenth century and continuing into the twentieth.

Special Case: Evangelicals, Slavery, and the Civil War

One of the characteristics of evangelicalism in America has been its Puritan tendency to view politics at times as an unambiguous, cosmic struggle between good and evil. We see this evangelical temper in one of the most momentous, religiously infused movements in the nation's history: the crusade against slavery. No issue so tormented the young nation as slavery, America's "original sin." Black people came to the New World in bondage, which was a contradiction with both professed political ideals and Christian beliefs from the beginning. Some early leaders such as George Washington and Thomas Jefferson acknowledged this contradiction but did almost nothing to address it. The Quaker faith expelled slaveholding members

---

BOX 1.1   ARE HIGHLY PAID MINISTERS THE SIGN OF A DECLINING CHURCH?

Yes, say Roger Finke and Rodney Stark. In their book *The Churching of America*, Finke and Stark demonstrate that there has been an inverse ratio between clergy salaries and church vitality throughout American history. Upstart churches with few material resources depend on ministers, who are willing to make extraordinary sacrifices for their cause.

Low-paid, circuit-riding clergy transformed the Methodist Church from a tiny sect in the mid-1700s into the largest denomination in the United States a century later. The Methodist Church grew rapidly in relation to Congregational, Episcopal, and Presbyterian churches, which paid their ministers far more. But as the Methodist Church became more affluent and comfortable with the world—and paid its clergy accordingly—it began to lose its vigor, stopped placing high expectations on its members, and slipped into decline. Methodism thus has lost its "market share" to Baptist and Pentecostal churches, both of which still have an abundance of low-paid clergy.

Source: Roger Finke and Rodney Stark, *The Churching of America 1776–2005: Winners and Losers in Our Religious Economy* (New Brunswick, NJ: Rutgers University Press, 2005).

in 1776, and antislavery societies sprouted among some churchgoing people, particularly in the North. But the practice of slavery was so entrenched by the late eighteenth century that the Constitution itself made a "pact with the devil" by accepting servitude and allowing southern states to count, for purposes of allocating members in the House of Representatives, three-fifths of their enslaved population.

A revolution against slavery began in northern thinking in the early 1800s as more antislavery societies sprang up in the wake of religious revivals. These revivals awakened Christian consciences against slavery, and churches increasingly became the fulcrum of antislavery agitation through the decades leading up to the Civil War. Many great revivalists and preachers eventually joined the cause. During debate over the Kansas-Nebraska Bill, which allowed the extension of slavery into new territories, Congress was presented with a petition from 3,000 New England ministers who opposed the bill.[26]

This heightened northern agitation served only to harden southern attitudes. White southern evangelicals came to view the defense of their land and institutions (including slavery) as divinely ordained, and biblical justifications for slavery became common.[27] The evangelical tendency to see political clashes as spiritual struggles between good and evil increasingly characterized both sides of the debate about slavery. Thus the irreconcilable conflict was, in some sense, a clash of evangelicals.

When war came, preachers in both camps depicted their cause in religious terms. From the pulpits of both the North and South came invocations of God's wrath toward the other side in martial prayers of vivid and bloody mien. Hymns similarly carried an almost apocalyptic message, as this stanza of Julia Ward Howe's "Battle Hymn of the Republic" shows:

> *I have read a fiery gospel, writ in burnished rows of steel.*
> *"As ye deal with my contemners, so with you my grace shall deal";*
> *Let the Hero, born of woman, crush the serpent with his heel,*
> *Since God is marching on.*

But how could both sides invoke God? And how could anyone find God's will in the carnage of the Civil War? These questions deeply vexed Abraham Lincoln, whose story is central to the religious and political history of America.[28] His thinking on the meaning of the Civil War reveals a great deal about the potential of religiously inspired politics.

The Second Inaugural Address (1865) was perhaps Lincoln's greatest speech. Reflecting on the bloodthirsty prayers of partisans, Lincoln observed that "both

North and South read the same Bible, and pray to the same God. . . . The prayers of both could not be answered; that of neither has been answered fully. The Almighty has his own purposes." Perhaps, pondered Lincoln, God had prolonged the war as the means to eradicate slavery, something neither side had expected. Perhaps the war was also God's punishment of *both* North and South for the sin of slavery. Lincoln prayed for a speedy end to the war but accepted that God might will that it last until "every drop of blood drawn with the lash, shall be paid by another drawn with the sword." For Lincoln, this decision was God's. The same God expected him to articulate a forgiving vision of reconstruction and reunification once the war was over: "with malice toward none, with charity for all."[29]

Special Case: Evangelicals and the Temperance Movement

The Temperance Movement—the crusade against intoxicating drink—constitutes another example of evangelical politics, and it provides some important practical lessons for religious partisans today. The crusade, which began in the early 1800s and lasted well into the twentieth century, was one of the landmark efforts by churches to affect American politics. Led by Protestant ministers and laity, it attained a remarkable public following. The Temperance Movement was in large part rooted in patterns of excessive alcohol consumption that had begun in the colonial period and continued long afterward. Alcohol use in the colonies was widespread and included the consumption of hard liquor by youth. Spurred by the difficulties of life on the frontier, consumption rose to extraordinary levels. Alcoholism was a pervasive problem, especially among men. Given the role of the male as breadwinner at the time, this posed an enormous threat to women and children and was debilitating to men's health and community life as well.

To understand the central role of churches in the Temperance Movement, it is helpful to trace the history of one of the most effective pressure groups in American political history, the Anti-Saloon League. Founded in 1895 by Rev. Howard Hyde Russell, the league united Protestant pietists across denominational lines in a strategic approach that led to political success. Because of its close ties to Protestant churches, which served as the grassroots basis for local organization, the league became a formidable national force, able to field 20,000 speakers nationwide for the cause.[30]

What made the Anti-Saloon League successful was its relentless pressure and clear strategic calculation. Knowing that state legislatures would resist, league leaders realized they would win only through ceaseless education, lobbying, and electioneering. The organization overcame the multitude of divisions within Protestantism with a simple message of democratic appeal: Fight for the right of local communities to regulate or close down saloons. League organizers compromised when necessary, formed alliances, flooded wavering legislators with mail, and played hardball with opponents. Where they could expand on Protestant fears of Catholic immigrants, they did. Where they could form alliances with Catholics, they would. State after state fell into line.

Moreover, once local "option laws" passed that allowed local governments to set their own policies on alcohol, the League moved to get local governments and communities on board. Where they were not powerful enough to close down saloons, they fought to regulate their hours, gambling, and locations. As more and more local communities acted, remaining wet areas became isolated, and most of a state went dry. Then organizers fought to repeal local option laws in favor of stricter statewide prohibition.[31]

The strategy of beginning a political effort in states before acting nationally worked extremely well. In 1900, five states were dry, and four held down the amount of drinking by enacting high license fees from sellers. All other states allowed local communities to regulate alcohol, but wet areas still predominated in many of them. The Anti-Saloon League increasingly began to avoid state legislatures, which were often responsive to beer and alcohol interests. They moved instead to get voters to decide about alcohol policy directly through state referenda. State after state enacted prohibition in this manner. Swept by a mood of optimism, the league finally turned its attention to the federal government, and Congress passed the Eighteenth Amendment to the Constitution banning the production and sale of intoxicating beverages. Only the heavily Catholic states of Connecticut and Rhode Island refused to ratify the amendment. Prohibition became the law of the land in 1920.

Although the common understanding today is that the Temperance Movement's effort to legislate morality failed, evidence suggests that the diverse efforts to curb alcohol consumption—from voluntary temperance to legal prohibition—succeeded in changing drinking habits. One study argues that per capita yearly consumption of alcohol went from an astonishing ten gallons of alcohol in the 1830s to a little over two gallons by 1850. With westward expansion, alcohol consumption went up again. But the Temperance Movement succeeded in changing that pattern as well. Even after the Eighteenth Amendment was repealed in 1933, consumption of alcohol remained below the 1910 level.[32]

Prohibition represented the high-water mark of the popularity and political clout of evangelical Protestantism. But its success ironically contributed to its downfall. Evangelicals increasingly became a social and political lightning rod throughout the

1920s. One reason is that while Prohibition reduced drinking, it also fueled political corruption and gangsterism and made lawbreakers out of millions of otherwise law-abiding citizens. Moreover, during the Roaring Twenties, American culture itself was changing. Religiously speaking, Catholics and Jews had grown in number and clout in just a few decades, so the religious pluralism of the nation had expanded again, eroding Protestant domination of the culture. The Great Depression was the final straw, making pietist moral concerns far less pressing than life-and-death economic ones. While many Protestant churches vigorously fought the repeal of Prohibition, the nation moved on, and the Twenty-First Amendment was passed, repealing the Eighteenth.

Nevertheless, much of the same evangelical energy continues to exist today and serves as a catalyst for modern-day religious reformers who wish to engage the world and redeem it. As we will see throughout this book, many citizens understand their work against smoking, crime, gambling, abortion, poverty, drunk driving, and myriad other social issues as an urgent religious response to a world marked by immorality and suffering.

THE POPULIST DIMENSION

Churches in America, as we have seen, depend upon the voluntary support of the faithful to survive, let alone thrive. But thrive many do. Churches were, and are, the most common means (apart from work and family) by which ordinary Americans meet voluntarily in large numbers. To a great extent religion in America is popular religion—and the churches that succeed understand this reality. Thus popular religion is often a way for people to discover and express their common hopes and concerns. It can be, therefore, a conservative force, helping to preserve traditions people cherish. It can also be a radical force, however, channeling mass discontent and challenging elites with prophetic denunciations of injustice. Whatever its specific directions, popular religion often fosters populist politics that focus on mass-based democracy and hold elites accountable to the people.

This populist dimension was evident in the religious Great Awakening of the eighteenth century, which fostered grassroots evangelism and prepared colonists for the Revolution. It was present in the crusades against slavery and alcohol. It is alive today in black churches that serve as vital social and political centers for many African Americans, directing both their hopes and their challenges. There is also a kind of populism alive today among Christian conservatives who lash out against the hegemony of "cultural elites." To understand this form of contemporary religious politics it is helpful to survey some important chapters in the evolution of popular democracy and populist politics.

The drafters of the Constitution did not view direct democracy or majority rule favorably at all. Key figures such as James Madison feared popular demagogues and knew that the masses could trample on liberty just as easily as a single tyrant could. The resulting Constitution, as well as standard suffrage restrictions (the exclusion of women and African Americans, for example) and the absence of strong political parties combined to ensure that politics in early American history remained far from fully democratic.

As historian Nathan Hatch suggests, however, a continuing democratization of Christianity advanced political democracy in the early 1800s. At the forefront of democratized religion were itinerant and often untutored grassroots preachers (especially Baptists and Methodists) who understood the special needs of people on the frontier.[33] Tent revivals, which brought souls to Christ by the thousands, originated in this period; Rev. Billy Graham and many subsequent evangelists later updated the setting and the technology. Clergy who arose from among the common people dominated religious life on the frontier because, as the eighteenth-century evangelist George Whitefield observed, Harvard and Yale divinity schools did not prepare their elite students "to spend half their days in the saddle going from one rural hamlet to another."[34]

Circuit-riding preachers endured many hardships to spread their message to the masses and brought with them a democratic faith that all are equal before God. Many people were profoundly moved by this populist Christianity and began refusing to see themselves as inferior to others. They pushed for elimination of property restrictions on voting and other measures that advanced democratization. By the late 1820s mass democracy (at least for white males) had come to America, propelled in part by Protestant evangelical forces in the young nation.

This link between popular religion and popular democracy emerged again toward the end of the nineteenth century, the era from which the term "populist" derives.[35] This was an era of great expansion in manufacturing, when industrialists garnered wealth while millions of farmers and workers struggled to survive. Along with rapid economic growth and ferment came a new set of ideas—especially the gospel of wealth, conspicuous consumption, and social Darwinism. In 1859 biologist Charles Darwin had shocked religious sensibilities with the publication of *The Origin of Species*, with its central argument that life forms develop and change slowly over time by a natural process of evolution. Herbert Spencer and William Graham Sumner popularized a social counterpart to this theory, with a competitive "survival of the fittest" model of human social evolution. Some saw captains of industry as the "fittest" by virtue of their success and wealth. To critics, this new doctrine provided a suspicious justification for the plunder perpetrated by nineteenth-century robber barons.

This new age and its justifying doctrine clashed sharply with rural Christian life, where more traditional, communal norms of barter, shared work, and extended families still operated. This clash of worldviews turned into a fierce political struggle beginning in the 1880s when hard times settled over much of agricultural America.

For our purposes, what is notable about the populist movement is its religious overtone. Many populists were evangelical Protestants. The crusade took on a distinct revivalist flavor, complete with camp meetings and stirring speeches. The crusade was "a pentecost of politics in which a tongue of flame sat upon every man."[36] Populists sought a series of religiously connected goals aimed at a moral structuring of society, which also was reflected in the Protestant-led Temperance Movement (many populists were also "temperance men"). They concluded that the threat posed by industrialists required that government act with vigor and authority to protect the people. They proposed a variety of radical ideas, from inflationary monetary policies to outright state ownership of the railroads and the telegraph.

In the presidential election of 1896, the Democratic Party nominated William Jennings Bryan, a fiery speaker who shared the populist repugnance for the emerging industrial society. Bryan could sound like a socialist one minute and a pietist preacher the next. For Bryan, as for many populists, the gospel of the New Testament was the proper basis for a good and caring society.[37]

To be sure, many other pietist Protestants branded the populists and Bryan as dangerous radicals. But systematic voting studies show that Bryan, as a Democrat, did better than expected among pietist Republican voters in the West. At the same time, he fared relatively poorly among many Democrats, especially Catholics and Lutherans who were uncomfortable with his particular brand of evangelical politics. Indeed, the two parties, for a time, seemed to have swapped characteristics. Many Republicans shifted from pietist concerns to embrace emergent entrepreneurial capitalism, whereas Bryan's Democratic followers lauded the pietist idea of creating a Bible-based moral social order, insisting, like Bryan did in his famous 1896 "Cross of Gold" speech, that "you shall not crucify mankind on a cross of Gold," a reference to the gold standard that Bryan hoped the United States would abandon to help farmers repay their substantial debts.[38]

Bryan's crusade was inherently limited, however, because it created an urban-rural cleavage and undercut traditional Democratic support among Catholics and some Protestants. But Bryan's legacy lived on. We even hear echoes of Bryan and populism today—from across the political spectrum—as religious and political leaders denounce the "business as usual" of elites and demand that "the people," especially those who are economically or culturally discontented, be heard.[39]

CONCLUSION

Threads of America's religious history are so intimately woven into the social and political fabric of the United States that they continue to shape public life today. To switch metaphors, as historian Mark Noll puts it, America's religious past "frames" its future. Noll points to numerous developments in the twentieth century that have had a surprising impact: the rise of new charismatic (spirit-filled) religious movements in the United States and abroad, the remarkable explosion of religious diversity combined with membership losses in some of the older Protestant denominations, increased Catholic-Protestant interaction, and a heightened importance of ethnicity within Christianity.[40] To varying degrees, these developments are the legacies of the Puritan, pluralist, evangelical, and populist dimensions of American religion that we have emphasized in this chapter. In later chapters, we will see how these themes, along with some new ones, help us understand politics and religion today.

FURTHER READING

Ahlstrom, Sydney. *A Religious History of the American People*. New Haven, CT: Yale University Press, 1972. The standard history of religion in the United States.

Butler, Jon. *Awash in a Sea of Faith: Christianizing the American People*. Cambridge, MA: Harvard University Press, 1990. A bold reinterpretation of the history of Christianity in America.

Butler, Jon, Grant Wacker, and Randall Balmer. *Religion in American Life: A Short History*. New York: Oxford University Press, 2003. A brief examination of religion in American history.

Clark, Norman H. *Deliver Us from Evil: An Interpretation of American Prohibition*. New York: W. W. Norton, 1976. A thoughtful modern history of the Prohibition experience.

Eck, Diana L. *A New Religious America: How a "Christian Country" Has Become the World's Most Religiously Diverse Nation*. San Francisco: HarperSanFrancisco, 2002. A recent history with a central theme of religious diversity in the United States.

Finke, Roger, and Rodney Stark. *The Churching of America, 1776–2005: Winners and Losers in Our Religious Economy*. New Brunswick, NJ: Rutgers University Press, 2005. Updated edition of a pioneering work on a market interpretation of the history of American religion.

Gaustad, Edwin S., and Leigh E. Schmidt. *The Religious History of America: The Heart of the American Story from Colonial Times to Today*. San Francisco: HarperSanFrancisco, 2004. One of the leading historical treatments of religion in America.

Marty, Martin E. *Pilgrims in Their Own Land: 500 Years of Religion in America*. Boston: Little, Brown, 1984. Sweeping history by one of the nation's foremost church historians.

McLoughlin, William. *Revivals, Awakening, and Reform: An Essay on Religion and Social Change in America, 1607–1977*. Chicago: University of Chicago Press, 1978. Especially useful discussion of the Great Awakening.

Miller, Perry. *Errand into the Wilderness*. Cambridge, MA: Belknap Press of Harvard University Press, 1956. The classic intellectual history of Puritanism.

Morgan, Edmund. *The Puritan Dilemma: The Story of John Winthrop*. Boston: Little, Brown, 1958. A readable introduction to Puritan religion and politics.

Noll, Mark, and Luke E. Harlow, eds. *Religion and American Politics: From the Colonial Period to the Present*. New York: Oxford University Press, 2007. Eminent historians reflect on religion and politics in the United States.

Reichley, A. James. *Faith in Politics*. Washington, DC: Brookings Institution, 2002. A superb historical introduction to its subject.

NOTES

1. See Perry Miller, *Errand into the Wilderness* (Cambridge, MA: The Belknap Press of Harvard University Press, 1956); and Edmund Morgan, *The Puritan Dilemma: The Story of John Winthrop* (Boston: Little, Brown, 1958).

2. A. James Reichley, *Faith in Politics* (Washington, DC: Brookings Institution, 2002), 54–73.

3. John Witte Jr., "How to Govern a City on a Hill: The Early Puritan Contribution to American Constitutionalism," *Emory Law Journal* 39 (1990), 41–64.

4. Sydney Ahlstrom, *A Religious History of the American People* (New Haven, CT: Yale University Press, 1972); and Reichley, *Faith in Politics*.

5. This point is made by Barry Allen Shain, *The Myth of American Individualism: The Protestant Origins of American Political Thought* (Princeton: Princeton University Press, 1994).

6. Alexis de Tocqueville, *Democracy in America,* trans. George Lawrence and ed. J. P. Mayer and A. P. Kerr (Garden City, NY: Doubleday/Anchor, 1969).

7. Shain, *The Myth of American Individualism.*

8. See Allen D. Hertzke, *Echoes of Discontent: Jesse Jackson, Pat Robertson, and the Resurgence of Populism* (Washington, DC: CQ Press, 1993), chap. 3.

9. Robert Booth Fowler, *Unconventional Partners: Religion and Liberal Culture in the United States* (Grand Rapids, MI: Eerdmans, 1989); Robert Putnam, *Bowling Alone: The Collapse and Revival of American Community* (New York: Simon & Schuster, 2000).

10. Mark Noll, ed., *One Nation Under God? Christian Faith and Political Action in America* (San Francisco: HarperSanFrancisco, 1988).

11. Ahlstrom, *A Religious History of the American People*; Leonard Levy, *The Establishment Clause: Religion and the First Amendment*, 2nd ed. (Raleigh: University of North Carolina Press, 1994).

12. Ahlstrom, *A Religious History of the American People*; Roger Finke and Rodney Stark, *The Churching of America 1776–2005: Winners and Losers in Our Religious Economy* (New Brunswick, NJ: Rutgers University Press, 2005); Andrew Greeley, *The Denominational Society: A Sociological Approach to Religion in America* (Glenview, IL: Scott, Foresman, 1972); Will Herberg, *Protestant-Catholic-Jew* (Garden City, NY: Doubleday, 1955).

13. Sydney Mead, *The Lively Experiment: The Shaping of Christianity in America* (New York: Harper and Row, 1963), 35. For an excellent general discussion of the theological and political ideas that presaged the Religion Clauses, see John Witte Jr., *Religion and the American Constitutional Experiment: Essential Rights and Liberties*, 2nd ed. (Boulder: Westview Press, 2005), chap. 2.

14. Gary Glenn, "Forgotten Purposes of the First Amendment Religion Clause," *Review of Politics* 49 (1987), 340–366; Michael Malbin, *Religion and Politics: The Intentions of the Authors of the First Amendment* (Washington, DC: American Enterprise Institute, 1978); Witte, *Religion and the American Constitutional Experiment*, chap. 4.

15. For example, see the first novel in the Left Behind series: Tim LaHaye and Jerry B. Jenkins, *Left Behind: A Novel of the Earth's Last Days* (Carol Stream, IL: Tyndale House, 1995).

16. Ahlstrom, *A Religious History of the American People*, 501–509.

17. Ibid.

18. Anson Phelps Stokes, *Church and State in the United States,* vol. 2 (New York: Harper, 1950), 275–285. For a brief and engaging discussion of Mormon experience in Utah in the mid–nineteenth century, see David Roberts, "The Brink of War," *Smithsonian Magazine,* June 2008.

19. *Pierce* v. *Society of Sisters*, 268 U.S. 510 (1925).

20. Finke and Stark, *The Churching of America*.

21. Laurence Iannaccone, "Why Strict Churches Are Strong," *American Journal of Sociology* 99 (1994), 1180–1211; Donald E. Miller, *Reinventing Protestantism: Christianity in the New Millennium* (Berkeley: University of California Press, 1997).

22. We use the term "church" here and in many subsequent contexts for linguistic economy. However, in this and future instances, blanket references to "church" may be read more broadly to encompass any organized faith tradition.

23. Robert N. Bellah, Richard Madsen, William M. Sullivan, Ann Swidler, and Steven M. Tipton, *Habits of the Heart: Individualism and Commitment in American Life* (New York: Harper and Row, 1985); Jack Miles, "Religion Makes a Comeback (Belief to Follow)," *New York Times Magazine*, December 7, 1997, 56–59.

24. Iannaccone, "Why Strict Churches Are Strong," Dean M. Kelley, *Why Conservative Churches Are Growing: A Study in Sociology of Religion* (San Francisco: HarperSanFrancisco, 1972).

25. Fowler, *Unconventional Partners.*

26. Luke Eugene Ebersole, *Church Lobbying in the Nation's Capital* (New York: Macmillan, 1951).

27. Ahlstrom, *A Religious History of the American People*, 653–654; David B. Chesebrough, *Clergy Dissent in the Old South, 1830–1865* (Carbondale, IL: Southern Illinois University Press, 1996).

28. On Lincoln and religion, see Allen C. Guelzo, *Abraham Lincoln: Redeemer President* (Grand Rapids, MI: Eerdmans, 1999); Richard J. Carwardine, *Lincoln* (New York: Longman, 2003).

29. Ronald C. White, *Lincoln's Greatest Speech: The Second Inaugural* (New York: Simon & Schuster, 2002).

30. Norman H. Clark, *Deliver Us from Evil: An Interpretation of American Prohibition* (New York: W. W. Norton, 1976).

31. Ibid.

32. Ibid.

33. Nathan O. Hatch, *The Democratization of American Christianity* (New Haven, CT: Yale University Press, 1989).

34. As quoted in Finke and Stark, *The Churching of America*, 87.

35. The literature on the populist movement, including its religious dimensions, is extensive and growing. It is summarized by Hertzke, *Echoes of Discontent*, chap. 2.

36. As quoted in John D. Hicks, *The Populist Revolt: A History of the Farmers' Alliance and the People's Party* (Lincoln, NE: University of Nebraska Press, 1961).

37. This point is developed more fully in Hertzke, *Echoes of Discontent*, chap. 2.

38. Paul Kleppner, *The Cross of Culture: A Social Analysis of Midwestern Politics, 1850–1900* (New York: Free Press, 1970).

39. Hertzke, *Echoes of Discontent*.

40. Mark A. Noll, "How the Religious Past Frames America's Future," in *Faith, Freedom, and the Future: Religion in American Political Culture*, ed. Charles Dunn (Lanham, MD: Rowman and Littlefield, 2003), 19–40.

2

CHRISTIANITY AND ITS
MAJOR BRANCHES

In this chapter and the next we analyze the status of religious traditions in America and chart their political impact. We focus in this chapter on the most prominent traditions of Christianity in the United States and their enduring yet changing roles in shaping public life. In Chapter 3 we examine Judaism, Islam, and other religious expressions that, despite size constraints and pressures from the broader culture, often exercise a significant voice in American society and politics. At one level, organized religion has enjoyed continuous vitality in the United States. At another level, however, the picture is complex: Secular voices, especially at the elite level, increasingly make an important mark on American culture. To understand the complexity of American religion and its interaction with politics, we must now embark on our two-chapter examination of the status of religion in contemporary American society.

THE STATUS OF RELIGION IN THE UNITED STATES

American religion today is alive, thriving, and diverse. Some 92 percent of Americans profess a belief in God or a universal spirit, with more than 70 percent claiming to be "absolutely certain" about God's existence.[1] Moreover, 83 percent of Americans claim an affiliation with one organized religious tradition or another, and 56 percent say that religion is "very important" in their everyday lives.[2] Although there is a sizable and growing segment of secular (religiously unaffiliated) citizens in the United

States,[3] a large majority of Americans continue to make religious faith an important part of their lives.

One way to understand the significance of faith in the United States is to compare Americans with citizens of other nations. The comparison lends some credence to the description of American culture as "exceptional."[4] On every measure—belief in God, belief in life after death, attendance at religious services, and daily prayer or meditation—the United States consistently ranks higher than most other nations. Only 61 percent of citizens in Great Britain, 56 percent in France, and 46 percent in Sweden profess a belief in God, as compared with more than 90 percent in the United States.[5] Whereas 76 percent of Americans believe in life after death, that view is shared by just 45 percent in Britain and 39 percent in France and Sweden.[6] Similarly, although more than a third of Americans report that they attend worship services weekly, the same can be said of just 5 percent or less of British, French, and Swedes.[7]

On the other hand, among nations outside of Europe and the Pacific Rim, the United States is not so exceptional. We see evidence of religion's continuing strength, and often its resurgence, from the Middle East to Latin America to Africa. Unlike Europe and Southeast Asia, where the average citizen rates the importance of God in everyday life at less than 5 on a 1-to-10 scale (where 10 denotes a belief that God is "very important"), Latin Americans rate God's importance as 8.7 and West Africans a remarkable 9.7.[8] Such data hint at the future prospects of religion across the globe. If demographic trends continue, well over 50 percent of the world's Christians will be in Africa, Latin America, and parts of Asia within twenty-five years—a clear shift from Christianity's traditional home in Europe and North America.[9] In addition, Islam, with more than a billion adherents worldwide, is the dominant faith in northern Africa, the Middle East, and other regions of Asia.[10] From this perspective, the United States is hardly unusual; it is Europe and the Pacific Rim that are the exceptions.

Another useful comparison is between groups of citizens within the United States itself. Faith is especially important to women and nonwhites, for example. Nearly two-thirds (63 percent) of women in the United States say religion is a significant guide in their day-to-day lives, compared to just under half (49 percent) of American men.[11] And African Americans typically register the highest average of any group in the world in Gallup surveys regarding the importance of God.[12] This high salience of religion is the basis for the tremendous political role of African American churches, which we explore in Chapter 10.

Despite growing religious diversity, the U.S. population remains decidedly Christian. Almost four in five Americans (78.5 percent) associate with some form of the Christian faith.[13] As many as eight in ten Americans claim to accept the traditional Christian view of God as a Trinity—Father, Son, and Holy Spirit[14]—and three-quarters feel "forgiveness of sins is only possible through faith in Jesus Christ."[15] Three-quarters of Americans believe in an afterlife, and half are absolutely certain of this belief.[16] A majority of Americans have a high view of holy scriptures as well, with 63 percent saying the scriptures of their faith tradition (for example, the Bible or the Qur'an) should be understood as the word of God.[17]

A sizable proportion of Americans say they have had extraordinary spiritual experiences, often through intense religious awakenings that change their lives. Of those, almost half claim to be "born-again" Christians, meaning they have had a profound, once-in-a-lifetime experience of repentance and commitment to Jesus Christ.[18] Many Americans also report experiencing gifts of the Holy Spirit, such as witnessing divine healings (29 percent) or receiving direct revelations from God (26 percent).[19] When sociologist and Catholic priest Andrew Greeley looked at the evidence, he proclaimed the United States a "nation of mystics."[20] This was an exaggeration, but for a notable portion of the population these religious experiences are a very real part of life.

Americans invest considerable trust in their religious institutions and clergy. For years, Americans have expressed more confidence in organized religion than in many other private and public institutions. Moreover, members of the clergy consistently rank highest among sets of social leaders in terms of public regard for their ethics and honesty. Confidence in the clergy dropped briefly in the wake of the televangelist scandals of the late 1980s, however, and has fallen for Catholic priests in the wake of child abuse accusations in the past decade.[21] Still, the public expresses more confidence in organized religion than it does in the U.S. Supreme Court, Congress, the health care system, banks, public schools, the press, organized labor, and big business.[22] Here again, Americans are distinct from people in other developed Western nations. Whereas Americans express more confidence in churches than they do in public schools, for example, these confidence figures are reversed in Germany, France, Great Britain, and many other European countries.[23]

Many Americans are also churchgoing Christians; in fact, 39 percent say they attend religious services at least once a week.[24] Some scholars, however, argue that people are less than truthful in responding to surveys about church attendance.[25] It is quite possible that many Americans have in fact become more secular in their habits but are unwilling to admit it. Yet even if attendance figures are inflated, the fact remains that church participation is the single most common group activity in the United States. Among Christian traditions, evangelical Protestants attend services most frequently, followed by Roman Catholics, with mainline Protestants trailing behind. As we will see in Chapter 4 when we discuss voting behavior, this pattern has increased the political clout of evangelical voters while reducing that of mainline Protestants.

On balance, the portrait of religious America is one of enduring faith. How much difference this makes in the daily lives of Americans, let alone in their politics, is another matter. Critics suggest that religion in America is like the proverbial prairie river: a mile wide and an inch deep. They note an obvious gap between high levels of apparent faith and considerable business dishonesty, tax fraud, sexual promiscuity, marital infidelity, family breakdown, cheating in school, crime, violence, and vulgarity in the popular culture. Pollster George Gallup Jr., whose surveys demonstrate the widespread appeal of religion in the United States, has concluded that much of American faith is indeed shallow and marked by a gap between faith and ethics.[26] A society that celebrates the individual pursuit of happiness, pervasive (and some argue destructive) popular culture, and capitalism will likely privilege hedonism and materialism over religion.[27]

On the other hand, there is evidence that religious belief and practice do make a difference in people's lives. Research suggests that religious conviction and practice are correlated with personal happiness, physical health, and general life stability.[28] But it is the salience and authenticity of religious conviction that matters more than nominal affiliation: the greater the faith or practice, the more intense the benefits, irrespective of denomination.[29] As we discuss more fully in Chapter 7, on the social and civic level, religious people are more likely than the secular to contribute to charities, vote, and otherwise become involved in the community.[30]

One reason American religion has so much vitality is its pluralism. In Europe, people who become alienated from the established church simply drift away from it, and usually from religion altogether, whereas in America people who leave one congregation often form or join a new one. A bewildering diversity of religious expression continues unabated in the United States and remains one of its primary defining characteristics. A constitutional doctrine that protects religious freedom, a relative openness to immigration, and a tradition of individualism that promotes the continual formation of new sects combine to foster tremendous American religious pluralism.

Part of this pluralism within Christianity, of course, is reflected in the division of people into the familiar categories of Protestant and Catholic. Additional diversity within each of these two broad traditions further increases the pluralism of American religion. The United States is home to virtually every Protestant denomination or sect in existence, some of which are very diverse in their own right. Consider the Baptists. There are black Baptist denominations and white Baptists,

RELIGIOUS AFFILIATION	PERCENTAGE OF U.S. POPULATION
Evangelical Protestant	*26.3*
Mainline Protestant	*18.1*
African American Protestant	*6.9*
Catholic	*23.9*
Jewish	*1.7*
Mormon	*1.7*
Muslim	*0.6*
Other	*4.7*
None	*16.1*

Table 2.1   A Profile of Current Religious Affiliations, 2008
Source: Pew Forum on Religion & Public Life, *U.S. Religious Landscape Study*, 2008.

fundamentalists and moderates, northern branches and southern ones. Indeed, there are several hundred distinct Baptist denominations. Moreover, within each denomination every church tends to consider itself sovereign and autonomous. There are also myriad independent evangelical churches, some affiliated with national organizations, others entirely separate (or "nondenominational"). Even the hierarchical Catholic Church is pluralistic. There are liberal and conservative Catholics, a host of religious orders from Jesuits to Maryknolls, and numerous religious lay groups from the most conservative to the decidedly radical. The patchwork of American pluralism also includes small pacifist churches, such as the Quakers, Brethren, Mennonites, and Amish, as well as Jews, Muslims, Mormons, Jehovah's Witnesses, Native American religionists, viewers of television ministries, pre- and postmillennial fundamentalists, Pentecostals and charismatics, evangelical Presbyterians, high church Episcopalians, and members of gay churches, just to name a few—not to mention people who join the host of new religious movements that sprout with regularity (Box 2.1).

Protestant Christianity remains the faith of a bare majority of Americans (roughly 51 percent), with Catholics accounting for a sizable 24 percent, and the remaining population is composed of Jews, Eastern Orthodox Christians, Mormons, Muslims, adherents of other faiths, the unaffiliated, and those who do not believe at all (Table 2.1).

Getting a good handle on actual church membership is harder than it might seem. Churches keep their own records, and they tend to count *members* according to their

BOX 2.1   THE MEGACHURCH PHENOMENON

Social scientists quite often use broad categories of religious affiliation as a key measure of a person's religion. Members of the United Church of Christ, for example, are put into the mainline Protestant category; Southern Baptists are catalogued as evangelicals. What about congregations that have no association with a denomination? Their status is an important question because nondenominational churches constitute a growing American trend. In fact, many of the largest churches in the United States—the so-called megachurches, with 2,000 or more members—are nondenominational. Willow Creek Church in Wheaton, Illinois, with more than 20,000 congregants on any given Sunday, is a pioneer among megachurches. Bill Hybels, its senior pastor, developed an outreach to religious "seekers" in the Chicago area in the 1970s and 1980s. More recently, Willow Creek has focused on a wide array of small group ministries that tap into the specific life experiences of its members. Saddleback Church in Southern California constitutes another prominent example of a megachurch. The brainchild of Rick Warren, who is perhaps best known as the author of the wildly popular book, *The Purpose Driven Life*, Saddleback has achieved such prominence that it hosted the only forum on religion and politics in the 2008 presidential campaign that included both major party candidates. Based on their core religious beliefs and behaviors, most nondenominational megachurches belong in the evangelical category, often sharing the political conservatism of their denominational brethren. But their size and detachment from the traditional organization of Protestantism make them an intriguing phenomenon in American culture.

Sources: http://www.willowcreek.org; www.saddleback.com; Mark Chaves, "All Creatures Great and Small: Megachurches in Context," *Review of Religious Research* 47 (June 2006), 329–346; Scott Thumma and Dave Travis, *Beyond Megachurch Myths* (Hoboken, NJ: Jossey-Bass, 2007).

own, often differing, methods; independent opinion surveys of people's *religious affiliation* look at another, broader picture of self-identification and do not always arrive at the same results. Nonetheless, the general outlines of affiliation provide a basic sketch of American religious pluralism.

The tremendous diversity that characterizes American religion frequently has given rise to cultural clashes. Roughly one-fourth of the American population is Catholic, slightly more than one-fourth white evangelical Protestant, less than one-fifth mainline Protestant, and about one-tenth African American Protestant.[31] When we categorize people by religious affiliation, evangelicals are most numerous.

The political significance of religious pluralism within Christianity is manifold. Pluralism acts as a check on the political influence of any religious group. No one group dominates, nor can it—a pluralist reality often ignored by those who fear that any single religious group could establish a "theocracy" or otherwise use government to enforce widespread oppression. Religious pluralism also requires a willingness on the part of activists to overcome theological differences in the interest of coalition building, which is a must for successful political endeavors. Deeply held convictions sometimes must be modified if effective political alliances are to result.[32]

THE MAJOR CHRISTIAN TRADITIONS AND POLITICS

The four dominant Christian traditions in the United States—Catholicism and evangelical, mainline, and African American Protestantism—are in many ways distinctive in their history, theology, and ethnic makeup. Moreover, these traditions are politically distinct, although, to be sure, the boundaries sometimes become blurry. The theological orientations of many African American Christians, for example, are evangelical, yet because of the American legacy of slavery and segregation, black churches developed in directions that diverge from white evangelical churches. We discuss the African American church tradition only briefly in this chapter, but Chapter 10 discusses it in detail. We treat Judaism, Islam, and several other, smaller religious traditions in Chapter 3.

Evangelical Protestantism

As we saw in Chapter 1, much of American history has been influenced by evangelical Protestant culture. By the 1920s, evangelicalism seemed to be in retreat from society, but it reemerged decades later with considerable vigor.

An important watershed for modern evangelicals came in 1976, when presidential candidate Jimmy Carter proclaimed himself a "born-again Christian." It was at that time that evangelicals burst into the broader public consciousness; a bevy of journalists made pilgrimages to the South to discover just what evangelicalism entailed. Before long, pollster George Gallup Jr. stunned the literati by announcing that fully one-third of Americans claimed to be born-again evangelicals. Conservative churches were growing because they offered precisely what their members found lacking in modern society: strong faith, concrete answers to life's challenges, and tight bonds of community.[33] One example of the tremendous growth in evangelicalism in the United States has been the presence of active evangelical student organizations on college campuses. Campus Crusade for Christ, for example, ministered to millions of college students in 2008 alone.[34]

The growth of evangelical Protestantism would not have been politically significant had a social movement known as the Christian Right not burst onto the scene as a political force in the late 1970s. The movement began with isolated protests by parents against public school texts in the mid-1970s; gained momentum through the movement to defeat the Equal Rights Amendment led by Phyllis Schlafly; hit its stride with the creation of the Moral Majority and other national groups in 1979; and had established itself as an effective political player by the 1990s.[35] Ronald Reagan acknowledged white evangelical voters in the 1980s and embraced their concerns, at least rhetorically, and to varying degrees Presidents Bill Clinton, George W. Bush, and Barack Obama followed suit.[36] By the early twenty-first century, white evangelicals had become one of the Republican Party's most loyal constituencies.[37]

What does it mean to be an evangelical? Some evangelicals simply self-identify as such; others may be classified as evangelicals as a result of their adherence to a specific set of orthodox religious beliefs. The most telling characteristic that separates evangelical Protestants from other Christians is an affirmative answer to the question, "Do you consider yourself a born-again or evangelical Christian?" This question taps a central tenet of Protestant evangelical Christianity—the need for a once-in-a-lifetime conversion, commonly known as a "born-again" experience. Evangelicals also hold an orthodox view of scripture—for all evangelicals the Bible is at a minimum the inspired word of God, and for some it is the literal word of God. Evangelicals also adhere strongly to the orthodox tenets of the Christian faith (Christ's divinity, his atoning death and resurrection, everlasting salvation or damnation in a literal heaven or hell) and are committed to Jesus' "great commission" to evangelize others by spreading the good news.[38]

Evangelicals also share a common language and at least a few basic assumptions. Evangelicals ask others, "Are you saved?" or, "When did you commit your life to Christ?" Born-again Christians are scattered throughout the Protestant world. Indeed, evangelical "renewal" groups occur within mainline denominations and congregations.[39] George W. Bush illustrates the point: He identifies strongly with evangelicalism but is a member of the United Methodist Church, a mainline denomination.

One of the most important distinctions within American evangelicalism is racial. Normally when scholars and commentators speak of evangelicals, they are referring to white evangelicals. Yet many black Baptists and Pentecostals also are fervent evangelicals. Moreover, decreased segregation and increased racial tolerance have brought increased interaction between white and black evangelicals. The Southern Baptist Convention, for example, now trumpets its growing black membership. And the burgeoning world of Pentecostal and charismatic congregations is truly interracial, largely because the Pentecostal movement began as an interracial religious revival in early twentieth-century California.[40] White religious conservatives have been modestly successful in building alliances with black clergy on such issues as school prayer, abortion, school choice, and pornography, and some white evangelicals have called for greater attention to racial justice among their brethren.[41]

Nonetheless, a considerable gulf remains between black and white evangelicals. African American churches feature a unique blend of theological conservatism and political liberalism; piety combines with prophetic witness. In black churches one hears the liberationist messages of God's mercy toward the poor, the captive, and the downtrodden and of considerable confidence in government as the temporal means to change. In this sense, God is an avenging liberator who can lift up the believer and provide both a refuge from the pain of the world and a means for counteracting injustice. This combination of messages lends itself naturally to political liberalism, at least on economic and civil rights issues.[42]

Beyond race, several significant theological and cultural divisions also exist within the evangelical world. Pluralism reigns here, just as it does elsewhere in religious America. There are "mainstream" evangelicals who believe scripture is inerrant but must be interpreted by humans; this group of evangelicals is largely ambivalent, rather than outwardly hostile, toward the broader culture. On the other hand, fundamentalists, who are true biblical literalists, are deeply suspicious of those who claim to "interpret" God's word and highly critical of the "fallen" culture they see around them.[43] Meanwhile, there are premillennialists, who expect certain biblical prophecies to come true before Jesus returns for a thousand-year reign on Earth (the best-selling Left Behind book series takes this approach), as opposed to postmillennialists, who believe a Christian reign will precede Jesus' second coming. An example of a postmillennialist group is the small but influential group of Christian Reconstructionists, who hold that believers should structure society as a theocracy on the basis of Old Testament law. Comprising another significant—and growing—category of American evangelicalism are Pentecostals and charismatics, who stress the availability of gifts of the Holy Spirit—such as speaking in tongues, faith healing, and prophecy.[44] Importantly, despite the fact that Pentecostals and charismatics are fervent believers in orthodox scriptural interpretation and traditional moral values, fundamentalists and many mainstream evangelicals

are skeptical of Pentecostals because of their strong emphasis on personal spiritualism, which they say diminishes the Bible as the sole source of divine authority.

One way to clarify the diversity within evangelical Protestantism is to think of
the evangelical community as a tree with several main branches and numerous
smaller ones. There are literally hundreds of evangelical denominations, or religious
organized subdivisions, the largest of which is the Southern Baptist Convention.
Many, but not all, evangelical congregations belong to these denominations, which
serve as a clearinghouse of sorts for worship and religious education materials and
as a touchstone for doctrine. Increasingly, evangelical churches in the United States
describe themselves as nondenominational, which usually means they are not affiliated with any formal religious organization outside of the congregation.

Nevertheless, evangelical Protestantism in the United States has grown along
three principal branches. The first and largest branch consists of mainstream evangelicals in the tradition of Rev. Billy Graham. This branch is well represented by
the National Association of Evangelicals (NAE), an umbrella group for numerous
evangelical churches and denominations, which works to transform the world spiritually and is generally conservative politically but is by no means militant. Another
branch is fundamentalism, which historically has been separatist, biblically literalist,
and rather strongly opposed to the secular world.[45] Finally, there is the fast-growing
Pentecostal or charismatic branch, whose members share many of the political
views of fellow evangelicals but whose vibrant religious practice and emphasis on
spiritual gifts set them apart. Whereas a fundamentalist church service usually features traditional Bible reading and preaching, charismatic congregations feature
contemporary music; speaking in tongues; and an emotional, free-form worship
style.[46] Although these distinctions may seem trivial to outsiders, to evangelical
leaders they present a very serious challenge to political unity.

Evangelical attitudes about political participation have changed dramatically in
recent decades. Evangelicals long viewed politics with distaste; political activity
constituted an engagement with the sinful world God meant them to eschew. To
be sure, many evangelical churches have always stressed the civic duty of voting,
but beyond occasional local issues involving gambling or alcohol, not much effort
was expended on politics. That stance left the political field open for mainline
Protestantism, which rode the crest of civil rights and antiwar activism in the
1960s.[47]

But by the 1970s all of that began to change. Many evangelical leaders came to
believe that the government and the broader culture had become dangerously secular and intrusive, so they felt they had to fight back. Others felt inspired to rekindle

the nineteenth-century evangelical commitment to bringing the gospel message to all corners of society. Moreover, evangelical congregations were growing rapidly by the 1970s. Their members were becoming better educated and more affluent than ever before, and their television and radio ministries were becoming more popular. They had the motivation to fight and, increasingly, the resources to do so.

Not all evangelicals, however, agree with each other politically. Many evangelicals oppose the tactics and even the aims of the Christian Right—some vigorously so. In recent years younger evangelical leaders, such as Rev. Rick Warren (of *The Purpose Driven Life*), have taken the Christian Right to task for ignoring issues that fall outside of the movement's tightly constructed political agenda of "family values" and sexual morality.[48] Some fundamentalists oppose involvement in national politics because such a turn means engaging with the fallen world. In the early days of the Christian Right, fundamentalist pastor and then-president of the South Carolina university that bears his name, Bob Jones Jr., once called Rev. Jerry Falwell the most dangerous man in America because he thought Falwell's political efforts would undermine the fundamentalist aim of separating from the broader (sinful) society. Television preachers, moreover, are by no means universally popular among evangelicals. In the 1988 presidential primaries, for example, many evangelicals voted against candidate Pat Robertson, who was best known at the time for his work as the Pentecostal host of a popular religious television program, *The 700 Club*.

Nor should it be assumed that all evangelicals are political conservatives. To be sure, most are conservative, but that does not preclude the existence of a small but growing "evangelical left." Represented most prominently by Jim Wallis of the progressive religio-political groups Sojourners and Call to Action, this movement focuses on poverty, civil rights, and the preservation of God's natural creation. Wallis gained national notice during the 2004 presidential campaign, during which his organizations launched a "God is not a Republican or a Democrat" information campaign. Wallis stayed on the national stage as a vocal critic of President George W. Bush during his second term in office and later advised the Obama campaign and Democratic Party on religious outreach in the 2008 presidential campaign.[49]

Real fissures belie the conventional wisdom that evangelicals constitute a disciplined army marching to take over America. Still, as we show in Chapter 4, most white evangelical voters have realigned into the Republican Party and now constitute a key GOP voting bloc in both national and local politics. Beneath tremendous diversity in theology and religious practice lies a broad-based consensus in support of conservative politics. How political leaders deal with this constituency will shape a key dimension of American politics in the years to come.

Mainline Protestantism

In the nineteenth and twentieth centuries, mainline Protestantism evolved into a tradition distinct and separate from evangelicalism. This tradition within Protestantism carries the label "mainline" because historically its denominations represented the dominant expression of organized Protestantism in the United States, a position that translated into exceptional political access. Mainline denominations, and many of its congregations, remain among the oldest and wealthiest in American religion. In terms of lay numbers and contemporary influence, however, the "mainline" nomenclature does not fit as easily as it once did because the Protestant center of gravity has shifted toward the evangelical community.

Some scholars refer to the tradition as "liberal Protestantism," with the adjective referring to theology, not politics. As theological liberals, mainline Protestants view the Bible as inspired by God but by no means literally true in every word. They also argue that scripture must be read in the context of history and modern science. In fact, the mainline-evangelical split crystallized in the early twentieth century when mainline Protestants embraced modernity and scientific theories such as Darwinism, of which evangelicals were wary.[50] This does not mean mainline Protestants abandon the central tenets of Christian faith, but they do place more emphasis on the goal of gradual, reflective spiritual development and less on the "born-again" conversion experience. Mainline Protestants are skeptical of the biblical literalism of fundamentalists and of the emotionalism and faith healing claims of Pentecostals.

As is the case in evangelicalism, considerable variation exists across mainline Protestant denominations. Mainline Lutherans (adherents of the Evangelical Lutheran Church in America, or ELCA) maintain a distinct liturgical tradition founded in ethnic German and Scandinavian roots; Methodists still stress doing good works in the world as a manifestation of faithfulness; Episcopalians often treasure a formal, traditional worship service that is not unlike Catholic mass; and the United Church of Christ is substantially more liberal in its theology than the other mainline denominations. Despite these differences, however, mainline Protestants share a lot in common, not only in theology but in worship style as well. In mainline Protestant churches one rarely hears sermons about hell or personal sin. More common are scholarly discussions of the meaning of divine incarnation or the ethical insights of Jesus' teachings. Services typically are orderly and include traditional musical offerings, but in recent times many mainline Protestant congregations have been experimenting with more contemporary worship styles as well. By and large, mainline Protestant churches are more accepting of skepticism about portions of the Bible than are their evangelical counterparts. Bible study, therefore, often focuses on moral precepts contained in the Bible and welcomes examinations of the context of biblical times. This is not to say that there are no traditional religionists sitting in the pews of mainline churches—there are many indeed—but most mainline church leaders do not reinforce their outlook.[51]

In many mainline churches, there is an emphasis on a general call to love one's brother or sister and to be active in "this world." Moreover, Christian love is often interpreted in collective ways as well as individual ones. For a century many mainline clergy have argued that Christians must address the world's injustices not merely by individual charity but by collective efforts to change societal structures. Mainline seminaries, liberal both in theological and political terms since the early twentieth century, became radicalized during the civil rights movement in the 1960s, exposing an entire generation of clergy to theologically grounded liberal politics.[52] It is in seminary that many clergy learn that, unless one changes political and economic structures, injustice and oppression will continue irrespective of personal acts of mercy and love.[53]

For mainline clergy and denominational leaders, theological liberalism often correlates with liberal political activism. Among their parishioners, the link between liberal theology and liberal politics is less well established.[54] A majority of mainline Protestants traditionally have voted Republican, but this pattern has been diminishing for more than a decade. In fact, in the 2008 presidential election, some election surveys suggested that a bare majority of mainline Protestants now identify with the Democratic Party, an indicator of an important historical shift.[55] These changes in partisanship reflect the clear correlation between theological liberalism and liberal attitudes among rank-and-file mainline Protestants on a wide range of socio-moral issues.[56]

The well-established Protestant denominations were the clearly dominant force in American religion through the 1950s. Methodists, Episcopalians, Congregationalists, most Presbyterians, many Lutherans, and northern (American) Baptists, along with members of a few other smaller mainline denominations and the National Council of Churches (a parachurch organization to which they all belong), constituted the principal political and social witness by religious people through most of the twentieth century.[57] From Main Street to Wall Street to Washington, mainline Protestants were well entrenched. When radical social movements gathered steam in the 1960s, influential mainline leaders voiced their solidarity with activists, and many mainline Protestants became foot soldiers in the movements.[58]

The 1960s exercised a strong influence on mainline Protestant leaders. They embraced—and continue to embrace—issues of poverty, racism, sexism, and oppression—and the unjust structures they see as incorporating these evils. Mainline church leaders typically view much of their work as championing peace and justice, especially for the poor and disadvantaged.[59] As a result, many mainline clergy favor expanded government funding for welfare at home and economic assistance for developing nations abroad. They also work for world peace (sometimes from a pacifist perspective) and frequently fault American foreign policy as too militaristic and too oriented toward gain for the U.S. economy. For example, the United Methodist Church ran a series of highly visible television advertisements in 2003 as the United States's war with Iraq was launched, in which church leaders stated, "We are President Bush's church, and we oppose war in Iraq."

Two significant challenges confront mainline clergy who wish to exercise political influence. First, many lay members either do not share the ideological orienta-

---

BOX 2.2   STRIFE INSIDE THE EPISCOPAL CHURCH

In recent years, the Episcopal Church in the United States (which is the American branch of the Church of England, or Anglican Church) has been wracked by so much strife that some observers wonder aloud whether the denomination will break in two. The reason for the dissension is that many of the Episcopal Church's more conservative members and leaders have found themselves in profound disagreement with some of the denomination's recent decisions and policies, especially around homosexuality. The greatest flashpoint of tension has been the 2003 installation of an openly gay man, Rev. Canon V. Gene Robinson, as the Episcopal Bishop of New Hampshire. Since Robinson's consecration, scores of conservative congregations have broken ties with the U.S. denomination and aligned themselves instead with Anglican communions in other countries, especially in Africa where traditional doctrines hold firm sway, most notably the Episcopal Church of Uganda. Some of these dissident congregations have wound up in court battles pitting them against the U.S. church over who owns their church buildings and other property. This crisis is far from over, and only time will tell if the Episcopal Church will remain intact as a denomination.

Sources: Neela Banerjee, "American Ruptures Shaking the Episcopal Church," *The New York Times*, October 3, 2004, A21; Peter J. Boyer, "A Church Asunder," *The New Yorker*, April 17, 2006, 54; Laurie Goodstein, "A Divide, and Maybe a Divorce," *The New York Times*, February 25, 2007, D1.

tions of their national leaders and local pastors or do not wish to conform to a particular political vision articulated from the pulpit. As an illustration of this phenomenon, consider the recent schisms within mainline denominations and congregations around homosexuality (Box 2.2).[60] Indeed, because of the process of political decision-making in these large denominations, lay members are not always consulted as official positions are developed.[61] Moreover, because mainline churches tolerate a wide diversity of views regarding theology, lay members are not accustomed to accepting concrete assertions of truth (about any matter, including politics) from their clergy. Thus, it can be difficult for mainline leaders to find support within their congregations for the political causes about which they care most.[62]

A second challenge is that mainline Protestantism has faced membership declines in recent decades. From 1990 to 2000, for example, the United Methodist, United Church of Christ, and Presbyterian USA denominations lost 6.7, 14.8, and 11.6 percent of their memberships, respectively.[63] Explanations for these losses abound, including the assertion that by turning more aggressively to politics in the 1960s and 1970s, the mainline churches turned off some of their parishioners.[64] Sociologist Dean Kelley offers the most convincing explanation in arguing that because the "business of religion is meaning," stricter and more demanding churches, especially conservative evangelical congregations, attract and keep members because they offer concrete answers to life's most vexing questions.[65] As we saw in Chapter 1, this theme echoes throughout American history; whenever churches relax their firm beliefs, they decline in proportion to more demanding churches.

Despite their numeric decline, however, mainline churches still possess a wealth of inherited capital in the form of buildings, institutions, and endowments, as well as the loyalty of millions of lay members. Local churches continue to operate a host of food banks, meal programs, homeless shelters, clothing closets, and day-care centers, and national church organizations operate large hospitals, charitable agencies, and highly respected international development organizations. Mainline Protestant churches are also key players in city coalitions designed to alleviate poverty and injustice. Thus extensive community involvement continues to thrive in mainline Protestantism, and mainline Protestants continue to exercise what sociologist Robert Wuthnow terms "quiet" but significant influence in American political and religious life.[66]

Roman Catholicism

In Chapter 1 we observed that the Catholic-Protestant split played an important role in shaping the first century and a half of American political culture. Catholics were seen as profoundly "other" in American society, living in ethnic neighborhoods and sustaining separate institutions to shield themselves from the dominance of Protestant culture. The result by the 1950s was a tremendously vibrant Catholic community dominated by an ethic of cultural separatism with an impressive number of Catholic churches, schools, hospitals, and social service agencies staffed by large numbers of priests and nuns.

This Protestant-Catholic division lingers in a few places, but it is mostly a memory. Today's suburban Catholics are hardly outsiders anymore. Indeed, complaints are heard among Catholics themselves that the distinctiveness of Catholic culture has been lost amid a homogenized mass society. Still, Catholics remain theologically distinct, preserving a sacramental approach to the "mysteries" of the faith and a unique intellectual tradition.[67]

Today, Catholics inhabit a highly strategic place in American politics. Catholics are key swing voters, and both mainline Protestants and evangelicals frequently seek political alliances with Catholic elites. Catholic bishops make news whenever they speak on political issues. But Catholics, especially at the parish level, hardly speak with a unified political voice; here pluralism reigns just as it does elsewhere in religious America. This lack of unity sometimes hampers Catholic political clout, although the size of the Catholic population (roughly one in every four Americans is Catholic) and the institutional strength of the Church ensure that Catholics are important players in the American system.

The Catholic Church is literally the oldest institution in the world; it is a truly global church with a distinct hierarchical structure headquartered in Vatican City. This internationalism adds a unique dimension to Catholic politics. One cannot focus merely on the American church; one must consider the hierarchical Church structure, the pope and other top Church leaders, and the relationship of the U.S. Church to this broader context. The Catholic organizational hierarchy is rooted in two millennia of history. All Catholics are geographically assigned based on their place of residence to a local neighborhood parish. Parishes comprise larger geographic areas known as dioceses or archdioceses, which are headed by a bishop or archbishop appointed by the pope. A few of these archbishops and other top Catholic bishops from around the world are named members of the College of Cardinals, the elite officials of the Church who are responsible for electing a new pope each time the "bishop of Rome" dies, as was the case in 2005 after the death of Pope John Paul II.[68]

At the heart of Church structure is the doctrine of apostolic succession, the idea that the pope is literally the successor of the apostle Peter. Although hierarchy remains a defining characteristic of the Catholic Church, American Catholicism leadership is characterized by pluralism. Diverse holy orders of monks and nuns, each with a distinct focus and élan, exist alongside the traditional structure of priests, bishops, and archbishops. Thus one finds left-wing Jesuits, feminist nuns, and Maryknoll missionaries spreading liberation theology alongside more conservative orders and groups of Catholic traditionalists (such as Opus Dei) that are fierce adherents of Catholic orthodoxy and the teachings of the pope.[69]

One of the distinctive features of the Catholic Church is its appreciation of politics. Throughout European history, for example, the Church was deeply enmeshed in statecraft. Politics was not alien to church leaders then, nor is it today. Catholic leaders and parishioners alike have been intensely involved in politics around the globe, from the Philippines to Latin America, from Eastern Europe to the United States.[70] In one sense this political comfort level is an asset: the Church and its activists do not need to overcome as much resistance to politics as do many evangelical Protestants. On the other hand, for much of American history the Catholic Church was seen as a suspect institution.

The Church's roots in the medieval world of kings and princes, along with its historical skepticism about democracy and religious freedom, placed it at odds with the American liberal tradition. Well into the twentieth century, for example, the Catholic Church resisted many liberal democratic reforms and allied itself with authoritarian governments.[71] This history created a huge problem for American Catholics, whom many Protestants and others viewed as lacking a fundamental commitment to American democracy and liberal freedoms even though most Catholics in fact embraced the American creed of democracy and individual liberty and were often ardent patriots and anticommunists.[72] Nevertheless, the question of whether or not the Catholic embrace of American liberal democracy was compatible with the tenets of their faith remained into the 1950s.[73]

Everything changed for American Catholics as a result of a profound revolution within the broader Church itself, a revolution in which the United States and its Catholic leaders played a pivotal role. In 1961 Pope John XXIII declared that the church needed to open its windows and get some fresh air. This declaration was just the second time in two millennia of Roman Catholic history that the pope called for a meeting of the world's bishops to modernize the Church. Vatican II, as this meeting came to be called, lasted from 1962 to 1965. It was a veritable earthquake for the Church, and its effects are still being felt decades later. As a result of Vatican II, the Catholic Church formally embraced democracy and ordered liberty, and for the first time Protestants were accepted as fellow Christians rather than as apostates. The Mass, which always had been said in Latin and thus was difficult for parishioners to follow, would thereafter be celebrated in hundreds of local languages. And the bishops in each country were given greater authority to speak on behalf of the church in their respective lands. One worldwide impact of the church's change, as political scientist Samuel Huntington has argued, was to encourage a wave of democratization in formerly authoritarian Catholic nations.[74]

In the United States, Vatican II legitimated the Catholic accommodation with liberal democracy and accelerated the assimilation process for Catholics. Even before Vatican II, leaders of the American Church had begun to assert themselves politically. After Vatican II, many others in the Catholic Church joined the bishops in political engagement. Nuns and priests marched in civil rights demonstrations, and Philip and Daniel Berrigan, radical antiwar priests, poured blood on the Pentagon to protest U.S. involvement in Vietnam. Two key Catholic organizations—Catholic Charities and the Campaign for Human Development—sponsored antipoverty projects in inner cities and rural backwaters. The Catholic Church also lent support to the farmworker movement led by César Chávez.[75]

Ultimately, Vatican II led to an increased role for the bishops' national organization, known today as the United States Conference of Catholic Bishops, or USCCB. Headquartered in Washington, D.C., and composed of several hundred leaders and former leaders of Catholic dioceses in the United States, the USCCB leads the Church's official social and political efforts. The politics of the bishops are not easily categorized, which is why American conservatives and liberals alike seek out alliances with Catholic bishops. On social welfare, labor, civil rights, and military policy, the bishops have taken a decidedly liberal posture over the years. At least some of this agenda stems from the Church's historical concern that untrammeled industrial capitalism exploits workers and undermines the dignity of work and the vitality of community and family. However, the Church's positions on abortion, divorce, and sexuality are conservative, and their support of "school choice" is libertarian in spirit.[76] Liberals celebrated when the bishops drafted "pastoral letters" on nuclear arms and the economy; conservatives applauded the bishops when they condemned abortion. Similarly, liberals welcomed the support of Catholics who lobbied against Reagan's support for the Nicaraguan Contras in the 1980s or the war in Iraq in the 2000s; conservatives appreciated the Catholic fight for day-care vouchers and school choice.[77] The Church is thus strategically placed as a sort of bridge between evangelical and mainline Protestants.

Ironically, at the very time that the Catholic Church is poised to exercise influence in American society and politics, it faces serious problems and shows some signs of decline. Since Vatican II, attendance rates at Mass have fallen off; perhaps as many as a third of all confirmed American Catholics pay little or no attention to the Church. Although another third are deeply committed to the Church and its teachings, most post–Vatican II American Catholics practice what is called "cafeteria-style Catholicism" in that they pick and choose what to take from the faith and what to leave.[78] Moreover, the number of people willing to enter the Catholic vocations—that is, to become priests and nuns—is very low. Many orders of nuns will die out entirely within a generation unless recruiting patterns change dramatically. Already there is a major shortage within the aging priesthood and the prospect for an even greater shortage in the near future.[79]

Of course, many of the Roman Catholic Church's challenges derive from the clash between its traditional values and American norms. Thus it defends celibacy for its all-male priesthood, a hierarchical authority structure, opposition to divorce, and even its official prohibition against "artificial" birth control. These stances have led not only to divisions within the Church but also to portrayals of Catholics in elite media and popular music that sometimes border on anti-Catholic bigotry.[80]

Other challenges, though, have been created by the Church's own leaders. Especially damaging has been the scandal that erupted in 2002 when it came to light that several American dioceses and archdioceses had failed to discipline Catholic priests who engaged repeatedly in the sexual abuse of minors. As of 2009, six American dioceses and archdioceses have been forced to file for bankruptcy due to financial settlements with victims of sexual abuse. To be sure, only a very small number of Catholic priests were engaged in this scandal, and sexual misconduct is hardly the exclusive domain of the Catholic Church. Nevertheless, this scandal has damaged the Church's credibility within its ranks and in the broader American society.[81]

But perhaps the most penetrating long-run explanation for the Catholic Church's challenges today is its evolution into a mainstream American religious tradition. As we saw in Chapter 1, church growth and decline in the American religious marketplace operate with a seemingly ineluctable logic. To the extent that the Catholic Church has become a mainstream institution in the United States, it has become subject to the profound encounter with the outside world that can have great effect. These encounters often point out where a church differs from the larger culture and encourages those more committed to values in that larger culture to move away from the church. This has certainly been the case with a number of feminist women for whom an all-male priesthood and hierarchy in the Catholic Church is not acceptable.[82]

This result should not surprise us. Catholics today are no longer found disproportionately among the working classes, as was the case at the turn of the twentieth century. Now Catholics and white Protestants have equal educational levels and are equally represented in professional and managerial occupations. And herein lies a paradox. When American Catholics were represented disproportionately at the lower end of the socioeconomic scale, they represented a much more distinct and unified community—and one that was much more likely to accept the authority of the Church and its teachings than is the case today among American Catholics. Today many Catholics do not feel bound by the dictates of the Church, let alone its political efforts. The Catholic Church, as a consequence, does not exercise as much political clout as it once did. Nonetheless, with its relatively large size, impressive organization, and long-standing openness to politics, it remains a major player.[83]

From another point of view, the reduction in size of Catholic numbers is potentially a plus in terms of political influence. The Church today is moving in a more conservative direction and so are many of its still-devoted millions of members. More conservative bishops, priests, and laity; more commitment to the Mass, the Virgin Mary, devotionals, and sometimes even experiences with versions of the Latin Mass; and standard Catholic moral positions may lead to a more cohesive, if much smaller, Church over time. Similarly, the rise of a vigorous evangelical movement in the Church, one devoted to inspiring Church members and others to a more spirited faith, is underway and making some impact.[84] A more unified and inspirited Church at all levels may in the end be a more powerful one than the present highly divided one. Unity and passion can make a lot of difference in politics.

CONCLUSION

Christianity in America flourishes with pluralism and vitality, yet it does so amid contrary secular forces, which creates a tension. On the one hand, professed faith seems to be strong and churches remain heavily involved in society and politics. On the other hand, moral and ethical problems abound, and many powerful institutions—such as the mass media, government, business, public schools, and universities—are driven primarily by secular logics that are relatively independent of religious influence.

One of the perennial questions, therefore, is why such an apparently thriving religious community does not exercise more political influence. The answer to this question lies in America's religious pluralism. Politicians hear a babel of competing religious voices on most issues. When religious groups do form a united front, they can be quite effective. But those instances are rare enough to prove the rule: Pluralism dilutes any group's power.

Religious influence is also checked by the defining characteristics of the American polity. As we discuss in Chapters 8 and 9, the First Amendment's requirement of religious disestablishment has fostered a separatist tradition and ethic in the United States that features wariness—even suspicion—of interaction between religion and government. This wariness is especially pronounced among secular elites, many of whom occupy positions of influence and power in government, media, and business.

The framers of the Constitution constructed a political order designed to disperse, fragment, and check power. A majority is required to pass national legislation, which can then be diluted or nullified by the actions of states, bureaucracies, or the courts. To achieve real clout, therefore, a movement or group must work successfully on a number of fronts—from the states to the national government, from Congress and the president to the courts and bureaucracies, from lobbying and electoral mobilization to the shaping of public opinion through the mass media. The challenge is formidable, and continuing success is rare. Although the framers saw to it that no single movement or voice can dominate the American political system, the system itself is open enough to provide access to even the smallest group. Thus our political structure ensures many religious groups the chance to have some political influence, and simultaneously it blocks each one from achieving dominance.

FURTHER READING

Gaustad, Edwin Scott, and Philip L. Barlow. *New Historical Atlas of Religion in America.* New York: Oxford, 2001. A valuable information resource that focuses on the geographic distribution of religion in America.

Green, John C. *The Faith Factor: How Religion Influences American Elections.* Westport, CT: Praeger, 2007. An excellent overview of American faith traditions and their political predilections.

Hemeyer, Julia Corbett. *Religion in America.* 6th ed. Englewood Cliffs, NJ: Prentice Hall, 2009. A good introduction to the sociology of religion in the context of the United States.

Kelley, Dean. *Why Conservative Churches Are Growing: A Study in Sociology of Religion.* San Francisco: Harper, 1977. The classic work on the rise of evangelical and the decline of mainline Protestantism.

Lindsay, D. Michael. *Faith in the Halls of Power: How Evangelicals Joined the American Elite.* New York: Oxford University Press, 2007. Massive study of evangelical elites in the United States.

Morris, Charles R. *American Catholic*. New York: Random House, 1997. A history of
American Catholicism.

Steinfels, Peter. *A People Adrift: The Crisis of the Roman Catholic Church in America*.
New York: Simon & Schuster, 2003. An examination of the contemporary challenges
facing the Roman Catholic Church.

Wuthnow, Robert. *The Quiet Hand of God: Faith-Based Activism and the Public Role of
Mainline Protestantism*. Berkeley: University of California Press, 2002. This text
argues that mainline Protestantism's political and social influence, though "quiet,"
nevertheless continues to be important.

————. *The Restructuring of American Religion: Society and Faith Since World War Two*.
Princeton: Princeton University Press, 1988. An extremely influential book reflecting
on the evolution of religion in the United States.

NOTES

1. Pew Forum on Religion & Public Life, *U.S. Religious Landscape Study*, http://religions
.pewforum.org/pdf/report2religious-landscape-study-chapter-1.pdf (2008), 23.

2. Ibid.

3. Ibid.

4. Seymour Martin Lipset, *American Exceptionalism: A Double-Edged Sword* (New York:
W. W. Norton, 1997).

5. Pippa Norris and Ronald Inglehart, *Sacred and Secular: Religion and Politics World-wide* (New York: Cambridge University Press, 2004), 90.

6. Ibid., 91.

7. Ibid., 17, 72.

8. Marita Carballo, "Religion in the World at the End of the Millennium," *Gallup International Millennium Survey* (Washington, DC: Gallup International, 1999). The report is
available at http://www.gallup-international.com.

9. Philip Jenkins, *The Next Christendom: The Coming of Global Christianity* (New York:
Oxford University Press, 2003); Norris and Inglehart, *Sacred and Secular*.

10. Tom Kington, "Number of Muslims Ahead of Catholics, Says Vatican," *Guardian*,
March 31, 2008, 18. For a fascinating cartographic description of global Islam, see Ninian
Smart, *Atlas of the World's Religions* (New York: Oxford University Press, 1999), 168–197.

11. Pew Forum, *U.S. Religious Landscape Study*, 24.

12. Robert Bezilla, ed., *Religion in American 1992–1993* (Princeton: Princeton Religion
Research Center, 1993).

13. Pew Forum, *U.S. Religious Landscape Study*.

14. Barna Research Group, "Americans Draw Theological Beliefs from Diverse Points of View," *Barna Research Online*, http://www.barna.org (October 8, 2002).

15. Barna Research Group, "Beliefs: Salvation," *Barna Research Online*, http://www.barna.org (n.d.).

16. Pew Forum, *U.S. Religious Landscape Study*, 31.

17. Ibid., 32.

18. Albert L. Winseman, "U.S. Evangelicals: How Many Walk the Walk?" *Gallup Poll News Service*, http://www.gallup.com/poll/16519/us-evangelicals-how-many-walk-walk.aspx (May 31, 2005).

19. Pew Forum on Religion & Public Life, *Spirit and Power: A 10-Country Survey of Pentecostals*, http://pewforum.org/surveys/pentecostal/ (2006).

20. Andrew Greeley, *The Denominational Society: A Sociological Approach to Religion in America* (Glenview, IL: Scott, Foresman, 1972).

21. National Opinion Research Center data, as reported in Tim O'Neil, "Scandal Rocks Church, but Faith Remains," *St. Louis Post Dispatch*, June 22, 2003, A1.

22. George H. Gallup Jr., *Gallup/CNN/USA Today Poll* (June 19, 2003).

23. International Social Survey Programme (ISSP), *Religion II: ISSP 1998 Codebook* (Cologne: Central Archive for Empirical Social Research, 2001), http://www.issp.org/data.htm, 26–27, 30–31.

24. Pew Forum, *U.S. Religious Landscape Study*, 36.

25. Figures on church attendance are disputed by C. Kirk Hadaway, Penny Long Marler, and Mark Chaves, "What the Polls Don't Show: A Closer Look at U.S. Church Attendance," *American Sociological Review* 58 (1993), 741–752. See also C. Kirk Hadaway and Penny Long, "Did You Really Go to Church This Week? Behind the Poll Data," *Christian Century* (May 6, 1998), 472–475.

26. George Gallup Jr., "Religion in America: Will the Vitality of the Churches Be the Surprise of the Next Century?" *The Public Perspective* 6 (October/November 1995), 1–8. See also Barna Research Group, "Survey Shows Faith Impacts Some Behaviors but Not Others," *Barna Research Online*, http://www.barna.org (October 22, 2002).

27. This argument is made by Allen D. Hertzke, *Echoes of Discontent: Jesse Jackson, Pat Robertson, and the Resurgence of Populism* (Washington, DC: CQ Press, 1993).

28. Linda K. George, Christopher G. Ellison, and David B. Larson, "Explaining the Relationship Between Religious Involvement and Health," *Psychological Inquiry* 13 (2002), 190–200; Harold G. Koenig, Michael E. McCollough, and David B. Larson, *Handbook of Religion and Health* (New York: Oxford University Press, 2001); Lynda H. Powell, Leila Shahabi, and Carl E. Thoreson, "Religion and Spirituality: Linkages to Physical Health," *American Psychologist* 58 (2003), 36–52; but see also Richard P. Sloan, Emilia Bagiella,

and Tia Powell, "Religion, Spirituality, and Medicine," *The Lancet* 353 (February 1999), 664–667.

29. Koenig, McCollough, and Larson, *Handbook of Religion and Health.*

30. Arthur C. Brooks, "Religious Faith and Charitable Giving," *Policy Review* 121 (October/November 2003), 39-50; David E. Campbell and Steven J. Yonish, "Religion and Volunteering in America," in *Religion as Social Capital: Producing the Common Good*, ed. Corwin E. Smidt (Waco, TX: Baylor University Press, 2003); Roger J. Nemeth and Donald A. Luidens, "The Religious Basis of Charitable Giving in America: A Social Capital Perspective," in *Religion as Social Capital: Producing the Common Good*; Mark Regnerus, Christian Smith, and David Sikkink, "Who Gives to the Poor? The Role of Religious Tradition and Political Location on the Personal Generosity of Americans toward the Poor," *Journal for the Scientific Study of Religion* 37 (1998), 481–493.

31. Pew Forum, *U.S. Religious Landscape Study*. See also John C. Green, *The Faith Factor: How Religion Influences American Elections* (Westport, CT: Praeger, 2007). For a discussion of methodological uses of denominations as indicators of religious traditions, see Lyman A. Kellstedt and John C. Green, "Knowing God's Many People: Denominational Preference and Political Behavior," in *Rediscovering the Religious Factor in American Politics*, eds. David C. Leege and Lyman A. Kellstedt (Armonk, NY: M. E. Sharpe, 1993); and Brian Steensland et al., "The Measure of American Religion: Toward Improving the State of the Art," *Social Forces* 79 (2000), 291–318.

32. See Paul A. Djupe and Laura R. Olson, *Religious Interests in Community Conflict: Beyond the Culture Wars* (Waco, TX: Baylor University Press, 2007).

33. Roger Finke and Rodney Stark, *The Churching of America, 1776–2005: Winners and Losers in Our Religious Economy* (New Brunswick, NJ: Rutgers University Press, 2008); Laurence Iannaccone, "Why Strict Churches Are Strong," *American Journal of Sociology* 99 (1994), 1180–1211; Dean M. Kelley, *Why Conservative Churches Are Growing: A Study in Sociology of Religion* (San Francisco: Harper, 1977).

34. Campus Crusade for Christ, *Annual Report 2008*, http://www.ccci.org/aboutus/donor-relations/annual-report/2008-ccc-annual-report.pdf (2008), 4. On Campus Crusade in general, see John G. Turner, *Bill Bright and Campus Crusade for Christ: The Renewal of Evangelicalism in Postwar America* (Chapel Hill: University of North Carolina Press, 2008).

35. For a fine discussion of the Christian Right, see Clyde Wilcox and Carin Larson, *Onward Christian Soldiers? The Religious Right in American Politics*, 3rd ed. (Boulder: Westview Press, 2006).

36. See, for example, Ronald Reagan, *Abortion and the Conscience of the Nation* (Nashville: Thomas Nelson, 1984). On the symbolic use of religion by presidents, see Colleen J. Shogan, *The Moral Rhetoric of American Presidents* (College Station, TX: Texas A&M University Press, 2006).

37. David E. Campbell, ed., *A Matter of Faith: Religion in the 2004 Presidential Election* (Washington, DC: Brookings Institution, 2007); Geoffrey Layman, *The Great Divide: Religious and Cultural Conflict in American Party Politics* (New York: Columbia University Press, 2001); Wilcox and Larson, *Onward Christian Soldiers?*

38. George M. Marsden, *Understanding Fundamentalism and Evangelicalism* (Grand Rapids, MI: Eerdmans, 1991).

39. Laurie Goodstein and David D. Kirkpatrick, "Conservative Group Amplifies Voice of Protestant Orthodoxy," *The New York Times*, May 22, 2004, A1.

40. Cecil M. Robeck Jr., *The Azusa Street Mission and Revival* (Nashville: Thomas Nelson, 2006).

41. Michael O. Emerson and Christian Smith, *Divided by Faith: Evangelical Religion and the Problem of Race in America* (New York: Oxford University Press, 2001).

42. Fredrick C. Harris, *Something Within: Religion in African-American Political Activism* (New York: Oxford University Press, 1999).

43. Joel A. Carpenter, *Revive Us Again: The Reawakening of American Fundamentalism* (New York: Oxford University Press, 1997); Mark Dalhouse, *An Island in the Lake of Fire: Bob Jones University, Fundamentalism, and the Separatist Movement* (Athens, GA: University of Georgia Press, 1996); Marsden, *Understanding Fundamentalism and Evangelicalism*.

44. Allan Anderson, *An Introduction to Pentecostalism: Global Charismatic Christianity* (New York: Cambridge University Press, 2004); Edith Blumhofer, *Restoring the Faith: The Assemblies of God, Pentecostalism, and American Culture* (Urbana, IL: University of Illinois, 1997); Donald E. Miller and Tetsunao Yamamori, *Global Pentecostalism: The New Face of Christian Engagement* (Berkeley: University of California Press, 2005); Grant Wacker, *Heaven Below: Early Pentecostalism and American Culture* (Cambridge, MA: Harvard University Press, 2001).

45. For a fine historical discussion of fundamentalism in the United States in the 1930s and 1940s, see Carpenter, *Revive Us Again*.

46. Anderson, *An Introduction to Pentecostalism*.

47. James F. Findlay Jr., *Church People in the Struggle: The National Council of Churches and the Black Freedom Movement, 1950–1970* (New York: Oxford University Press, 1993).

48. Michael Luo and Laurie Goodstein, "Emphasis Shifts for New Breed of Evangelicals," *The New York Times*, May 21, 2007, A1.

49. Jim Wallis, *The Great Awakening: Reviving Faith and Politics in a Post-Religious Right America* (New York: HarperCollins, 2008).

50. H. Richard Niebuhr, *Christ and Culture* (New York: Harper and Row, 1951); Peter J. Thuesen, "The Logic of Mainline Churchliness," in *The Quiet Hand of God: Faith-Based Activism and the Public Role of Mainline Protestantism*, eds. Robert Wuthnow and John H. Evans (Berkeley: University of California Press, 2002).

51. James L. Guth, John C. Green, Corwin E. Smidt, Lyman A. Kellstedt, and Margaret M. Poloma, *The Bully Pulpit: The Politics of Protestant Clergy* (Lawrence, KS: University Press of Kansas, 1997).

52. Jeffrey Hadden, *The Gathering Storm in the Churches* (Garden City, NY: Doubleday, 1969); Harold E. Quinley, *The Prophetic Clergy: Social Activism Among Protestant Ministers* (New York: Wiley, 1974).

53. Jackson W. Carroll, Barbara G. Wheeler, Daniel O. Aleshire, and Penny Long Marler, *Being There: Culture and Formation in Two Theological Schools* (New York: Oxford University Press, 1997).

54. Campbell, *A Matter of Faith*; Green, *The Faith Factor*; Jeff Manza and Clem Brooks, "The Changing Political Fortunes of Mainline Protestants," *The Quiet Hand of God: Faith-Based Activism and the Public Role of Mainline Protestantism*, eds. Robert Wuthnow and John H. Evans (Berkeley: University of California Press, 2002).

55. See Corwin Smidt et al., *The Disappearing God Gap? Religion and the 2008 Presidential Election* (New York: Oxford University Press, forthcoming).

56. Green, *The Faith Factor*.

57. Findlay, *Church People in the Struggle*; Allen D. Hertzke, *Representing God in Washington* (Knoxville: University of Tennessee Press, 1987).

58. Findlay, *Church People in the Struggle;* Michael B. Friedland, *Lift Up Your Voice Like a Trumpet: White Clergy and the Civil Rights and Antiwar Movements, 1954–1973* (Chapel Hill: University of North Carolina Press, 1998); Mitchell K. Hall, *Because of Their Faith: CALCAV and Religious Opposition to the Vietnam War* (New York: Columbia University Press, 1990).

59. Crawford and Olson, *Christian Clergy in American Politics*; Guth et al., *The Bully Pulpit*; Smidt, *Pulpit and Politics*.

60. See Wendy Cadge, "Vital Conflicts: The Mainline Protestant Denominations Debate Homosexuality," in *The Quiet Hand of God*.

61. Hadden, *The Gathering Storm in the Churches*; Quinley, *The Prophetic Clergy*; A. James Reichley, *Faith in Politics* (Washington, DC: Brookings Institution, 2002), 264.

62. Djupe and Gilbert, *The Political Influence of Church*; Guth et al., *The Bully Pulpit*; Hadden, *The Gathering Storm in the Churches*; Smidt, *Pulpit and Politics*.

63. Dale Jones et al., *Religious Congregations and Membership: 2000* (Nashville: Glenmary Research Center, 2002).

64. Phillip Hammond, *The Protestant Presence in Twentieth-Century America: Religion and Political Culture* (Albany: State University Press of New York, 1992).

65. Finke and Stark, *The Churching of America*; Iannaccone, "Why Strict Churches Are Strong"; Kelley, *Why Conservative Churches Are Growing*; Robert Wuthnow, *The Crisis in the Churches* (New York: Oxford University Press, 1996).

66. Nancy Ammerman, *Pillars of Faith* (Berkeley: University of California Press, 2005); Djupe and Olson, *Religious Interests in Community Conflict*; Ram A. Cnaan, *The Invisible Caring Hand* (New York: New York University Press, 2002); Stephen Hart, *Cultural Dilemmas of Progressive Politics: Styles of Engagement Among Grassroots Activists* (Chicago: University of Chicago Press, 2001); Wuthnow and Evans, *The Quiet Hand of God.*

67. Richard John Neuhaus, *The Catholic Moment: The Paradox of the Church in the Postmodern World* (San Francisco: Harper and Row, 1987).

68. John L. Allen Jr., *The Rise of Benedict XVI: The Inside Story of How the Pope Was Elected and Where He Will Take the Catholic Church* (Garden City, NY: Doubleday, 2005).

69. John L. Allen Jr., *Opus Dei: An Objective Look Behind the Myths and Reality of the Most Controversial Force in the Catholic Church* (Garden City, NY: Doubleday, 2005).

70. Paul Christopher Manuel, Lawrence C. Reardon, and Clyde Wilcox, eds., *The Catholic Church and the Nation-State: Comparative Perspectives* (Washington, DC: Georgetown University Press, 2007).

71. For a brief survey in the European context, see Martin Conway, "Introduction," in *Political Catholicism in Europe, 1918–1965*, eds. Tom Buchanan and Martin Conway (New York: Oxford University Press, 1996).

72. See, for example, Paul Blanshard's critique of the Church in *American Freedom and Catholic Power* (Boston: Beacon Press, 1949). For a balanced historical treatment, see John T. McGreevy, *Catholics and American Freedom: A History* (New York: W. W. Norton, 2003).

73. See John Courtney Murray, *We Hold These Truths: Catholic Reflections on the American Proposition* (New York: Sheed and Ward, 1960). Murray concludes that the American experiment, properly understood, is compatible with Church teachings.

74. Samuel Huntington, *The Third Wave: Democratization in the Late Twentieth Century* (Norman: University of Oklahoma Press, 1991). On Vatican II, see Melissa J. Wilde, *Vatican II: A Sociological Analysis of Religious Change* (Princeton: Princeton University Press, 2007).

75. Timothy A. Byrnes, *Catholic Bishops in American Politics* (Princeton: Princeton University Press, 1991); Friedland, *Lift Up Your Voice Like a Trumpet*, chap. 6–9; Murray Polner and Jim O'Grady, *Disarmed and Dangerous* (Boulder: Westview Press, 1997); Marco G. Prouty and César Chávez, *The Catholic Bishops, and the Farmworkers' Struggle for Social Justice* (Tucson: University of Arizona Press, 2008).

76. Byrnes, *Catholic Bishops in American Politics*; Clarke E. Cochran and David Carroll Cochran, *Catholics, Politics, and Public Policy: Beyond Left and Right* (Maryknoll, NY: Orbis, 2003).

77. Cochran and Cochran, *Catholics, Politics, and Public Policy*; Hubert Morken and Jo Renee Formicola, *The Politics of School Choice* (Lanham, MD: Rowman and Littlefield, 1999).

78. Peter Steinfels, "When Is a Catholic Not a Catholic?" *New York Times Magazine*, December 7, 1997, 63–65.

79. On the priest shortage in the Catholic Church, see Richard A. Schoenherr, *Goodbye Father: The Celibate Male Priesthood and the Future of the Catholic Church* (New York: Oxford University Press, 2002).

80. Philip Jenkins, *The New Anti-Catholicism: The Last Acceptable Prejudice* (New York: Oxford University Press, 2003).

81. United States Conference of Catholic Bishops, *The Nature and Scope of the Problem of Sexual Abuse of Minors by Catholic Priests and Deacons in the United States*, http://www.usccb.org/nrb/johnjaystudy/ (2004). For extended coverage of the scandal in Boston, see "Spotlight Investigation: Abuse in the Catholic Church," *The Boston Globe*, http://www.boston.com/globe/spotlight/abuse/; see also Peter Steinfels, *A People Adrift: The Crisis of the Roman Catholic Church in America* (New York: Simon & Schuster, 2004).

82. Finke and Stark, *The Churching of America*.

83. Two important books on the contemporary Roman Catholic Church are Steinfels, *A People Adrift*; and David Gibson, *The Coming Catholic Church: How the Faithful are Shaping a New American Catholicism* (San Francisco: HarperSanFrancisco, 2003).

84. See also evangelicalcatholic.com.

3

JUDAISM, ISLAM, AND OTHER EXPRESSIONS OF RELIGIOUS PLURALISM

Most of the discussion of religion and politics in the United States concentrates on the political activity of familiar and well-established Christian groups, meaning Catholics and various Protestant denominations. This focus makes sense because these groups are the largest and most prominent among the complex and pluralistic mix of religions in the United States. But these major religious groups hardly constitute the entire story of religion—or of religion and politics—in the United States.

After all, there are literally hundreds of religions and thousands of religious communities and churches in the United States. Every one of them is a part of the larger nation, and that simple fact necessarily affects each of them. Of course, each American religious group has political objectives—even if it simply wishes to be left alone. And each exercises political influence, however small, indirect, or unintended. Smaller religions have important lessons to teach about what they do, how they protect themselves, and how they advance their values. Their stories become ever more relevant as the pluralism of American religion continues to grow.

It is not obvious how to study the political dimensions of smaller religious groups in the United States. Few have done so, and as we proceed we are acutely aware that our approach represents only one possible method. We approach smaller religions with respect—not as strange phenomena. Religious movements deserve to be taken seriously, both on their own terms and for their political implications.

In this chapter we divide small religious movements into three groups: first, Judaism and Islam, both of which present major alternatives to Christianity in American public life; second, religious traditions that maintain a clear separation from mainstream politics and culture; and third, non-separatist traditions that have reached beyond their own walls to engage the broader culture. For each category we give attention to attitudes toward, and involvement in, political life. We argue that distinctive religious beliefs and behaviors combine with a host of other factors—geography, relative size, and so on—to explain differences in how smaller religious groups approach public life.

MAJOR NON-CHRISTIAN RELIGIONS

Judaism and Islam, both in terms of their size and public exposure, are the most prominent non-Christian religious traditions in America. Jews have lived in the United States since before the founding of the nation and have carved out a highly successful niche in American society. Islam, by contrast, is a relative newcomer and is struggling to address unique political and social challenges.

Jews and Judaism

Jews are among the most successful minority groups in America. After suffering persecution for centuries throughout the world, Jews have found the United States, with its doctrine of religious tolerance, a remarkably hospitable place. This is not to say that they have not faced serious disadvantages; many Jews have been subjected to outright discrimination and cultural hostility. But the constitutional protection of religious liberty, combined with a social system that rewards strong families, hard work, and education, has enabled Jews to prosper in the United States. Jews rank high on every aggregate socioeconomic measure, including educational attainment, income, and professional status. They have moved into positions of prominence in business, law, higher education, politics, journalism, and entertainment.[1]

However, we need to avoid reinforcing unfair stereotypes of Jewish cabals ruling the world. In fact, Jewish influence is often exaggerated. Constituting less than 2 percent of the population, Jewish voting strength makes an impact only in cities and states where their numbers are concentrated, and migration patterns suggest increasing vote dilution as Jewish Americans disperse across the United States.[2] In some cases, Jews' influence on some issues—backing for Israel, for example—is enhanced due to broad support from Christians. Still, due to their activism around civil liberties and civil rights issues and their support for Israel, Jews often have had an impact on American politics that is more profound than their relatively small size would suggest.

Most Jews who are formally associated with a synagogue fall into one of three major groupings—Reform (41 percent), Conservative (29 percent), and Orthodox (18 percent)—that reflect the diversity within American Judaism.[3] Yet many Jews are in fact largely secular and committed to a secular approach to life. As a result, one dimension of the politics of religion—the conflict between secular forces and religious ones in the American public square—attracts many Jewish voices strongly opposed to government interaction with religion.

Among Jewish Americans, synagogue attendance rates are low—only a third attend on a monthly basis[4]—and many Jews admit to agnostic views. Nevertheless, there is a cultural dimension to Judaism that ties even the least religious Jews together out of a sense of shared history and culture. Many Jews proudly describe themselves as Jewish even though they never set foot in a synagogue. One of the serious issues in Jewish circles today is the challenge of maintaining a distinctive Jewish culture without much of a religious dimension.[5] Roughly half of all American Jews today marry people of other faith traditions, and children often are raised with only a vague sense of their Jewish heritage.[6] Moreover, birthrates for Jewish women are lower than the rate needed to replace the population.[7] Myriad calls to reclaim Jewish heritage only confirm the concern.[8]

Jews have a well-deserved reputation for political liberalism that derives from several factors. The majority of religious American Jews belong to one of the two largest (and theologically liberal) branches of Judaism: the Reform and Conservative traditions. Reform Jews in particular have roots in the liberal Enlightenment period and are assertive champions of civil liberties and church-state separation. Moreover, because of their historical experience of persecution, most Jews believe in the need to maintain a society that tolerates minorities and cares about the disadvantaged. Support for progressive taxation, civil rights, and other liberal causes often places Jews in the vanguard.[9]

Jews exercise political power through a host of robust organizations. The oldest of these is the American Jewish Committee (AJC), which was formed in 1906. Interest groups such as the AJC exercise influence because they have thriving local chapters, seasoned leaders, and a clear political agenda. Even though these groups' agenda is undeniably liberal, there is pluralism within American Jewish politics as well.[10] Indeed, Orthodox Jews and the Ultraorthodox (see Box 3.1) often oppose abortion, support government aid to religious schools, applaud the enforcement of antipornography laws, back various measures to check the advance of secular culture, and vote Republican. But this is not the extent of Jewish pluralism. A highly influential group of Jewish intellectuals, including former liberals Norman Pod-horetz and Irving Kristol, were leaders of the neoconservative movement, helping to formulate the reaction against perceived excesses of the 1960s and 1970s.[11] That movement continues to the present day, as illustrated by Irving Kristol's son, William, who now heads the conservative magazine *The Weekly Standard* and frequently appears as a commentator on Fox News Channel. There were key links between such neoconservatives as Kristol and the presidential administration of George W. Bush, especially in the person of Paul Wolfowitz, the deputy secretary of defense and a Jewish American.[12] Wolfowitz and other neoconservatives were stalwart advocates of the war in Iraq.

BOX 3.1   THE HASIDIM IN AMERICA

There are several distinct Ultraorthodox Jewish communities in the United States, but the largest of these are Hasidic Jews, who are concentrated primarily in several neighborhoods in New York City, Los Angeles, and New Jersey. It is important to note that the Hasidim are not a thoroughly unified group; they are in fact divided into several tight subgroups, each organized under a *rebbe* (master) and devoted to the laws and teachings of ancient scripture. Unlike many other Ultraorthodox Jews, however, the Hasidim do not single-mindedly study the scriptures. For the Hasidim, such an approach is much too formal and scholarly; it downplays the essential importance of emotion in their worship of God.

The political tradition of the Hasidim mostly has been one of political withdrawal from larger, usually Christian, societies. Hasidic Jews are similar to many other fundamentalist religious groups in that they seek distance from societies they judge to be corrupting or otherwise dangerous to the faithful. At the same time, however, the Hasidim do sometimes participate in politics. In the United States this has included regular voting. Because the Hasidim are social conservatives, they have often voted Republican. Moreover, the Hasidim have on occasion tried to elect their own candidates in local or state legislative contests where crucial issues are at stake and where they have a chance to win (as in a few parts of New York State).

Sources: Samuel C. Heilman and Steven M. Cohen, *Cosmopolitans and Parochials: Modern Orthodox Jews in America* (Chicago: University of Chicago Press, 1989); William M. Kephart and William W. Zellner, *Extraordinary Groups*, 7th ed. (New York: Worth, 2001), chap. 6; Jack Wertheimer, *A People Divided* (New York: Basic Books, 1993).

For many of the conservative and Republican Jewish minority the real explanation for the overwhelming Jewish orientation toward liberalism on so many issues and in voting stems from a rejection of Judaism itself in any traditional sense. Instead of the ancient Jewish law critical of abortion and opposing same sexual relations, modern secular liberal attitudes hold force. For these outnumbered critics, if there is a religion that affects dominant Jewish attitudes today, it is the religion, so to speak, of liberalism to which "they give the kind of steadfast devotion their forefathers gave to the religion of the Hebrew Bible."[13]

Support for Israel, of course, is a major cause for many American Jews because the connection between American Jews and Israelis traditionally has been deep. No other nation has as many Jewish citizens as the United States; in fact, more Jews live in the United States than in Israel itself. There is a great deal of contact between Jews in both lands. But for many American Jews, Israel is more than a familiar land where close friends and relatives often live. It is also the Jewish homeland and a place that has been a refuge for Jews (off and on) for several millennia. This is another reason for the strong commitment American Jews have to the preservation of Israel, despite plenty of disagreements with particular Israeli leaders and policies. Thus many American Jews support Israel both politically and financially. In turn, Israeli leaders keep in close contact with Jewish leaders and organizations in the United States.

Muslims and Islam

Islam today receives a great deal of media attention, especially as many observers finally became aware of American Muslims in the wake of the September 11, 2001, attacks on the World Trade Center and the Pentagon. The number of Muslims living in the United States is estimated to be between 1.4 and 6 million.[14] The exact number is difficult to count accurately because surveys must be adjusted for the fact that many American Muslims today are immigrants who sometimes do not speak English well or at all. A reasonable estimate is that about 1 percent of the U.S. population is now Muslim. There is no doubt that that number is growing. As recently as fifty years ago no more than 20,000 Muslims lived in the United States.

The number of Muslim places of worship in the United States has grown as well. In the early 1930s, there was just one mosque in the United States, but by 2001 there were at least 1,200 Islamic religious centers.[15] Today there are also a host of Muslim voluntary organizations including charities, civic groups, publishers, private schools, Boy Scout troops sponsored by mosques, college clubs, and political organizations. There is no reason to think that this pattern of growth will not continue, particularly because in the aggregate Muslim Americans are young and have relatively large families.[16]

Although many American Muslims are first- or second-generation immigrants, a sizable proportion of the Muslim population is African American. Most African American Muslims adhere to mainstream Islam, although assorted splinter groups exist, including the much-discussed Nation of Islam led by Louis Farrakhan (see Chapter 10). Perhaps the most influential African American Muslim leader of recent years was Warith Deen Mohammed. Until his retirement from the American Society of Muslims (an umbrella organization for mainstream black Muslims) in 2003, Mohammed led his followers toward mainstream Islam and away from Farrakhan's racially separatist theories. Mohammed died in 2008.

The ethnic diversity that characterizes American Muslims is remarkable. Muslim immigrants have come to the United States in considerable numbers and from no fewer than eighty countries, especially Pakistan, Iran, Bangladesh, Nigeria, Egypt, the Philippines, Indonesia, and various other nations in Asia and Africa. Perhaps 20 percent of American Muslims today are African American. About a third's origins are in South Asia, a fourth in Arabic countries, and less than 10 percent in Africa, with the remainder arriving from East Asia and other regions.[17]

Such ethnic diversity ensures that contemporary U.S. Muslims represent both major traditions of Islam: Sunni and Shi'a, traditions that differ primarily over the question of who succeeded the Prophet Muhammad after his death. However, although there is a sizable Shi'a population in Southern California today, Sunni Muslims predominate in the United States, as they do in the Islamic world as a whole.

Today there are signs of organization that may lead to greater political influence for American Muslims. The aftermath of September 11, 2001, created urgent public policy concerns in the American Muslim community, which a variety of groups has worked to address through interfaith relations, lobbying, and partnership with government agencies. The primary umbrella organization of Islamic groups in the United States is the Islamic Society of North America. September 11 pushed groups such as the Muslim Public Affairs Council (MPAC) to the forefront.

Such groups as MPAC focus primarily on protecting the civil liberties and rights of Muslim American citizens.[18] Since September 11, MPAC and other Muslim organizations have been spending much of their time confronting and debunking the false perception that most Muslims are terrorists or even anti-American. Muslim leaders understand that such stereotypes must be dismantled if Muslims are to gain political influence in the United States. Another way these myths will be debunked is through the growing visibility of some younger Muslims, who are assimilating into American culture with relative ease.[19]

Before September 11, given the racial and ethnic divisions inherent in American Islam—divisions which are especially keen between black Muslims and the remainder of the Muslim population—collective Muslim political muscle seemed unlikely to develop. That is changing now as Muslims of all backgrounds worry about their future in the United States. Security issues aside, however, Muslims come in every political persuasion and do not yet agree on the key components of a political agenda for the Islamic community in the United States. Many Muslims, however, tend to be conservative on social and moral issues such as abortion, gender roles, and sexual behavior. Indeed, many people who convert to Islam from other religions are attracted to its confident discipline and clear boundaries.

It is possible that as adherence to Islam in the United States grows and as it becomes more organized, it may become something of a partner in the rest of the conservative movement in American religion, which today includes evangelical Protestants, traditional Catholics, and Orthodox Jews. However, there are many obstacles to such a partnership. Criticism of the USA PATRIOT Act, the roundup and detention of thousands of Muslims by the U.S. government, and the war in Iraq combined to make the Bush administration highly unpopular with American Muslims by 2004—despite the fact that Muslims had given Bush a plurality of their votes in the 2000 presidential election. Increasingly, Muslims are identifying themselves as Democrats, and they gave large majorities of their votes to John Kerry in 2004 and Barack Obama in 2008.[20] Even if the events of September 11, 2001, had never happened, there would have been obstacles to a Muslim-Christian-Jewish political alliance, not the least of which is deep-seated religious differences.

Another possibility, of course, is that policy concerns affecting Islamic countries such as Iraq will become the core of a political agenda for Muslims in the United States, mirroring American Jews' concern for Israel. To some extent this is true already, although it has not necessarily led to a single set of policy priorities on the part of Muslim interest groups, given the diversity both of Islamic nations and of Muslims in America. The one exception is the existence of strong, universal support among Muslims for the Palestinian cause.[21]

It may turn out that Muslims will never obtain substantial political leverage in the United States regardless of what agenda (or agendas) they pursue. This lack of leverage could result if Islam remains divided and subdivided along ethnic and racial lines, which would undercut the development of a unified Muslim political

BOX 3.2   A MUSLIM FROM MINNESOTA IN THE
U.S. HOUSE OF REPRESENTATIVES

When asked about religion and their vote choices, Americans routinely say they are less likely to cast their ballot for candidates from religions perceived as being outside the mainstream. Hence the election of Keith Ellison to the U.S. House of Representatives in 2006 marked an unusual moment in American political history. Ellison, a Democrat representing Minnesota's 5th Congressional District, became the first Muslim elected to Congress. Raised in Detroit, Ellison became a member of Islam while attending college in the mid-1980s. He earned a law degree at the University of Minnesota and went on to a legal and political career at the state level. During his congressional campaign and in its aftermath, he was no stranger to controversy. Although he did not wear his Muslim faith on his sleeve, it inevitably became a campaign issue, especially when it came to light that as a law student he had defended Louis Farrakhan, the contentious leader of the Nation of Islam who often is linked to anti-Semitism. After making amends with the Jewish community in Minneapolis–St. Paul and handily winning the congressional seat, Ellison also sparked criticism by choosing to place his hand on a copy of the Qur'an that was once owned by Thomas Jefferson during a photo opportunity reenactment of his congressional oath. Despite this and other controversies, he won a second term in 2008, and he remains a committed advocate for greater Muslim engagement in American politics, as well as for American engagement with global Islam.

Source: Neil Macfarquhar, "Democrat Poised to Become First Muslim in Congress," *The New York Times*, October 8, 2006, A10; Richard Wolf, "First Muslim Lawmaker Takes Oath with Qur'an," *USA Today*, January 5, 2007, A4.

agenda in the United States. In time, however, assimilation may render ethnicity less important in defining and dividing American Muslims. In that event, a more politically unified Islam could well emerge in the United States. For this to happen, several things need to occur. A serious effort must be made to fashion a more positive image of Islam in America, a focused political agenda is a must, and so is improved relations with American Jews (Box 3.2).

However, features of Islam that clash with mainstream American culture pose difficulties.[22] This is true, for example, of Islam's patriarchal attitudes toward women.[23] More broadly speaking, Islam is not well understood in most parts of the United States, a reality that must be acknowledged and overcome. But these difficulties can be addressed; other groups, including both Roman Catholics and Jews, already have overcome similar obstacles in American history.

SEPARATIST RELIGIONS

Several smaller religious traditions in the United States take a distinctly separatist orientation toward the broader culture. By the term "separatist," we mean that these religious communities set stricter moral boundaries for their members than do mainstream religions, and that these boundaries necessarily separate members of the religious group from the larger society to a degree. Most of these groups are deeply critical of the larger society, which they portray as immoral, evil, or wrong-headed. Some have an interest in reaching out to the larger society to gain converts, but many enjoy only limited success in such efforts because of the heavy demands placed on group members by their religious beliefs and practices.

It is helpful to subdivide small, separatist religions into two types. The first type includes religious traditions whose members share a common history or ethnic origin. Such characteristics provide a powerful basis for community, but they also limit growth. The second type consists of groups with no such "built-in" basis for unity, so they substitute some other foundation as the premise for their tightly bound community.

The Amish are a good example of a religious group whose community is based on a shared history. Most Amish originally came from the sixteenth-century Anabaptist movements that arose during the Protestant Reformation in Switzerland. The Amish broke away from one Anabaptist branch over issues that are now dusty with time. They began their formal existence as a separate religious group in 1693, although it was not until the eighteenth century that Amish people began migrating to the United States. Since 1992, the Amish population has grown by 84 percent. This is not surprising given the group's strong emphasis on having many children and its success in having about 85 percent of its teenagers opt to join. Today more than 230,000 Amish reside in 28 states, with their best-known communities located in southern Pennsylvania.[24]

The religious beliefs of the Amish are reasonably familiar in the American Protestant context. At the same time, however, the Amish are not part of mainstream American religion or culture. Their focus on maintaining a tightly knit and separatist religious community, as well as their buggies, plain clothes, and rejection of electricity in the home, make this obvious. This separatism is particularly clear to the Amish themselves as they struggle to maintain their way of life against an indifferent and occasionally hostile American culture.[25]

The Amish traditionally have displayed little interest or faith in politics or government. Their numbers are tiny, and their chances of having much political influence are extremely modest. In the United States the Amish usually have had only the most minimal contact with the government. Nevertheless, some Amish citizens vote, and there have been some Amish efforts to lobby state legislatures over issues of urgent importance to them. In 1972, the Amish were involved in a noted U.S. Supreme Court case in which they won the right not to send their teenagers to high school (*Wisconsin* v. *Yoder*). Mostly, though, the Amish have turned away from politics, for their stance reflects the politics of noninvolvement and withdrawal.

Because it is dictated by a sense of religious and cultural separatism, political disengagement has worked well for the Amish. They have acquired a reputation as a quaint and inoffensive people who just wish to be left in peace. This is why they have escaped significant persecution and interference. The broader American culture seems to accept the Amish as a charming expression of a past and a people who pose no threat (with perhaps the small exception of some local drivers who find slow-moving Amish buggies an annoyance). Amish separatism has turned out to be a de facto form of politics that has provided protection from the broader society.

Unlike the Amish, new religious movements, or "cults," are the prime illustration today of small, separatist religions that reach into the society for converts but usually encounter opprobrium. Every so often, television, radio, and newspapers seem to be full of reports of one cult religion or another and the seemingly strange, dangerous, or fanatical activities of its members.[26] Use of the term *cult* is prejudicial because its meaning is always negative. The terms *new religious movement* or *unconventional religion* are more value-neutral, but there are many new or unconventional religions that are very unlike cults. This is why we reluctantly continue to use the term *cult* to describe a specific type of highly dissident, alternative religion organized into tight communities and that exists in extreme tension with the broader culture.

Often such religious groups are headed by a single charismatic leader whom the group's members are willing to follow—sometimes to death, as in the cases of Jim Jones and his 914 Peoples Temple followers in 1978 and Marshall Herff Applewhite and his 39 Heaven's Gate followers in 1997.[27] Estimates range from as many as 5,000 to as few as 700 cults in the United States at any given moment, depending on how strictly one interprets the definition. Few are, or have been, as well known as Peoples Temple or Heaven's Gate. Most cults are nonviolent and shun both politics and the public eye.

In recent decades, few cults have had much political influence, but some have locked horns with the government. Before Jim Jones moved his Peoples Temple from northern California to Guyana (where they ultimately perished), he and his church enjoyed substantial influence in San Francisco politics as an organized voice for various progressive causes.[28] The fiery April 1993 demise of David Koresh and his Branch Davidian religious community outside Waco, Texas, is another example of a cult in conflict with the state. The Branch Davidian community was a breakaway group of another breakaway group of the Seventh-day Adventist Church. Under Koresh, the Branch Davidians soon became a classic illustration of a strictly separatist community led by a charismatic leader. Its eventual destruction had a definite political impact, especially on the Bureau of Alcohol, Tobacco, and Firearms and the Federal Bureau of Investigation, while dramatically demonstrating the Branch Davidians' own lack of political influence.[29]

The Unification Church of Rev. Sun Myung Moon (and now his son, Hyung Jin Moon) presents another exception to cults' standard strategy of political avoidance. This movement and its followers, who are universally known derisively as "Moonies," are committed to being involved in politics. How influential the Unification Church is, however, is another matter. The membership, financial resources, and political influence of the Unification Church are not well understood, but we do know that the church in the United States is part of a larger movement, based in South Korea, that has substantial financial resources. The Unification Church has been willing to commit these resources, for example, to funding the politically conservative *Washington Times*, a newspaper that is the major alternative to the more liberal *Washington Post*.[30]

On the extreme fringe of American religious life is the tiny but noteworthy Christian Identity movement, which is made up of small separatist organizations whose leaders preach hate through religion. Most Christian Identity groups are extremely hostile toward racial and ethnic minorities, gay and lesbian people, and those who practice faiths other than Christianity. They embrace what they term the "Israel message" that white people are chosen by God and that Jews and persons of color are subhuman. In the view of Christian Identity followers, an apocalyptic holy war will destroy all people except white Christians. As postmillennialists, Christian Identity followers see the End Times as imminent, so they often arm themselves heavily and live together in remote compounds. The Christian Identity movement's political approach is sometimes violent; convicted and executed Oklahoma City bomber Timothy McVeigh had links to the movement.[31]

There is little doubt that the extent of the cult phenomenon gets exaggerated when sporadic outbursts of media attention flare up. This is doubly true if we think about cults in political terms because most of their adherents stay out of politics as much as they possibly can. They know society does not like them and that the public eye can be cruel. Although they seek converts, they also seek withdrawal. They may not want to let society alone, but they certainly want society to leave them alone.

OTHER SMALL RELIGIONS

Some alternative religions are not especially separatist, though their size renders their political involvement and impact modest. Nevertheless, religious expressions defined by ethnic characteristics or even sexual orientation can provide a means for smaller religious communities to build social capital, group solidarity, and civic skills.

Consider religion among Native Americans, a highly complex phenomenon. Native American religion includes diverse tribal practices, Christian congregations, and a number of syncretic expressions that blend aspects of Christian worship with traditional native ritual. Most Native American religious groups today are fairly loosely organized and organic, though some are institutionalized in familiar senses.

Because of its use of the drug peyote as a part of worship, the Native American Church is one of the best known of these syncretic faiths. Influenced to some extent by Christianity, this religion shares with other Native American religious expressions a belief in a supreme being; the reality and power of spirits, visions, and ghosts; life after death; and the omnipresence of a spiritual aspect, usually unseen but of great significance in the empirical world. The church has developed a clergy and other facets of organization. Yet in most instances its formal religious organization and institutionalization are modest in comparison with other American religions.[32] Not surprisingly, the main political effort of this religion is defensive—such as going to court to defend peyote use, not always successfully.

Although peyote use may grab headlines, a more widespread expression of Native American spirituality takes place within Christian churches both on and off of reservations. Many prominent Native American leaders have been and are members. Because Christian churches represent a legacy of conquest, many early political efforts by Native American activists were directed both within and against Christianity itself. This campaign to gain self-determination within the churches contributed to the Red Power consciousness that emerged in the late 1960s and 1970s.[33]

We see this consciousness in the work of such figures as Vine Deloria Jr., a Yankton Sioux and seminary graduate. His book *Custer Died for Your Sins* served as a "manifesto" of Native American activism.[34] Though damning of the way Christian proselytizing divided people and undermined tribal ways, he embraced the vision of a more ecumenical and truly Native American Christianity. In much the same way that African American clergy have developed fresh understandings of the Christian message, Deloria and others have attempted to do the same for Native Americans.

The most tangible aspect of organizing through Christian churches involved the Indian Ecumenical Conference, founded in 1969. As James Treat shows, the conference began as an effort to mend divisions between tribal and Christian traditions. This vision of building unity across tribes was the same one that occupied Deloria. Although focused mostly on religious matters, the thousands who gathered every summer in the 1970s helped stimulate a kind of "cultural revival" among Native people that contributed to other political efforts.[35]

Native American groups have become more politically involved and sophisticated in recent times because of tribal involvement in the gaming industry and the high-stakes politics surrounding it. The money and clout gaming provides are enabling tribes to defend their sovereignty and traditions, sometimes thanks to the work of high-powered lobbyists. To the extent that religion is woven together with tribal affairs, as it often is, Native American spiritual practices may benefit from the power and visibility this new era represents, though some remain dubious about the source of that clout.[36]

If Native American spirituality must overcome tribal and regional divisions, the Fellowship of Metropolitan Community Churches (MCC), a ministry directed specifically to gay and lesbian people, faces other obstacles. It illustrates another way that a small religion can sometimes make a modest impact by fostering group solidarity and confidence, even if their larger political role is minimal. Even though MCC churches are Christian, and not "alternative" in that sense, their largely gay membership and focus often brings them more controversy than acceptance in the broader Christian community. Even the liberal National Council of Churches, an ecumenical parachurch organization, has not agreed to admit the MCC as a member.

The fellowship includes about 300 congregations, with many thousands of members worldwide, and a large headquarters in Los Angeles.[37] Although the church itself has not been particularly influential in the broader society, it plays a role in various gay rights campaigns, most notably its recent Marriage Equality project. It is on the local level, perhaps, where some gay congregations exercise a more distinct, if still modest, role. Scholar Debra St. John followed the activity of a small MCC congregation in a west Texas city. She observed how it fostered civic skills among formerly sheepish members who became more confident over time, to the point of engaging in a visible political campaign over the town's library policy on books dealing with homosexuality.[38]

Such examples illustrate the disparate character of the MCC's political impact. If the Fellowship of Metropolitan Community Churches wished to exert broader collective political clout, it would be hard pressed to succeed because of its still-small numbers. The only way for small religious groups to exercise broad political clout is to work in coalition with larger, more powerful groups.

A COMPARATIVE CASE STUDY:
MORMONS AND JEHOVAH'S WITNESSES

The example of the Church of Jesus Christ of Latter-day Saints (LDS Church), or the Mormons, seems to belie the picture of only modest political effectiveness of the religions we have been considering. Mormons constitute an important political force in American politics. In contrast, the Jehovah's Witnesses illustrate our argument that smaller religions often have little political sway. Comparing and contrasting these two religious communities sheds light on the problems and challenges politics presents for minority religions today in the United States.

Due to a unique combination of factors, Mormons are major players in modern American religion and politics. Two of these factors are their size and steady growth. The LDS Church claims about 6 million faithful in the United States and has even more adherents worldwide outside the United States.[39] The church experienced nearly 20 percent growth from 1990 to 2000, and its numbers continue to increase steadily today.[40] But this growth in numbers and political influence has not come easily. The LDS story presents a remarkable case study of an unconventional religion overcoming tremendous disadvantages. In their early days, Mormons had no influence. Indeed, it accurately may be argued that no religious group has suffered more discrimination in the United States—often severe and deadly persecution—than did the Mormons in the nineteenth century.

Yet today the Mormons' situation is entirely different. Headquartered in Salt Lake City, the LDS Church is highly organized and thriving. Its members are engaged in local, state, and national politics all across the country, but especially in western states. The church itself sometimes involves itself in politics, but mostly behind the scenes.

There has been some debate about where the LDS faith fits into the rest of the Christian tradition. Some traditional Protestant and Catholic groups dispute the authenticity of the Mormon expression of Christianity.[41] Disagreements over the LDS

Church's place in the Christian tradition have impeded Mormon efforts to reach across religious barriers for political (and other) purposes. LDS leaders have worked to enhance Mormons' direct engagement with mass culture, most recently through concerted efforts to showcase their mainstream credentials during the 2002 Winter Olympics in Salt Lake City.[42] In 2008, the LDS Church received additional attention when former Massachusetts governor Mitt Romney—who had chaired the Salt Lake Olympic Organizing Committee—ran unsuccessfully for the Republican presidential nomination. Speculation abounded about whether Romney's Mormon faith played a role in the failure of his campaign, but the fact that he was a serious candidate in the race speaks to the LDS Church's emergence as a respected participant in the mainstream of American religious traditions.

Both Christianity and Judaism inspired Joseph Smith in 1830 when he founded the LDS Church in western New York. Yet his interpretations of those faiths inevitably clashed with the traditional Protestantism that dominated American culture of the time. Smith contended that the angel Moroni directed him to golden plates that translated into the Book of Mormon. The plates explained the history of a tribal branch of Israelites who came to the Americas after about 600 BCE. This tribe was visited by Jesus Christ and eventually was destroyed because its members failed to follow God's will. Mormons believe that in his earthly life, Moroni was the son of a prophet, Mormon, who repeatedly warned the tribe of its impending doom. They also hold that Mormon himself recorded most of the history recounted on the golden plates and that he buried them several thousand years before they were revealed to Joseph Smith.[43]

Nineteenth-century Mormon history is filled with often heroic and always controversial accounts. From the founding of the LDS Church in 1830 to the murder of Joseph Smith in 1844 to the settlement of Utah a few years later, Mormons clashed with the broader American culture. The result was a great deal of pain and suffering for Mormon people—which intensified with increased awareness of the (now long-abandoned in the official LDS church) Mormon practice of polygamy.

The LDS belief system affirms the three persons of the Christian Trinity—the Father, Son, and Holy Spirit—but maintains that they are separate entities, not three persons in one. Mormons also believe that all people were with God before creation and they move on after death to live with God. The LDS Church teaches that present-day Mormons may save people who lived before Smith's revelation and thus could not have known Mormon truth. This is why Mormons have amassed the United States's leading genealogical archive; they are seeking past relatives to help them toward salvation.

Mormons are typically middle class, well-educated, overwhelmingly white, and commonly established in stable marriages with children. Mormons are especially likely to vote, and they tend to be more conservative than the population as a whole on almost every policy issue. They are also distinctly Republican in their party affiliation and voting behavior; they are an even more reliable part of the GOP base than evangelical Protestants.[44] In the 2008 presidential election, a remarkable 88 percent of all Mormon voters preferred John McCain over Barack Obama.[45] Much of the reason for this distinctiveness lies in Mormon commitment to family life, individual responsibility, and moral conservatism. Another reason is a deep suspicion of government authority rooted in the nineteenth-century Mormon experience of conflict with the federal government. This attitude can lead some Mormons to adopt liberal political causes, but much more often it creates a consistent conservatism that is almost unrivaled among other religious groups.

The LDS Church contends that it is not really political. This is so in large part because the church does not take political stands unless its president, whom Mormons view as a prophet, experiences and shares a specific revelation. Like most religious groups in the United States, the LDS Church does not endorse candidates for office, nor does it contribute directly to candidate campaigns; doing so would be illegal on the part of any tax-exempt religious organization. Evident in the LDS Church's general political reticence is the fact that Mormons learned from their tumultuous experiences in the nineteenth century, when popular and governmental hostility forced them to try to fashion a political theocracy—a nation of Zion—in Utah. That effort brought Mormons only grief in the end. Although the LDS Church lost this political struggle, it learned how to fashion an effective political voice in the process.

The fact is that the LDS Church is political in several senses, but most of its activism happens behind the scenes. Mormon leaders encourage involvement in politics and foster a setting where conservative values and politics are a way of life. From time to time the LDS quietly advances specific public policies. For example, the LDS Church played significant roles, both financially and organizationally, in the 2008 campaign to pass Proposition 8, which amended California's constitution to recognize only heterosexual marriages as valid.[46] The approval of Proposition 8, which passed with 52 percent of the vote, illustrates the reality that the LDS Church has the ability to exercise substantial political muscle in certain circumstances.

Jehovah's Witnesses are another story altogether. Although the Witnesses achieved some notable political victories through their use of the legal system, at least in the 1940s, they have no political impact today. They are correctly cited as a prime example of the more typical pattern of small religious groups having little political power.[47]

Jehovah's Witnesses emerged in the United States in the 1870s under the leadership of their founder, Charles Russell. The movement has undergone steady growth despite a strict morality that rejects much of the conventional world. The Witnesses' growth is due in good part to the group's well-known intensive evangelism and its communal ethics. Witnesses are unusually integrated racially and ethnically for a religion in the United States and continue to enjoy steady growth; they now number roughly 2 million adherents in the United States.[48]

Witnesses declare that they are true followers of the Bible. They affirm Jehovah (God the Father) and acknowledge Jesus Christ as the Son of God—indeed, as God's first creation. However, Witness theology contends that though Christ is the Son of God, Christ is not God. This marks a crucial difference from Christian belief. Witnesses also believe that at the end of the world there will be 144,000 disciples who will be glorified with God. The rest of the dead will live again on an Earth that will have become a wonderful land of peace and happiness. Their view is that the end of the world is near, so no one ought to waste time trying to help others via politics or government. Helping individuals to discover religious truth is the answer now. This is why Witnesses distance themselves from government, politics, and even the nation itself. They refuse to salute the flag, serve in the military, or otherwise do anything that might violate their beliefs or indicate that they value the nation. For them, loyalty must be to God, so they have opted for strict separatism.[49]

Still, it would be inaccurate to say that Witnesses have made no political impact. Over the years their involvement in court cases to defend their religious freedom has expanded religious liberty for all kinds of small religious groups, especially against the government (see Chapters 8 and 9 for discussion). Realistically, minority religions may not be able to have any greater political success. In terms of day-to-day politics and policymaking in the United States, however, Witnesses do not wish to play an important role. Although not all small religious groups share this goal of noninvolvement, most encounter the same political fate whether they like it or not.

POLITICAL ASSESSMENTS

Pluralism defines religion in the United States, but all religious groups are not politically equal, and the overall political strength of most non-Christian and unconventionally Christian religious groups in the United States is modest at best. Few of them have much political influence. Some have made a political mark in the courts by seeking to protect themselves, as has been the case with the Jehovah's Witnesses. The few exceptions that do have some measure of political clout, such as Jews and Mormons, are comparably large groups composed of members who are well integrated into American life—and who are also willing and able to undertake political action.

Of course, size is a factor that can hardly be ignored in explaining why some religious groups play such a minor role in American politics. We know that most alternative religions are small, comprising a tiny fraction of a country with more than 300 million people. Many of these faith groups are not growing, either. Only a few, such as the LDS Church, are growing rapidly enough to increase their share of the nation's population. To be sure, numbers are not everything, but they do matter in politics. They furnish activists, supporters, and much more. A group begins at a serious disadvantage without those numbers, even if the politics it practices is almost entirely defensive, as is the case with Jehovah's Witnesses or the Amish.

The issue of isolation is important as well. Many small religious communities self-consciously choose withdrawal or isolation because they fear the corrupting power of the larger culture (the Amish constitute a good example). Sometimes the decision to withdraw also reflects a realistic analysis of the slim chances these groups have to affect the broader culture. Often, however, disengagement is rooted in theological belief. Jehovah's Witnesses hold that the true believer should not be concerned with governments and nations, so political engagement becomes almost sacrilege.

Islam, like Judaism, may have an advantage politically because its religious principles *encourage* political involvement. Islam holds that religion should pervade every aspect of life. Thus Muslim leaders have argued that politics and government are legitimate and important realms. This tenet should provide hospitable theological and ideological support for Muslims as they venture further into American politics.

Geography can also influence isolation. This has been true throughout Mormon history. It is still true today, at least to some extent, because the majority of American Mormons still reside in Utah and surrounding Mountain West states. Today Mormons are mostly integrated into the larger culture, but this is much less true of many Native Americans who live on reservations. For them, geography has played a major role in fostering separation. This separation can pose major problems for political influence but has not been a hindrance for tribes generating large sums of money from the gaming industry, some of which they put toward politics.

Socioeconomic isolation also has an effect. Many smaller religious traditions have a high number of adherents who lack financial resources, sometimes because of restrictions imposed by their faiths. This situation limits their potential political influence. They have fewer resources, from money to highly educated members, to bring to bear on politics than do religious communities with affluent and well-educated memberships. A small religion of the poor faces daunting odds if it seeks to make a political impact. This has been the case for Jehovah's Witnesses. Judaism and Mormonism, whose members are more affluent on the whole, do not face this constraint.

Something that also matters a great deal is what we might call "respectability." Many alternative religions are unknown and thus not automatically respected by mainstream religions. In some cases they acquire a reputation as less-than-respectable groups, especially if they are perceived as unusual or vaguely threatening, and for this they pay a considerable political price. Such has been the fate of cults. Fashion, though, can make unheralded groups and their religions popular, which benefits them. This is increasingly true of Native Americans in the United States—and thus of Native American religions, which could increase their political clout in the long run.

FURTHER READING

Bromley, David G., and Anson Shupe. *Strange Gods: The Great American Cult Scare.* Boston: Beacon, 1981. A discussion of cults in the United States.

Conklin, Paul K. *American Originals: Homemade Varieties of Christianity.* Chapel Hill: University of North Carolina Press, 1997. Excellent account of Mormons, Jehovah's Witnesses, and Pentecostals, among others.

Esposito, John L. *The Oxford History of Islam.* New York: Oxford University Press, 1999. A broad history of Islam.

Haddad, Yvonne Yazbeck, and Jane Idelman Smith, eds. *Muslim Communities in North America.* Albany: State University of New York Press, 1994. The best book on American believers in Islam.

Heilman, Samuel C., and Steven M. Cohen. *Cosmopolitans and Parochials: Modern Orthodox Jews in America.* Chicago: University of Chicago Press, 1989. Very interesting discussion of Orthodox Jews.

Maisel, L. Sandy, and Ira N. Forman, eds. *Jews in American Politics.* Lanham, MD: Rowman and Littlefield, 2001. An excellent collection of essays on many aspects of Jewish politics in America.

Ostling, Richard, and Joan K. Ostling. *Mormon America: The Power and the Promise,* rev. ed. San Francisco: HarperSanFrancisco, 2007. A journalistic account of the LDS Church, past and present.

Schaeffer, Richard T., and William W. Zellner. *Extraordinary Groups*, 8th ed. New York:
   Worth, 2007. Good study that considers a number of the same groups as does this
   chapter.

Treat, James. *Around the Sacred Fire: Native Religious Activism in the Red Power Era.*
   New York: Palgrave Macmillan, 2003. A historical case study of the role of religion in
   Native American politics.

NOTES

1. J. J. Goldberg, *Jewish Power: Inside the American Jewish Establishment* (Reading, MA: Addison-Wesley, 1996); Bernard M. Lazerwitz, *Jewish Choices: American Jewish Denominationalism* (Albany: State University of New York Press, 1988); L. Sandy Maisel and Ira N. Forman, eds., *Jews in American Politics* (Lanham, MD: Rowman and Littlefield, 2001).

2. In 1966, 84 percent of American Jews lived in the East; by 2008, that percentage had declined to only 41 percent, with dramatic percentage increases in the South. See The Pew Forum on Religion & Public Life, *U.S. Religious Landscape Study*, http://religions .pewforum.org/portraits, 2008.

3. Pew Forum, *U.S. Religious Landscape Study*, http://religions.pewforum.org/affiliations, 2008.

4. Pew Forum, *U.S. Religious Landscape Study*, http://religions.pewforum.org/portraits, 2008.

5. Samuel G. Freedman, *Jew vs. Jew: The Struggle for the Soul of American Jewry* (New York: Simon & Schuster, 2000).

6. United Jewish Communities, *The National Jewish Population Survey 2000–01* (New York: United Jewish Communities, 2003), 16.

7. Ibid., 4.

8. Alan Dershowitz, *The Vanishing American Jew: In Search of Jewish Identity for the Next Century* (Boston: Little, Brown, 1997); Ari Goldman, *Being Jewish: The Spiritual and Cultural Practice of Judaism Today* (New York: Simon & Schuster, 2000); Michael Lerner, *Jewish Renewal: A Path to Healing and Restoration* (New York: Putnam, 1994).

9. On the ideological commitments of American Jews, see Anna Greenberg and Kenneth D. Wald, "Still Liberal After All These Years: The Contemporary Political Behavior of American Jewry," in *Jews in American Politics*, 161–193.

10. On this point, see Lazerwitz et al., *Jewish Choices.*

11. On Jewish conservatism, see Edward Shapiro, "Right Turn? Jews and the American Conservative Movement," in *Jews in American Politics,* 195–211.

12. Ilan Peleg, *The Legacy of George W. Bush's Foreign Policy: Moving Beyond Neoconservatism* (Boulder: Westview Press, 2009).

13. Norman Podhoretz, "Why Are Jews Liberals?" *Wall Street Journal,* September 10, 2009, A23.

14. The higher figure often cited by American Muslim leaders comes from an analysis by Ilyas Ba-Yunus and Kassim Kone based on an extrapolation of membership counts from mosques and various other Muslim organizations. Ba-Yunus and Kone concluded that the Muslim population was close to 6 million and probably larger, which would make it roughly the same size as the American Jewish population. See Ilyas Ba-Yunus and Kassim Kone, "Muslim Americans: A Demographic Report," in *Muslims' Place in the American Public Square: Hopes, Fears, and Aspirations,* ed. Mumtaz Ahmad (Walnut Creek, CA: Alta Mira Press, 2004). Lower figures come from Andrew Kohut et al., *Muslim Americans: Middle Class and Mostly Mainstream,* http://pewforum.org/surveys/muslim-american/ (2007); and Tom W. Smith, "The Muslim Population of the United States: The Methodology of Estimates," *Public Opinion Quarterly* 66 (2002), 404–417.

15. Ihsan Bagby, Paul M. Perl, and Bryan T. Froehle, *The Mosque in America: A National Portrait* (Washington, DC: CAIR, 2001), 2.

16. For a straightforward introduction to Islam, see John Esposito, *The Oxford History of Islam* (New York: Oxford University Press, 1999); and Ninian Smart, *Atlas of the World's Religions* (New York: Oxford University Press, 1999), 168–197. On Muslims in America, see Steven Barboza, *American Jihad: Islam After Malcolm X* (Garden City, NY: Doubleday, 1993); Yvonne Yazbeck Haddad and John Esposito, eds., *Muslims on the Americanization Path?* (New York: Oxford University Press, 2000); Yvonne Yazbeck Haddad and Jane I. Smith, eds., *Muslim Communities in North America* (Albany: State University of New York Press, 1994); Pew Research Center, "Muslim Americans"; Jane I. Smith, *Islam in America* (New York: Columbia University Press, 2000).

17. *Project MAPS: Muslims in the American Public Square* (Washington, DC: Georgetown University Center for Christian-Muslim Understanding, 2001).

18. See the Muslim Public Affairs Council's website at http://www.mpac.org/.

19. Selcuk Sirin and Michelle Fine, *Muslim American Youth: Understanding Hyphenated Identities Through Multiple Methods* (New York: New York University Press, 2008).

20. Drummon Ayres Jr., "The 2000 Campaign: Campaign Briefing" (October 24, 2000), A27; *Project MAPS.*

21. Yvonne Yazbeck Haddad, *Not Quite American? The Shaping of Arab and Muslim Identity in the United States* (Waco, TX: Baylor University Press, 2004).

22. Ibid.; Sirin and Fine, *Muslim American Youth.*

23. See Asma Gull Hasan, *American Muslims: The New Generation,* 2nd ed. (New York: Continuum, 2002).

24. Alexandra Alter, "They're No Bodice Rippers, but Amish Romances Are Hot," *The Wall Street Journal,* September 9, 2009, A19; Daniel Burke, "Surging Amish Spreading Out,"

The Washington Post, October 11, 2008, B8. See also Richard T. Schaeffer and William W. Zellner, *Extraordinary Groups*, 8th ed. (New York: Worth, 2007); Donald B. Kraybill and Carl Desportes Bowman, *On the Backroad to Heaven: Old Order Hutterites, Mennonites, Amish, and Brethren* (Baltimore: Johns Hopkins University Press, 2001).

25. Tom Shachtman, *Rumspringa: To Be or Not to Be Amish* (New York: North Point Press, 2006).

26. On cults and topics in the discussion that follows, see Willa Appel, *Cults in America: Programmed for Paradise* (New York: Holt, Rinehart and Winston, 1983); David G. Bromley and Anson Shupe, *Strange Gods: The Great American Cult Scare* (Boston: Beacon, 1981), chap. 2; Robert Booth Fowler, *The Dance with Community* (Lawrence, KS: University Press of Kansas, 1992), 147–153; J. Gordon Melton and Robert L. Moore, *The Cult Experience: Responding to the New Religious Pluralism* (New York: Pilgrim, 1982); Catherine Wessinger, *How the Millennium Comes Violently: From Jonestown to Heaven's Gate* (New York: Chatham House, 2000).

27. Rebecca Moore, *Understanding Jonestown and Peoples Temple* (Westport, CT: Praeger, 2009); Wessinger, *How the Millennium Comes Violently.*

28. Moore, *Understanding Jonestown and Peoples Temple.*

29. "Adventists Disavow Waco Cult," *Christian Century*, March 17, 1993, 285–286; David Gelman, "From Prophets to Losses," *Newsweek*, March 15, 1993, 62; "The Messiah of Waco," *Newsweek*, March 15, 1993, 56–58.

30. On the Unification Church, see Eileen Barker, *The Making of a Moonie: Choice or Brainwashing* (New York: Blackwell, 1984); Irving Louis Horowitz, ed., *Science, Sin, and Scholarship: The Politics of Rev. Moon and the Unification Church* (Cambridge, MA: MIT Press, 1978).

31. The Christian Identity movement is monitored closely by the Southern Poverty Law Center. See *False Patriots: The Threat of Antigovernment Extremists* (Montgomery, AL: Southern Poverty Law Center, 1996); http://www.splcenter.org/intel/map/hate.jsp.

32. Lawrence E. Sullivan, ed., *Native American Religions: North America* (New York: Macmillan, 1987).

33. Joane Nagel, *American Indian Ethnic Renewal: Red Power and the Resurgence of Identity and Culture* (New York: Oxford University Press, 1996); James Treat, *Around the Sacred Fire: Native Religious Activism in the Red Power Era* (New York: Palgrave Macmillan, 2003).

34. Vine Deloria Jr., *Custer Died for Your Sins: An Indian Manifesto* (New York: Macmillan, 1969).

35. Nagel, *American Indian Ethnic Renewal*; Treat, *Around the Sacred Fire.*

36. Dale Mason, *Indian Gaming: Tribal Sovereignty and American Politics* (Norman, OK: University of Oklahoma Press, 2000).

37. "Metropolitan Community Churches: Fact Sheet," http://www.mccchurch.org/media room/index.htm (2009).

38. Debra St. John, "Unexpected Participants in Democracy: Refuge, Community, and Activism in a Congregation of the Metropolitan Community Church" (PhD dissertation, University of Oklahoma, 2001).

39. Church of Jesus Christ of Latter-day Saints, "Key Facts and Figures," http://www.newsroom.lds.org/ldsnewsroom/eng/statistical-information (2009).

40. Jones et al., *Religious Congregations and Membership: 2000*; for a contemporary and thorough discussion of the Mormons in detail, see "A Portrait of Mormons in the U.S." Pew Forum.org, 2009.

41. For a brief survey of the debate, see Ostling and Ostling, *Mormon America,* chap. 19.

42. Kenneth L. Woodward, "A Mormon Moment," *Newsweek*, September 10, 2001, 44.

43. Ostling and Ostling, *Mormon America.*

44. David E. Campbell and J. Quin Monson, "Dry Kindling: A Political Profile of American Mormons," in *From Pews to Polling Places: Faith and Politics in the American Religious Mosaic*, ed. J. Matthew Wilson (Washington, DC: Georgetown University Press, 2007).

45. "Another place where Obama gained was with the composite category of White Other Christians: He received more than one-quarter of the vote, up from Kerry's one-fifth in 2004. This result is also a surprise, because the largest denomination in the category is the Latter-day Saints, one of the most Republican religious communities in the nation. True to past form, the Other Christians were consistently conservative on the issues, especially cultural ones, though they gave the economy high priority in 2008. It is also possible that Mormon controversies of the Republican primary season redounded to Obama's benefit. This group is another place where Obama made modest gains in a Republican constituency." John C. Green, at http://www.firstthings.com/article/2009/02/005-bwhat-happened-to-the-values-voterb-19, 2009.

46. Jesse McKinley and Kirk Johnson, "Mormons Tipped Scale in Ban on Gay Marriage," *The New York Times*, November 14, 2008, A1.

47. On the Jehovah's Witnesses, see Robert M. Anderson, *Vision of the Disinherited* (New York: Oxford University Press, 1979); James A. Beckford, *The Triumph of Prophecy* (Oxford: Basil Blackwell, 1975); Schaeffer and Zellner, *Extraordinary Groups*, chap. 8.

48. This estimate is based on data from the Pew Forum, *U.S. Religious Landscape Survey*, http://religions.pewforum.org/affiliations. See also Edwin Scott Gaustad and Philip L. Barlow, *New Historical Atlas of Religion in America* (New York: Oxford University Press, 2000), 165–173.

49. Beckford, *The Triumph of Prophecy.*

4

VOTING AND RELIGION
IN AMERICAN POLITICS

Throughout American history, religious currents have flowed powerfully, defining partisan attachments and shaping voting behavior. In this chapter we chart the voting patterns of the key American religious traditions and offer evidence for the existence of value- and religion-based cleavages in the American electorate. The nature and intensity of such cleavages have varied widely throughout American history, often because of religion's interaction with a host of other social and cultural influences on how people vote. In recent years those cleavages have emerged as a major force in national elections, owing to the salience of religiously based value differences. But we caution that "value difference" does not necessarily make for a "culture war."[1] Some religious activists see themselves engaged in a struggle against mortal enemies, but most voters do not see things in that way. Instead, they vote simply and straightforwardly based on their perception of which candidate or party most closely represents their values and interests.

A HISTORICAL REVIEW

Religion has played an important role in national elections since the founding of the United States. In the first contested presidential campaign (in 1800), Thomas Jefferson's Democratic-Republican Party challenged the Federalists, led by incumbent President John Adams. Adherents of the era's establishment religions, especially Episcopalians and Congregationalists, aligned closely with the status-quo Federalists, whereas Jefferson gained support from the religious innovators of the day, such as Baptists, Methodists, and Presbyterians. Part of this alignment may be traced to the class profiles of these churches: Members of higher-status churches often supported the Federalists, whereas populist upstarts backed Jefferson.[2]

The debate about state establishment of religion also was related to social class. Even though the Constitution prohibited a national religion, several states retained legally established churches. Federalists generally backed this sort of religious establishment, but the Jeffersonians did not. Religious minorities thus aligned with Jefferson despite the fact that he was not a particularly religious person. During the campaign, in fact, the Federalists mounted attacks accusing Jefferson of rejecting the Christian faith. But Jefferson's personal beliefs were less important to his supporters than the fact that he was committed to protecting religious minorities and ending government preferences for one faith over others at all levels. Thus Baptists, with their commitment to the separation of church and state, flocked to Jefferson.[3]

After the demise of the Federalist Party, a similar religio-social division persisted, manifesting itself especially clearly in the two elections of Andrew Jackson (in 1828 and 1832), who attracted the support of more populist churches but not established ones. By 1833, however, all states had disestablished their churches, no longer aiding one church over all others in various ways, and the era of formal church establishment in the United States was over.[4]

Immigration of Catholics from Europe, which increased significantly in the 1830s and continued unabated until 1920, resulted in a softening of earlier cleavages between Protestant denominations and the development of something far more durable: a Catholic-Protestant political divide. This division profoundly shaped political and voting patterns for more than a century. While Catholics quickly became heavily Democratic, northern Protestants gravitated toward their opponents: first the Whigs, then the Republicans. This alignment also shaped partisan positions on important issues. State aid to Catholic parochial schools, a perennial issue in American politics, found its strongest resistance among Republicans, who took many of their cues from Protestant activists. Moreover, the Republican Party's platforms of the late nineteenth and early twentieth centuries contained "strict separationist" planks designed to block Catholics from making social inroads.[5]

The Catholic-Protestant split was not the only way in which religious culture played itself out in nineteenth-century elections and politics. Careful studies by historians suggest that those Protestants least prone to evangelical pietism often joined Catholics in voting Democratic in the nineteenth and early twentieth centuries. Thus one way to understand the division of the electorate was that it pitted pietists against others, who sometimes were termed ritualists.[6] The pietist-ritualist political division, which also was tied to ethnic differences, drew deep and enduring lines on the American political map. The pietists included evangelical Methodists, Baptists, Congregationalists, Presbyterians, and less ritualistic Lutherans. These groups were overwhelmingly Republican in nearly every region, from California to Rhode Island. The ritualists included Roman Catholics as well as many Lutherans; both groups usually voted Democratic.

What distinguished pietists from ritualists were their incompatible visions of the "good life" and the role government ought to play in it. As heirs to the Puritan evangelical spirit, pietists stressed religion's connection with morality. They saw themselves as moral reformers, and they favored active government involvement through laws and policies designed to accomplish their moral ends. Whether the perceived evil was alcoholism, gambling, dueling, or the breaking of the Sabbath, pietists were comfortable bringing their desire to reform society into the public realm, just as modern-day religious moralists favor government regulation of abortion, gambling, pornography, and television violence.[7]

Ritualists, on the other hand, emphasized church liturgies and sacraments, as opposed to moral crusades, in their conception of religion. Compared to pietists, they were more tolerant regarding personal behavior and less likely to support government regulation of morals. This religious and cultural divide between pietists and ritualists was powerful enough to transcend class and immigrant status. In the North, Catholics were Democrats and Methodists were Republicans regardless of their socioeconomic status.[8]

In the South, of course, religious factors often were supplanted by the politics of race and regional pride. During post–Civil War Reconstruction (1865–1877), southern whites saw the Republican Party literally as a conquering army of occupation, so they voted Democratic. African Americans voted overwhelmingly for Republicans, but when southern whites reasserted control of politics in their region, they disenfranchised and otherwise kept African Americans subordinate and made the South solidly Democratic. Thus, despite the fact that the white southern population was heavily Baptist and Methodist, these pietists voted Democratic—unlike their northern counterparts.[9]

The contemporary movement of evangelical Protestants into the Republican fold that began in the 1960s represents a return to nineteenth-century patterns. In order to appreciate the significance of this trend, we must examine an important component of 1930s American politics: Franklin Delano Roosevelt's New Deal coalition. Its breakup reconfigured religio-political alignments in contemporary America.

The economic upheavals of the Great Depression produced what scholars term a "critical election," resulting in a partisan realignment of voters and creating a relatively stable majority for the new Democratic coalition. Roosevelt's New Deal coalition rested on three interrelated factors: region, class, and religion.[10] A fourth dimension, race, was not a major factor during Roosevelt's time—the black electorate was very small because of the systematic disenfranchisement of southern black voters. Only later did African Americans, securely enfranchised by the Voting Rights Act of 1965, come to represent a major voting bloc. Since the 1930s, black voters overwhelmingly have supported the Democratic Party and its candidates.[11]

President Roosevelt received his highest vote margins in the solidly Democratic South. The Civil War legacy and the Democratic Party's total domination of southern politics played key roles here. But so did Roosevelt's activist policies regarding the economy; his initiatives to overcome the Great Depression were popular among many white southerners, the majority of whom were poor evangelical Protestants who had been hit especially hard by the Depression. The kind of moral cleavages we see in today's American politics were largely absent from national partisan politics in the 1930s and thus presented few cross-pressures for southern Democrats.[12]

In the rest of the United States as well, class cleavages were vital to President Roosevelt's electoral fortunes. He was popular among poor and working-class voters, labor union members, and others of modest means. Much of his appeal to northern pietists (both traditional evangelicals and Pentecostals) flowed from the fact that many of them were far less affluent than their mainline Protestant counterparts. This same kind of appeal brought northern black voters into the New Deal coalition despite their previously longstanding loyalty to the party of Lincoln.

Despite the political significance of social class in the early twentieth century, various religious groups also formed quite cohesive elements of the New Deal coalition. Catholics at every socioeconomic level were far more likely to identify themselves as Democrats and vote that way than were similarly situated Protestants. Indeed, Catholics constituted one of the central New Deal constituencies.[13] Also solidly aligned with the Democrats under Roosevelt were Jewish voters. In earlier years, many Jews had been Republicans because they viewed the GOP as the more liberal party. The Depression and Roosevelt led Jews to gravitate heavily to the Democratic Party, where most have stayed ever since.[14]

Who, then, opposed Roosevelt? Northern white Protestants (especially those from mainline denominations), wealthier individuals, and traditional Yankee Republicans formed the core of his opposition. Many modest-income Protestants in the North remained loyal to the GOP, especially in more traditional rural areas. The problem for the Republicans, of course, was that this base was too narrow to mount a serious challenge to the Democratic Party's hegemony. Republican war hero Dwight Eisenhower interrupted the Democrats' dominance at the presidential level in the 1950s, but Roosevelt's coalition enabled the Democrats to remain the clear majority party at all levels of government until at least 1968.[15]

The point here is that religion combined with socioeconomic status and region to shape voting patterns and political outcomes in the Roosevelt years and for several decades after his death. By the beginning of the twenty-first century, though, the New Deal coalition had crumbled, producing new alignments in which religion has assumed a more direct and decisive political role.

THE POSTINDUSTRIAL ERA

In the 1960s, divisive new cultural issues began to fracture the New Deal coalition, producing new political alignments that have elevated religion's political significance. Scholars attribute these phenomena to the nature of postindustrial society.[16] Value differences and disputes over moral issues now join traditional class-based and ethnic differences to structure voting patterns. In addition, since the mid-1960s, the immigration of Muslims, Hindus, and others has added new ethno-religious communities to the tapestry of American life. Religious currents intersect in complex ways with value-based concerns and ethno-religious identities. This process has a powerful and sustained effect on American citizens' political attitudes and behaviors—and requires careful analysis to understand (Box 4.1).

To understand the role of religion in elections, it is important to make note of both voting patterns and turnout. The electorate is made up of the 60–65 percent of adult citizens in the United States who vote in a given presidential election (this figure is lower in midterm congressional elections and in elections for state and local offices). Diverse religious groups record different rates of voting participation, which shapes their electoral clout. High voting rates among Jews and Mormons serve to increase their relative share of the electorate, whereas lower turnout among Hispanics (whether Catholic or Protestant) reduces their electoral clout. Moreover, specific circumstances in a given election year affect turnout. Barack Obama's unprecedented candidacy increased African American turnout by 2 million votes, raising it to a rate that equaled white turnout for the first time in history (around 65 percent).[17]

Table 4.1 provides one snapshot of the religious composition of the potential electorate (different surveys come up with slightly different figures, but the overall patterns generally hold). The reader will find it helpful to note the relative size of these groups as we provide summaries of how they voted. It should be obvious that

BOX 4.1   THE CHALLENGE OF MEASURING
RELIGIOUS VOTING

Given the growing complexity of the American religious electorate, it is no surprise that the measurement of religious voting presents challenges. One problem
is the trade-off between survey size and number of questions. The largest surveys
are exit polls conducted by news organizations on the day of the election. Their
large sample size allows us to capture smaller voting groups more accurately.
However, such polls cannot ask many questions, and news organizations are notorious for not always asking the same religion questions from election to election. More problematic is the fact that the 2008 exit polls did not ask the same
religion questions in every state, calling some of their findings into question.

Surveys conducted by scholars are more sophisticated, ask more religion questions, and provide us with more meaningful breakdowns. The problem with these
surveys, however, is that they have smaller sample sizes, so subgroupings often
have few respondents, making generalizations questionable. Because of these
challenges, we use several sources of data, which vary in their findings and do
not always categorize "religion" in the same way. The important thing is to grasp
general patterns and not dwell on precise statistical summaries. One final note
about religious categorization: We realize that speaking of "whites" is reduction-
ist and subsumes older ethnic identities (Irish, German, Italian, Polish, etc.), and
we know that a growing number of American families represent a blend of racial
and ethnic backgrounds. However, we find that drawing the simpler distinctions
contained in this chapter gives us the best purchase on religious voting with the
least complication.

it is even more advantageous for a candidate to hold a small edge with a large religious group than it is to have a larger edge with a small religious group.

Electoral dynamics can be fluid, as voting outcomes hinge in part on the appeal
of particular candidates and the changing salience of issues. In the 2004 presidential
election, for example, Republican George W. Bush won in large part thanks to a
surge of conservative religious voters who said "values" issues mattered most to
them in their vote decision.[18] With the economic meltdown of 2008, fewer voters
ranked values issues as their top concern; instead, the economy was preeminent,
and swing voters went for Democrat Barack Obama.[19]

Even though we do see such shifts from one election to another, the basic structure of faith-based voting is more enduring. Certain religious groups, for example,
strongly affiliate with one political party or another, whereas others are not as uni-

RELIGIOUS TRADITION	% OF VOTING AGE POPULATION
White Evangelical Protestants	23.0
White Mainline Protestants	14.0
Hispanic Protestants and Other Minority Christians	7.0
African American Protestants	9.0
Catholics	25.0
Mormons and Other White Christians	3.0
Jews	1.5
Muslims, Hindus, Buddhists, and Other Faiths	3.0
Unaffiliated	15.0

Table 4.1   Religious Traditions as a Percentage of Voting Age Population, 2008
Source: University of Akron, *Fifth Annual Survey of Religion and Politics*, 2008.

formly partisan but nevertheless cast their votes in fairly regular patterns (with some variation from election to election). As we see in Table 4.2, white evangelicals are strongly Republican in their party identification, but large majorities of African American Protestants, Jews, and Hispanic Catholics identify as Democrats. Other groups fall somewhere in between. Table 4.3 shows the partisan identification of several smaller religious groups. As we see here, Mormons are even more loyally Republican than evangelicals, whereas Muslims, Buddhists, and Hindus are quite strongly Democratic. Although party identification is not a perfect predictor of vote choice in a given election, it is one of the strongest indicators.[20]

In the current postindustrial era, religious influence on voting is more complex than it ever was in the past, manifesting itself in three different ways:

Religious affiliation, or the religious tradition to which people belong, has a direct effect on vote choice. Because of the political significance of different theological traditions, it matters politically whether people are evangelicals, mainline Protestants, Catholics, Mormons, Jews, or Muslims.

Ethno-religious identity, in which racial or ethnic ties blend with religion to create distinct political groups, also matters. Out of their collective experience, for example, African American Protestants and Latino Catholics have developed

RELIGIOUS TRADITION	% REPUBLICAN	% INDEPENDENT	% DEMOCRAT
Evangelical Protestants	56	20	25
Mainline Protestants	40	20	40
Hispanic Protestants	36	16	48
African American Protestants	7	7	86
Hispanic Catholics	6	33	62
Non-Hispanic Catholics	36	20	44
Jews	27	13	60
Other Faiths	27	26	47
Unaffiliated	16	41	42

Table 4.2   Partisan Identification of Religious Traditions Following the 2008 Election
Source: Paul B. Henry Institute, *National Survey on Religion and Public Life*, 2008.

RELIGIOUS TRADITION	% REPUBLICAN	% INDEPENDENT	% DEMOCRAT
Mormons	65	8	22
Orthodox Christians	35	8	50
Muslims	11	10	63
Buddhists	18	9	67
Hindus	13	13	63

Note: This survey included in the party categories those Independents who lean toward one party or the other. Figures do not equal 100 percent because some respondents said "Don't Know."

Table 4.3   Partisan Identification of Selected "Other" Religious Traditions, 2007
Source: Pew Forum on Religion & Public Life, *U.S. Religious Landscape Study*, 2008.

cultural and political identities that are distinct from their white counterparts. We also see a similar phenomenon (across U.S. history) for new immigrant groups.

Religious salience, in which the *intensity* of religious practice creates subgroups
within religious traditions, may now be the most significant way in which
religion affects voting. It is no longer very meaningful to speak of "the white
Catholic vote," for example, because there are such big voting differences between more and less observant Catholics. Religious salience typically is measured by frequency of worship attendance.[21]

We can see how these three factors operate by examining a summary breakdown
of the 2008 presidential vote by different religious traditions (see Figures 4.1 and
4.2). Although there were some notable changes from the previous presidential
election (which we discuss later), the 2004 breakdown was remarkably similar in
its basic structure.

In 2008, Barack Obama received his strongest support from ethno-religious
groups—African American Protestants, Hispanic Catholics, Jews, Muslims, and
members of other non-Christian faiths—along with people who have no religious
affiliation. In a way, Obama's victory represented the growing ethnic and religious
diversity of the nation. Republican challenger John McCain, on the other hand, won
majorities of white Christians, including evangelicals; Mormons; and observant
mainline Protestants and Catholics. The 2008 vote also shows how religious affiliation blends with salience to produce key outcomes. Larger percentages of evangelicals and Mormons backed McCain than was the case among mainline
Protestants and Catholics. Weekly worship attendance magnified McCain's edge
over Obama among white evangelicals and added significantly to his votes among
mainline Protestants and Catholics. On the other hand, Obama gained an edge
among less observant mainline Protestants and Catholics, which is a clear indication
that religious salience (intensity of practice) matters at least as much as religious
tradition does for voting behavior.

We also can understand how these factors interact by looking at attitudes that
often help shape voting behavior. The Pew Forum on Religion & Public Life recently
conducted a massive survey of religion in America that charted the social and political attitudes of different religious traditions and communities.[22] Figure 4.3 provides a particularly vivid example from the Pew Forum survey: how religion
correlates with attitudes toward the highly charged issue of abortion. Here we see
some evidence of how—and to a limited extent, why—Jews tend to be liberal

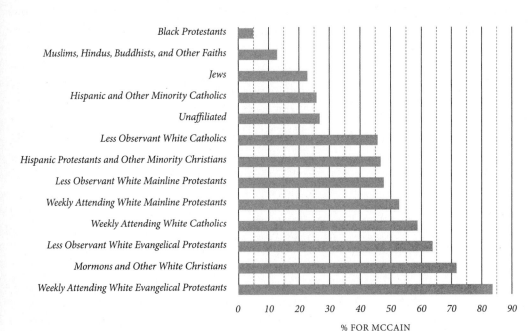

Figure 4.1   Vote for John McCain by Religious Tradition and Observance, 2008
Source: University of Akron, *Fifth National Survey of Religion and Politics*, 2008.

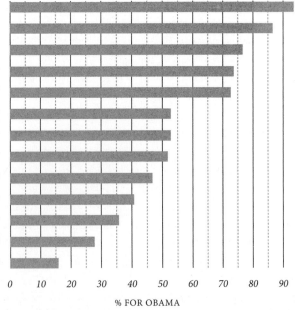

Figure 4.2   Vote for Barack Obama by Religious Tradition and Observance, 2008
Source: University of Akron, *Fifth National Survey of Religion and Politics*, 2008.

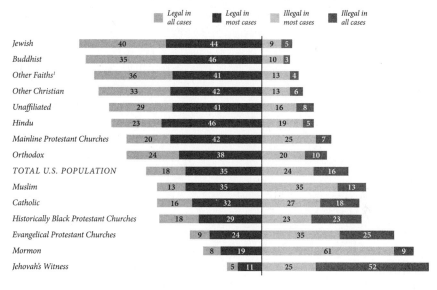

% WHO SAY ABORTION SHOULD BE . . .

Legend: Legal in all cases | Legal in most cases | Illegal in most cases | Illegal in all cases

	Legal all	Legal most	Illegal most	Illegal all
Jewish	40	44	9	5
Buddhist	35	46	10	3
Other Faiths¹	36	41	13	4
Other Christian	33	42	13	6
Unaffiliated	29	41	16	8
Hindu	23	46	19	5
Mainline Protestant Churches	20	42	25	7
Orthodox	24	38	20	10
TOTAL U.S. POPULATION	18	35	24	16
Muslim	13	35	35	13
Catholic	16	32	27	18
Historically Black Protestant Churches	18	29	23	23
Evangelical Protestant Churches	9	24	35	25
Mormon	8	19	61	9
Jehovah's Witness	5	11	25	52

% WHO SAY ABORTION SHOULD BE ILLEGAL IN
ALL OR MOST CASES, AMONG AMERICANS WHO...

Attend church weekly or more	Say religion is very important	Pray at least daily	Have absolutely certain belief in a personal god
61	56	53	54
All others 31	All others 26	All others 28	All others 30

1. "Other Faiths" includes Unitarians and other liberal faiths, New Age groups, and Native American religions. "All Others" reflects those who gave other responses except "don't know," for example, those who responded that they don't attend church weekly. Rows do not add up to 100 percent, reflecting those who said "don't know" or gave no response.

Figure 4.3 Abortion Attitudes by Religious Tradition, 2007
Source: Pew Forum on Religion & Public Life, *U.S. Religious Landscape Survey*, 2007.

RELIGIOUS TRADITION	2004		2008	
	% FOR BUSH	% FOR KERRY	% FOR McCAIN	% FOR OBAMA
Evangelical Protestants	77	23	76	24
Mainline Protestants	51	49	46	54
Hispanic Protestants	63	37	57	43
African American Protestants	17	83	7	93
Hispanic Catholics	31	69	31	69
Non-Hispanic Catholics	53	47	53	47
Jews	27	73	29	71
Other Faiths	45	55	41	59
Unaffiliated	28	72	24	76

Note: Evangelical and Mainline categories include whites and minorities other than African Americans and Hispanics.

Table 4.4   Presidential Vote by Religious Tradition, 2004–2008
Source: University of Akron, *Fourth National Survey of Religion and Politics*, 2004; and Paul B. Henry Institute, *National Survey on Religion and Public Life*, 2008.

whereas evangelicals are conservative. We also see how ethno-religious identity among Democratic-voting Muslims or African American Protestants trumps their frequent opposition to abortion or gay marriage. Finally, we see how religious salience shapes opinion, with more religiously observant people commonly taking more conservative views on abortion than those who are less involved in religious practice.

To better understand how various religious factors operate in today's American electoral politics, we now analyze in more detail the voting behavior of each of the major American religious groups, noting evolution over time as well as short-term shifts from one election to another. As we move along, the reader may find it useful to refer back to Tables 4.4 and 4.5, which provide slightly different breakdowns of the religious vote and changes from 2004.

Roman Catholics: A Demographic Transformation
We begin with Roman Catholics because they vividly illustrate how religious, demographic, and sociological changes interact and affect American elections. The

RELIGIOUS TRADITION & OBSERVANCE	% FOR McCAIN	% FOR OBAMA	DEMOCRATIC PARTY % CHANGE FROM 2004
Weekly Attending White Evangelical Protestants	84	16	-1
Less Observant White Evangelical Protestants	64	36	0
Weekly Attending White Mainline Protestants	53	47	0
Less Observant White Mainline Protestants	48	52	-1
Hispanic Protestants and Other Minority Christians	47	53	+25
African American Protestants	5	95	+12
Weekly Attending White Catholics	59	41	+3
Less Observant White Catholics	47	53	-6
Hispanic and Other Minority Catholics	26	74	+9
Mormons and Other White Christians	72	28	+7
Jews	23	77	+3
Muslims, Hindus, Buddhists, and Other Faiths	14	86	+8
Unaffiliated	27	73	+1

Table 4.5   Two-Party Presidential Vote by Religious Tradition and Observance, with Democratic Party Percentage Change, 2004–2008
Source: University of Akron, *Fourth National Survey of Religion and Politics, Post-Election Survey*, 2004; and University of Akron, *Fifth National Survey of Religion and Politics, Post-Election Survey*, 2008.

transformation of the Catholic electorate is an important part of the story of recent American politics. It illustrates the dynamic nature of religious life and the different ways in which religion operates to shape voting behavior. To understand this transformation we begin in 1960, the election in which the old Catholic-Protestant cleavage began to give way to different—and more complex—voting patterns.

From the middle of the nineteenth century through the 1960s, Democrats could count on the votes of a large majority of Catholics. Indeed, white Catholics, comprising about a quarter of the electorate, provided more than a third of the total Democratic presidential vote during the New Deal and in later eras.[23] The cultural divide between Catholics and Protestants continued to be a strong predictor of both partisanship and voting behavior through the early 1960s, especially when Catholic voters were directly mobilized. This especially happened when Catholic John F. Kennedy earned the Democratic presidential nomination in 1960. His candidacy electrified the Catholic world, and he received an overwhelming 80 percent of the votes of self-identified Roman Catholics. Kennedy's candidacy also provoked intense Protestant opposition. Both mainline and evangelical leaders expressed grave reservations about having a Catholic in the White House. Would his loyalties be divided? Would he be under pressure to take directions from the Vatican? As a Catholic, how could he serve the entire American population? Anti-Catholic tracts appeared by the thousands, reminiscent of nineteenth-century broadsides against "Romanism" and "papists."[24]

In spite of Kennedy's adroit political handling of the way his religion was made an issue in the campaign, his Catholicism nearly cost him the election. Gains among Catholic voters were more than offset by losses among the larger group of Protestant Democrats, particularly in border states, but also in places as different as Pennsylvania, New Mexico, California, and Wisconsin.[25] Kennedy probably lost about 1.5 million votes because he was Catholic.[26] His razor-thin victory margin of 100,000 votes easily could have vanished had he not personally blunted at least some of the anti-Catholic prejudice that was circulating around his candidacy by his deft reassurance that he would never allow the Pope to determine U.S. government policy. In the end, however, Kennedy's presidency and assassination, coupled with changes in the Catholic Church after Vatican II, put to rest the deep political cleavage between Catholics and Protestants that had existed for more than a century.

Kennedy's election represented the high-water mark of Catholic loyalty to the Democratic Party. Now we can see that it also marked a high point for Church vitality—a time of plentiful priests and nuns, well-appointed parochial schools, high Mass attendance, large families, and general success in passing the faith on to the next generation. The brief Kennedy years also represented the end of an era of Catholic solidarity reinforced by ethnic pride (among Irish Catholics, Polish Catholics, Italian Catholics, etc.), embeddedness in parish life, and complementarity between Catholic social teaching and the platform and policies of the Democratic Party (such as support for labor unions and a social safety net).[27]

Today there no longer is a cohesive Catholic electorate; instead, numerous Catholic subgroups vote in distinct ways. Catholic voting, in fact, differs by frequency of Mass attendance, ethnicity, race, gender, and generation. Moreover, as we will see, religious switching and immigration are changing the composition of the Catholic population in politically salient ways.

Loyalty to the Democratic party has trailed off notably since 1960 among white Catholics, especially frequent Mass attenders. The most observant Catholics now are less Democratic for many of the same reasons that reduced Catholic-Protestant tension. White Catholics today have integrated into the larger society, and most no longer feel much tension with it or with the Protestant majority. This assimilation process happened naturally over successive generations, as time separated people from the social significance of the immigrant experience. Assimilation also was facilitated by Vatican II (1962–1965), which replaced the use of Latin in Mass with local languages, eliminating one of the principal features that set Catholics apart from Protestants. Most white Catholics, now well educated and relatively affluent, have moved out of ethnic enclaves to the suburbs, where they often send their children to public schools to mix with children from all sorts of other religious backgrounds.[28]

Issues—such as abortion and same-sex marriage—also have fractured the Catholic population and chipped away at Catholic support for the Democratic Party. No issue has so agonized Catholic leaders and laity alike as has abortion. Most Democratic politicians today embrace an abortion-rights position that the American Bishops decry because it is contrary to Church teaching affirming life. In fact, a few Bishops have made news by saying they will withhold communion from Catholic politicians who stray from Church teaching on abortion.[29] Yet many lay Catholics hold pro-choice views, which is a source of frustration for Church leaders.

Here a real divide has emerged between less-observant Catholics, who tend to have more liberal social views, and weekly Mass attenders, who register stronger pro-life sentiment. A Pew Forum study found that whereas 47 percent of Catholics thought abortion should be legal in most cases, only 30 percent of weekly attenders held that view.[30] Moreover, a distinct Catholic pro-life subculture has arisen that expresses tension with the broader culture and consciously votes that way, normally for Republicans who endorse their position. In response, prominent lay Democrats in 2008 formed a pro–Barack Obama group, arguing that even though he supports abortion rights, his health care and social welfare policies would reduce the need for abortions.[31]

Unlike the majority of evangelicals, though, white Catholics are not reliably Republican because they reflect the distinctive Catholic ideological blend of conservatism on abortion and other socio-moral issues and progressivism on other

CATHOLIC CATEGORY	% FOR McCAIN	% FOR OBAMA	DEMOCRATIC PARTY % CHANGE FROM 2004
Weekly Attending White Catholics	59	41	+3
Less Observant White Catholics	47	53	-6
Hispanic and Other Minority Catholics	26	74	+9

Table 4.6   Catholic Two-Party Presidential Vote, with Percentage Change, 2004–2008
Source: University of Akron, *Fourth National Survey of Religion and Politics, Post-Election Survey,* 2004; and University of Akron, *Fifth National Survey of Religion and Politics, Post-Election Survey,* 2008.

matters, such as health care, social safety nets, and environmental protection.[32] These stances are not idiosyncratic, either; Catholic social teaching emphasizes the imperative of affirming life in all its forms, so the Catholic inclination is to protect, defend, and improve human life from the moment of conception until the moment of natural death.[33] Thus, depending on the candidates and the salience of particular issues in a given race, Catholics today often are swing voters.

Since the 1980s, in fact, the overall Catholic vote has switched back and forth, acting like a bellwether predicting the outcome of the general election. Ronald Reagan won the Catholic vote in 1980 and 1984, whereas Bill Clinton carried it in 1992 and 1996. Al Gore had the edge among Catholics in 2000 in an election in which he won the popular vote, but George W. Bush carried Catholics in 2004. True to form, exit polls in 2008 showed Barack Obama recapturing the Catholic vote.[34] All the while the Catholic share of the total electorate remained steady, at about 25 percent.

But beneath the surface of these patterns lies a far more complex story. As Table 4.6 shows, there are huge differences in the votes cast for McCain and Obama among three distinct Catholic groups. What gave Obama the edge with Catholics was a surge in votes from Catholics who are Hispanic or members of other racial or ethnic minority groups. The lesson for Republicans is that they need to recapture some of these constituencies—which are growing in size and political clout—if they are to be competitive with the new Catholic electorate.

There is another part of the American Catholic story that has long-term political implications. In brief, the Catholic Church in the United States today has lost some of the vitality and solidarity it once enjoyed. Mass attendance is down; fewer children attend parochial school; many fewer adults choose religious vocations (resulting in a dire priest shortage); and there is considerable lay dissent from certain Church teachings. A sign that this reflects a deeper problem is that the Church is lagging behind other religions in passing on the faith from one generation to the next. A massive Pew Forum survey of the American religious landscape in 2008 discovered an enormous amount of religious switching in the United States. Half of all adults had switched denominations, and more than a quarter joined an entirely new religious tradition. What struck the Pew researchers was that the Catholic Church suffered the greatest losses. Those leaving the Church outnumbered those entering by roughly a 4-to-1 margin. Remarkably, one in ten American adults are *former* Catholics.[35]

These departures are not necessarily a bad thing from some Catholic points of view, however. The Church is now much smaller among whites than it once was, but to many more conservative or orthodox Catholics this is a regrettable good. They welcome a Church that is now increasingly composed of more committed Catholics, those more devoted to the Mass, to Mary, to devotionals, and to the Church itself and less composed of casual, cultural Catholics who are not really serious about either Catholicism or Christianity.

This loss of members obviously undercuts the overall impact of Catholic voters. However, the decrease in the American Catholic population at large has been masked by a massive infusion of new Catholic immigrants, especially from Latin America, which is changing the composition of the Catholic electorate. In 1960, the Catholic electorate was largely white, but by 2008 nonwhites constituted more than a third of Catholic voters. Latino Catholics have arrived in waves from such places as Puerto Rico, Cuba, Mexico, and Central America. There also are many Filipino and some African American Catholics, as well as adherents hailing from a variety of Asian and African countries. With the exception of Asian Americans, these minority Catholics are far more Democratic in their voting loyalties than are their white counterparts. Thus their growing numbers have masked a significant slide in white Catholic support for Democratic presidential and congressional candidates.

Table 4.7 shows the collective impact of the decrease in membership, the decline in religious observance, and immigration on the composition of the Catholic electorate. White Catholics who attend Mass weekly represent less than 8 percent of the American electorate and only 31 percent of the Catholic vote, a far cry from their heyday in the 1960s. The minority Catholic proportion, on the other hand, will continue to grow for a simple reason: the continuing growth of the American Hispanic population. Already many Catholic parishes have overflowing Spanish language Masses, a reflection of this tectonic shift.[36]

CATHOLIC CATEGORY	% OF VOTING AGE POPULATION	% OF CATHOLIC POPULATION
Weekly Attending White Catholics	7.6	31
Less Observant White Catholics	8.5	34
Hispanic and Other Minority Catholics	8.6	35
TOTAL	24.7	100

Table 4.7   Catholic Voter Profile, 2008
Source: University of Akron, *Fifth Annual Survey of Religion and Politics*, 2008.

RELIGIOUS CONSTITUENCY	% OF TOTAL McCAIN VOTERS	RELIGIOUS CONSTITUENCY	% OF TOTAL OBAMA VOTERS
Evangelical Protestants	40	Unaffiliated	22
Non-Hispanic Catholics	19	Mainline Protestants	18
Mainline Protestants	18	African American Protestants	17
Unaffiliated	9	Non-Hispanic Catholics	14
Hispanic Catholics	5	Evangelical Protestants	10
Other Faiths	5	Hispanic Catholics	9
Hispanic Protestants	2	Other Faiths	6
African American Protestants	1.5	Jews	2
Jews	1	Hispanic Protestants	1

Note: Evangelical and Mainline categories include whites and minorities other than African Americans or Hispanics.

Table 4.8   The Religious Composition of Presidential Voting Coalitions, 2008
Source: University of Akron, *Fourth National Survey of Religion and Politics*, 2004; and Paul B. Henry Institute, *National Survey on Religion and Public Life*, 2008.

One way to understand the changing nature and impact of the Catholic vote is by its importance in party coalitions. As Table 4.8 shows, the total Catholic vote is approximately of equal importance to both of the major party coalitions (24 percent of McCain's and 23 percent of Obama's), but the details differ. Non-Hispanic Catholics were the second most important religious component of McCain's electoral coalition, whereas they ranked fourth for Obama. Minority Catholics constituted a significant part of Obama's coalition.

Other factors suggest further splintering of the Catholic electorate. Generational splits are emerging that may presage enhanced Republican affiliation among observant white Catholics, and perhaps others. Today, older Catholics are more likely to identify with the Democratic Party, whereas younger Catholics are more Republican in their identification and voting. Despite Obama's general appeal to young voters, a majority of younger Catholics, especially regular Mass attenders, voted for McCain.[37] On the other hand, gender works in the other direction: As in the population at large, Catholic women are more likely than Catholic men to vote Democratic.

Because they remain a significant segment of the American electorate, Catholics will continue to be courted by politicians and parties. But our analysis suggests that general appeals to Catholics inevitably may give way to the targeting of specific subgroups on the basis of ethnicity, religious salience, age, or gender. Perhaps this confirms the adage making its way around political circles: There is no Catholic vote, but the Catholic vote matters.

Evangelical Protestants, Mormons, and Other Pietists: A Revival for the GOP

It is important to note at the outset of this section that the American evangelical community includes a large number of minorities (whom we discuss elsewhere), but because of distinct voting patterns, we consider here the white evangelical voting bloc specifically.

Two momentous developments have influenced the partisanship and voting behavior of white evangelical Protestants. The first has been the rapid growth of evangelical churches over the past several decades and the relative decline of mainline denominations. In 1960, more than 40 percent of all white adults claimed membership in mainline denominations, compared with only 27 percent in evangelical churches. Today, however, there are many more evangelicals than there are mainline Protestants. Moreover, because regular church attendance and other measures of commitment tend to be lower in mainline churches than in evangelical ones,[38] this estimate exaggerates the number of people who are involved in mainline church life (see Table 4.9). Thus whereas mainline Protestants remain an important segment of the electorate, evangelical Protestants have moved toward the strategic center of the Protestant world.

The second development has been the realignment of evangelical Protestants to the Republican Party that began in roughly 1980—a development made all the more

PROTESTANT POPULATION	% OF VOTING AGE CATEGORY	% OF WHITE PROTESTANT POPULATION
Weekly Attending White Evangelical Protestants	*13.6*	*37*
Less Observant White Evangelical Protestants	*9.5*	*25*
Weekly Attending White Mainline Protestants	*5.5*	*15*
Less Observant White Mainline Protestants	*8.7*	*23*
TOTAL	*37.3*	*100*

Table 4.9   White Protestant Voter Profile, 2008
Source: University of Akron, *Fifth Annual Survey of Religion and Politics*, 2008.

significant by their numerical growth over the past several decades. These two developments have altered the dynamics of internal GOP politics dramatically. The old Republican Party was an alliance of business interests and mainline Protestants, but the new GOP also relies heavily on its "values constituency," which is composed primarily of evangelicals.[39] As a result, the Democratic Party's strategy also has changed, particularly by solidifying Jewish and secular support for Democrats.[40]

For much of the twentieth century, many Baptists, Pentecostals, and other evangelicals were Democrats, in spite of general Protestant loyalty to the Republican Party. Many evangelicals, especially conservative Baptists and Methodists, lived in the South where loyalty to the Democratic Party was almost universal, reflecting the Civil War legacy of opposition to the party of Lincoln.[41] Second, a class dimension reinforced Democratic tendencies among evangelicals. During the New Deal era, for example, lower-status Protestants (most of whom were evangelical) were more likely to vote for Franklin Roosevelt than were upper-class Protestants, who tended to belong to mainline denominations. Thus Pentecostals, independent Baptists, and other evangelicals were quite a bit more likely to be Democrats than were Presbyterians, Episcopalians, United Methodists, and Congregationalists.

However, things began to change in the 1960s. Some southern Protestants began voting Republican at the presidential level at the same time that the Democratic Party was embracing civil rights and other agendas. The 1960s and 1970s introduced a new kind of cultural politics associated with the counterculture, the sexual revolution, newly legalized abortion, women's rights, and gay rights. As liberalism— and by extension the Democratic Party—became associated in some minds with rapid social change and rejection of tradition, including traditional religion, Republicans made sizable gains among conservative Protestants.[42]

Jimmy Carter, a born-again Baptist from Georgia, temporarily stalled the transition of evangelical voters into the Republican Party with his 1976 presidential victory. Analysts concluded that Carter probably did better at the polls among evangelicals than he did among mainline Protestants.[43] But many evangelicals later felt betrayed by Carter's policy priorities as president, and simmering cultural forces combined to bring about the emergence of a new "Christian Right" movement on the eve of the 1980 presidential election. Ronald Reagan courted the evangelical constituency, who were ripe for mobilization by conservative forces, and they proved a major factor in his 1980 victory over Carter.

From the 1980s onward, evangelicals' loyalty to the Republican Party grew. Although the evangelical vote was indistinguishable from the overall white Protestant vote in 1980, white evangelicals have become increasingly Republican since then, routinely providing some three-quarters of their votes to Republican presidential candidates. The importance of the evangelical constituency to the Republican Party is well recognized. One of the major reasons John McCain chose Sarah Palin as his 2008 running mate was because of her appeal to this constituency. Republican get-out-the-vote drives specifically target the evangelical community, as was most famously the case with George W. Bush's 2004 presidential campaign.[44] But even among evangelicals, religious salience matters: Republican voting is magnified by religious observance, with weekly attenders providing some 84 percent of their votes for McCain in 2008 as opposed to 64 percent of the less observant (see Table 4.10). As a rule, however, evangelicals across the board are more reliably Republican than either Catholics or mainline Protestants. A final indication of the thoroughness of the evangelical realignment to the Republican Party is their voting behavior in races below the presidential level, which solidified for Republicans starting with the 1994 elections.[45]

It is important to note that the term *evangelical* is not synonymous with the Christian Right. Indeed, many evangelicals historically have not supported either the rhetoric or the policy agenda of major Christian Right interest groups. Sometimes religious differences among evangelicals have made mobilization difficult as well. Many Southern Baptists, for example, look askance at spirit-filled Pentecostal beliefs and practices and so were not necessarily thrilled when Pentecostals began flooding into state- and local-level Republican Party meetings. Realignment, therefore, has brought a series of different, and sometimes competing, evangelical groups into the Republican fold.

EVANGELICAL/ PIETIST CATEGORY	% FOR MCCAIN	% FOR OBAMA
Weekly Attending White Evangelical Protestants	*84*	*16*
Less Observant White Evangelical Protestants	*64*	*36*
Mormons and Other White Christians	*72*	*28*

Table 4.10   Two-Party Presidential Vote, Evangelical Protestants and Other Pietists, 2008
Source: University of Akron, *Fourth National Survey of Religion and Politics, Post-Election Survey*, 2004; and University of Akron, *Fifth National Survey of Religion and Politics, Post-Election Survey*, 2008.

Although many contemporary evangelicals vote Republican for economic reasons, a strong element of cultural conservatism clearly is behind the evangelical-Republican marriage. Evangelicals are more conservative than other Americans on a host of issues, from abortion and marriage to health-care reform and national defense.[46] Evangelical clergy, too, are most likely to be politically active (and Republican partisans) when they are cultural conservatives.[47] Unlike the electorate as a whole, evangelicals rank the nexus of abortion and family values as more important than economic issues. Moreover, the salience of socio-moral issues is even higher for frequent church attendees and middle-aged citizens, who often are involved in raising children—and who are most likely to vote.[48] The salience of these issues may wax and wane with the times but is likely to endure. Indeed, the issue of same-sex marriage, which cuts to the core of conservative evangelical concerns about traditional family values, looks to reinforce the place of evangelicals within the Republican Party due to its general opposition to legalizing same-sex marriage.[49]

Much was made in 2008 about Barack Obama's concerted efforts to reach out to the evangelical community and an evangelical left proved enthusiastic about Obama's candidacy. For his part, Obama made broad overtures to evangelicals especially through the work Joshua DuBois, a young black Pentecostal minister, did as his chief religious campaign liaison. DuBois later was appointed head of the White House Office for Faith-Based and Neighborhood Partnerships.[50] In the immediate aftermath of his victory, exit polls showed that Obama gained 26 percent of the white evangelical vote, up five points from the 21 percent John Kerry won in 2004, with most of that increase coming from young evangelicals.[51] Other surveys, however, show no gain for Obama and no youth surge.[52] In short, white evangelicals remain heavily in the Republican camp.

It is important to note that other pietist groups share the cultural conservatism of evangelicals. The most notable of these groups are adherents of the Church of Jesus Christ of Latter-day Saints (Mormons), who have become one of the strongest Republican voting blocs. With their high levels of religious salience, conservative moral values, large families, and relative affluence, Mormons form a very cohesive political community, routinely giving at least 75 percent of their votes to Republican candidates. Although today Mormons still are a relatively small group, the LDS Church is growing, and Mormons' geographic concentration in a few states in the Mountain West magnifies their impact there. In yet another irony of American politics, a group vilified by Republicans and evangelicals alike in the nineteenth century is now firmly embedded in the conservative alliance.[53]

Mainline Protestants: The New Swing Voters?

As noted, the size of the mainline Protestant component of the American electorate has declined over the past several decades. Nevertheless, mainline voters remain a significant electoral force despite their declining numbers because they are well educated and have a strong commitment to civic participation, which makes them likely voters.[54] Along the way, this constituency also has become less conservative and Republican. Mainline Protestants seem to be reevaluating their ties to the Republican Party because of the heavy emphasis it has placed on moral issues since the Reagan era. It is now fair to say that mainline Protestants make up an important swing constituency, even if they are not collectively mobilized as such.[55] To be sure, Table 4.2 above shows that the partisan split among mainline Protestants is now even. Table 4.11 reveals that a bare majority of mainline Protestants voted for Bush in 2004, but this margin switched to Obama in 2008. The movement toward the Democratic Party is especially strong among mainline clergy, a substantial majority of whom are solidly Democratic and liberal across a range of issues, but it now appears that more laity are following this lead than was once the case.[56]

Whatever the reasons, this partisan shift among mainline Protestants is a striking political development. In a reversal of a more than century-long pattern, one survey in 2008 found mainline voters giving the edge to Obama whereas a majority of white Catholics were backing McCain (see Table 4.4 above). Other surveys showed white mainline voters giving a slight edge to McCain but still registering as less Republican than white Catholics.[57] This truly is a sea change; as recently as the 1960s, no observer ever would have thought such a religio-political alignment would have been possible.

As Table 4.5 above shows, there is a worship attendance gap in mainline voting, but it is modest compared to other religious traditions. More telling is the liberal

YEAR	% FOR DEMOCRATIC CANDIDATE	% FOR REPUBLICAN CANDIDATE	% FOR INDEPENDENT CANDIDATE
1968	27	65	< 9 (Wallace)
1972	28	72	< 1
1976	38	61	1
1980	30	62	8 (Anderson)
1984	28	70	< 2
1988	36	63	< 1
1992	35	41	24 (Perot)
1996	46	47	7 (Perot)
2000	48	50	< 3 (Nader)
2004	49	51	--
2008	54	46	--

Table 4.11   White Mainline Protestant Presidential Vote, 1968–2008
Source: *National Election Studies, 1968–2000;* University of Akron, *Fourth National Survey of Religion and Politics,* 2004; and Paul B. Henry Institute, *National Survey on Religion and Public Life,* 2008. Analysis courtesy of John C. Green, University of Akron (via personal communication).

shift of mainline political attitudes. On social issues like abortion and same-sex marriage, mainline Protestants are more liberal than evangelicals and Roman Catholics. A majority also hold relatively liberal views on fighting poverty, helping the disadvantaged, and protecting the environment; this liberalism often is comparable with that of Catholics, as Table 4.12 illustrates.[58] Today's liberal mainline Protestants may be ripe for mobilization by Democratic candidates who can connect their policy goals with the longstanding mainline religious imperative of fighting for social justice.[59]

Jews, Liberalism, and Democratic Loyalty

In one sense, American Jews always have been in the vanguard of a secular vision of American politics. The vast majority of Jews in the United States are liberals who celebrate the Enlightenment ideal of the nonsectarian state. Thus most behave like secular voters, are very socially liberal, and show loyalty to the Democratic Party.

ISSUE POSITION	% EVANGELICAL PROTESTANTS	% MAINLINE PROTESTANTS	% BLACK PROTESTANTS	% CATHOLICS	% JEWS	% UNAFFILIATED
The government should spend more to fight hunger and poverty even if it means higher taxes for the middle class. (2008)	43	51	65	52	66	59
The economically disadvantaged need governmental assistance to obtain their rightful place in America. (2004)	57	54	62	57	72	62
Gays and lesbians should be permitted to marry legally. (2008)	19	50	37	42	68	64
Strict rules to protect the environment are necessary even if they cost jobs or result in higher prices. (2008)	42	52	52	52	74	65
The U.S. should support Israel over the Palestinians in the Middle East. (2004)	53	33	24	30	75	21

Table 4.12   Selected Issue Positions by Religious Tradition

Source: University of Akron, *Fourth National Survey of Religion and Politics*, 2004; and Paul B. Henry Institute, *National Survey on Religion and Public Life*, 2008.

Their commitment to liberalism extends to encompass economic and civil rights issues.

Jewish voters remain one of the true paradoxes of American politics. It is only a slight exaggeration to say that, although they look like Episcopalian Republicans in socioeconomic status, they vote more like Hispanic Democrats. Here we see the impact of a kind of value-based voting that is independent of social class. And in this case, the values are liberal ones because, as political scientist Lee Sigelman puts it, liberalism constitutes a kind of "lay religion" among American Jews.[60] Jews are among the most liberal of all American voting groups and are far more likely than other citizens to describe themselves as liberal, despite the negative connotations now attached to that term.[61]

This commitment to liberal ideals helps explain the loyalty of many Jews to the Democratic Party. Jewish Democratic loyalty solidified during the New Deal era (during which Roosevelt received an estimated 85 percent of the Jewish vote),[62] continued through the 1960s (when John Kennedy, Lyndon Johnson, and Hubert Humphrey each also received more than 80 percent), and remains to this day. In some cases support is even higher among rabbis.[63]

Beginning in the mid-1970s, however, Republicans began to see opportunities to make political inroads into the Jewish community and attempted to co-opt some of the Jewish activism and financial support that have been mainstays of the Democratic Party. As we see in Table 4.13, these hopes sometimes were realized, as Jimmy Carter did less well among Jews than did previous Democrats. Republican hopes for further gains among Jewish voters in the 1980s were buoyed by Ronald Reagan's strong pro-Israel outlook and the rise of Rev. Jesse Jackson in the Democratic Party, which produced a good deal of anxiety among Jews who believed him to be hostile to Israel and to Judaism. But these Republican hopes proved futile in the long run. One reason was that Jackson did not receive the Democratic nomination in 1984 or 1988, which allayed Jewish fears.[64] Moreover, no clear partisan lines have been drawn on support for Israel.

The most important reason for the return of Jews to the Democratic Party was the influence of Christian Right organizations in the Republican coalition. Jewish groups opposed the Christian Right's agenda on abortion, gay rights, and church-state issues, and we can see the corresponding rebound of Jewish loyalty to the Democratic Party. From Bill Clinton onward, Democratic presidential candidates routinely have received about three-quarters of the Jewish vote, margins congressional candidates normally share.[65]

In the post–September 11 era, one might have expected to see Republican gains in the Jewish electorate. Concern over Israel's security has been heightened since the

YEAR	% FOR DEMOCRATIC CANDIDATE	% FOR REPUBLICAN CANDIDATE	% FOR INDEPENDENT CANDIDATE
1976	64	36	--
1980	45	39	15 (Anderson)
1984	67	31	--
1988	64	35	--
1992	80	11	9 (Perot)
1996	78	16	3 (Perot)
2000	79	19	1 (Nader)
2004	74	25	--
2008	78	21	--

Table 4.13   Jewish Presidential Vote, 1976–2008
Source: Data for 1976–2000 from Ira N. Forman, "The Politics of Minority Consciousness: The Historical Voting Behavior of American Jews," in *Jews in American Politics*, eds. L. Sandy Maisel and Ira N. Forman (Lanham, MD: Rowman and Littlefield, 2001), 153; data for 2004–2008 from Pew Forum on Religion & Public Life, *National Exit Polls*, http://pewforum.org/docs/?DocID=367.

September 11 attacks, and during his presidency George W. Bush took an aggressive posture toward regimes (Iraq and Iran) and movements (Hamas and Hezbollah) viewed as serious threats to the Jewish state. Moreover, many adherents of Orthodox strains of Judaism share the moral conservatism of evangelicals and traditional Catholics, which has led them to vote Republican in the past few elections.[66]

But we have yet to see broad Republican gains among Jewish voters. Orthodox Jews comprise only a small portion of the Jewish population, so their conservatism alone will not register as a major shift. In addition, despite vigorous attempts by Republican leaders to court the broader Jewish community, and despite a sustained effort by vocal Jewish neoconservatives to dismantle traditional Jewish liberalism, Jewish voters have not abandoned the Democratic Party.[67] They remain firmly on one side of the cultural divide, as the 2008 vote suggests. Some surveys show a slight decrease and others a slight increase in Jewish support for Obama in 2008 compared to 2004 levels of Jewish support for John Kerry; what they all show is that Republican candidates cannot seem to garner much more than a quarter of the Jewish vote.

One ominous sign for Jews is that their share of the electorate, though always small, has been declining. With little new infusion of immigrants, Jewish population growth simply has not kept pace with other religious groups or with the overall U.S. population. With the exception of Orthodox communities, Jews tend to have small families. Intermarriage is also a challenge, as it tends to dilute Jewish identity in future generations. These long-term trends, combined with the dramatic expansion of voter participation by African Americans, Hispanics, and other minorities in 2008, produced the smallest Jewish share of the electorate in recent history. Although it was once as high as 4 percent, the Jewish share of the electorate is now barely 2 percent and is likely to decline further. This is of obvious concern to Jewish leaders, but it is not clear what they can do about it.[68]

African American Protestants: Loyal Democrats

African Americans in the United States are overwhelmingly Christian and mostly evangelical. Well over half of all African Americans, for example, consider themselves born-again Christians and biblical literalists.[69] Moreover, religious salience is quite high in the African American community: 85 percent (more than in any other demographic or ethnic group) say that religion is important in their lives, and a sizable majority say they attend worship services at least once a week.[70]

Even though a great many African Americans are evangelicals, they also are decidedly Democratic in their voting behavior. As is the case with the voting behavior of American Jews, African American voters are paradoxical. Their paradox differs substantively from that of their Jewish counterparts, however. Part of the African American paradox is explained by the uniquely American tradition of black Christianity, which blends evangelical pietism with prophetic and liberationist messages. African American churches were, and are, infused with a keenly visceral understanding of the biblical narratives of captivity and freedom, of God's judgment on oppressors, and support and comfort for the downtrodden. Many African American Christians, and especially their clergy, see themselves as chosen carriers of God's prophetic message of justice to a troubled land. What this means is that black voters often combine religious and moral traditionalism with decided support for government welfare policies and civil rights. Thus black voters surpass white voters in their support for school choice and school prayer and are less liberal than Jews, secularists, and mainline white Protestants on same-sex marriage and abortion. Yet they are far more liberal than other groups in their support for government jobs programs, health care, civil rights, and affirmative action.[71]

This blend of issue positions often receives little attention in voting studies of African Americans because what really seems to matter most is their almost monolithic (roughly 90 percent) support for the Democratic Party. African Americans have been loyal to the Democrats because of their crucial support for the civil rights movement and because the party remains committed to government-sponsored welfare programs and affirmative action.

Black church life, however, also affects political behavior in ways that aggregate voting studies cannot capture. First, because the church traditionally has been the central social institution in the African American community, it is a focal point for political organizing, voter registration drives, and overt campaigning. Unlike most white clergy, many African American pastors invite political candidates to speak to their congregations from the pulpit. Some also endorse specific candidates at election time. The church is, in a sense, often the precinct for black politics. Democrats now routinely campaign in black churches. It is no wonder that in the African American community, church membership connects people to politics and increases voter turnout. Black church members are far more likely to vote than nonmembers. And contrary to the pattern for whites, frequent church attendance is correlated with increased identification with the Democratic Party.[72]

Another important development has been the expansion of the African American voting population. Strong black support for Democratic candidates tells us nothing about the relative size of that proportion of the electorate and its impact on national politics. The Voting Rights Act of 1965 officially ended the systematic disenfranchisement of African American voters, but its promise was not realized immediately. After relatively slow progress, black voter registration mushroomed in the 1980s, especially in the South, owing in part to Jesse Jackson's presidential bids in 1984 and 1988. The black electorate grew again as African Americans, inspired by the candidacy of Barack Obama, flooded the polls in 2008 (to comprise 12 percent of the total U.S. vote). Although many organizations played a part in voter registration and mobilization, African American churches have been crucial to the galvanizing of the black portion of the U.S. electorate. The growing number of African American voters has had a profound effect on the political calculi of numerous political figures. It also has enhanced the clout of black leaders in the Democratic Party.[73]

The impact of the Obama candidacy among African American Protestants is illustrated by the combined impact of increased turnout and Democratic loyalty. After the disputed election of 2000, George W. Bush actively courted people in black churches. He enlisted African American pastors in his faith-based initiative and promoted federal grants to religious charities at national black denominational meetings. He appointed prominent African Americans to his cabinet. This outreach may have paid off, as he significantly increased his support among black Protestants from less than 5 percent in 2000 to more than 17 percent in 2004.[74] That benefit was short-lived, however, as Obama carried 95 percent of a dramatically expanded black electorate. Thus, whereas African American Protestants comprised 13 percent of John Kerry's electoral base in 2004, they were nearly 17 percent of Obama's base. And that figure grows when African American Catholics and Muslims are added to the mix.[75]

There is a final sense in which African American religious conviction has implications for politics. Because of their relatively conservative views on many sociomoral issues, including abortion and gay rights, African American Protestants are being courted as potential allies by white religious conservatives. These efforts are based on the premise that even though African Americans vote for Democrats, moral conservatism may lead some African Americans to join in issue-based coalitions with white evangelicals. We see this most dramatically in the numerous nonpartisan state ballot measures banning same-sex marriage. Many African American pastors have campaigned actively against same-sex marriage, and black voters have responded in kind. Exit polls from 2008 found that 70 percent of African Americans in California (who turned out in record numbers for Barack Obama) voted in favor of the Proposition 8 ballot initiative against same-sex marriage.[76]

Latino Christians: A Diverse Constituency

Like African Americans, Latinos in the United States combine a deep consciousness of ethnic identity with high levels of religiosity. More than nine in ten claim a religious affiliation; nearly 40 percent say they are born-again (including over a quarter of Hispanic Catholics); and two-thirds say religion is very important to them. Religious affiliation and commitment among Latinos account for a certain degree of social conservatism, with large majorities supporting school vouchers and opposing abortion and gay marriage, for example. But ethnic identity is just as important as religion in shaping Hispanic views on other issues and voting. Although many Latinos have lived in the United States for generations, the majority are foreign born; worship in Spanish in ethnic churches; and celebrate distinct Latin religious traditions, festivals, and rituals. On many issues related to immigration and economics, Latinos lean to the left of the ideological spectrum. They are strong supporters of government health insurance and services for poor people. Some Hispanics in the United States are not citizens, but a shared culture makes immigration a pressing concern for those who are able to vote. Indeed, a remarkable one-quarter of all Latinos have participated in a demonstration or protest on immigration.[77]

The most important religious distinction within the Latino community is a familiar one: Catholic versus Protestant. A large majority (roughly 70 percent) of

Latinos are Catholic, due in good part to immigration from traditionally Catholic countries in Latin America, especially Mexico. Approximately 25 percent are charismatic Catholics. About 15 percent of Latino Americans today have found church homes within Pentecostalism and other branches of evangelical Protestantism. In many cases Protestant Latino services are in Spanish with Latino preachers not submerged in a still largely white Catholic setting. Moreover, a great many Latino Protestant churches and services are frankly experiential, promoting a direct and passionate relationship with Jesus, a widely popular piety among Latinos.[78]

The distinction between Protestant and Catholic Latinos explains some significant differences in political attitudes and partisan voting.[79] Evangelical Latinos are more likely to describe themselves as conservative and to prioritize socio-moral issues. They are far more likely to self-identify as Republican than are Latino Catholics (who identify strongly as Democrats). This partisan distinction registers in voting patterns. In 2000, Al Gore received nearly 70 percent of the Latino Catholic vote but only 50 percent of that of Latino Protestants. The gap grew more pronounced in the 2002 congressional elections, when GOP candidates received 56 percent of the Latino Protestant vote versus 28 percent of Latino Catholics, [80] and then again in 2004 when George W. Bush gained the votes of 64 percent of Hispanic Protestants (most of whom are evangelicals).[81] Table 4.4 above shows that this trend continued in 2008 as well, with Obama earning the votes of 69 percent of Hispanic Catholics but only 43 percent from Hispanic Protestants. This trend has buoyed Republican strategists who envision making continuing inroads into the growing Hispanic evangelical constituency.

Latino voters provide a clear illustration of how one issue, in this case illegal immigration, can influence electoral fortunes. George W. Bush worked closely with Hispanics as governor of Texas and understood the overwhelming significance of the immigration issue to this population: Millions of undocumented Hispanic immigrants worry about possible deportation or family separation. As president, Bush pressed for comprehensive immigration reform that would have provided some means for undocumented workers to move toward citizenship. This ignited vehement opposition among some conservatives, who mounted a successful campaign against immigration reform during Bush's presidency.[82]

Whatever the merits of various policy arguments, opposition to President Bush's immigration reform proposal came to be associated in the minds of some as hostility toward Latinos, and the Republican Party paid a price in 2008: Hispanic support for Republican candidates down the ticket decreased.[83] Whether this drop in Republican support is an anomaly or a new trend is one of the current puzzles of religious voting in America.

Latinos illustrate the three ways religion operates in voting. As we have seen, ethno-religious identity operates for the community as a whole, but differences among subgroups also are salient; for example, Cuban Americans are more Republican than Mexican Americans. Religious affiliation also matters, with key differences between Catholic and evangelical Latinos. Finally, religious observance plays a role by magnifying moral traditionalism; the most conservative Latinos are weekly attending evangelicals. Because the Latino electorate will continue to grow in the years to come, these distinctions will play an increasingly significant role in American politics.

Muslims: Increasing Democratic Allegiance

Muslims comprise slightly less than one percent of the American voting public. But their concentration in certain states, rapid growth, and heightened political consciousness make them more important than their numbers might suggest. As a political community, American Muslims are ideologically complex. They tend to oppose same-sex marriage, abortion, and pornography but support public vouchers for families to send their children to private religious schools.[84] We easily might hypothesize that this cultural conservatism, combined with solid socioeconomic status, high marriage rates, and entrepreneurial skills, would make Muslims look like typical Republican voters. Indeed, before September 11, many Muslims were drawn to the GOP, and Republican operatives actively courted them. In 2000, a coalition of American Muslim leaders made a strategic decision to flex their political muscle by collectively endorsing George W. Bush, who won a plurality of the Muslim vote against Al Gore (but not quite a majority because of a large number of votes cast for Independent candidate Ralph Nader, who is of Lebanese descent). When African and African American Muslims are separated out, the margin for Bush among other Muslims increases to nearly 60 percent.[85] Given Bush's razor-thin margin in Florida in 2000, his edge among Muslims may have given him the presidency.

This support earned Muslim leaders invitations to White House functions and some access to executive branch agencies. White House sensitivity to the Muslim population continued in the immediate aftermath of the attacks of September 11, 2001. President Bush proclaimed Islam a religion of peace, called upon Americans not to discriminate against Muslim citizens, and spoke about protecting "women of cover." He also hosted end-of-Ramadan Eid celebrations at the White House. By the end of 2001, the majority of Muslims gave what turned out to be short-lived approval of Bush's handling of the war on terror.

Muslim attitudes never fully conformed to the economically libertarian agenda of today's Republican Party. Perhaps reflecting both their immigrant status and the social justice tradition of Islam, American Muslims overwhelmingly favor universal health care, government assistance to the poor, stricter environmental protection, funding for after-school programs, and increased foreign aid to impoverished nations.[86] These views incline Muslims toward the agenda of the Democratic Party, and as sentiment toward the Bush administration soured with the war in Iraq and substantial controversies surrounding the Abu Ghraib and Guantánamo Bay prison camps, they moved with alacrity into the Democratic camp.

Indeed, American politics seldom has seen such a rapid electoral turnaround as the shift in the Muslim electorate between 2000 and 2004. Questions about the USA PATRIOT Act of 2001, domestic surveillance of Muslim groups and citizens following September 11, the detention of several thousand Muslim people in prison camps, and the war in Iraq combined to make the Bush administration highly unpopular among American Muslims by 2004. Not only did they overwhelmingly give their votes to John Kerry (82 percent), but increasing numbers also had come to identify themselves as Democrats.[87] This trend strengthened with the candidacy of Barack Obama, who enjoyed substantial support from the American Muslim community. Internal surveys by Muslim groups put Obama's share of the Muslim vote at nearly 90 percent.[88] Only time will tell if this level of Democratic support can be sustained, but because of Muslim population growth rates, this group will play an increasingly important role in American elections.

The Secular Vote: A Growing Democratic Stronghold

In 1960, Americans were decidedly a society of churchgoers. The Democrats depended on churchgoing Catholics and some evangelicals (especially in the South) to offset Republican strength among most Protestant faithful. Only a small percentage of the population claimed no religious preference, and those who were not religious had relatively low voting rates. Thus secular citizens had a negligible influence on American elections.

By the 2000s, however, religious observance had declined among a much larger segment of the American public, and secular citizens were voting differently from the religiously observant. Figure 4.4 shows the yawning partisan gap by frequency of worship attendance, indicating that the less embedded people are in religious communities, the more they vote for Democratic candidates. This pattern is especially pronounced among whites, where ethnic or racial solidarity does not confound the influence of worship attendance on moral traditionalism.

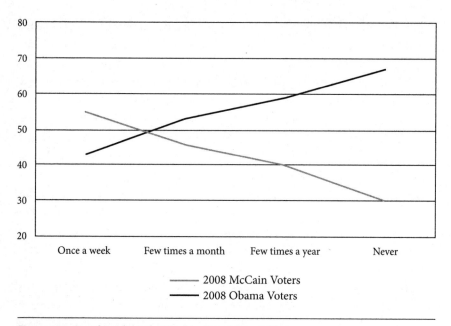

Figure 4.4   Presidential Vote by Worship Attendance, 2008
Source: Pew Forum on Religion & Public Life, "How the Faithful Voted," *2008 Exit Poll*,
http://pewforum.org/docs/?DocID=367.

An increasing number of Americans (around 15 percent) claim no religious
affiliation at all. Because this group has shown greater cohesiveness over time, scholars are concluding that they really are an important new sector of the electorate.[89]
President Obama specifically mentioned "nonbelievers" in affirming tones during
his inaugural address. Until recently, this socially liberal but economically moderate
group lacked clear political direction. Some would vote for Republican candidates
who emphasized libertarian themes of limited government. But in the postindustrial era, as polarization on social and moral issues has come to define the two parties, secular voters have moved increasingly away from a Republican Party that is
closely associated with religious traditionalism.[90] Thus secular voters have become
a crucial part of the Democratic coalition. Indeed, they comprised more than a fifth
of the total voter base for Obama's victory in 2008 (see Table 4.8).

This partisan split along religious lines traces its roots to the Democratic convention of 1972. Prior to that time, as political scientists Louis Bolce and Gerald De
Maio observe, "There was something of a tacit commitment among elites in both

parties to traditional Judeo-Christian values regarding authority, sexual mores, and the nuclear family."[91] That consensus was shattered as secular activists took a more prominent place in some state- and local-level Democratic Party organizations. Ever since, Democratic activists have been far more likely than their Republican counterparts to describe themselves as secular or marginally attached to religion.[92]

Over time, this division has trickled down to average voters. This trend is especially clear in the increasing vote margins for Democrats among secular Americans during the last three presidential cycles, with exit polls showing Gore with 61 percent in 2000, Kerry with 67 percent in 2004, and Obama with 75 percent in 2008[93] (see also Table 4.4). In fact, the voting gap between secular and religious Americans is larger than differences in education, gender, income, age, and numerous other factors.[94]

Some Democrats fear that secularism within the party may alienate the important religious vote.[95] This fear recently has led Democratic Party officials and candidates to initiate outreach efforts to various religious constituencies.[96] The need to balance religious and secular constituencies will continue to be a challenge in the years ahead for Democratic politicians. The growing importance of the secular voting bloc within the Democratic Party, coupled with the continued loyalty of religious conservatives to the Republican Party, might portend continued religious polarization along partisan lines. Will some devout Hispanic or African American Christians find Democratic politics too secular? Will Republican elites try to appeal to secular voters and alienate their religious backers? Will new issues emerge that undercut existing divides?

CONCLUSION

The growing divide between religiously observant and more secular Americans has led some commentators to wonder if a European-style party alignment is emerging in the United States, pitting a Christian conservative party (the Republicans) versus a more secular, liberal party (the Democrats). As we have seen, this pattern is only partly accurate because many progressive mainline Protestants, Catholics, religious minorities, and immigrant groups inhabit the same political coalition with secular voters. What this chapter illustrates, instead, is how dynamic and complex religious voting is in the United States. It is dynamic because we see important changes over time—sometimes dramatic ones. It is complex because religion can operate on several different levels, often simultaneously. One simply cannot understand elections in the United States without comprehending the impact of religion upon them. There is no doubt that religion remains a defining characteristic of American political life.

FURTHER READING

Campbell, David E., ed. *A Matter of Faith: Religion and the 2004 Election.* Washington, DC: Brookings Institution, 2007. A collection of essays analyzing various aspects of religion's substantial significance in the 2004 election.

Green, John C. *The Faith Factor: How Religion Influences American Elections.* Westport, CT: Praeger, 2007. A thorough, empirical look at the various ways in which religion affects American electoral politics.

Layman, Geoffrey. *The Great Divide: Religious and Cultural Conflict in American Party Politics.* New York: Columbia University Press, 2001. A provocative examination of the changing role of religion and culture in American voting patterns.

Menendez, Albert. *Religion at the Polls.* Philadelphia: Westminster, 1977. The classic study of religious voting in American politics.

Pew Forum on Religion & Public Life. http://pewforum.org/. This website contains some of the most up-to-date surveys of the religious composition of the United States and religious voting patterns.

Reichley, A. James. *Faith in Politics.* Washington, DC: Brookings Institution, 2002. In a rich book, a good discussion of the voting behaviors of various religious groups placed in historical perspective.

Wilson, J. Matthew, ed. *From Pews to Polling Places: Faith and Politics in the American Religious Mosaic.* Washington, DC: Georgetown University Press, 2007. Contains in-depth case studies of the political attitudes and voting behavior of different religious traditions.

NOTES

1. Morris P. Fiorina, *Culture War? The Myth of a Polarized America*, 2nd ed. (Upper Saddle River, NJ: Longman, 2006).

2. A. James Reichley, *Faith in Politics* (Washington, DC: Brookings Institution, 2002).

3. Edwin S. Gaustad, *Sworn on the Altar of God: A Religious Biography of Thomas Jefferson* (Grand Rapids, MI: Eerdmans, 1996); Reichley, *Faith in Politics.*

4. Allen D. Hertzke, *Echoes of Discontent: Jesse Jackson, Pat Robertson, and the Resurgence of Populism* (Washington, DC: CQ Press, 1993), 3.

5. On the subject of Catholics and the Republican Party during this period, see Reichley, *Faith in Politics.*

6. See Paul Kleppner, *Continuity and Change in Electoral Politics, 1893–1928* (Westport, CT: Greenwood Press, 1987); and Paul Kleppner, *The Cross of Culture: A Social Analysis of Midwestern Politics, 1850–1900* (New York: Free Press, 1970).

7. Robert Booth Fowler, *Religion and Politics in America* (Metuchen, NJ: Scarecrow Press, 1985), chap. 3. See also Andrew R. Murphy, *Prodigal Nation: Moral Decline and Divine Punishment from New England to 9/11* (New York: Oxford University Press, 2009).

8. Fowler, *Religion and Politics in America*, chap. 3.

9. For an excellent history of religion and politics in the African American experience, see Barbara Dianne Savage, *Your Spirits Walk Beside Us: The Politics of Black Religion* (Cambridge, MA: Belknap Press of Harvard University Press, 2008).

10. A good summary of the New Deal coalition appears in Everett Carll Ladd Jr. with Charles D. Hadley, *Transformations of the American Party System: Political Coalitions from the New Deal to the 1970s*, 2nd ed. (New York: W. W. Norton, 1975). On critical electoral realignment, see Walter Dean Burnham, *Critical Elections and the Mainsprings of American Politics* (New York: W. W. Norton, 1970).

11. Fredrick C. Harris, *Something Within: Religion in African-American Political Activism* (New York: Oxford University Press, 1999); Savage, *Your Spirits Walk Beside Us*.

12. Lyman A. Kellstedt, John C. Green, James L. Guth, and Corwin E. Schmidt, "Has Godot Finally Arrived? Religion and Realignment," in *Religion and the Culture Wars: Dispatches from the Front*, eds. John C. Green, James L. Guth, Corwin E. Smidt, and Lyman A. Kellstedt (Lanham, MD: Rowman and Littlefield, 1996), 291–299; V. O. Key Jr., *Southern Politics in State and Nation* (New York: Knopf, 1949); Ladd and Hadley, *Transformations of the American Party System*.

13. Ladd and Hadley, *Transformations of the American Party System*.

14. Ibid, chap. 1.

15. Earl Black and Merle Black, *The Rise of Southern Republicans* (Cambridge, MA: Harvard University Press, 2002).

16. Ronald Inglehart, *Culture Shift in Advanced Industrial Society* (Princeton: Princeton University Press, 1990); Ronald Inglehart, *The Silent Revolution: Changing Values and Political Styles Among Western Publics* (Princeton: Princeton University Press, 1977).

17. Pew Hispanic Center, "Dissecting the 2008 Electorate: Most Diverse in U.S. History," http://pewhispanic.org/reports/report.php?ReportID=108 (April 30, 2009).

18. David E. Campbell, ed., *A Matter of Faith: Religion and the 2004 Presidential Election* (Washington, DC: Brookings Institution, 2007).

19. Pew Research Center for the People and the Press, "Independents Take Center Stage in Obama Era—Trends in Political Values and Core Attitudes: 1987–2009," http://people-press.org/report/517/ (May 21, 2009).

20. The classic statement of the relationship between party identification and vote choice is Angus Campbell, Philip E. Converse, Warren E. Miller, and Donald J. Stokes, *The American Voter* (Chicago: University of Chicago Press, 1960), especially chap. 6.

21. John C. Green, *The Faith Factor: How Religion Influences American Elections* (Westport, CT: Praeger, 2007).

22. Pew Forum on Religion & Public Life, *U.S. Religious Landscape Survey*, http://religions .pewforum.org/ (2008).

23. Robert Axelrod, "Presidential Election Coalitions in 1984," *American Political Science Review* 80 (1986), 281–284.

24. Albert Menendez, *Religion at the Polls* (Philadelphia: Westminster, 1977).

25. Ibid., chap. 7.

26. Phillip E. Converse, *Religion and Politics: The 1960 Elections* (Ann Arbor: University of Michigan Survey Research Center, 1961).

27. Clarke E. Cochran and David Carroll Cochran, *Catholics, Politics, and Public Policy: Beyond Left and Right* (Maryknoll, NY: Orbis, 2003); Matthew J. Streb and Brian Frederick, "The Myth of a Distinct Catholic Vote," in *Catholics and Politics: The Dynamic Tension Between Faith and Power*, eds. Kristin E. Heyer, Mark J. Rozell, and Michael A. Genovese (Washington, DC: Georgetown University Press, 2008), 93–112.

28. Andrew M. Greeley, *The Catholic Revolution: New Wine, Old Wineskins, and the Second Vatican Council* (Berkeley: University of California Press, 2005).

29. Margaret Ross Sammon, "The Politics of the U.S. Catholic Bishops: The Centrality of Abortion," in *Catholics and Politics*; Peter Slevin, "St. Louis Prelate Aims to Bring Flock in Line," *The Washington Post* (May 29, 2007), A2.

30. Pew Forum on Religion & Public Life, *Obama, Catholics, and the Notre Dame Commencement*, http://pewforum.org/docs/?DocID=413 (April 30, 2009).

31. Douglas W. Kmiec, *Can a Catholic Support Him: Asking the Big Questions About Barack Obama* (Woodstock, NY: Overlook Press, 2008).

32. Cochran and Cochran, *Catholics, Politics, and Public Policy*.

33. Joseph L. Bernardin, *The Seamless Garment: Writings on the Consistent Ethic of Life*, ed. Thomas A. Nairn (Maryknoll, NY: Orbis, 2008).

34. Pew Forum on Religion & Public Life, *How the Faithful Voted*, http://pewforum .org/docs/?DocID=367 (2008).

35. Pew Forum on Religion & Public Life, *Faith in Flux: Changes in Religious Affiliation in the U.S.*, http://pewforum.org/events/?EventID=215 (April 27, 2009).

36. David A. Badillo, *Latinos and the New Immigrant Church* (Baltimore: Johns Hopkins University Press, 2006).

37. Paul B. Henry Institute, *National Survey of Religion and Public Life* (2008).

38. Pew Forum, *U.S. Religious Landscape Survey*, http://religions.pewforum.org/portraits (2008).

39. Geoffrey Layman, *The Great Divide: Religious and Cultural Conflict in American Party Politics* (New York: Columbia University Press, 2001); Albert J. Menendez, *Evangelicals at the Ballot Box* (New York: Prometheus, 1995).

40. Layman, *The Great Divide*; Louis Bolce and Gerald De Maio, "Our Secularist Democratic Party," *The Public Interest* 154 (Fall 2002), 3–20.

41. Key, *Southern Politics*.

42. Black and Black, *The Rise of Southern Republicans*.

43. Paul Lopatto, *Religion and the Presidential Election* (New York: Praeger, 1985). Lopatto concluded that Carter split the theologically conservative (or evangelical) vote with Ford but lost among Protestants more generally. See also Albert Menendez, *Religion at the Polls* (Philadelphia: Westminster, 1977). Menendez gave the evangelical edge to Ford but also concluded that Carter did better with evangelicals than he did with mainline Protestants (who backed Ford by a wide margin).

44. J. Quin Monson and J. Baxter Oliphant, "Microtargeting and the Instrumental Mobilization of Religious Conservatives," in *A Matter of Faith*.

45. Kellstedt et al., "Has Godot Finally Arrived?"; Mark J. Rozell and Clyde Wilcox, eds., *God at the Grassroots: The Christian Right in the 1994 Elections* (Lanham, MD: Rowman and Littlefield, 1995).

46. Layman, *The Great Divide*.

47. James L. Guth et al., "The Political Activity of Evangelical Clergy in the Election of 2000: A Case Study of Five Denominations," *Journal for the Scientific Study of Religion* 42 (2003), 501–514; James L. Guth, John C. Green, Corwin E. Smidt, Lyman A. Kellstedt, and Margaret M. Poloma, *The Bully Pulpit: The Politics of Protestant Clergy* (Lawrence, KS: University Press of Kansas, 1997).

48. For a fuller discussion of the issues important to evangelicals and other religious groups, see Green, *The Faith Factor*; Andrew Kohut, John C. Green, Scott Keeter, and Robert C. Toth, *The Diminishing Divide: Religion's Changing Role in American Politics* (Washington, DC: Brookings Institution, 2000), chap. 4; Clyde Wilcox and Carin Larson, *Onward Christian Soldiers? The Religious Right in American Politics*, 3rd ed. (Boulder: Westview Press, 2006).

49. Katharine Q. Seelye, "Conservatives Mobilize Against Ruling on Gay Marriage," *The New York Times*, November 20, 2003; Adam Nagourney, "Decision on Gay Marriage Creates a Thorny Issue for 2004 Race," *The New York Times*, November 19, 2003.

50. Alex Altman, "Joshua DuBois: Obama's Pastor-in-Chief," *Time*, February 6, 2009.

51. Pew Forum, *How the Faithful Voted*.

52. Both the University of Akron and the Henry Institute surveys showed no evangelical gains by Obama.

53. David E. Campbell and J. Quin Monson, "Dry Kindling: A Political Profile of American Mormons," in *From Pews to Polling Places: Faith and Politics in the American Religious Mosaic*, ed. J. Matthew Wilson (Washington, DC: Georgetown University Press, 2007).

54. Laura R. Olson and Adam L. Warber, "Mainline Protestants and the American Presidency," in *Religion, Race, and the American Presidency*, ed. Gaston Espinosa (Lanham, MD: Rowman and Littlefield, 2008).

55. Ibid.

56. James L. Adams, *The Growing Church Lobby in Washington* (Grand Rapids, MI: Eerdmans, 1970); Guth et al., *The Bully Pulpit*; Ted G. Jelen, *The Political World of the Clergy* (Westport, CT: Praeger, 1993); Norman B. Koller and Joseph D. Retzer, "The Sounds of Silence Revisited," *Sociological Analysis* 41 (1980): 155–161.

57. University of Akron, *The Fifth National Survey of Religion and Politics, 2008*, shows mainline Protestants voting more for Obama than white Catholics. Exit poll data provided by staff at the Pew Forum on Religion & Public Life.

58. See also Pew Forum, *U.S. Religious Landscape Survey*.

59. Olson and Warber, "Mainline Protestants."

60. Lee Sigelman, "Jews and the 1988 Election: More of the Same?" in *The Bible and the Ballot Box: Religion and Politics in the 1988 Election*, eds. James L. Guth and John C. Green (Boulder: Westview Press, 1991); see also Anna Greenberg and Kenneth D. Wald, "Still Liberal After All These Years: The Contemporary Political Behavior of American Jewry," in *Jews in American Politics*, eds. L. Sandy Maisel and Ira N. Forman (Lanham, MD: Rowman and Littlefield, 2001), 161–193.

61. Greenberg and Wald, "Still Liberal."

62. Sigelman, "Jews and the 1988 Election."

63. Paul A. Djupe and Anand E. Sokhey, "American Rabbis in the 2000 Elections," *Journal for the Scientific Study of Religion* 42 (2003), 563–576; Greenberg and Wald, "Still Liberal."

64. Adolph L. Reed, *The Jesse Jackson Phenomenon: The Crisis of Purpose in Afro-American Politics* (New Haven, CT: Yale University Press, 1986).

65. Green, "The Undetected Tide," *Religion in the News* (2003), 5; Greenberg and Wald, "Still Liberal."

66. Greenberg and Wald, "Still Liberal."

67. Edward Shapiro, "Right Turn? Jews and the American Conservative Movement," in *Jews in American Politics*.

68. Elliott Abrams, *Faith or Fear: How Jews Can Survive in a Christian America* (New York: Free Press, 1997).

69. Pew Research Center, *Evenly Divided and Increasingly Polarized: 2004 Political Landscape* (Washington, DC: Pew Research Center, 2003), 66.

70. Pew Forum, *U.S. Religious Landscape Survey.*

71. Harris, *Something Within*; Pew Forum, *U.S. Religious Landscape Survey.*

72. Harris, *Something Within*, chaps. 6–7; see also Steven Peterson, "Church Participation and Political Participation: The Spillover Effect," *American Politics Quarterly* 20 (1992), 123–139.

73. This development is elaborated in Hertzke, *Echoes of Discontent.*

74. University of Akron, *Third National Survey of Religion and Politics* (2000); University of Akron, *Fourth National Survey of Religion and Politics* (2004); Eric L. McDaniel, "The Black Church: Maintaining Old Coalitions," in *A Matter of Faith.*

75. University of Akron, *Fourth National Survey of Religion and Politics*; and Paul B. Henry Institute, *National Survey of Religion and Public Life* (2008).

76. Karl Vick and Ashley Surdin, "Most of California's Black Voters Backed Gay Marriage Ban," *The Washington Post*, November 7, 2008.

77. Pew Forum on Religion & Public Life and Pew Hispanic Center, *Changing Faiths: Latinos and the Transformation of American Religion* (2006); Gaston Espinosa, Virgilio Elizondo, and Jesse Miranda, eds., *Latino Religions and Civic Activism in the United States* (New York: Oxford University Press, 2005).

78. For an excellent look at Latino Pentecostals, see Arlene Sanchez Walsh, *Latino Pentecostal Identity: Evangelical Faith, Self, and Society* (New York: Columbia University Press, 2003); "Separated Brothers," *The Economist*, July 18, 2009, 31.

79. Nathan J. Kelly and Jana Morgan Kelly, "Religion and Latino Partisanship in the United States," *Political Research Quarterly* 58 (2005), 87–95; Nathan J. Kelly and Jana Morgan, "Religious Traditionalism and Latino Politics in the United States," *American Politics Research* 36 (2008), 236–263.

80. John C. Green and Mark Silk, "The New Religion Gap," *Religion in the News* 5 (2003), 3.

81. University of Akron, *Fourth National Survey of Religion and Politics.*

82. Richard Wolffe, Holly Bailey, and Evan Thomas, "Bush's Spanish Lessons," *Newsweek*, May 29, 2006, 24.

83. The 2008 Henry Institute *National Survey of Religion and Public Life* found a drop of 7 points in McCain's vote among Hispanic Protestants (from 64 to 57 percent), whereas the University of Akron's *Fifth National Survey of Religion and Politics* recorded a drop to 47 percent (but that category included other minorities). Exit polls estimate an even larger drop of 29 percent. It appears that the outlier was the Henry survey, suggesting a double-digit drop.

84. Project MAPS, *American Muslim Poll 2004*. www.wr.mea.com/archives/Dec._2004/0412058.html.

85. Ahmed Younis, national director of the Muslim Public Affairs Council described how the American Muslim Political Coordinating Council, consisting of several of the major American groups, endorsed Bush because the candidate came out against secret evidence. Younis, who felt that this position was not enough to warrant an endorsement, described the 2000 initiative as a "fiasco." Ahmed Younis, personal interview with Allen Hertzke, Washington, DC, June 14, 2006.

86. Project MAPS, *American Muslim Poll 2004*.

87. Ibid.

88. American Muslim Taskforce on Civil Rights and Elections, http://muslimmedia network.com/mmn/?p=3203 (November 7, 2008).

89. Green, *The Faith Factor*; Kohut et al., *The Diminishing Divide*; Layman, *The Great Divide*.

90. Pew Forum on Religion & Public Life, *Clinton and Giuliani Seen as Not Highly Religious*, http://pewforum.org/surveys/campaign08/ (2007).

91. Louis Bolce and Gerald De Maio, "Secularists, Antifundamentalists, and the New Religious Divide in the American Electorate," in *From Pews to Polling Places: Faith and Politics in the American Religious Mosaic*.

92. Layman, *The Great Divide*.

93. Pew Forum on Religion & Public Life, *How the Faithful Voted*.

94. Laura R. Olson and John C. Green, "The Religion Gap," *PS: Political Science & Politics* 39 (2006), 455–459.

95. Tony Carnes, "Swing Evangelicals," *Christianity Today*, January 9, 2004.

96. Peter J. Boyer, "Party Faithful," *The New Yorker*, September 8, 2008, 24.

5

THE POLITICS OF ORGANIZED
RELIGIOUS GROUPS

Even though Americans love individualism and celebrate the heroic individual in literature and history, political power in the United States flows mostly from collective action. Organizing is an essential key to success in American politics. In this chapter we examine organized religious groups that work to affect politics and policy by tracing their roots and exploring their responses to front-burner political issues.[1]

Although religious interest groups vary widely in organizational style, ideology, and focus, collectively they have engaged in the full range of political activities—lobbying legislatures and executive branch officials, mobilizing their constituents, and attempting to influence public opinion and sometimes elections. Elsewhere we consider judicial strategies, but it must be noted in passing that for some groups litigating in the courts seamlessly supplements other forms of lobbying.

Religious group leaders generally eschew the term "lobbying," with its unsavory connotations of shady dealings and corruption, and instead often speak of themselves as "advocates." We use the term lobbying neutrally in reference to any organized effort to influence public policy.

For all religious interest groups there is a practical dimension to terminology. Most operate as tax-exempt nonprofit organizations that, under Section 501(c)(3) of the Internal Revenue Code, cannot devote a "substantial" part of their time and resources to actual lobbying. This is generally not a problem for large organizations that undertake a wide range of activities, and the law is sufficiently vague so that most groups can avoid officially registering as "lobbies" (which would result in for-feited tax-exempt status).

Nevertheless, some religious groups do register themselves as lobbies, which gives them greater flexibility in strategies, such as producing scorecards on the voting records of individual members of Congress. Rarer still in the religious community are political action committees (PACs), which make campaign contributions and endorse candidates. For most religious groups partisan electioneering is simply too divisive and risky, although some "Christian Right" groups have striven to influence elections, and black churches can be formidable venues for electoral mobilization.

The dominant characteristic of religious advocacy is its tremendous diversity, which tends to prevent dominance by any single group. Despite claims to the contrary by one group or another, no religion or coalition has been politically dominant in our modern times, and continued pluralism makes such dominance unlikely in the future. To be sure, some religious groups clearly play the political game better than others, but even the best operate in a challenging environment and can appreciate that their political fortunes naturally rise and fall with the times.

Religious lobbying also is constantly evolving. It has dramatically grown over time, with the appearance of more and different kinds of groups. Moreover, the issue agenda of religious organizations is much broader than it used to be, touching on just about every imaginable public policy concern. Finally, religious advocacy is increasingly globalized, sophisticated, and high-tech.[2]

THE EVOLUTION OF NATIONAL RELIGIOUS LOBBIES

Religious advocacy, as we saw in Chapter 1, is as old as the Republic. At first, this advocacy was episodic and restricted to the state and local level, largely because the federal government's role in the lives of American citizens was limited. Issues of importance to religious people, such as child welfare, prison reform, and education, were state and local matters, and the common pattern was that temporary coalitions of religious groups would come together when issues arose.

As the nation grew, however, religious groups periodically were drawn into national lobbying campaigns, from seemingly trivial battles over Sunday mail delivery and dueling to the momentous issues of slavery and Native American removal.[3] Some of the most formidable church-based activism in American history involved the Prohibition movement. The Anti-Saloon League, a religiously based coalition in favor of Prohibition, was a principal force behind the passage of the 18th Amendment in 1919, banning the sale of alcoholic beverages throughout the nation.[4]

In the twentieth century, the increasing prominence and reach of the federal government acted as a catalyst in the growth of ongoing church lobbying. Early groups included the International Religious Liberty Association, established by the Seventh-day Adventists at the turn of the century; the United Methodist Church, which established a Washington office in 1916 to promote prohibition and social reform; the National Catholic Welfare Conference, which set up shop in 1919; the Quakers, who opened the first full-time registered religious lobby in 1943, primarily to protect conscientious objector status; and Jewish and Baptist organizations that arrived in Washington by mid-century. A study published in 1950 found at least sixteen national religious groups that had offices in Washington representing Protestant, Jewish, and Catholic constituencies.[5]

Since 1950, the number of religious lobbies has grown substantially. A major 2009 study by the Pew Forum on Religion & Public Life identified more than 180 national religious organizations that engage at least occasionally in public policy advocacy.[6] Included in this number are significant Catholic, mainline Protestant, evangelical, African American Protestant, and Jewish interest groups. Today there is also a range of organized groups representing the political interests of a number of smaller religious communities as well, including Orthodox Jews, Muslims, Baha'is, Hindus, Tibetan Buddhists, Sikhs, and Chinese Uyghurs.

In addition to religious communities, religious lobbies advocate on behalf of a wide array of professional associations (for example, evangelical doctors, Muslim female lawyers, homeschoolers, leaders of Catholic religious orders, and Latino clergy) and institutions (such as religious charities, international relief organizations, hospitals, schools, colleges, and immigration agencies). A host of membership groups also represent broad faith-based concerns (ranging from "traditional values" to "social justice") and particular issues, such as abortion, the death penalty, and hunger. Finally, a number of faith-based think tanks operate to provide new policy ideas and shape the broader intellectual discourse.

Why has there been all of this growth in the organized political representation of religious interest groups? There are many reasons. One is the flowering of American religious pluralism and the growing sense that such pluralism creates an imperative for religious groups to get organized to protect their collective interests. In the 1950s, Baptists established a lobby to "watch" Catholics. Much more recently, Muslim Americans have coalesced in part to counteract the influence of Jewish interest groups. Another explanation is that as the federal government's size and scope of responsibility have expanded, many groups have arisen to monitor its impact on their religious organizations—hospitals, schools, charitable organizations, and development agencies—as well as on their basic religious freedom. The third reason is that many religious people have come to the conclusion that they must get organized and enter politics to promote or defend the values of their religious traditions. This realization is consistent with the greater emphasis on socio-moral issues in American politics since the 1960s.[7] Finally, the huge influence of the United States on the global stage serves as a catalyst for groups seeking American support for their persecuted fellow believers abroad. To take but one example, the national Baha'i organization regularly petitions policymakers to address the plight of Baha'is in Iran and elsewhere.[8] For these and other reasons, the diversity, scope, and number of religious groups lobbying in Washington has never been greater (Box 5.1).

STRATEGIES FOR EFFECTIVE ADVOCACY

In one sense, the politics of pressure groups has not changed fundamentally since the nineteenth century.[9] Effective advocacy is—and always has been—a combination of outside pressure and inside influence coalescing in favorable circumstances. Nonetheless, new dimensions have been added to the craft, particularly Internet-based tools that connect constituents, lobbyists, and policymakers.

Outside Pressure

To be effective, interest groups must rely on a loyal network of members or influential institutions at the grassroots level that can bring pressure to bear on members of Congress and state legislators. The threat of electoral defeat remains a powerful motivator of modern politicians. All elected officials know that groups with many members or well-heeled contributors can have an effect on their fortunes on Election Day. The kinds of outside pressure brought by interest groups vary tremendously

---

**BOX 5.1   PEW FORUM REPORT ON
RELIGIOUS ADVOCACY AND PUBLIC POLICY**

In 2009, the Pew Forum on Religion & Public Life published a major study of religious lobbies—who they are, what they do, and how they do it. The study charts the growth in the diversity of groups, the breadth of the issues they tackle, and the high-tech methods they increasingly are using in their public policy advocacy efforts. The study may be found on the Pew Forum's webpage: http://pewforum.org/.

by group and context. Mass mobilization, a technique commonly used by conservative Protestant organizations, represents one approach. Television and radio ministry connections, huge computer lists of contributors, and affiliated activist churches can generate a groundswell of communication to elected officials, which can attract attention and occasionally affect policy.[10]

Mass mobilization is necessary but rarely sufficient for success. Members of Congress often discount the "artificially inseminated" constituent communication that results from mass mobilization. More modest but well placed and informed constituent communication can be as effective. Members of the liberal nuns' lobby, NETWORK, for example, have some influence because their members are well read, knowledgeable about politics, and hooked into informational networks around the globe through their religious orders. In an era when members of Congress receive millions of e-mails every year, Bread for the World continues to employ its traditional "offering of letters" strategy. Leaders specify the goal for the year (for example, raising more money for international food aid), identify members of Congress who serve on pertinent committees and subcommittees, then organize congregations in those members' districts or states to collect an offering of letters that are delivered to their offices in Washington (because regular mail to Congress receives intensive security screening, personal delivery is imperative).[11]

As a supplement to mass mobilization, sophisticated groups also activate smaller lists of key contacts who may be reached via e-mail or Twitter for quick response. This is effective because sometimes a few influential community leaders and party contributors who personally know their member of Congress can have greater clout than thousands of relatively unsophisticated supporters or newcomers to politics. But not all groups are equally adept or positioned to do this. Jewish groups are renowned for deploying key contacts because local rabbis or Jewish civic leaders tend to be prominent members of their communities. The same is true of Catholic bishops, pastors of megachurches, and leading African American clergy.

A related form of "elite mobilization" involves the leaders of religious institutions that are woven into the life and economy of the local community. Religious institutions—such as parochial schools, hospitals, colleges, charities, international relief organizations, and mission societies—are multimillion-dollar enterprises. Thus policymakers pay attention when the president of a religious college or the director of a religious hospital calls in regard to legislation.

The key contact approach represents the perfect marriage of the Washington lobbyist and the grassroots following. To appreciate the effectiveness of this strategy, imagine a member of Congress at a hearing. At one point the member expresses skepticism about a bill's provisions. A lobbyist in the room notices this lack of support and immediately communicates with contact people from the member's home district. The contact people receive an e-mail or voice mail and immediately communicate their concern to the member of Congress or top staff. Stories circulate in Washington about how the most sophisticated groups are able to deliver protests to members of Congress even before a day's hearing is over. Whether or not that happens, members of Congress know that their moves are being watched and being communicated at the speed of light to influential contributors, community leaders, and even their personal friends back in the district or state. And because most members of Congress want to be reelected,[12] they have to care deeply about what such people think.

Money, of course, speaks loudly in contemporary politics. Most religious groups, however, do not form political action committees (PACs), organizations that donate money to candidates. Nor are clergy normally in the position to make substantial individual contributions to candidates, political parties, or PACs. Thus religious groups are not major players in the money game, with a few exceptions. Jewish organizations, especially pro-Israel groups, do support PACs; they constitute important sources of money for both individual congressional candidates and political parties. Some Jewish citizens also are major contributors and fund-raisers—particularly for the Democratic Party—and this provides access. Like other religious bodies, African American churches are tax-exempt institutions and thus cannot form PACs or make direct financial contributions, but they do sometimes allow their property to be used for political fund-raisers. They also frequently invite candidates to speak during services. Because overt political involvement is more accepted in the African American religious community than in the rest of organized religion in the United States, favored candidates are sometimes able to raise money through direct appeals made in churches.

By and large, however, religious actors are not big players in the political money game. Some argue that this protects them from the corrupting influences of fundraising and allows them to present a clearer moral message to leaders. And sometimes this may be true; religious leaders, at their best, present politicians with visions of the public good undiluted by narrow self-interest. But money does speak, and religious leaders often resign themselves to the fact that they will not have that tool at their disposal.

Outside pressure involves efforts by religious actors to shape public opinion on key issues of the day. When a religious interest group demonstrates the ability to shape public opinion, it brings indirect pressure on politicians. Strategies and success rates for this activity, however, vary. Events staged for media coverage have become common. Demonstrations, dramatic testimony, publicized fact-finding reports, and statements by bishops all are aimed at the mass media and the broader public.

Here it is crucial that the religious group enjoy the sympathies of the elite press. Conservative evangelicals and pro-life activists complain bitterly that they are not given a fair hearing in the mass media and that they are either ignored or stereotyped. As surveys of elite journalists show, there may be some truth to this analysis.[13]

Sometimes a religious leader captures invaluable media attention through a propitious convergence of timeliness and message. Jim Wallis did this with the publication of his book, *God's Politics*, in January 2005.[14] The book's denunciation of the Christian Right by a self-identified progressive evangelical, coming right after George W. Bush won a second term with substantial help from conservative religionists, catapulted Wallis into the media stratosphere and made him the de facto leader of religious progressives in America. His book tour became a major media event, and he was feted by Democrats desperately seeking a way to demonstrate that they were faith-friendly. One of those Democrats was Barack Obama, who spoke on the "proper connection" between faith and politics at a Sojourners gathering in 2006. With Obama's election to the presidency, Wallis gained the kind of access most religious leaders only dream of—and put Sojourners into a leadership role among progressive religious groups.[15]

Inside Influence

No matter how much outside pressure an interest group can mount, it means little if group leaders are not skilled at gaining and keeping elite access. To have any measure of political success, a group needs the chance to tell sympathetic policymakers about its agenda. Here, too, not all religious groups are equal. Some enjoy excellent access; others have to fight for every bit. During the 1980s, for example, when so much was made of the rise of the Christian Right, the Moral Majority actually suffered because they had poor access. Later more sophisticated Christian Right groups cultivated better access with the Republican Congress of the 1990s and the administration of George W. Bush, but that access began to dissipate after the 2006 midterm election.[16]

The quality of interest group leadership matters greatly.[17] Some groups employ lobbyists with years of experience and strong reputations; others suffer from lack of experience or little perceived gravitas. Experienced interest group leaders have a strong strategic sense, developing a clear, limited set of attainable objectives on the basis of the current political climate. One of the recurrent problems faced by mainline Protestant lobbies is a lack of sharp focus and a tendency to take on too many issues at the same time, although some mainline leaders are striving to address this problem.[18]

A national lobby's effectiveness also is governed by the total quality of its operation, resources, staff, research facilities, and technological ability to reach members. All of that takes money and institutional support. Conservative Christian groups such as the Family Research Council, Focus on the Family, and Concerned Women for America have enjoyed such backing. And Catholic lobbies benefit from the institutional strength of the Catholic Church and its schools, hospitals, charities, and universities. Interestingly, the size of the religious community does not always determine the sophistication of the lobbying operation. The Society of Friends, or Quakers, have a tiny membership in the United States. However, their members are affluent, well educated, and highly motivated to make a political difference, so the Quakers support one of the best-staffed, experienced, and sophisticated lobby operations in Washington. In turn, Jewish organizations are well funded and well staffed.[19] In contrast, mainline Protestant churches have met with declining financial and institutional backing as national denominational offices have cut back on their Washington operations.[20] By way of comparison, the National Spiritual Assembly of the Baha'is of the United States has a larger advocacy staff in Washington than several mainline denominations.[21]

In spite of the growing presence and diversity of religious lobbies, most remain small affairs compared to such giants as the National Education Association, the American Association for Retired Persons, or the National Association of Manufacturers (the one exception is the huge American Israel Public Affairs Committee). A large religious lobby may have twenty-five staff people (a few have upwards of seventy or so), but many operate with only a handful of people. A major secular lobby, on the other hand, could have 300 or more professional lobbyists. This is part of the reason that—despite periodic exceptional cases of high impact—religious organizations exercise mostly modest political influence in the grand scheme of Washington, or statehouse, politics.

A treatment of outside and inside influence would be incomplete without a discussion of the constantly evolving revolution in communications technology that is transforming the lobbying craft in novel ways. To varying degrees, virtually all religious groups are employing new technology. This means that even offices with small staffs can maintain e-mail communications with thousands of supporters, which has expanded the grassroots reach of mainline Protestant Washington offices and small religious interest groups alike. Lobbying software enables groups to facilitate e-mails by constituents at the click of a mouse and monitors which constituents send e-mails to which members of Congress. Social networking modalities such as Twitter, Facebook, blogs, and podcasts connect lobbyists, lay members, and policymakers in an increasingly interactive web. National religious leaders now receive more feedback from members, who interact with each other and with people in wider networks. Thus the most effective mobilizations are those that "go viral," where, say, not just Quakers but friends of Quakers are activated by a national campaign. The most sophisticated religious leaders are attempting to ride this new wave, sometimes to great effect.

THE LEGISLATIVE PROCESS, COMPROMISE, AND COALITION BUILDING

At the heart of the legislative process—whether in Congress or in statehouses—is compromise. Although compromise is a dubious concept to some religious activists, legislators themselves view it as the key to action, and seasoned religious advocates accept its necessity. They know it is the only way to build the coalitions that are necessary to get political goals accomplished. In order to understand why compromise is so vital, it is important to recall that the American system of government frustrates swift action. The framers of the Constitution wanted to limit power because they feared tyranny. The checks and balances they built into the system are there to delay proposals and to allow many groups the chance to block proposed legislation. Political insiders know this, so they work to build the strongest possible coalition of supporters. Indeed, Washington politics is renowned for its "strange bedfellows" alliances. There are no permanent friends or enemies, so the saying goes, just shifting coalitions.[22]

Religious leaders realize that it is essential to build coalitions with other lobbies to magnify their voices. Coalitions are effective because a kind of specialization operates: Different groups rotate the lead in different lobbying campaigns because of their special expertise or focus. Thus Quakers might lead the coalition on nuclear proliferation but Bread for the World would do so on hunger. Concerned Women for America might spearhead an alliance against cloning whereas the Family Research Council takes the lead on expanding child tax credits. Moreover, different groups have access to different policymakers, so when groups join hands, the collective clout is greater.

At the national and state levels we see contending progressive and traditionalist alliances, often formalized into steering bodies. But shifting coalitions belie the simplistic view of continuous "culture war" polarization. People who fight like cats and dogs over abortion and gay marriage have joined forces to defend the autonomy of religious institutions, the fight against HIV/AIDS in Africa, and measures against human trafficking.

Sometimes temporary alliances form around a single issue. The conservative evangelical group Concerned Women for America teamed up with Muslim groups and the Catholic Church to spearhead a United Nations resolution banning cloning. Legislation to enable the Food and Drug Administration to regulate tobacco was backed by the Southern Baptist Convention and the United Methodist Church, two bodies that tend to disagree on hot-button cultural issues. On the prevention of prison rape, Prison Fellowship, a conservative evangelical group, teamed up with liberal groups to gain passage of legislation trying to curb the problem. More recently, conservative Chuck Donovan of the Family Research Council teamed up with liberal Ron Sider of Evangelicals for Social Action to propose policies that would enhance the take-home pay of working-class and poor Americans.[23]

On other issues normal allies have become serious ongoing adversaries. On Israel, for example, liberal Protestant groups part company with their Jewish counterparts in staking out a critical posture toward Israeli policies that they see as unjust to Palestinians. Most evangelical Protestants, on the other hand, are strongly supportive of Israel, both because of a theology that sees the formation of Israel as providential[24] and because Israel represents a bulwark against what they see as the militant Islamist forces arrayed against the United States.

The religious community can be formidable when groups across the ideological and theological spectrum get together. For example, in 1990, a Supreme Court decision in *Employment Division* v. *Smith* narrowed the grounds for religious free exercise claims. In response, a virtual unanimity of religious groups coalesced to lobby Congress for the Religious Freedom Restoration Act (RFRA), which decreed that government had to show a "compelling interest" before burdening religious freedom. This sparked a decade-long battle between Congress and the Supreme Court over the contours of free exercise of religion (see Chapter 9). The breadth of the coalition for RFRA reflected the reality that in modern pluralist America every group can conceive of itself as a minority in need of protection. Perhaps in that sense the bedfellows were not so strange after all.

The relationships forged during the campaign for RFRA in turn helped facilitate broad religious alliances on global human rights. Since the 1990s, true left-right religious coalitions have backed legislation promoting international religious free-dom, peace in Sudan, human rights in North Korea, and multiple measures against human trafficking. Again, under the right circumstances, a broad religious alliance can be formidable.[25]

A MODEL OF RELIGIOUS GROUP EFFECTIVENESS

What makes for religious group effectiveness?[26] We suggest that five factors con-tribute to success: amenable traditions and theological beliefs; internal strength and unity; strategic location; constraints and opposition from other groups; and a fa-vorable "spirit of the times," that is, whether the political culture is open to a group's political advocacy.

Traditions and Theological Beliefs

Historical traditions and theological beliefs influence whether a religious group will enter politics at all, and if so, how it will approach that task. Some religions are so otherworldly that they eschew politics altogether; others get involved only when they feel a direct threat. The Jehovah's Witnesses are a group that generally stays out of politics, with the exception of occasional forays into the courts to protect their religious freedom. Others, such as Lutherans, have a deep tradition of teaching civic responsibility for the individual but resisting corporate political witness by the church, a tendency that sometimes frustrates Lutheran activists.[27]

Other religious traditions lend themselves to political action more readily. The American Catholic Church has long been at ease with politics and has a deep scholastic tradition of reflection on statecraft. Jewish groups, drawing upon a the-ology rooted heavily in justice, tend to approach public action with enthusiasm. Muslims, though they are newcomers to the advocacy scene, also arise from a reli-gious tradition steeped in government and law. And more than any other American religious group, African American Protestantism has long been deeply involved in political activism. The civil rights movement was organizationally based in black churches, and many African American clergy say they could not imagine their pas-toral role without a political component.[28]

Proclivities are not etched in stone, however, and change does occur. For exam-ple, for most of the twentieth century evangelical Protestant churches taught that politics was a realm to be avoided; today they are a formidable political force.[29] Tra-dition and theological beliefs also structure the political agendas of religious groups and their clergy; certain theological orientations are associated with different types of issue concerns.[30] A belief in the sanctity of traditional marriage comes naturally to Southern Baptists and Catholics. Jewish groups champion civil liberties. Pacifist denominations, such as the Quakers and Mennonites, make issues of war and peace central to their advocacy.[31]

Internal Strength and Unity

No religious group will be able to make much of a political impact without supportive lay members. It is strategically important to have a large and unified membership. At the same time, the existence of internal dissent, disputes among leaders, and resistance from members all detract from political clout. This is a major challenge within American Catholicism because some lay members, including important political officials, dissent from the official positions of the Catholic hierarchy.[32] Catholic Democrats in Congress mostly take pro-choice positions on abortion, for example, and some prominent lay Catholic Democrats endorsed Barack Obama, despite his support for abortion rights, a view that Catholic conservatives rejected.

Equally important is the intensity of group members' commitment. Are laity willing to write only an occasional letter to Congress? Or are they ready to sacrifice hours of their time building the organization, participating in telephone trees, and attending endless meetings? Are they willing to speak, vote, demonstrate, or even go to jail for their convictions?

Even the most committed participants need effective leaders. Strong leaders must exhibit energy, drive, and conviction. They also must have the ability to think strategically, form alliances, and articulate their messages in an appealing manner— often to elites who do not share their religious values. As in any organization, however, there is a risk that leaders may become overbearing and, in the case of membership organizations, inattentive to the members themselves. Indeed, Theda Skocpol suggests that leadership of many advocacy organizations has become highly professionalized and that ordinary members today make fewer decisions about the direction of organizations than they did just a few decades ago.[33] Because this situation can diminish members' sense of having a stake in the organization, the best leaders try to balance the inevitable need for management at the top with attentiveness to the goals and energies of members at the grassroots. Some religious groups, as we shall see, have been highly successful at achieving this balance, but others struggle.

Finally, resources, especially financial resources, are an absolute necessity for any political organization. Are members affluent, and are they willing to make financial contributions? Do they have time for politics? Are they well connected already, as contributors to political parties, as personal friends of members of Congress, or as leaders in their communities? Do they have expertise that the organization might need, perhaps in legal advocacy, policy analysis, or marketing? Many Jewish groups, for example, combine all of these components of internal strength and unity and are therefore politically effective, as are Quakers. Other groups enjoy a different kind of resource base. The International Campaign for Tibet, which represents the exiled community of Tibetan Buddhists, benefits from a large and intense international following of the Dalai Lama and the support of Hollywood celebrities.

Even religious groups without such advantages may stand a good chance of building a reasonable degree of political effectiveness. When people are deeply involved in any of a religious group's activities (such as serving on a church council), they learn valuable "civic skills," such as organizing, speaking, and letter writing. These civic skills make people better equipped and more willing to participate in politics.[34]

Strategic Location

Another factor that is crucial to political success is a religious interest group's "strategic location." Does the group enjoy natural access to elites in government? Or does it have to beat down the door just to get noticed? Meaningful access does not just involve securing one meeting with a few members of Congress or their staffs. It means getting serious hearings with congressional leaders and committee chairs, top White House officials, high-ranking bureaucrats and administrators (who formulate much policy), and the courts. Meaningful access also involves working with the assorted network of think tanks, law firms, foundations, and influence peddlers in Washington who know how the political game is played. It is useful to have connections with state and local officials, some of whom retain enormous influence over the federal government as well. The best access of all is to the elite national press. In a town where the words of *The Washington Post*—and more recently *The Washington Times*—often matter a good deal, the ability to gain favorable media exposure is crucial.

Some groups, such as the American Israel Public Affairs Committee (AIPAC), are able to maintain wide access over time and under changing circumstances. Others, as we saw above, are affected deeply by shifting party control of government or events. Still others have mixed success. As newcomers to the political scene, Muslim groups today have limited access to Congress. But because they are seen as important allies in the war on terror, they do have notable access to executive branch agencies, such as those within the U.S. Departments of Justice and Homeland Security.

Constraints and Opposition

The power, intensity, and access of a group's opponents matter. Some groups, of course, ignite more opposition than others. This has perennially been the case for Christian conservatives, who face groups, such as the Interfaith Alliance, that intentionally present themselves as opponents of the Christian Right. Muslim groups, too, face serious opposition from vehement critics and the serious constraint of skeptical public opinion. In mainline Protestant and Catholic circles, we often see tougher struggles against opposition within their own ranks. Such opposition is sometimes based in policy disputes. In other instances, members simply see political involvement of any kind as a divisive diversion from their view of the church's mission: providing meaning, spiritual comfort, forgiveness, or conciliation. Moreover, suspicion of religious activism is endemic in American culture. The tradition of church-state separation in the United States encourages skepticism about church involvement in politics. How effectively a group overcomes these hurdles often determines how far it can go politically.

Zeitgeist: Spirit of the Times and Political Context

The fortunes of a religious group are governed in part by how well its agenda conforms to the spirit of the times and the dominant political context. A spirit of liberal political activism in the 1960s aided mainline Protestant churches, just as a more conservative tone in the 1980s helped conservative evangelicals.[35] Rising concern for religious persecution in the 1990s buoyed the political fortunes of religious minorities, from Baha'is to Tibetan Buddhists, whereas the environment since September 11, 2001, has presented a major challenge to Muslims.

Religious groups usually cannot affect the prevailing zeitgeist, but they can recognize it and adapt their strategies—defensive or offensive—accordingly. For example, during the presidency of George W. Bush, evangelical groups enjoyed good access (if not always influence) with administrative officials and pursued an ambitious agenda. Mainline Protestant lobbyists and other progressive religious groups largely were shut out, so they took an oppositional posture to much of what Bush pursued. The election of Barack Obama with a Democratic congressional majority dramatically reversed fortunes and political strategies. Faced with aspects of a new policy agenda that they see as antithetical to their concerns, conservative evangelical groups have shifted to a defensive posture, mostly trying to blunt any initiatives by the Obama administration around abortion or gay rights. Progressive lobbyists, from Jim Wallis to mainline Protestant leaders and liberal Catholics, now enjoy much better access and have been able to pursue an ambitious agenda they could never have dreamed possible in previous years. Of course, another aspect of the times—the 2008–2009 economic meltdown—adversely affected the capacity of some religious groups, which had to cut back their staff as their budgets tightened.

To show how these five factors influence the actions and effectiveness of different American religious groups, we now turn to some examples.

PROGRESSIVE PROTESTANT GROUPS

As we noted in Chapter 2, mainline Protestants enjoyed a strategic location in American society through much of the twentieth century. One embodiment of this is the actual location of the United Methodist Building right across the street from the U.S. Capitol. It houses a number of liberal Protestant lobbies and rents space to other progressive groups. Moreover, beginning with the Social Gospel movement of the early twentieth century, mainline church leaders came to share a liberal theology that encouraged, and even expected, their involvement in "this world," which would include the political realm.[36] Thus they were, and continue to be, both receptive to political action and in a position to have some influence.

The most vivid illustration of this combination came with the civil rights movement. Inspired by Dr. Martin Luther King Jr., mainline denominational leaders became pivotal advocates and strategists for the landmark Civil Rights Act of 1964. They mobilized laity and brought delegations of clergy to Washington to lobby members of Congress, which was especially effective in gaining the swing votes of Midwestern Republicans who belonged to their denominations. Summing up the role of churches, Hubert Humphrey wrote that without them, "This bill could never have become law."[37]

The campaign for the Civil Rights Act served as a catalyst for expanded mainline political activism, and national church leaders continue to lobby on a host of liberal causes.[38] The 1960s, however, represented the high-water mark for the mainline denominations in Washington. Weakened by declining church memberships and diminishing financial support from the pews, and sometimes criticized as out of touch with lay members, mainline church lobbies are no longer as prominent as they were in the past.[39] This is especially the case for their umbrella organization, the National Council of Churches. On the other hand, mainline lobbyists today are buoyed by the proliferation of allied groups, so it is helpful to treat progressive Protestants more generally and examine the alliances they form with Catholics, Jews, progressive evangelicals, and secular liberals.

The progressive Protestant lobbying community in Washington does include the government relations offices of the mainline denominations, particularly the

Episcopal Church, the Evangelical Lutheran Church in America, the Presbyterian Church (U.S.A.), the United Church of Christ, the American Baptist Churches USA, and the United Methodist Church. Their work is bolstered by the robust organizational presence of the peace churches—the Quakers and the Mennonites (see Box 5.2), Unitarian Universalists, and African American denominations. One of the more intriguing developments is the way that progressive evangelical groups, such as Evangelicals for Social Action and Sojourners, have provided fresh energy for causes dear to religious liberals. The recent broadening of the agenda of the usually conservative National Association of Evangelicals to include environmental concerns and poverty has created new alliance opportunities as well.[40]

The progressive Protestant lobby also benefits from the expertise and reach of domestic service providers (such as Lutheran Social Services) and international agencies (such as Church World Service and Lutheran World Relief). Such membership groups as Bread for the World provide leadership for progressive Christians on federal food programs. Liberal Christians also have formed a number of issue-specific coalitions, such as the Religious Coalition for Reproductive Choice and the National Religious Campaign Against Torture (which was formed to challenge the interrogation techniques of the Bush administration). On church-state

---

BOX 5.2   MENNONITE CENTRAL COMMITTEE: A PACIFIST LOBBY

The story of the Mennonite Central Committee illustrates how the actions of the federal government have spurred the growth of church lobbies. One of the perennial issues for pacifist denominations (such as the Mennonites) is how to protect their members from compulsory military service. Thus the Mennonites were shocked in 1967 when they learned that proposed selective service legislation during the Vietnam War would not allow the kind of broad conscientious objector provisions that had protected them from military service during World War II. Church leaders traveled to Washington, testified at congressional hearings, and ultimately saw changes made in the law. In the wake of conscientious-objector battle, the Mennonite Central Committee established a permanent Washington office in 1968. Its first director was Deton Franz, a pastor who directed Mennonite lobbying until his retirement in 1994. Although it is small by Washington standards, the Mennonite office remains a visible player in the religious community.

Source: Keith Graber Miller, *American Mennonites Engage Washington: Wise as Serpents, Innocent as Doves?* (Knoxville, TN: University of Tennessee Press, 1996).

issues mainline Protestants often join in coalitions with "separationist" groups, including the Baptist Joint Committee for Religious Liberty and Americans United for Separation of Church and State.

The political agenda of progressive Protestants is wide-ranging. The National Council of Churches and affiliated religious bodies, for example, took a turn to the left on foreign policy in the late 1960s and early 1970s, repeatedly objecting to U.S. military activities abroad, most recently the wars in Afghanistan and Iraq. On domestic affairs, progressive Protestants have embraced a broad agenda that includes poverty, health care, women's equality, environmental protection, affirmative action, and in some cases, abortion rights and gay rights. During the presidency of George W. Bush, progressive religious leaders formed the now-defunct Clergy Leadership Network as an alternative to religious conservatism in politics—and in direct opposition to the Bush administration.[41]

One of the challenges facing progressive Protestant groups is convincing lay members of the value and urgency of their agenda. Sometimes this challenge reflects an ideological gap between clergy and laity, and sometimes it demonstrates a lack of effort by leaders to persuade and mobilize members. But with the technological revolution, most progressive Protestants have expanded grassroots networks.[42] Moreover, there is some evidence to suggest that the "clergy-laity gap" may not be as salient in low-income urban congregations, where economic hardship presents incentives for political action through churches as well as heightened resonance of the social justice message.[43]

ROMAN CATHOLIC GROUPS

Catholic interest groups enjoy an advantageous strategic location. On the one hand, they have been allied with the Democratic Party for much of American history and were strongly supportive of the New Deal. Most Catholic leaders are generally comfortable with—and in some cases stand to the left of—the Democrats' approach to such issues as welfare spending, labor laws, civil rights, and the death penalty. On the other hand, they join with the Republicans in opposing abortion, promoting parental choice options in education, and criticizing some elements of popular culture. Thus religio-political activists from across the spectrum—from conservative evangelicals to ecumenical liberals—view Catholics as potential allies.[44]

The American Catholic Church has maintained a Washington presence since just after World War I, when the National Catholic Welfare Conference was established. Today, the United States Conference of Catholic Bishops (USCCB) represents the

official political positions of the Church. The clear Catholic organizational structure, along with a strong hierarchical tradition, allows its leaders to speak with authority for the Catholic Church. This fact represents a distinct political advantage.
Thus even if lay opinion is divided on an issue, the official Church position can be
articulated clearly. Bishops therefore are guaranteed extensive press coverage when
they express their stands on issues.

The Catholic lobby, however, is far from monolithic. It includes a host of associations, religious orders, and membership organizations. In most cases these
groups do not oppose the bishops directly, but there are large differences in emphasis and even ideology. On the left we find groups such as Pax Christi, known
for its opposition to wars; NETWORK, a membership organization composed
mostly of activist nuns; and the Maryknoll order, known for its support of liberation
theology. [45] These groups are decidedly more liberal than the USCCB, especially
on foreign policy issues. Also quite liberal are the Jesuit Conference, the Franciscan
Action Network, and Catholic Charities, all of which lobby on issues of poverty
and justice.

A different posture emerges, however, from large associations of Catholic hospitals and parochial schools, which have tangible financial interests to protect and
are generally treated with some respect by policymakers. On church-state issues
we find the Catholic League for Religious and Civil Rights, headed by William
Donohue, which vigorously combats anti-Catholic bigotry in news and entertainment media. Finally, there are organizations sustained in part by sizable Catholic
memberships, including National Right to Life, the nation's oldest antiabortion
group.

Among the strengths of the Catholic lobby are a theological comfort with politics, a scholastic tradition of serious reflection on issues, clear lines of leadership,
and a potentially strategic position in broader political alignments. There is a considerable degree of cohesion about the theological reasons for political engagement.
Given the formal authority of clergy in the Catholic Church, these attitudes provide
an important resource for mobilization.[46]

One of the weaknesses of Catholic political groups is the diversity of opinion in
the pews and among Catholic politicians.[47] The recent sex abuse scandals in the
Church also have diminished the legitimacy of Catholic leaders, exacerbating the
problem of creating a unified Catholic voice in politics.[48] A look at some particular
issues illustrates the challenge.

Even before and certainly since the U.S. Supreme Court struck down restrictive
state abortion statutes in *Roe* v. *Wade* in 1973, the Catholic Church has been at the

center of pro-life lobbying, both in Washington and at state legislatures.[49] No issue so clearly illustrates the constraints facing the Catholic Church. Despite the Church's enormous investment of political capital around the issue, its successes have been modest. Abortion remains legal in the United States despite three decades of agitation by pro-life forces.[50] Another constraint pro-life Catholics face is the highly partisan nature of the abortion issue. Most Democratic politicians are solidly pro-choice; hence, many Catholic leaders have become ambivalent or, in some cases, highly critical of the Church's historical link to the Democratic Party, and some have left the party altogether.

Finally, lack of lay unity has hurt the Church's ability to exercise political power in the United States. Although polls on abortion sometimes are ambiguous, there is no question that a sizable number of Catholics support some degree of reproductive freedom, and women who identify themselves as Catholic are just as likely to have abortions as are non-Catholic women. However, pro-life support is strongest among those who most faithfully attend Mass, whereas nominal Catholics are the most likely to reject the Church's pro-life position.[51]

Even in the face of these impediments, the Catholic Church has had periodic success in gaining provisions banning federal funding for abortion or restricting late-term abortions.[52] Political gains, however, are always vulnerable to changing political contexts. Upon entering office, President Obama reversed some Bush-era abortion restrictions, and the Church shifted to a defensive strategy in its abortion advocacy, in particular fighting for "conscience clauses" to protect Catholic institutions from being forced to offer abortion services in new federal healthcare programs.[53]

The Catholic Church has achieved a certain prominence on issues of war and peace. The USCCB exercised some influence on debates over nuclear arms and American military involvement in Central America in the 1980s,[54] and the bishops continue to address military issues. But this does not mean that their efforts are always successful. Catholic opinion about the Gulf War of 1991 and the Iraq war provides lessons about the limits of Catholic (or religious) influence regarding the momentous national decision to go to war. In response to Saddam Hussein's 1990 invasion of Kuwait, the Catholic hierarchy offered conditional support for the U.S. effort to keep the Iraqis from occupying Saudi Arabia, but it opposed the first Bush administration's decision to expel them from Kuwait. When Congress voted to authorize the use of force, allowing President George H. W. Bush to begin Operation Desert Storm, Roman Catholic parishioners strongly backed the view that it was a just war, so the reservations of Church leaders were ignored.[55] Roughly the same picture emerged before the Iraq war began in 2003, but in this case the bishops seemed prescient in warning of the dangers of sectarian strife and refugees in the wake of the war.

Catholics lobby about a host of domestic economic and welfare issues, often in an effort to secure public money to support Church schools or to provide assistance to the poor. Since the nineteenth century, the American Catholic Church has battled to obtain state support for its school system, in recent times especially by promoting legislation allowing choice in education through state support in the form of vouchers for parents sending their children to nonpublic schools. Every step of the way the Church has faced vigorous and effective opposition from public teacher unions, civil liberties groups, Protestant organizations such as the Baptist Joint Committee, and the formidable Americans United for Separation of Church and State. Even though the Church has achieved some success, for example, modest voucher programs in Milwaukee and Cleveland, it has not realized its major educational goal of broadening parental choice through vouchers for parochial school attendance. Indeed, Democrats in Congress killed an experimental voucher program in the District of Columbia in 2009.

Catholic groups have had much greater success regarding the public funding of various domestic social service agencies associated with the Church. Part of the reason for this success is the Catholic tendency to separate religion from the actual method of providing the service. Unlike evangelical "gospel missions" and other pervasively religious groups, Catholic agencies such as Catholic Charities do not expect clients to engage in religious behavior as a condition of receiving food assistance, job training, housing, or other benefits. Consequently, public funding of these agencies, with federal and state grants worth millions of dollars, has never raised serious constitutional challenges.[56] Even though President George W. Bush strove to expand the range of grant-making to other ministries, Catholics maintain an edge in this form of church-state partnership.

JEWISH GROUPS

The Jewish proportion of the population in the United States is small—less than 2 percent—but it is also highly educated, relatively affluent, and politically active. These characteristics by themselves translate into significant political resources, but other factors also account for the success of Jewish interest groups, especially in Washington.[57]

The first Jewish national interest group, the American Jewish Committee (AJC), was not formed until 1906, in response to a horrible Russian pogrom. Since then, the AJC has sought to protect Jews both at home and abroad. In 1913, the Anti-Defamation League of B'nai B'rith was founded to combat domestic anti-Semitism, followed by the American Jewish Congress, which was made up at first of Jews devoted to the creation of a Jewish homeland in Palestine.[58]

Jewish theological diversity is reflected in national organizations of the three major branches of Judaism—Reform, Conservative, and Orthodox—which are active in civic and political affairs. In Washington, DC, both the Reform and Orthodox branches of Judaism maintain national lobbying offices. Of these, the most active is the Religious Action Center of Reform Judaism, which represents the largest branch of American Judaism and is decidedly liberal. Orthodox Jews, represented by the Union of Orthodox Jewish Congregations of America, part company with their more liberal counterparts on abortion, marriage, and school vouchers.[59]

In a class by itself, of course, is AIPAC, one of the most formidable lobbies in Washington. AIPAC's sole aim is to coordinate American support for the Jewish state of Israel, and it has become a model for a whole range of other interest groups that wish to influence U.S. foreign policy. With a staff of some 250 in Washington and an equal number in branches around the country, AIPAC is respected and even feared in Washington politics. It has combined excellent research resources in its Washington office, a grassroots network of activist members, and a host of affiliated PACs that contribute money to pro-Israel candidates for federal office. And there is, in fact, tangible evidence of AIPAC's effectiveness in Congress. Largely because of AIPAC's efforts, the billions of dollars in foreign aid that the United States sends to Israel no longer comes in the form of loans; it is now given as outright grants.[60]

AIPAC has not gone unchallenged. In 2008, two prominent political scientists published a book that is highly critical of the "Israel Lobby," which they see as distorting U.S. foreign policy.[61] The book generated enormous press attention and debate. This dustup, however, has not seriously dented the clout of AIPAC, in part because American public opinion remains strongly supportive of Israel.

On most issues, Jewish political groups are liberal. They have championed abortion rights, opposed school prayer and school voucher programs, sought strict separation of church and state, and backed gay rights and full gender equality. They have consistently opposed the Christian Right in the political realm. On matters involving Israel, of course, most Jewish groups have welcomed conservative evangelical support, although some are very skittish about the theological rationale for it.[62]

The growing political clout of Orthodox Jews, particularly since the 2000 vice-presidential nomination of Sen. Joseph Lieberman (I–Connecticut), himself an Orthodox Jew, has increased the pluralism of the American Jewish political witness. On such issues as opposition to abortion and gay rights and support for public recognition of faith, Orthodox and Ultraorthodox Jews often have the same perspective as evangelicals and conservative Catholics. The Rabbinical Council of America—the national organization of Orthodox rabbis—also has become more politically active on issues such as public support for religious schools. Christian conservatives, of course, have leapt at the chance to build alliances with Orthodox Jews.

Why do Jewish groups enjoy such excellent elite access in Washington and elsewhere? First, Jewish faith and tradition promote political participation. Like mainline Protestantism, Judaism emphasizes worldly engagement. In Jewish scripture, for example, the ancient Hebrews lived under God's mercy and judgment on the basis of how faithfully they organized their communal affairs. Jewish communities in America also foster a robust public life in which people feel at home with the debates and compromises of politics. Indeed, if one compares Jewish Americans with other Americans of similar economic standing, it is striking how much more interested in the world of politics many Jews tend to be. This ease with politics is, of course, a major resource. Jewish leaders do not have to spend time and energy convincing their members that politics is a legitimate activity. Often their members already are politically involved.[63]

Second, Jewish political organizations build on many internal resources. At the local level, American Jews operate vibrant community organizations and chapters of national groups. Thus, when national leaders seek to mount political pressure, they can call upon a wide range of people and organizations. Even in regions with small Jewish populations, prominent Jewish citizens sometimes know their congressional representatives personally. Relative affluence is also a real resource—and one that leaders have no timidity about tapping. Jews are major contributors to a range of interest groups and to political parties, candidates, and pro-Israel PACs.[64]

Jewish political resources are maximized by a host of strong leaders. Indeed, some of them have been legends in Washington: confidants of presidents, friends of members of Congress, quintessential insiders.[65] One reason for this sustained access is the longevity of senior Jewish leadership, a product of stability in the Washington community. For example, the head of the Religious Action Center of Reform Judaism, Rabbi David Saperstein, has served for more than three decades in Washington and is widely known and respected in religious, political, and intellectual circles. In 2008, President Obama named Saperstein, along with other distinguished American religious leaders, to his Advisory Council on Faith-Based and Neighborhood Partnerships. Longevity fosters not only wisdom in the ways of politics but a long view of lobbying strategy. National Jewish leaders encourage workshops to build political awareness and foster college clubs to bring a new generation into the fold. They help build relationships with local politicians, mayors, and state representatives, especially because years later these people may be elected to Congress.

Third, Jews enjoy excellent strategic access to political elites. In part their strategic location is a function of the presence of Jews in a variety of elite circles. It is, of course, hard to speak of this fact without promoting unfair stereotypes or feeding conspiracy theories that suggest a vast Jewish ruling cabal. The truth is that American Jews strongly embrace education and civic engagement. This results in a mathematical overrepresentation of Jews at elite levels of government, media, and the academy.

Jewish leaders employ resources to cultivate political elites throughout the system. Whether they are targeting a Democratic or Republican White House, a Democratic or Republican Congress, or a conservative or liberal Supreme Court, Jewish leaders endeavor to win. They also work assiduously with top bureaucrats and cabinet members. They cultivate the media, and they build alliances with the vast network of Washington lobbies and law firms. Finally, they benefit from the broadly positive sentiment non-Jewish Americans have of Jews.[66]

EVANGELICAL PROTESTANT GROUPS

No other organized religious advocacy has received as much attention as the efforts of evangelicals in the past three decades. Evangelical Protestantism thrives in the free marketplace of American religion, producing many entrepreneurial leaders, a vital resource for interest group formation and maintenance. Moreover, as political scientist Robert Putnam observes, American evangelicals have built "the largest, best organized grassroots" social movement network of the last quarter-century.[67] Thus, groups such as the Family Research Council, Concerned Women for America, Focus on the Family, and the Traditional Values Coalition draw upon the resources of a host of conservative Protestant denominations and the extensive network of nondenominational megachurches, local activist groups, alternative schools, Christian colleges, parachurch organizations, broadcast ministries, and publishing houses. Lobbying activity thus is melded into the multifarious social movement activities of institutional development, electoral mobilization, litigation, media campaigns, and demonstrations.[68]

But here too, pluralism reigns. Not all expressions of organized evangelical advocacy fit the stereotypical mold of the Christian Right. Indeed, the National Association of Evangelicals recently has moved away from an exclusive focus on the core Christian Right issues of abortion and family structure to embrace concern for the poor, "Creation Care" environmental concerns, and international human rights. And some evangelicals, such as the aforementioned Jim Wallis, are in overt contention with the Christian Right.[69]

There also is diversity among conservative evangelicals. There are legal advocacy groups such as the Christian Legal Society that take a self-consciously moderate posture, whereas others, such as the Rutherford Institute and the American Center for Law and Justice, present a harder edge. There are denominational organizations, such as the Ethics & Religious Liberty Commission of the Southern Baptist Convention, which take strong positions against abortion and gay marriage but hold a more accommodating posture on immigration. There are single-issue groups, such as the Home School Legal Defense Fund, led by Michael Farris, that see themselves in a fierce battle to maintain autonomy against an overweening state. Other groups, such as Prison Fellowship, created by Charles Colson, promote prison reforms also embraced by liberals. Finally, broad-based membership groups appeal to distinct if sometimes overlapping constituencies. Thus Concerned Women for America, headed by Wendy Wright, has a robust and heavily female membership, whereas the Family Research Council, led by Tony Perkins, relies more on large donors to sustain itself.

Despite periodic announcements of its death, the Christian Right movement endures with successive waves of mobilization. When the movement's first major organization, the Moral Majority, went defunct, Pat Robertson founded a new group, the Christian Coalition, to pick up the mantle. When the Christian Coalition foundered, the Family Research Council moved into the breach. As long as cultural discontent with American society remains, there very likely will be Christian Right interest groups at all levels of society. Indeed, a heightened sense of threat—as felt by some evangelical leaders after the election of Barack Obama and strong Democratic majorities in Congress—often leads to increased fund-raising and group formation. Christian Right groups enjoy infusions of new energy through continued social movement mobilization.[70]

The cyclical nature of movement mobilization is illustrated by the recent battle over same-sex marriage. The Massachusetts Supreme Court ignited a national debate in 2003 when it ruled that the state must allow gay and lesbian couples to marry. Christian conservatives, both evangelical and Catholic, along with some Orthodox Jews, mobilized against this decision by promoting "defense of marriage" amendments to state constitutions that prohibit same-sex marriage. Between 2004 and 2008, defense of marriage amendments passed in twenty-six states, the most notable of which was California. There, black pastors and Hispanic clergy joined evangelicals, Catholics, and Mormons in backing Proposition 8, which amended the state constitution to overturn court-ordered same-sex marriage. In one sense, this movement against same-sex marriage demonstrated the political clout of religious conservatives. But in another sense, it illustrates limitations because the campaigns were entirely defensive. Thus evangelicals succeeded only in part, and their success hinged on support of other religionists and favorable public opinion that could change over time.[71]

Like black church organizations, but unlike most other religious interest groups, Christian Right groups focus heavily on electoral mobilization, and some have even formed PACs to help finance campaigns, a rarity among religious lobbies. From the Moral Majority to the Christian Coalition to the Family Research Council, evangelical groups have engaged in massive voter mobilization initiatives so successfully that a definable Christian conservative voting bloc has become an important part of the Republican Party.[72] The paradox, as Wilcox and Larson note, is that the Christian Right has been "the most successful social movement in influencing elections and party politics over the past century," but it has been largely unsuccessful in winning major policy change around its core agenda.[73] The structure of American national government, with its numerous veto points, plus the countermobilization produced by threatened opponents, ensures that most Christian conservative victories will be modest and incremental.

Indeed, the political system has a way of filtering the demands of the movement into more modest outcomes. A good example is the campaign for a school prayer amendment to the U.S. Constitution in the 1980s. Popular with the public, but contrary to the weight of constitutional scholarship, it failed to obtain the two-thirds congressional vote necessary to move on to a vote by the states. In the wake of that defeat, however, Congress passed the Equal Access Act of 1984, a more modest and broadly supported measure. The law stipulated that if public high schools provided space before, during, or after school for noncurricular-related student clubs, it could not deny the same space to religiously oriented clubs. Thus, although the Christian Right set the agenda with its school prayer mobilization—in a sense signaling to Congress that something should be done about "secular" public schools—it did not determine the outcome, which in the end was so carefully crafted that it gained support of religious lobbies across the spectrum.

One of the unmistakable legacies of organized evangelical mobilization has been a kind of citizen education. Conservative evangelical groups have invested an enormous amount of resources in "leadership schools" and various voter awareness programs that explain matters such as where to register to vote and how to attend a caucus. Some initiatives generate understandable controversy, such as distributing voter guides in churches that attempt to circumvent Internal Revenue Service guidelines against endorsements by showing side-by-side comparisons of presidential candidates' stands on issues that leave little doubt for whom congregation members should vote. In other cases, citizen awareness programs constitute basic civic education, leading at least one scholar to argue that the Christian Right promotes "democratic virtues."[74] Whatever one thinks of the Christian Right, one thing is clear: We will continue to hear about evangelical groups in politics in the years to come.

MUSLIM GROUPS

Relative newcomers to organized politics, American Muslims illustrate several crucial themes regarding religious lobbying: the growing pluralism of religious advocacy, its globalization, and the ways new groups adapt over time to the norms of the system.

In the current political environment, Muslims face unique challenges. Critics charge that some American Muslim interest groups are fronts for militant Islamist movements abroad, and exposés have documented the influence of foreign (especially Saudi) money in promoting a fundamentalist strain of Islam in some American mosques that is hostile to Jews, Christians, and liberal democracy. Muslim groups also operate under intense scrutiny by the U.S. government, which has shut down some Muslim charities with links to Hamas or Hezbollah and has convicted a few leaders of supporting terrorist organizations abroad. Yet American Muslim organizations are also crucial government allies in rooting out and combating potential terrorists, so they enjoy a considerable degree of political access to law enforcement agencies and other government officials.[75]

Amid this cloudy picture, one thing is clear: In the wake of the September 11 attacks, Muslim Americans have responded in a characteristically American fashion, increasing their civic engagement and getting organized to lobby for their interests. Groups have intensified fundraising, registered voters, and expanded operations in Washington, DC.

American Muslim groups voice understandable concern about U.S. foreign policy toward Muslim nations. But they also object to domestic surveillance, profiling, and detentions. On these issues they have gained Jewish allies committed to civil liberties, illustrating how sometimes Middle East adversaries can work together.

Muslim groups also lobby on social justice issues such as health care, poverty, and the environment.

One indication of growing sophistication is that groups are carving specialized niches. The Muslim American Society emphasizes grassroots mobilization; the Muslim Political Affairs Committee lobbies and works with government agencies; and the American Muslim Alliance focuses on promoting office seekers. A key umbrella organization is the Islamic Society of North America, whose annual convention attracts an estimated 30,000 participants and a host of institutional representatives.

But pluralism reigns in the American Muslim community as elsewhere, and a vigorous debate is occurring about the proper direction of Muslim advocacy. Indeed, a growing number of groups and individuals have emerged to challenge established Muslim organizations (Box 5.3). Among these self-conscious reformist

---

BOX 5.3 ZAINAB AL-SUWAIJ: AN AMERICAN MUSLIM LEADER WITH A GLOBAL FOCUS

The granddaughter of the leading cleric in Basra, Iraq, Zainab Al-Suwaij was one of the few women to join the armed Shi'ite uprising against Saddam Hussein in the wake of the First Gulf War in 1991, at one point joining a group that stormed a prison to free dissidents. When Hussein crushed the rebellion, she was injured, went into hiding, fled to Jordan, and eventually made her way to the United States.

Al-Suwaij was teaching at Yale University in 2001, but the shock of seeing the attacks of September 11 occur in the name of her religion led her to create the American Islamic Congress. Headquartered in Washington, DC, and with offices in Boston, Cairo, and Basra, the organization promotes "responsible" moderate Muslim leadership, interfaith understanding, women's equality, and civil rights. Al-Suwaij runs women's empowerment programs in Iraq, sponsors an essay contest on civil rights for Muslim youth in the Middle East, and runs workshops on nonviolent reform for young Arab activists. Her organization widely distributes an Arabic language comic book on the Montgomery bus boycott led by Rev. Martin Luther King Jr. A critic of some American Muslim groups she sees as being too sympathetic to Islamist militants, she also runs a Capitol Hill lecture series on Muslim issues sponsored by the congressional caucuses on religious freedom and antiterrorism. She vividly illustrates the globalization of American religious advocacy.

Source: http://www.aicongress.org/about/leadership.html; personal interview with Allen D. Hertzke, December 2008.

groups are the Islamic Supreme Council of America (a Sufi group), the American Islamic Forum for Democracy, the Center for Islamic Pluralism, the Free Muslims Coalition, and the American Islamic Congress.

We also see evolution over time, particularly as second-generation professionals take the reins of Muslim American organizations. Some groups are cutting the tether to foreign money and emphasizing Islam's compatibility with American liberal democracy. Other groups demonstrate such commitments through powerful symbolic gestures. The Islamic Society of North America, for example, selected Ingrid Mattson, a woman who has criticized the Muslim community for lack of female inclusion, to head the association. A professor at Hartford Seminary in Connecticut, Mattson declared that she aims to "give worshipers more control over who preaches in their Mosques" and intends to "help keep out extremists."[76]

THE POLITICS OF RELIGIOUS MINORITIES

Religious scholar Diana Eck argues that the United States, because of its openness to global immigration, has become the world's most religiously diverse nation.[77] This diversity is manifested in the growing pluralism of organized political advocacy. Thus there are now national organizations representing the political concerns of Buddhists; Hindus; Baha'is; Sikhs; Copts; and Falun Gong, a Chinese meditation sect that routinely protests in front of the Chinese embassy in Washington, DC. In the Islamic community there are not just Sunni organizations but Shi'ite, Sufi, Ahmadiyya, and Uyghur advocacy groups. The Ahmadiyya adhere to the teachings of a nineteenth-century prophet who they believe clarified true Islamic practice, but they are persecuted as heretical by other Muslims. Uyghurs are a Turkic Muslim ethnic group in western China who are seen as a security threat by the Chinese government and thus suffer repression similar to that faced by Tibetan Buddhists. The Uyghur American Association, not surprisingly, advocated on behalf of the Uyghur refugees who were swept up in Afghanistan and detained by the United States at the Guantánamo Bay prison camp.

As we note below, such religious minority groups naturally focus on defending their counterparts abroad, thus widening the coalition lobbying on behalf of religious freedom in American foreign policy. But concerns for domestic religious liberty also animate these groups as they seek to carve out space for their religious practices.

Take the case of Sikhs, who trace their faith to a fifteenth-century guru from the Punjab territory of the Indian subcontinent. Sikhs sometimes are mistaken for Muslims or Hindus but come instead from an entirely separate faith tradition that stresses equality of all people, including gender equality—an egalitarian tradition Sikh Americans take pride in. Sikh men stand out because of their practice of wearing a turban around uncut hair, and like many Muslims, some Sikhs were attacked, profiled, or subjected to humiliating airport screening in the wake of September 11. In response, the Sikh American Legal Defense & Education Fund, led by second-generation young professionals, engaged in a broad public awareness campaign that sent educational materials to various law enforcement agencies. Its most notable achievement was getting the Transportation Safety Administration to provide a training video for all of its 45,000 airport screeners about the Sikh faith. This success illustrates how even very small religious groups can gain a sympathetic hearing when they assert their very American case for the freedom to practice their faith. Successes like the one won by Sikhs after September 11 also serve to bolster the patriotic allegiance of religious minorities, who appreciate the ability to maintain their religious identity and still participate fully in civic life.[78]

THE GLOBALIZATION OF RELIGIOUS ADVOCACY

From the beginning of the Republic, national religious interest groups periodically have focused on international relations. Mainline Protestant groups, for example, were pivotal in pressing for the United Nations' 1948 Universal Declaration of Human Rights,[79] and most religious groups since then have been drawn into contentious foreign policy issues—from the Vietnam War, to clashes over communism in Central America, to the Iraq war and terrorism. However, globalization—the process by which people around the world increasingly are interlinked through commerce, travel, and communication—has heightened international awareness and increased international engagement by religious interest groups.

Specific American religious groups often lobby on behalf of their coreligionists in other regions of the world. Jews lobby for Israel, Muslims for the Palestinian cause, Buddhists on behalf of their beleaguered counterparts in Tibet, American Baha'is for Iranian Baha'is, Falun Gong practitioners and Muslim Uyghurs for religious freedom in China, and Ahmadis for their persecuted brethren in Pakistan.

But advocacy is more than just defense of fellow religionists. Falun Gong members have become adept at breaking computer firewalls that Chinese authorities erect against dissent, enabling other groups to piggyback to get their messages through. Global connections also facilitate the work of the Center for the Study of Islam and Democracy, founded by Radwan Masmoudi, a Tunisian immigrant, who conducts workshops on democratic theory in Muslim nations. Concerned that President Obama might distance himself from the Bush administration by backtracking on the promotion of democracy in the Middle East and other regions of Asia, Masmoudi worked with allies to present an open letter to the new president, calling upon him to make human rights and democracy central to his engagement with the Islamic world. Because this initiative solicited signatories from hundreds of group leaders and activists around the world, Masmoudi in a sense helped to bring a global lobbying campaign to the new administration.[80]

We also see globalization in advocacy specific to the mission of particular groups. The Church of Jesus Christ of Latter-day Saints maintains a Washington staff but does little congressional advocacy. Instead it maintains relationships with embassies of foreign governments to facilitate access for its thousands of Mormon missionaries. Similarly, the Ultraorthodox Hasidic Jewish movement, Chabad-Lubavitch, which also has a missionary impulse, opened a Washington office to help its members navigate complex laws of foreign countries.

In some cases, American religious groups actually lobby before agencies of the United Nations and other international organizations. Advocates for global religious freedom and human rights, in particular, realize that the U.S. government can only do so much; they must make their case before international tribunals. Thus representatives of such organizations as the Becket Fund for Religious Liberty and the Institute on Religion and Public Policy frequently testify before the UN Human Rights Council or the Organization for Security and Co-operation in Europe.[81]

In other cases, religious groups have concluded that they need to lobby on the international level to defend their values at home. Cultural issues, in fact, have migrated globally as the UN and other international bodies debate women's rights, population control, secularism, or any number of other issues with socio-moral implications. Thus conservative religious groups that often criticize the UN nevertheless have found themselves drawn into its orbit, sometimes lobbying against the positions of the U.S. government. Leaders of Concerned Women for America (CWA), for example, have gained official observer status at the UN and often find themselves allying with delegates from developing nations who espouse conservative views on marriage or abortion. In one instance, Germany introduced a resolution before the UN that would have promoted the practice of therapeutic cloning. Representatives of CWA worked with delegates from developing nations who were concerned that impoverished women would be exploited for their eggs; the UN instead passed a resolution in 2005 recommending a ban on all cloning.[82]

In a still different vein is the work of Advocates International, founded by Sam Ericsson. It is a global network of Christian evangelical lawyers who pledge to defend the vulnerable and advance religious freedom by representing litigants in court, training lawyers and judges, and pressing for changes in laws. One indication of how the "culture wars" have gone global is that Ericsson personally provided legal defense to a Swedish pastor, Ake Green, who was sentenced to prison in 2004 for violating a hate crimes law by preaching a sermon against homosexuality. Green's case gained international attention, and Ericsson successfully made the case on appeal that if Green were imprisoned, Sweden would have no legitimacy to criticize other nations that imprison pastors.

Nowhere has this global engagement manifested itself so vigorously as in campaigns for religious freedom and human rights abroad. Beginning in the mid-1990s, a movement of unlikely religious allies burst unexpectedly onto the international scene in a faith-based quest to advance human rights through the machinery of American foreign policy. Thanks to successful lobbying of Congress, this movement effectively built a new human rights architecture in American government.[83]

BOX 5.4 MICHAEL HOROWITZ: A JEWISH ACTIVIST FOR GLOBAL HUMAN RIGHTS

Major credit for helping force the issue of religious persecution onto the national agenda belongs to Michael Horowitz, who attended an Orthodox Yeshiva school as a youth in the Bronx and thought about becoming a rabbi. A Washington think tank lawyer, he became involved in the fight against religious persecution when his Ethiopian housekeeper, who was threatened with deportation, told him of being tortured because of his Christian faith. Horowitz connected with other advocacy groups and drafted a "statement of conscience" that was adopted by the National Association of Evangelicals. He then helped assemble a lobbying coalition for religious freedom legislation that included evangelical Protestants, the United States Catholic Conference, the Episcopal Church, a variety of Jewish organizations, Baha'is, and Tibetan Buddhists. Horowitz later worked to forge left-right coalitions around human trafficking and the quest for peace in southern Sudan.

Source: Allen D. Hertzke, *Freeing God's Children: The Unlikely Alliance for Global Human Rights* (Lanham, MD: Rowman and Littlefield, 2004).

Initially activated by concern about religious persecution abroad, religious groups across the theological spectrum fought for passage of the International Religious Freedom Act of 1998. This legislation established a permanent office in the U.S. Department of State charged with reporting on the status of religious freedom in every country on Earth, and it required that actions be taken by the U.S. government against countries that egregiously persecute religious believers (see Box 5.4).

Galvanized by their legislative successes on religious freedom, coalition leaders mounted campaigns for peace in Sudan. From the early 1990s onward, such groups as Christian Solidarity International, Christian Solidarity Worldwide, Voice of the Martyrs, and Samaritan's Purse publicized the massacres, slave raids, and ethnic cleansing committed by the government of Sudan against the African population of its southern region, made up of Christians and tribal religionists. These advocacy groups joined with African American religious leaders and the Congressional Black Caucus in gaining passage of the Sudan Peace Act in 2002, which pressured the Sudanese regime to negotiate a cessation of conflict. When conflict then erupted in the western province of Darfur, resulting in harsh ethnic cleansing, Jewish groups led a religious coalition calling for tough international measures against the regime.[84]

One of the most dramatic examples of faith-based international involvement concerns human trafficking. As many as a million women and children each year are trafficked across international boundaries into prostitution and other forms of forced labor; many are bought and sold until they die of disease and abuse.[85] Congress passed the Trafficking Victims Protection Act of 2000,[86] as a result of the United States's faith-based human rights leadership composed of voices from Jewish, evangelical Protestant, and secular feminist groups.[87] The law provides harsh penalties for international traffickers, equips enforcement agencies with new tools to deal with organized crime syndicates that run the traffic, penalizes countries that fail to criminalize and appropriately punish trafficking, and provides protection for victims. The law also established an anti-trafficking office at the State Department (formally known as the Office to Monitor and Combat Trafficking in Person), which has become one of the most aggressive human rights centers in the federal government.[88]

The campaign against human trafficking that brought together such an unlikely coalition of Jewish groups, evangelical Protestants, and feminists was impressive. Evangelical leaders not only joined in coalition with feminist groups but actively plotted strategy with them, indicating a willingness to work face-to-face with people who otherwise would be their adversaries in the "culture wars" of American politics. Even in a city known for unexpected alliances, this coalition was a classic. At the pivotal last stage of the legislative campaign, members of Congress were simultaneously receiving letters from Gloria Steinem and other prominent feminist leaders and being lobbied by leading evangelical figures such as Charles Colson of Prison Fellowship, Richard Land of the Southern Baptist Convention, Janice Crouse of Concerned Women for America, Richard Cizik of the National Association of Evangelicals, and John Busby of the Salvation Army.[89]

The growing global religious agenda is illustrated by the sense of mission that animates the work of an emerging evangelical leader, Gary Haugen, founder and president of the Christian-based International Justice Mission (IJM). A former lawyer in the U.S. Department of Justice and the chief UN genocide investigator in Rwanda, Haugen felt called to reclaim the vocabulary of justice for the evangelical Christian community. As he writes in a book for fellow believers, the "good news about injustice" is that "God is against it."[90] To provide a tangible way for believers to redress injustice, his organization intervenes in egregious cases of child prostitution, bonded servitude, and exploitation. In 2003 the IJM helped shut down Cambodia's most notorious brothels, freeing the captive children and placing them in the care of Christian aid workers. This dramatic event, followed by others around the world, prompted the head of the State Department's Trafficking Office to proclaim boldly that U.S. policy was now aimed at nothing less than abolishing "modern day slavery."[91]

One driving force behind this global agenda is the tectonic shift of the globe's Christian population to the developing world. Whereas in 1900, 80 percent of Christians lived in Europe and North America, by 2000 at least 60 percent of all Christians could be found in Asia, Africa, and Latin America. [92] This shift is likely to accelerate, nesting Christian congregations amid vulnerable people afflicted by poverty, violence, exploitation, and persecution. Global communication, travel, and international mission and development networks channel awareness of these conditions to American churches and advocacy groups, which lobby for ameliorative U.S. policies. For the evangelical community, this means that the political networks built out of domestic social concerns now are being put in service of human rights and justice concerns normally associated with progressive politics.

To illustrate how many American denominations are now smaller arms of larger global ministries, consider the Seventh-day Adventist Church. Although the Adventist faith was born in the United States, today only 1 million of its 16 million members are American. The Adventist Relief and Development Agency, headquartered in Washington, D.C., now operates with indigenous leadership in more than a hundred countries. Thus when its leaders testify on global food security, they draw upon research from their field offices around the world. This global perspective lends tremendous legitimacy to Adventist efforts to affect public policy in the U.S.

The growing international role of nongovernmental organizations (NGOs) that promote economic development, peace, or human rights also has a substantial religious component. Large relief and development agencies such as World Vision, Catholic Relief Services, Lutheran World Relief, and Church World Service have moved from solely delivering services to engaging in political advocacy. With teams on the ground in some of the most forbidding places on earth, these NGOs gain unique insight into U.S. military, trade, and aid policies, which they share in testimony before Congress or in meeting with executive agencies. Because of the size of the U.S. government's footprint on the global stage, NGO leaders have become aware of how small changes in U.S. policy can magnify their efforts. Moreover, as Stephen Monsma has shown, the U.S. government contracts with NGOs to deliver famine relief, provide refugee services, and undertake development projects, which creates another powerful motivation for political advocacy.[93]

NGOs also can raise awareness around issues previously invisible to the international community. World Vision, for example, noticed that illegal diamond traffic in central Africa was fueling violent militias and exploiting child soldiers. In cooperation with other organizations and business, World Vision succeeded in its effort to establish an international protocol on the sad costs of "conflict diamonds" (later exposed in the 2006 movie *Blood Diamond*).

Poverty, disease prevention, and economic development increasingly receive the attention of the religious advocacy community. In 2000, Pope John Paul II joined American religious groups, secular organizations, and such celebrities as Bono in the "Jubilee 2000" campaign for global debt relief. The problem this coalition had identified was that interest payments on debt accumulated by deposed governments represented a crushing burden on poor countries, which were unable to fund health, education, and economic development programs. Taking its inspiration from the "Year of Jubilee" in Hebrew scripture in which debts were forgiven, the movement sought debt write-offs by lender nations, the International Monetary Fund, and the World Bank. In the United States, the debt-relief effort focused on gaining a large congressional appropriation to leverage other international actions. This successful campaign was led by the chief Washington lobbyist for the Episcopal Church, Thomas Hart, who heard from his Anglican counterparts in Africa and elsewhere how debts incurred by former dictators sap development efforts.[94]

Out of the Jubilee 2000 initiative came a new global organization, the ONE Campaign, created by religious and secular NGOs and with the prominent backing of

Bono, to combat extreme poverty by fighting HIV/AIDS and malaria, to provide clean water and sanitation, to support maternal health, and to promote agricultural development. By 2009, Hart was leading the ONE Campaign's ambitious Washington lobbying agenda.

The nexus of global religion, American churches, and U.S. foreign policy is illustrated vividly by the distinct role evangelicals played in the development of the U.S. President's Emergency Plan for AIDS Relief (PEPFAR), which was launched in 2003. Evangelical development organizations such as World Vision saw the devastating impact of HIV/AIDS firsthand, especially in Africa, and had begun developing their own relief programs in the 1990s. In addition, many lay members learned about the AIDS crisis in Africa as a result of the growing number of mission trips sponsored by American congregations. Employing the access they enjoyed with President George W. Bush, evangelical leaders joined others to lobby the president on AIDS, and he ultimately made it a signature issue. From the launch of the PEPFAR initiative in 2004, AIDS funding more than tripled. AIDS activists criticized its abstinence component, but the program succeeded in delivering antiretroviral treatment to more than 2 million HIV-positive Africans by 2008 (up from just 50,000 before PEPFAR), extending many lives and contributing to economic development.[95]

Global engagement also includes mediation initiatives by American religious NGOs with international networks. This so-called track-two diplomacy supplements formal efforts by the U.S. State Department. The Institute on Religion and Democracy, for example, works to build better relations between religious communities in different countries as a means of promoting peace. The Institute for Global Engagement (IGE), headed by Chris Seiple, strives to create conditions conducive to religious freedom by working simultaneously with leaders of governments to relax restrictions and with religious communities to practice freedom responsibly. Working parallel to efforts of the State Department, IGE contributed to the recent liberalization of religious laws in Vietnam, allowing a number of Christian and Buddhist communities to operate more openly.

RELIGIOUS ADVOCACY AT THE STATEHOUSE

One of the more noteworthy recent developments in religious lobbying is the increasing extent to which religious groups lobby state governments. This new focus has been driven in part by the devolution of more policymaking authority to the states. In a sense, this development brings religious advocacy back to the level of government from which it originated. Especially now that the stakes are higher, a full range of religious groups now battle in statehouses over policy matters including abortion, same-sex marriage, education, health care, social welfare spending, the death penalty, immigration, and state budget priorities.[96]

As is the case at the national level, religious advocacy is distinct from the professional and economic lobbies that tend to dominate interest group politics. Religious lobbyists are not hired guns who wine and dine legislators or who make PAC contributions to campaigns; instead, they rely on moral appeals and information from their various ministries. Indeed, what distinguishes religious interest groups from across the theological and ideological spectrums is the fact that they represent broad moral visions that transcend the agendas advanced by typical lobbies. "From family policy to gambling, abortion to euthanasia, homelessness to child poverty, sentencing guidelines to treatment of prisoners, religious advocates articulate faith-based arguments into the often grubby world of state lobbying."[97]

Because states vary greatly in their level of party competition, legislative professionalism, and guiding political culture, there is tremendous variation in the religious groups that lobby in different statehouses, as well as their relative effectiveness.[98] Professional state legislatures with extensive staffs, as in California and Michigan, tend to provide more access points for religious lobbyists, whereas part-time legislatures that meet infrequently, as in Virginia and Alaska, tend to blunt the efficacy of religious groups. And a state's political culture has a profound impact on the political fortunes of different religious communities. Thus, in some states the Christian Right maintains a robust presence, partly as a result of intense electoral mobilization; in others, it barely registers.[99] In some states mainline Protestant councils have substantial clout; in other states black church groups have an inside track. Jewish group engagement varies widely from state to state as well.

One of the most striking patterns of statehouse religious advocacy, however, is the consistency of a Catholic presence, even in such states as Utah that have relatively small Catholic populations.[100] The institutional structure of the Catholic Church, which has state-level Catholic conferences that parallel the federal structure of American government, along with the presence of Catholic schools, hospitals, charitable agencies, and religious orders in nearly every state, ensures a robust lobbying operation. Moreover, as noted above, Catholic groups defy neat right-left characterization. They join with conservative evangelicals on abortion, same-sex marriage, and educational vouchers, but ally with mainline Protestants, Jews, and African American Protestants on an array of social justice issues, from welfare policy to job training to health care for the poor.[101] In part because of its heavy Latino population, the Catholic Church also backs lenient immigration policies at the state level.

As noted, the emergence of same-sex marriage as a major issue has activated alliances between evangelical groups, Catholic lobbies, black churches, and Mormons. Notably, the normally cautious LDS Church saw opposition to same-sex unions as fundamental to its understanding of marriage and societal organization, so in 2008 it endorsed California's high-profile defense of marriage amendment initiative, Proposition 8, and provided substantial backing to the successful campaign to pass it. However, the LDS Church faced a fierce backlash from people who support gay rights, illustrating the dangers of visible lobbying by religious organizations.[102]

LOCAL-LEVEL ADVOCACY

Religious congregations are woven intimately into the fabric of local social life in America. They run an array of service activities: food pantries, drug and alcohol rehabilitation, after-school programs, community improvement initiatives, and the like. This puts them in close and constant contact with disadvantaged people, which sometimes leads to various forms of local advocacy.[103]

One form such efforts take is community development, which focuses on marshaling the resources of a community for the betterment of citizens.[104] A prominent example is the work of John Perkins, an African American pastor in Mississippi, along with the Christian Community Development Association he helped to found.[105] Perkins' model induces clergy and other religious leaders to live among the poor and initiate self-help efforts. These efforts show the religious leaders how political structures can inhibit or buoy their ministries, which leads periodically to organized initiatives aimed at making city or county government work better for the less powerful members of society.

More overt political action is the aim of community organizing programs, which gained notice in 2008 because of President Barack Obama's background as a community organizer in Chicago. Faith-based community organizing traces its roots to the work of Saul Alinsky,[106] who founded a networking organization called the Industrial Areas Foundation (IAF) in 1940. IAF's initiatives involved creating tough-minded organizations aimed at confronting local power structures and making them responsive to neglected neighborhoods. Alinsky and IAF initially treated faith communities only as useful instruments for organizing, with modest results. But as Richard Wood recounts, a crucial change occurred when the Pacific Institute for Community Organizing (PICO), headquartered in Oakland, California, began to develop true partnerships with local congregations. PICO grew from a few projects in California to a nationwide network with more than a thousand participating churches in 150 cities and towns. Along with IAF and several similar networking organizations, PICO sparked successful initiatives involving enhancement of city services, eyesore removal, improved local schools, changes in policing, and infrastructure development.[107]

Faith-based organizing has proven especially important for Hispanics and African Americans. Hispanic churches were crucial to the United Farm Workers movement, and a pioneering community organization, Communities Organized for Public Service (COPS) of San Antonio, grew out of Hispanic churches.[108] In turn, many activist black churches form the core of civil society in many urban areas, where people gather, learn civic skills, and develop the social capital necessary for group action.[109] In cities such as Atlanta, Chicago, Boston, New York, Cleveland, Buffalo, and Miami, African American ministerial organizations act as highly effective lobbying groups, making them a crucial part of the political landscape.[110] In many cases, black pastors can produce dramatic political results. In the 1990s, for example, a coalition of local pastors formed a partnership with the Boston Police Department to tackle the problem of youth violence. With an emphasis on community policing and faith-based antigang initiatives, murder rates plummeted and working relations between the police and community residents improved substantially.[111]

Conservative religionists have turned to the local level as well, fighting battles over school curricula, sex education, and public expressions of faith. By far the most intense arena for Christian Right groups has been the public schools, which evangelical parents often see as overly steeped in secular values. This has led to highly publicized school board campaigns by conservative Christian candidates. Political scientist Melissa Deckman has found that Christian Right school board members were less successful in enacting controversial policies (such as teaching creationism) than when they pursued goals that enjoyed broad public resonance, such as back-to-basics curricula, better discipline, and character education.[112] As in the national arena, religious groups face many obstacles in altering the trajectory of such major institutions as public schools.

Meanwhile, the study of religious advocacy at the local level is still in its infancy. However, case studies do show tangible impact on such varied issues as gambling, health care, homelessness, race relations, and urban development. Political culture plays an even greater—and more varied—role at the local level. Ministerial organizations and coalitions that reach across religious dividing lines are often well positioned for political success, especially when they choose to tackle issues around which consensus is possible.[113]

DO RELIGIOUS GROUPS PLAY A DISTINCTIVE ROLE IN AMERICAN DEMOCRACY?

Religious group leaders may disagree with each other substantially about public policy, but one thing they share is a conviction that they should offer something distinctive to the political system. Evidence suggests that collectively they do act as a modest counterweight to what scholars describe as the "elite bias" of the pressure system. The fact is that most of the thousands of activists engaged in secular lobbying represent the self-interests of the well-heeled who have the financial resources to form national organizations or hire high-priced lobbyists. In light of this reality, religious advocates are distinctive in broadening the representativeness of the lobby world.[114]

For one thing, religious advocates provide a moral perspective on public policy. Most of the time they are not lobbying in their own self interest but rather for what they see as the humanitarian impulse of their tradition. Virtually all religious traditions have something to say about justice and the most vulnerable members of society, and the most skilled religious activists apply these moral and theological principles in conducting policy analysis of, and lobbying around, complex issues. Indeed, religious advocates often see themselves as representing "the least, the lost, and the left out." This vision takes tangible form, as we have seen, in advocacy for some of the most vulnerable people around the world, such as trafficking victims, the religiously persecuted, war refugees, and famine victims.[115]

To be fair, self interest does play some role in religious lobbying. Religious groups work to defend their own liberties and autonomy, and some receive government grants for faith-based social services or international development ministries. But religious leaders make the argument that this kind of government support merely facilitates their charitable work. By representing the interests of their social institutions at home and abroad, such as charities, international relief organizations, treatment programs, homeless shelters, refugee resettlement operations, schools, colleges, and hospitals, religious lobbyists work to protect services that assist a large number of people in need. As a practical upshot, religious lobbyists are in a unique position to provide useful information to policymakers on how well public policies are working or what might make them better. Religious advocacy, in this sense, represents a swath of civil society that transcends organized religion: the volunteer, nonprofit, nongovernmental sector. One of the things religious lobbyists do is protect the autonomy of this entire sector from governmental intrusion, enabling it to continue contributing meaningfully to society.

More dubious is a relatively new phenomenon: lobbying by religious entities for "pork barrel spending," or budgetary earmarks sponsored by individual members of Congress to benefit constituents in their home districts or states. As earmarks have mushroomed into a multibillion-dollar enterprise, religious interests have been enticed into seeking funding for special projects, in some cases hiring professional lobby firms to gain funding. A major *New York Times* study found that Congress recently has approved nearly 900 earmarks for individual projects at church colleges, hospitals, charities, and other institutions. Most of this funding came during the 109th and 110th Congresses (2005–2007), when earmarks reached their peak. Some lobbying firms even have developed a specialty in working with the religious community to obtain earmarks, a practice that most religious advocates find troubling because they do not wish to be perceived as participating in anything that looks like nakedly self-interested lobbying. Publicity about such practices, moreover, has resulted in some groups reevaluating their use.[116]

CONCLUSION

As this chapter shows, religious advocacy is an important part of the American political scene today. But how effective are religious lobbies? Effectiveness is a notoriously difficult concept to measure. If it is to pass, most legislation requires the support of broad coalitions and diverse policymakers responding to complex events and shifting public opinion, so determining any single group's influence is exceedingly difficult. However, sometimes particular policies can be traced to the efforts of particular groups. Thus Jewish groups have worked hard to secure and maintain U.S. foreign aid for Israel, but even here sympathetic public opinion and diverse allies have been crucial. In the context of the vast amount of policymaking and budgeting that goes on in Washington and in each state capital, most religious advocacy results in modest gains. For example, in spite of enormous effort over several decades, religious pro-life groups have gained only moderate, and tenuous, restrictions on abortion, but not much else.

When religious lobbies do have a meaningful impact on public policy, it is usually the result of fortuitous circumstances and unusual coalitions. Religious advocacy was a driving force in the successful campaign to secure major debt relief for poor countries. Similarly, religious groups have played an important role in convincing the federal government to increase funding to address world hunger, AIDS in Africa, and human trafficking. Thus when religious groups come together, their impact can be dramatic, but since those occasions are rare, we must be cautious about claiming too much for the religious advocacy community.

One trend worth watching is the growing importance of intellectual discourse, including the war of ideas fought in elite journals and magazines, think tank reports, policy institute advocacy, and academic research. Ideas clearly matter, and so does the marshaling of facts and analysis. Religious groups cannot depend solely upon pressure or skilled maneuvering in Washington; they also must participate in the intellectual debate where the ideas that drive policy germinate. In Washington today, as in many statehouses, this new brand of advocacy is teeming. Ideas are an important currency of twenty-first century American politics. Every day some institute is releasing a new report, calling for a new program, or presenting new facts to support a particular agenda. Similarly, such magazines as the *Weekly Standard, New Republic, The Nation, National Review, Commentary, The Atlantic,* and *First Things* provide venues for intellectuals to present ideas publicly and propose solutions to the problems of the day. Religious groups must insert themselves into this elite world of public discourse, or they will see their influence wane.

Finally, it is clear that political influence flows from the depth of a religious community's cultural reach, which is rooted primarily in its congregations, schools, colleges, media outlets, and other institutions. For example, evangelicals developed their political clout through a vibrant network of budding cultural institutions in the 1980s. Thus, if we wish to make meaningful predictions about the future political efficacy of any American religious tradition, we should look to their present culture-building activities. Effective national advocacy ultimately rests on the vitality of each religious group's institutional presence and the constituencies they represent.

FURTHER READING

Cleary, Edward L., and Allen D. Hertzke, eds. *Representing God at the Statehouse: Religion and Politics in the American States.* Lanham, MD: Rowman and Littlefield, 2006. A collection of essays about religious lobbying at the state level.

Hertzke, Allen D. *Freeing God's Children: The Unlikely Alliance for Global Human Rights.* Lanham, MD: Rowman and Littlefield, 2004. A detailed look at coalition-building among religious groups around issues of international religious freedom and human rights.

———. *Representing God in Washington: The Role of Religious Lobbies in the American Polity*. Knoxville, TN: University of Tennessee Press, 1988. The classic guide to religious interest groups today.

Hofrenning, Daniel J. B. *In Washington But Not of It: The Prophetic Politics of Religious Lobbyists*. Philadelphia: Temple University Press, 1995. The most recent book-length treatment of religious lobbies, which is comprehensive and stimulating in its perspective.

Wood, Richard L. *Faith in Action: Religion, Race, and Democratic Organizing in America*. Chicago: University of Chicago Press, 2002. A valuable study of the role of religion in community organizing.

NOTES

1. For a summary of the political science literature on religious interest groups, see Allen D. Hertzke, "Religious Interest Groups in American Politics," in *Oxford Handbook of Religion and American Politics*, eds. Corwin E. Smidt, Lyman A. Kellstedt, and James L. Guth (New York: Oxford University Press, 2009).

2. See Pew Forum Report on Religious Advocacy and Public Policy, http://pewforum.org, 2009.

3. Daniel J. B. Hofrenning, *In Washington But Not of It: The Prophetic Politics of Religious Lobbyists* (Philadelphia: Temple University Press, 1995).

4. Ann-Marie Szymanski, *Pathways to Prohibition* (Durham, NC: Duke University Press, 2003).

5. For an account of the formative years, see Luke Eugene Ebersole, *Church Lobbying in the Nation's Capital* (New York: Macmillan, 1951).

6. http://pewforum.org/.

7. Jeffrey M. Berry, *The New Liberalism: The Rising Power of Citizen Groups* (Washington, DC: Brookings Institution, 1999).

8. See Allen D. Hertzke, *Freeing God's Children: The Unlikely Alliance for Global Human Rights* (Lanham, MD: Rowman and Littlefield, 2004).

9. A fuller development of strategies may be found in Allen D. Hertzke, *Representing God in Washington: The Role of Religious Lobbies in the American Polity* (Knoxville, TN: University of Tennessee Press, 1988).

10. On interest group strategy, one good source is Kenneth M. Goldstein, *Interest Groups, Lobbying, and Participation in America* (New York: Cambridge University Press, 1999).

11. Hertzke, *Representing God in Washington*; Hofrenning, *In Washington But Not of It*.

12. David R. Mayhew, *Congress: The Electoral Connection* (New Haven, CT: Yale University Press, 1974).

13. S. Robert Lichter, Stanley Rothman, and Linda S. Lichter, *The Media Elite* (Bethesda, MD: Adler, 1986). In this controversial work the authors argue that elite journalists are in fact highly secular in their behavior and attitudes. But see also John Schmalzbauer, *People of Faith: Religious Conviction in American Journalism and Higher Education* (Ithaca, NY: Cornell University Press, 2003).

14. Jim Wallis, *God's Politics: Why the Right Gets It Wrong and the Left Doesn't Get It* (San Francisco: HarperOne, 2005).

15. Jane Lampman, "Rev. Jim Wallis Searches for Old-Time Justice," *The Christian Science Monitor*, March 12, 2008.

16. Clyde Wilcox and Carin Larson, *Onward Christian Soldiers? The Religious Right in American Politics*, 3rd ed. (Boulder: Westview Press, 2006).

17. This is especially true for public interest groups, a category into which many religious lobbies fit. See Anthony J. Nownes and Grant Neeley, "Public Interest Group Entrepreneurship and Theories of Group Mobilization," *Political Research Quarterly* 49 (1996), 119–146.

18. See Laura R. Olson, "Mainline Protestant Washington Offices and the Political Lives of Clergy," in *The Quiet Hand of God: Faith-based Activism and the Public Role of Mainline Protestantism*, eds. Robert Wuthnow and John H. Evans (Berkeley: University of California Press, 2002). Interviews by Allen Hertzke for the Pew Forum in 2009 suggest that some mainline leaders are developing more strategic focus in their work.

19. Hertzke, *Representing God in Washington*; Hofrenning, *In Washington But Not of It*.

20. Allen D. Hertzke, "An Assessment of the Mainline Churches Since 1945," in *The Role of Religion in the Making of Public Policy*, eds. James E. Wood Jr. and Derek Davis (Waco, TX: Dawson Institute of Church-State Studies, 1991); Olson, "Mainline Protestant Washington Offices."

21. This information comes from Allen Hertzke's study of national religious lobbies for the Pew Forum on Religion & Public Life in 2009.

22. Kevin W. Hula, *Lobbying Together: Interest Group Coalitions in Legislative Politics* (Washington, DC: Georgetown University Press, 1999).

23. Poverty Forum, http://thepovertyforum.org/.

24. Deborah Caldwell, "Why Christians Must Keep Israel Strong: An Interview with Richard Land," available at http://www.beliefnet.com; Todd Hertz, "The Evangelical View of Israel?" *Christianity Today*, June 11, 2003; Tatsha Robertson, "Evangelicals Flock to Israel's Banner," *The Boston Globe*, October 21, 2002, A3.

25. Hertzke, *Freeing God's Children*.

26. This model is a revised version of one developed by Robert Booth Fowler, *Religion and Politics in America* (Metuchen, NJ: Scarecrow Press, 1985).

27. Lawrence Kersten, *The Lutheran Ethic: The Impact of Religion on Laymen and Clergy* (Detroit, MI: Wayne State University Press, 1970).

28. R. Drew Smith and Fredrick C. Harris, eds., *Black Churches and Local Politics: Clergy Influence, Organizational Partnerships, and Civic Empowerment* (Lanham, MD: Rowman and Littlefield, 2005).

29. Wilcox and Larson, *Onward Christian Soldiers?*

30. James L. Guth, John C. Green, Corwin E. Smidt, Lyman A. Kellstedt, and Margaret M. Poloma, *The Bully Pulpit: The Politics of Protestant Clergy* (Lawrence, KS: University Press of Kansas, 1997).

31. Keith Graber Miller, *American Mennonites Engage Washington: Wise as Serpents, Innocent as Doves?* (Knoxville, TN: University of Tennessee Press, 1996).

32. Gregory Allen Smith, *Politics in the Parish: The Political Influence of Catholic Priests* (Washington, DC: Georgetown University Press, 2008).

33. Theda Skocpol, *Diminished Democracy: From Membership to Management in American Civic Life* (Norman, OK: University of Oklahoma Press, 2003).

34. Sidney Verba, Kay Lehman Schlozman, and Henry E. Brady, *Voice and Equality: Civic Voluntarism in American Society* (Cambridge, MA: Harvard University Press, 1995).

35. Hertzke, *Representing God in Washington*; Harold E. Quinley, *The Prophetic Clergy: Social Activism Among Protestant Ministers* (New York: Wiley, 1974); Wilcox and Larson, *Onward Christian Soldiers?*

36. Guth et al., *The Bully Pulpit*; Quinley, *The Prophetic Clergy*.

37. James F. Findlay Jr., *Church People in the Struggle: The National Council of Churches and the Black Freedom Movement, 1950–1970* (New York: Oxford University Press, 1993).

38. Findlay, *Church People in the Struggle*; Quinley, *The Prophetic Clergy*.

39. Hertzke, "An Assessment of the Mainline Churches"; Olson, "Mainline Protestant Washington Offices."

40. Frances Fitzgerald, "The New Evangelicals," *The New Yorker*, June 30, 2008, 28.

41. Lynette Clemetson, "Clergy Group to Counter Conservatives," *The New York Times*, November 17, 2003, A17.

42. Olson, "Mainline Protestant Washington Offices."

43. Sue E. S. Crawford, "Clergy at Work in the Secular City" (PhD dissertation, Indiana University, 1995); Sue E. S. Crawford and Laura R. Olson, "Clergy as Political Actors in Urban Contexts" in *Christian Clergy in American Politics*, eds. Sue E. S. Crawford and Laura R. Olson (Baltimore: Johns Hopkins University Press, 2001); Laura R. Olson, *Filled with Spirit and Power: Protestant Clergy in Politics* (Albany: State University of New York Press, 2000).

44. Timothy A. Byrnes, *Catholic Bishops in American Politics* (Princeton: Princeton University Press, 1991).

45. Liberation theology, which originated in Latin America, teaches that churches must work to liberate those who are oppressed by economic and political inequality. See Paul E. Sigmund, *Liberation Theology at the Crossroads* (New York: Oxford University Press, 1990).

46. Ted G. Jelen, "Catholic Priests and the Political Order: The Political Behavior of Catholic Pastors," *Journal for the Scientific Study of Religion* 42 (2003), 597; Smith, *Politics in the Parish.*

47. William D'Antonio, ed., *Laity, American and Catholic: Transforming the Church* (Kansas City, MO: Sheed and Ward, 1996).

48. NORC data, as reported in Tim O'Neil, "Scandal Rocks Church, But Faith Remains," *St. Louis Post Dispatch*, June 22, 2003, A1.

49. See Timothy A. Byrnes and Mary Segers, *The Catholic Church and Abortion Politics: A View from the States* (Boulder: Westview Press, 1991).

50. See Mary Ann Glendon, *Abortion and Divorce in Western Law* (Cambridge, MA: Harvard University Press, 1987).

51. This point is made on the basis of national survey data as analyzed in Hertzke, *Representing God in Washington,* chap. 5. See also Chapter 4 here, Figure 4.3.

52. Richard W. Stevenson, "Bush Signs Ban on a Procedure for Abortions," *The New York Times*, November 5, 2003, A1.

53. Jacqueline L. Salmon, "Bishops Call Obama-Supported Abortion Rights Bill a Threat to Catholic Church," *The Washington Post*, November 12, 2008.

54. Byrnes, *Catholic Bishops in American Politics*. For an excellent overview of various aspects of just war theory, see Terry Nardin, ed., *The Ethics of War and Peace: Religious and Secular Perspectives* (Princeton: Princeton University Press, 1996).

55. For an excellent discussion of churches' activism around the 1991 Gulf War, see Andrew R. Murphy, "The Mainline Churches and Political Activism," *Soundings* (Winter 1993), 525–549. See also James Turner Johnson and George Weigel, *Just War and the Gulf War* (Washington, DC: Ethics and Public Policy Center, 1991), who argue that the Gulf War did meet just war criteria, much along the lines that Bush did in his speech to religious broadcasters. What weakened the Catholic Church's influence, in part, was the natural ambiguity inherent in deciding whether criteria are met or not.

56. Stephen V. Monsma, *When Sacred and Secular Mix* (Lanham, MD: Rowman and Littlefield, 1996).

57. L. Sandy Maisel and Ira N. Forman, eds., *Jews in American Politics* (Lanham, MD: Rowman and Littlefield, 2001).

58. American Jewish Congress, http://www.ajcongress.org/allabout.htm; Jerome A. Chanes, "Who Does What? Jewish Advocacy and Jewish 'Interest,'" in *Jews in American Politics*.

59. Chanes, "Who Does What?"

60. American Israel Public Affairs Council, http://www.aipac.org; Chanes, "Who Does What?"

61. John J. Mearsheimer and Stephen M. Walt, *The Israel Lobby and U.S. Foreign Policy* (New York: Farrar, Straus, and Giroux, 2008).

62. Eun Lee Koh, "Robertson's Speech Backing Israel Gets Ovation at Temple," *The Boston Globe*, April 14, 2003, B1.

63. Maisel and Forman, *Jews in American Politics*.

64. Ibid.

65. Ibid.

66. Nearly three-quarters of Americans say they have either a very favorable or mostly favorable opinion of Jews, and only 9 percent have unfavorable feelings. See Pew Research Center and Pew Forum on Religion & Public Life, *2003 Religion and Public Life Survey* (June 24, 2003), available through the Roper Center, http://www.ropercenter.uconn.edu.

67. Robert Putnam, *Bowling Alone: The Collapse and Revival of American Community* (New York: Simon & Schuster, 2000), 162.

68. Wilcox and Larson, *Onward Christian Soldiers?*

69. Fitzgerald, "The New Evangelicals."

70. Napp Nazworth, "The Institutionalization of the Christian Right" (PhD dissertation, University of Florida, 2006).

71. The Pew Forum on Religion & Public Life offers an excellent summary of the gay marriage debate and the status of state laws: http://pewforum.org/docs/?DocID=288.

72. Lyman A. Kellstedt, John C. Green, Corwin E. Smidt, and James L. Guth, "Faith Transformed: Religion and American Politics from FDR to G. W. Bush," in *Religion and American Politics: From the Colonial Period to the Present*, 2nd ed., eds. Mark A. Noll and Luke E. Harlow (New York: Oxford University Press, 2007).

73. Wilcox and Larson, *Onward Christian Soldiers?*

74. Jon A. Shields, *The Democratic Virtues of the Christian Right* (Princeton: Princeton University Press, 2009).

75. Information for this section is from Allen D. Hertzke, "American Muslim Exceptionalism," *Borders of Islam*, ed. Stig Jarle Hansen (London: C. Hurst, 2009).

76. Sarah Childress, "Islam: Ingrid Mattson," *Newsweek*, December 25, 2006.

77. Diana L. Eck, *New Religious America: How a "Christian Country" Has Become the World's Most Religiously Diverse Nation* (San Francisco: HarperOne, 2002).

78. Interview by Allen Hertzke, May 2009, with national leaders of the Sikh American Legal Defense & Education Fund.

79. John Nurser, *For All Peoples and All Nations: Christian Churches and Human Rights* (Washington, DC: Georgetown University Press, 2005).

80. For the letter and signatories, see https://www.csidonline.org/sign-open-letter.

81. Hertzke, *Freeing God's Children.*

82. From an interview by Allen Hertzke with Wendy Wright, president of Concerned Women for America, May 2009. See also http://www.cwfa.org/articledisplay.asp?id=7659&department=CWA&categoryid=.

83. Hertzke, *Freeing God's Children.*

84. Ibid.

85. William Branigin, "A Different Kind of Trade War," *The Washington Post,* March 20, 1999.

86. Victims of Trafficking and Violence Protection Act of 2000, Public Law 106–386, October 28, 2000.

87. Elisabeth Bumiller, "Evangelicals Sway White House on Human Rights Issues Abroad," *The New York Times,* October 26, 2003.

88. Hertzke, *Freeing God's Children.*

89. Ibid.

90. Gary A. Haugen, *Good News About Injustice* (Downers Grove, IL: InterVarsity Press, 1999).

91. John Miller, speech delivered at Georgetown University, February 20, 2003.

92. Philip Jenkins, "The Next Christianity," *The Atlantic Monthly,* October 2002.

93. Stephen V. Monsma, "Faith-based NGOs and the Government Embrace," in *The Influence of Faith: Religious Groups & U.S. Foreign Policy,* ed. Elliott Abrams (Lanham, MD: Rowman and Littlefield, 2001).

94. Joshua William Busby, "Bono Made Jesse Helms Cry: Jubilee 2000, Debt Relief, and Moral Action in International Politics," *International Studies Quarterly* 51 (2007), 247–275.

95. Scott Baldauf and Jina Moore, "Bush Sees Results of His AIDS Plan in Africa," *The Christian Science Monitor,* February 20, 2008, 7.

96. Edward L. Cleary and Allen D. Hertzke, *Representing God at the Statehouse: Religion and Politics in the American States* (Lanham, MD: Rowman and Littlefield, 2006).

97. Kevin R. den Dulk and Allen D. Hertzke, "Conclusion: Themes in Religious Advocacy," in *Representing God at the Statehouse,* 226.

98. Cleary and Hertzke, *Representing God at the Statehouse.*

99. John C. Green, Mark J. Rozell, and Clyde Wilcox, eds., *The Christian Right in American Politics: Marching to the Millennium* (Washington DC: Georgetown University Press, 2003).

100. Cleary and Hertzke, *Representing God at the Statehouse*; David Yamane, *The Catholic Church in State Politics: Negotiating Prophetic Demands and Political Realities* (Lanham, MD: Rowman and Littlefield, 2005).

101. Cleary and Hertzke, *Representing God at the Statehouse*.

102. Jesse McKinley and Kirk Johnson, "Mormons Tipped Scale in Ban on Gay Marriage," *The New York Times*, November 14, 2008, A1; Ashley Surdin, "Protesters Target Supporters of Gay Marriage Ban," *The Washington Post*, November 15, 2008, A12.

103. Nancy Tatom Ammerman, *Pillars of Faith: American Congregations and Their Partners* (Berkeley: University of California Press, 2005); Mark Chaves, *Congregations in America* (Cambridge, MA: Harvard University Press, 2004); Ram A. Cnaan, *The Invisible Caring Hand: American Congregations and the Provision of Welfare* (New York: New York University Press, 2002); Laura R. Olson, *Filled with Spirit and Power: Protestant Clergy in Politics* (Albany: State University of New York Press, 2000).

104. Michael L. Owens, "Doing Something in Jesus' Name: Black Churches and Community Development Corporations," in *New Day Begun*, ed. R. Drew Smith (Durham, NC: Duke University Press, 2003).

105. John M. Perkins, *Beyond Charity: The Call to Christian Community Development* (Grand Rapids, MI: Baker Books, 1993).

106. Saul Alinsky, *Rules for Radicals* (New York: Random House, 1971).

107. Stephen Hart, *Cultural Dilemmas of Progressive Politics: Styles of Engagement Among Grassroots Activists* (Chicago: University of Chicago Press, 2001); Heidi J. Swarts, *Organizing Urban America: Secular and Faith-based Progressive Movements* (Minneapolis: University of Minnesota Press, 2008); Mark R. Warren, *Dry Bones Rattling: Community Building to Revitalize American Democracy* (Princeton: Princeton University Press, 2001); Richard L. Wood, *Faith in Action: Religion, Race, and Democratic Organizing in America* (Chicago: University of Chicago Press, 2002).

108. Gaston Espinosa, Virgilio Elizondo, and Jesse Miranda, eds., *Latino Religious and Civic Activism in the United States* (New York: Oxford University Press, 2005).

109. Allison Calhoun-Brown, "What a Fellowship: Civil Society, African American Churches, and Public Life," in *New Day Begun*.

110. Smith and Harris, *Black Churches and Local Politics*.

111. Christopher Winship, "End of a Miracle? Crime, Faith, and Partnership in Boston in the 1990s," in *Long March Ahead: African American Churches and Public Policy in Post–Civil Rights America*, ed. R. Drew Smith (Durham, NC: Duke University Press, 2004).

112. Melissa M. Deckman, *School Board Battles: The Christian Right in Local Politics* (Washington, DC: Georgetown University Press, 2004).

113. Paul A. Djupe and Laura R. Olson, eds., *Religious Interests in Community Conflict* (Waco, TX: Baylor University Press, 2007).

114. For a summary of scholarship on interest groups and religious advocacy, see Hertzke, "Religious Interest Groups in American Politics."

115. Hertzke, *Freeing God's Children*.

116. Diana B. Henriques and Andrew W. Lehern, "Religious Groups Reap Federal Aid for Pet Projects," *The New York Times*, May 13, 2007; and interview of Henriques by Allen Hertzke.

6

RELIGION AND POLITICAL
AND CULTURAL ELITES

Religious activism, as we have seen, can be directed toward shaping culture, influencing elections, or lobbying government. To a large degree, the success or failure of religious activism hinges on the accessibility and responsiveness of leaders in government, media, and entertainment. As we explore the connections between religious politics and American elites, we must ask: How much do elites listen and respond to religious groups and activists? We ask this question with the understanding that elites are not empty vessels. Their own religious backgrounds, worldviews, and biases affect how open they are to religious groups and faith-based arguments.

One might think that much is known about elite religious views, but we know substantially less about their religious outlooks than we do about those of the general public. In part this reflects the problem of access. For example, busy members of Congress, executive branch officials, party leaders, or judges can, and often do, refuse to answer questionnaires. Rarely do they agree to provide more than the most cursory interview. Thus we have too little data on elites that can compare to standard national surveys of the religious public, such as those that the Gallup Organization or the Pew Forum on Religion & Public Life regularly conduct. Still, we do have enough information to come to a basic understanding of religion's relevance in the lives and work of political and social elites.

As we chart what we know of the religious perspectives of elites and the broader environment in which they work, we observe some important religious differences among political elites, just as we see among the general public. But we also note that the religious perspectives of elites as a group are not necessarily representative of those of the general public. Some religious perspectives are overrepresented while others are underrepresented—and this fact has political implications.

RELIGION AND THE PRESIDENCY

The outcomes of presidential elections clearly matter to religious activists. After all, the president appoints top officials in the executive branch, federal judges, U.S. Supreme Court justices, and diplomats. The president also has great influence over domestic policy and charts the nation's defense and foreign policies. Thus it matters tremendously who occupies the Oval Office, and the president can be a powerful ally or foe for activists who wish to further a political agenda based on religious principles. Presidents, for their part, realize the importance of religious constituencies and religious interest groups, and for many years they have designated White House officials to serve as liaisons to them.[1]

But every president also must contend with a wide range of compelling demands, and a pragmatic logic easily can override the moral pleas of religious petitioners. In the high-stakes world of realpolitik, religious niceties often give way to Machiavellian calculations. Moreover, the presidency is really a diverse office in which a host of White House aides jockey for influence, calling on religious leaders when it is expedient but ignoring them when it is not. Charles Colson recalls how he and other aides to President Richard Nixon consciously used religious figures to add legitimacy to his presidency, or awed them with tours of the White House to mute their criticism. Religious figures, he has remarked, are often well-meaning but gullible people who understand little of the cutthroat nature of White House politics.[2] Some evangelical leaders now suspect that they were naive about what they could get out of the Reagan White House in the 1980s. They have also raised pointed questions as to whether the Clinton White House used certain religious leaders for its own political purposes. Another chorus of critics has raised similar questions about the treatment of evangelicals by the George W. Bush administration; allegations emerged during Bush's second term that his administration's much-touted commitment to evangelicals was designed strictly for electoral gain.[3] The point is that religious influence does not flow in just one direction. Religious groups may attempt to use politics to advance their values, but political leaders also can manipulate these groups in the process.[4]

The chief executive's response to religious groups is constrained by the unique religious dimension of the Office of the President. As head of state, the president serves a "civil religious" function.[5] Part of every president's responsibilities includes offering prayers to grieving families of soldiers killed in action, invoking God's blessing on the nation on holidays such as Thanksgiving and Memorial Day—and even during the presidential inauguration itself. Because of the nation's religious pluralism, presidents typically avoid clearly sectarian references on these occasions and employ only broad, vague kinds of religious imagery. In fact, President Barack Obama gained substantial notice for breaking with this precedent in his inaugural address, when he noted: "We are a nation of Christians and Muslims, Jews and Hindus—and nonbelievers."

Americans' expectation that the president will serve, in an important sense, as an informal "pastor of the nation" can have the ironic effect of diminishing the political clout of religious tradition to which the president belongs. The classic illustration of this phenomenon involves John Kennedy. His election to the presidency in 1960 brought enormous legitimacy to the American Catholic population, but his policy priorities did not intersect well with the agenda of the Catholic Church (for instance, government support for parochial schools). Kennedy bent over backward to avoid the hint of favoritism, and some Catholic critics argued that this made his administration even less hospitable to the Catholic Church than previous Protestant administrations had been.[6]

In general, what can we make of the relationship between religion and the presidency? We should note at the outset that almost all U.S. presidents have professed to be Christians. Harry Truman was a Baptist, Dwight Eisenhower a Presbyterian, and Lyndon Johnson a member of the Disciples of Christ (a small mainline Protestant denomination). But it has only been in the last two decades or so that the issue of religion in the White House itself has become so visible and important. This is a manifestation of the growing politicization of religion. By contrasting presidents Richard Nixon, Jimmy Carter, Ronald Reagan, George H. W. Bush, Bill Clinton, George W. Bush, and Barack Obama, we will see both the scope and the limits of religious influence at 1600 Pennsylvania Avenue.

Richard Nixon

Richard Nixon, president from 1969 to 1974, offers perhaps the easiest case.[7] Though he was raised a Quaker, Nixon demonstrated little personal connection between his declared Christian faith and his politics. Nixon's approach to politics was strategic, not religious or moralistic. Both his successes and his failures were closely connected to his calculating political personality. His approach produced one of the most enduring cautionary tales for would-be religious activists. That tale involved this century's most celebrated evangelist, Rev. Billy Graham.[8]

Born in 1918, Graham had emerged as the premier Protestant evangelist in the United States by mid-century, and by virtue of that role he became a sort of unofficial pastor to presidents. Indeed, he visited the White House of every president from Harry Truman to George W. Bush. It does not take a cynic to see why these presidents welcomed Graham's blessing and association. Graham relished his role, especially in the 1950s, 1960s, and early 1970s, playing golf with Eisenhower and spending a lot of time with Lyndon Johnson and even more with Nixon.

Graham got to know Nixon during the Eisenhower years, when Nixon served as vice president. Graham came to count Nixon as a friend. When Kennedy opposed Nixon in the 1960 presidential election, Graham was like many evangelicals in not supporting Kennedy for religious reasons, but his sympathies also lay with Nixon as a friend. When Nixon gained the Republican nomination in 1968, Graham emerged as a visible supporter. He visited the Nixon headquarters at the Republican National Convention, introduced the candidate at one of his trademark evangelistic crusades, and took the dramatic step of announcing five days before the election that he planned to vote for Nixon (a public endorsement he repeated in Nixon's 1972 reelection campaign). After Nixon's 1968 victory, Graham was welcomed in the White House and often was included in the presidential entourage.

We now know, however, that Graham was never a member of Nixon's inner circle, nor was he privy to important decisions or secrets. Neither did Graham, as he came to realize, have a real friendship with Nixon, a man he knew much less well than he originally thought.[9] The Watergate scandal became the crucial moment in the Nixon-Graham relationship. When the Watergate drama unfolded, Graham initially refused to believe that Nixon had done—or could have done—anything illegal. But as evidence piled up, and tapes revealed Nixon's personal vulgarity, meanness, and calculating manner, Graham changed his mind. The whole experience tempered Graham, leaving him substantially more cautious about the blandishments of politicians and the temptations of power.[10]

Jimmy Carter

Jimmy Carter's presidency (1977–1981) provided a contrast to the Nixon years. Lauded for his strict personal morality, Carter was also criticized for his naïveté and lack of strategic ability. A born-again Southern Baptist, a Sunday school teacher, and by all accounts a devout man, Carter has always drawn close conscious links between his faith and his politics.[11] This was true in his general view of the presidency as a trusteeship; he believed he should act in the public interest despite any adverse political fallout.[12] Carter also connected his faith to his policy priorities. For example, his approach to environmental politics was based on a framework of biblical stewardship of God's creation. But the religion-politics connection was most obvious in the realm of Carter's foreign policy, where he sought to advance what he viewed as Christian mandates of human rights and peace. As president, Carter brokered the historic peace agreement between Egypt and Israel that stands to this day. He has continued his faith-inspired work for peace, human rights, and economic development in the decades since he left office and was rewarded for his efforts with the 2002 Nobel Peace Prize. Ironically, many who later rose to prominence in the Reagan White House criticized Carter as naive, claiming that he failed to provide a robust defense of American national interests and charging that Carter was simply not Machiavellian enough to be a good president.[13]

Carter's greatest triumph as president—the Camp David Accords, which sealed the peace between Egypt and Israel—reflected core aspects of his faith. His belief in redemption, his stubborn determination to foster reconciliation, and his embrace of both sides of the conflict (Egypt and Israel) as religious kin of the "blood of Abraham" made a real difference in the delicate negotiations.[14] Critics of Carter's international role since his presidency, which has taken him to Bosnia, North Korea, Haiti, and the Middle East, among many other conflict-riddled regions, claim that he seeks peace at any price and that he places too much stock in the good faith of dictators.[15] But it is an indisputable fact that Jimmy Carter's political endeavors, which flow from his understanding of Christian faith, have made an enduring mark on the world.

Ronald Reagan

Perhaps the deepest irony of Carter's commitment to living out his faith through political work is that he lost the support of members of his own religious tradition—evangelical Protestants—during the course of his presidency. Not only did evangelicals reject Carter, but they began a wholesale rejection of the Democratic Party as well.[16] Evangelicals became upset because Carter interpreted his faith in a more liberal way than many of his fellow Southern Baptists. Moreover, the Democratic coalition Carter led as president continued liberal policies—and produced some new ones—that angered and insulted many evangelicals. Carter's opponent in the 1980 election, Ronald Reagan, understood this discontent and played on it. Speaking before a convention of mostly evangelical religious broadcasters in 1980, Reagan acknowledged that as religious leaders they could not endorse him without risking their organizations' tax-exempt status. He assured Christian evangelicals, however, that he supported their policy goals, making his view clear in one succinct declaration: "I endorse *you*."

Many Protestant evangelicals flocked to Reagan's candidacies in 1980 and 1984, although critics noted that he was not much of a churchgoer, had been divorced, and had risen to political prominence out of Hollywood—hardly an evangelical bastion. They also pointed out that his wife, Nancy Reagan, put some stock in astrology. Still, Reagan remained popular among evangelicals because he defended "traditional values," nuclear families, patriotism, and the faith of the framers—with rhetorical skill and apparent sincerity.[17]

The case of Reagan and his appeal to evangelicals illustrates a key problem in sorting out the role that faith plays in the life of the occupant of the Oval Office. A president's electoral coalition often is based much more on political stands than on personal practices or worldview. This is not to gainsay Reagan's religion; he did affirm conservative religious beliefs and even shared in speculation about the End Times prophesied in scripture.[18] Moreover, his White House staff paid close attention to evangelicals, as well as to Jews and Catholics, while shunning most liberal religious groups. In retrospect, however, questions remain about what, if anything, evangelicals and other religious conservatives gained during the Reagan years (1981–1989). To be sure, many applauded Reagan's stand against communism, and new moderate-to-conservative jurists were appointed to the U.S. Supreme Court and the lower federal courts. But most of the evangelical political agenda went nowhere during the Reagan years.[19] For example, legal abortion continued with few restrictions and prayer stayed out of public schools, leading some evangelical leaders to grumble that the Reagan administration paid only lip service to their agenda.

Reagan's vigorous denunciation of the Soviet Union, which he called the "Evil Empire," led him to form ties with Pope John Paul II that had an historic global impact. Prior to his election as pope, John Paul II served as Archbishop of Krakow, Poland, and was a leader in the Polish opposition to communist rule. As pope, he set about using his authority and freedom to travel as a means of subtly encouraging growing opposition to communist regimes in Eastern Europe.[20] The Reagan administration was aware of these efforts and bolstered them with initiatives of its own aimed at destabilizing Soviet rule. The alliance between Reagan and John Paul II (and some would add British prime minister Margaret Thatcher to the equation as well) was a dramatic example of the effectiveness of religious and political authorities working together.[21] What is less clear is how to disentangle whether Reagan's faith played any role in his papal alliance against communism.

George H. W. Bush

This brings us to George H. W. Bush, Connecticut Yankee, blue blood, and president from 1989 to 1993. In his case we again encounter the ironies of faith versus strategic politics. Bush is an Episcopalian and is decidedly uncomfortable with pietistic politics.[22] Evangelical-style public witnessing and dramatic accounts of sin and redemption are as alien to Bush as they are to most other mainline Protestants. And when Bush was president and tried publicly to affirm his faith, his statements came across as strained and awkward.

In spite of his lack of comfort with public religion, Bush worked hard to earn the votes of various religious groups, particularly evangelicals, in the 1988 presidential election. He succeeded, actually garnering a greater share of the evangelical vote than Reagan had in 1984. At least some of this success must be attributed to the fact that by 1988, a thorough partisan realignment had swept the evangelical community; evangelicals likely would have given a majority of their votes to whomever the Republican Party nominated at that point.[23] Like his predecessors, Bush was not seen as an ideal president by conservative evangelicals, or by Catholics, mainline Protestants, or members of other religious groups. He generated considerable anger in conservative religious circles when he hosted a meeting of gay and lesbian activists at the White House, and he was criticized more generally for his tepid advocacy of the Christian Right's political agenda. On the other hand, religious conservatives were pleased with his work to block abortion funding and his appointment of a staunch conservative, Clarence Thomas, to the U.S. Supreme Court. Even in defeat in 1992, Bush received more support from evangelical Protestants than he got from any other religious group.[24]

Bill Clinton

In many respects, Bill Clinton, president from 1993 to 2001, was his predecessor's opposite. From an early age he was immersed in evangelical Protestantism, and he remained at ease with its messages and cadences as an adult. Clinton was raised in Bible Belt Arkansas, where he attended Baptist churches and Pentecostal summer camps as a youngster. As governor of Arkansas he joined a prominent Baptist church in Little Rock. He is fluent in the evangelical language of sin and redemption, and he is equally comfortable in both black and white evangelical congregations (often joining in gospel singing from memory). His wife, Secretary of State Hillary Rodham Clinton, has been an active United Methodist who embodies the social justice agenda of her denomination, which undoubtedly gave President Clinton a deep appreciation for mainline Protestantism as well.[25] However, Clinton's liberalism on social issues hurt any support he might have received from evangelicals or other religious traditionalists. By the 1990s, a powerful "religion gap" had come to characterize partisan politics, with committed evangelicals, Catholics, and mainline Protestants all favoring the Republican Party and its candidates by substantial margins.[26]

Until sexual scandal tarnished Clinton's presidency late in his second term, the Clintons' presence in Washington was a boon to the liberal religious community.

From the National Council of Churches to the United Methodist Church, religious activists who had been shut out of the White House during the Reagan-Bush years were welcomed back. Clinton also proved to be intensely popular among African Americans, but his social liberalism made him unpopular with white evangelicals. And the sexual scandal involving Clinton and a White House intern doomed his relations with many religious leaders and groups.

George W. Bush

No recent presidency is more important to consider in the context of religion and politics than that of George W. Bush, who served from 2001 to 2009. Bush grew up in west Texas, where his religious upbringing was decidedly mainline Protestant. He attended a Presbyterian church with his family until he left for an elite preparatory school (and later college and graduate school) in the Northeast. Upon returning to Texas years later, he joined the same United Methodist church his wife, Laura Bush, attended, where he became a respected and dutiful member of the congregation. But his personal relationship to religion changed, by most accounts dramatically, when he began participating in a Bible study during a time of personal struggle with alcohol and family life. In 1986 he gave up drinking and embraced a more evangelical Christianity.[27]

This conversion became part of his public life, too, first during Bush's stint as a liaison to evangelicals during his father's 1988 presidential bid, then as governor of Texas, and finally as president.[28] During a 2000 presidential debate, for example, he famously declared that Jesus was his favorite philosopher, and he repeatedly said that Jesus "changed my heart"—statements that resonate deeply with many evangelicals.[29]

What really set Bush apart from his predecessors in the White House were his open affirmation of religious commitment and his eager public support for many kinds of religious groups. Some policy decisions underlined his credentials as a religious conservative, such as his establishment of the White House Office for Faith-Based and Community Initiatives, an office that worked to increase partnerships between the federal government and religious organizations that participate in welfare-delivery programs.[30]

When Bush's presidency took on a heavy foreign policy focus, he declared that the United States faced an "axis of evil," which he specifically construed as Iraq, Iran, and North Korea. After September 11, 2001, the evangelical overtones of the "Bush Doctrine" justifying military action in Afghanistan and then Iraq in particular were clear, pleasing some Americans and rankling critics at home and abroad.[31]

Every president's use of religion necessarily remains somewhat suspect to the skeptical citizen. How much are his invocations of religion a matter of sincere expressions of personal faith and how much a deliberate effort to use faith for political purposes? Sorting out religious motivations from political calculations is a difficult business. As we have seen, every president's faith matters under some circumstances, but the dynamics of political interest and advantage may count for as much, if not more. Presidents are political animals, and they are in the business of making political judgments and calculations.

Barack Obama

It remains to be seen exactly how President Barack Obama will connect religion with politics during his presidency. Obama was not raised in a religious environment; his mother was a religious skeptic, and his father was not a part of his life.[32] Obama later embraced Christianity as an adult while working with a faith-based community-organizing group in Chicago. There he attended Trinity United Church of Christ, a large African American congregation headed by Rev. Jeremiah Wright.[33] Wright became a highly controversial figure during the 2008 presidential campaign when inflammatory clips from some of his sermons appeared on the Internet. Obama cut ties with Wright and has gone on to surround himself with a variety of other clergy, establishing Evergreen Chapel at the Camp David presidential retreat as his new home church.[34] The most visible religion-relevant action Obama took in his early days as president was his outreach to the Muslim world, including a speech given in Cairo in which he emphasized "the truth that America and Islam are not exclusive, and need not be in competition."

A different approach to the role of religion in presidential politics is to consider the possibility that what might matter most is not presidents' own religious beliefs but rather their symbolic use of religious rhetoric. From this point of view, presidential rhetoric can set a broad national tone from the top, which might be even more politically expedient than any specific policy initiative. Much of the criticism of George W. Bush's incorporation of religion in his administration, for example, was directed at his willing use of religious terms and imagery in his rhetoric. Recent research on presidential rhetoric since the early 1970s shows that successive presidents do use recognizably religious language, but that Republican presidents have employed it far more often than have Democratic ones. This may come as a surprise considering that both Democratic presidents in this period were quite open about their Christian religious convictions. However, recent Democratic presidents appear to have been more likely than their Republican counterparts to address religion in substantive terms (such as in reference to international human rights concerns).[35] These differences are real, but what is constant is the use of religious language by one American president after another. Every president knows that religion is a source of cultural influence. As political scientist David Leege and his colleagues argue, political elites have recognized this influence for centuries and have sought to exploit it for political gain.[36] In this sense, religion is inextricably linked with the American presidency despite the constitutional separation between church and state.

RELIGION AND CONGRESS

Congress today reflects the religious pluralism of America more than many other elite institutions. Yet the membership of Congress does not mirror the population perfectly. Some religious groups, such as mainline Protestants, Jews, and Catholics, are overrepresented relative to their proportion of the U.S. population, whereas Baptists and other evangelical Protestants are underrepresented.[37] Several factors are at work here, including different religious groups' socioeconomic status, their openness to politics, and their geographic concentration.

One way to assess religion's role in Congress is to look at patterns in the religious affiliation of members over time. In the 1950s, for example, congressional membership was weighted heavily toward mainline Protestant denominations, with Catholics, evangelical Protestants, and other religious groups underrepresented. The first big change in this pattern occurred in 1958, when huge Democratic gains in midterm elections brought an unprecedented number of Catholics to Congress. Indeed, it was this influx of Catholics, coupled with Kennedy's presidential candidacy two years later, that motivated scholars and journalists alike to begin studying the faith of members of Congress.[38]

Since 1960, congressional membership has become even more religiously diverse (see Table 6.1). One striking example concerns Jewish representation. Only 2 percent of the members of the House and Senate were Jews in 1960, which was less than their share of the total population at the time. In 2008, by contrast, 7 percent of House members and 13 percent of senators were Jewish, which is considerably more than their 2 percent of the U.S. population today.[39] Among the reasons for this change are the increased acceptance of American Jews at large, strong political interest within the Jewish community, and high levels of Jewish economic status and educational attainment, which enables Jews to run for office more readily than people of lower socioeconomic status.

RELIGIOUS AFFILIATION	HOUSE	SENATE	TOTAL	PERCENT OF CONGRESS	PERCENT CHANGE SINCE 1960
Protestant (total)	239	53	292	54.6	-25.9
Baptist	58	8	66	12.3	+6.5
Methodist	47	10	57	10.7	-41.2
Presbyterian	31	12	43	8.0	-41.1
Episcopalian	32	6	38	7.1	-42.4
Lutheran	20	4	24	4.5	+14.3
United Church of Christ	2	4	6	1.1	-77.8
Pentecostal	2	0	2	0.4	N/A
Other/Unspecified Protestant	47	9	56	10.5	+16.7
Catholic	135	26	161	30.1	+61.0
Jewish	32	13	45	8.4	+275.0
Mormon	9	5	14	2.6	+100.0
Other	19	3	23	4.3	N/A

Table 6.1   Religious Affiliations of Members of Congress, 2008
Source: Pew Forum on Religion & Public Life, *Faith on the Hill: The Religious Affiliations of Members of Congress*, http://pewforum.org/docs/?DocID=379 (2008).

Catholics compose about 25 percent of the U.S. population. Although they were slightly underrepresented in Congress in 1960 (19 percent), they had achieved more than parity by 2008, when they accounted for 30 percent of congressional membership.[40] In fact, Catholic congressional representation has consistently mirrored or exceeded the Catholic proportion of the U.S. population since 1980.[41] Politically, however, Catholic members of Congress hardly constitute a monolith in terms of party affiliation, ideology, issue priorities, or anything else beyond religious identification.[42]

Mainline Protestant denominations continue to be overrepresented relative to their share of the population. Their congressional numbers have declined since 1960, paralleling declines in mainline church membership. We see this trend across mainline denominations; as Table 6.1 shows, the size of the Methodist, Presbyterian, and Episcopalian congressional delegations has shrunken by more than 40 percent since 1960. Although their membership in Congress is down substantially, mainline Protestants still retain robust representation relative to the size of their lay membership.[43] This again reflects the importance of socioeconomic status. Mainline Protestants, as a group, are relatively well educated and economically advantaged, so some of their members are well positioned to run successfully for political office.

Of course, congressional representation does not by definition translate into automatic clout for mainline Protestant lobbies in Washington, which on the whole tend to be more liberal than mainline members of Congress. Members of Congress can disagree with each other on political issues, after all, and they also can disagree about how religious they are and thus how much religion matters in their political lives. And in some instances, it is the religious backgrounds of the constituents, rather than those of the members themselves, that bear a strong relationship to congressional voting behavior.[44] Nonetheless, having members of one's own denomination in the halls of Congress may provide at least some access.

We do not have complete data on evangelicals in Congress because they are diffused across many denominations. For example, some Presbyterian members of Congress, such as Sen. Jim DeMint (R–South Carolina), belong to the conservative, evangelical Presbyterian Church in America, rather than its mainline counterpart, the Presbyterian Church (U.S.A.). It is clear that the number of evangelical members of Congress has increased since 1960. Still, they remain underrepresented relative to their share of the population, in part because of the overrepresentation of mainline Protestants and growth in Catholic representation. The Baptist contingent in Congress, which contains many traditional evangelicals, illustrates this fact. Baptist representation has increased by 6.5 percent since 1960, but Baptists remain slightly underrepresented in comparison with their numbers in the U.S. population. Despite the fact that they make up 17 percent of the population, Baptists make up 12 percent of congressional membership.[45] This should not surprise us considering the historically modest economic and educational profiles of Baptists as a group. The Baptist congressional delegation is also diverse, containing a healthy share of black Baptists, whose politics often diverge from the white evangelical agenda, and some adherents of the American Baptist Churches U.S.A., a moderate mainline denomination.

The Church of Jesus Christ of Latter-day Saints is notable in that, unlike most small faith groups, it has at least as large a proportion of adherents in Congress as it does in the population at large. Mormons comprised 1.3 percent of the Congress in 1960, but this share doubled by 2008. The Mormon congressional delegation (2.6

percent) is proportionately larger than the Mormon share of the U.S. population, which has been steadily increasing but is still less than 2 percent.[46] The best explanation for this phenomenon is that Mormons are concentrated in Utah and neighboring western states, the very places where most Mormons win elections. Also, Mormons are mostly middle-class people with access to the educational and financial resources that matter in politics.

Outside the Judeo-Christian orbit, the United States has experienced significant growth in the population of Muslims, Hindus, and Buddhists since 1960. Although none of these groups has reached the size of the Jewish or Mormon voting populations, their share of the electorate would warrant representation in Congress. Yet currently there are just two Muslims, two Buddhists, and no Hindus in Congress, and until 2007, no member of any of these faiths had ever served.[47] Muslims may have the greatest potential to fill their representational gap because their numbers are growing quickly in the United States, but as a heavily immigrant community they will probably need to become more numerous, more strategically concentrated, and better organized to do so.

The U.S. Senate provides an interesting laboratory for analyzing the representation of different religious faiths. The Senate features a decidedly more elite religious profile than the House of Representatives. Mainline Protestants comprise the largest religious group in the Senate, accounting for roughly a third of the entire membership but just 18 percent of the U.S. population.[48] Episcopalians historically have been overrepresented in the Senate, and this continues to be true: Six senators (6 percent) are Episcopalian, even though the Episcopal Church claims just 1.5 percent of the U.S. population.[49] Catholics are the second–best represented religious group in Congress with 26 percent of the membership, followed by Jews at 13 percent and Baptists with 8 percent; by and large, evangelicals are underrepresented relative to their share of the population.[50]

The crucial issue, however, is not about the declared affiliation of members of Congress. What matters is whether Catholic, mainline Protestant, Jewish, or Baptist members of Congress constitute distinct voting blocs. The evidence on this is mixed at best. A study of Catholic legislators in the late 1950s, for example, found some evidence of Catholic solidarity in congressional voting, but only at the margins of normal party voting.[51] Mary Hanna's study of Catholics in the 1970s showed that Catholic members of Congress were not even aware of their own sizable numbers, so they were definitely not cohesive in their votes.[52] This appears to be true today as well. It is not really surprising because partisan differences, varying regions, specific constituencies, and personal perspectives diffuse the unity and impact of any religious group in Congress.[53] One of the few exceptions seems to be unified Jewish support for Israel, but beyond that, religion-based issue cohesiveness disappears.[54] With regard to the congressional delegations of other religious groups, it is hard to find even a single unifying issue. Even though one study does suggest that the most religiously committed evangelicals in Congress tend to coalesce around issues associated with the Christian Right, there is considerable partisan and ideological difference even among evangelical Protestant legislators.[55] In short, political diversity reigns.

Even acknowledging this diversity, we still must ask if religious affiliation might make a subtler impact on congressional politics. After all, affiliation is often less important than *how* one experiences faith.[56] If only we could get inside the minds of members of Congress, we might see how their religious worldviews (as opposed to their nominal religious affiliations) shape their roll call votes. Surely this would be the best guide of all as to how religion affects politics on Capitol Hill. This was exactly the premise of an ambitious study by Peter Benson and Dorothy Williams titled *Religion on Capitol Hill.*[57]

The authors conducted in-depth interviews with a large sample of members of Congress in the 1980s. The religious themes explored in the interviews reached beyond affiliation to the personal experience of faith. How did members of Congress understand God or religion—as comforting or challenging? As restricting or releasing? As an individual or a member of a community? What did they see as the central demand of their religion—reverence for God or service to fellow humans? How did they view God—as a judge or a loving presence? Benson and Williams discovered that members of Congress fell into six religious "types": legalistic, self-concerned, integrated, people-concerned, nontraditional, and nominal. These categories did not correlate with particular religious denominations or political parties, but they proved widely predictive of voting behaviors. In fact, members' religious attitudes predicted their voting patterns better than did their party affiliations. Religious worldviews clearly structured members' value systems and their political behaviors.

What Benson and Williams help us appreciate is the complexity of religious experience and its relationship with politics. Thus a "legalistic" Catholic member of Congress may have more in common with a Protestant colleague of the same type than with a fellow Catholic whose faith experience falls into a different category.[58] As Benson and Williams and subsequent scholars, especially political scientist Elizabeth Oldmixon, have shown, members of Congress are not empty vessels. Rather, they bring to their jobs years of socialization and religious experiences that mold their worldviews. Those views, in turn, are likely to contribute, consciously and unconsciously, to their politics.[59]

Another way to study the impact of religion on Congress is to examine specific members for whom religion matters a great deal. As in American society, religious convictions among members of Congress take a wide range of forms, sometimes even within the same religious tradition or denomination. These expressions of religious belief and devotion often help us make sense of a member's political actions.

One illustration concerns minority faiths. Mormons in Congress, for example, tend to mirror the strong commitment to conservatism on cultural and family issues that exists within the LDS Church as a whole. A prominent example is Sen. Orrin Hatch (R–Utah), who has been a vocal critic of the role of judicial "activism" in supporting abortion rights and other liberal causes. For example, in 2009 he expressed various concerns about Supreme Court Justice Sonia Sotomayor's approach to jurisprudence during her confirmation process. One ought not to assume that all Mormon members of Congress are conservatives, however. Sen. Harry Reid (D–Nevada) is a Mormon and a Democrat who is known for his strong commitment to environmental protection, stem cell research, and gun control.[60]

Offering a contrasting case are Jews, who tend to be liberal Democrats, although it is often hard to sort out the ethnic from the religious influences. That is not the case, however, for the most celebrated Jewish legislator, Sen. Joseph Lieberman (I–Connecticut). Lieberman became a national figure as the result of his 2000 vice-presidential nomination and subsequent bid for the Democratic presidential nomination in 2004. An Orthodox Jew, Lieberman's political liberalism is tempered by his high-profile efforts to have warning labels placed on CDs featuring sexually explicit and violent lyrics, his openness to school choice and similar policies, and his supportive position on the war in Iraq (though not its aftermath). Each of these positions, in fact, reflects his Jewish orthodoxy. Meanwhile, his support for abortion rights, domestic-partnership benefits for same-sex couples, universal healthcare coverage, and other policies have endeared him to liberal groups. Lieberman made many enemies within the Democratic Party in 2008 when he openly endorsed and campaigned for the Republican nominee for president, Sen. John McCain (R–Arizona). Although Lieberman now technically classifies himself as an Independent (after losing in the Democratic primary election during his 2006 reelection bid, he won in the general election as an Independent), he caucuses with the Democratic Party in the Senate. At a minimum, it is safe to classify Lieberman as among the most unusual of all nominal Democrats in the Senate.[61]

The Republican Party has been particularly keen on moving religiously committed legislators into prominent roles. Rep. Eric Cantor (R–Virginia) is the sole Jewish Republican in the House of Representatives and is among the highest-ranking members of the leadership team of the House Republican caucus. He is distinct from most Jews in his fiscal conservatism, pro-life position, and support for school prayer. But he shares with Joe Lieberman and many other Jewish legislators a passionate pro-Israel stance.[62] Another example is Sen. Jim DeMint (R–South Carolina), regarded by many as one of the most conservative individuals in all of Congress. An evangelical Presbyterian, he has emerged as a key spokesperson for moral traditionalism. DeMint is an especially strong supporter of school prayer and a staunch opponent of abortion. He ruffled feathers during his 2004 Senate campaign when he contended in a debate: "If a person is a practicing homosexual, they should not be teaching in our schools."[63] DeMint apologized for this statement but did not retract it, and in 2009 he emerged as the leading congressional opponent of an effort to cover gay and lesbian people in hate-crimes legislation.[64]

As with DeMint, many Republicans' religious convictions contribute to their conservatism on hot-button moral issues. But for some members, religious convictions simultaneously lead them to champion causes commonly associated with liberal groups, such as international human rights. Consider the case of Rep. Frank Wolf (R–Virginia). A conservative evangelical, he has focused attention on the spread of gambling in the United States, which is no surprise for a religious traditionalist. But Wolf is also one of the House's leading crusaders for human rights. *The Washington Post* profiled him as the capitol's first "bleeding heart conservative," a human rights champion who "has traveled the world in search of famine, death and war, trying to find ways to help."[65] He sees his career in Congress as a response to the maxim, "To whom much is given, much is required." Wolf cochairs the bipartisan Tom Lantos Human Rights Commission, named for the late Rep. Tom Lantos (D–California), who was the only Holocaust survivor ever to serve in the U.S. Congress. In this capacity, he has held hearings, conducted fact-finding trips (sometimes incognito), toured foreign prisons, and secured the release of dissidents. Wolf takes inspiration from the martyrdom of Dietrich Bonhoeffer, the German Lutheran pastor who opposed the Nazis. For Wolf, Christian faith demands that he do all he can for the "Dietrich Bonhoeffers" around the world.[66]

A good friend of Wolf's, Rep. Chris Smith (R–New Jersey), presents another illustrative case. A devout Catholic, Smith traces his political convictions to his upbringing in the faith. As the former director of New Jersey Right to Life, Smith entered Congress in 1980 as a fierce opponent of abortion, which led some observers to lump him in with conservative adherents of the Christian Right. But throughout his career Smith generally has been supportive of labor unions, government aid for impoverished children, international relief programs, and global human rights. For Smith this blend of issue positions reflects his Catholicism. Describing himself as a "Matthew 25 Christian," Smith sees both his pro-life and international humanitarian work as flowing from the same injunction ("Whatsoever you do to the least of my brethren you do to me"). When Republicans took control of the House after the 1994 elections, Smith became chair of the International Relations Subcommittee on Human Rights. In subsequent years Smith has held hundreds of hearings on human rights abuses and has sponsored legislation on such diverse issues as promotion of religious freedom, support for victims of torture, sanctions against human trafficking, and Sudanese peace.[67]

Another interesting case in the Senate is Sam Brownback (R–Kansas). He came to Congress with the new Republican class of 1994 and quickly lived up to its conservative profile on economic and social issues. A Methodist when he entered the Senate, Brownback converted to Catholicism in 2003, partly out of admiration for the humanitarian work of the late Mother Teresa. He has worked closely with a range of conservative religious groups, for example, to restrict stem cell research and ban human cloning. But his record on international humanitarian causes has earned him respect among liberals. He was the principal Senate sponsor for major legislation on human trafficking with the late Sen. Paul Wellstone (D–Minnesota); peacemaking in Sudan; North Korean refugees with the late Sen. Ted Kennedy (D–Massachusetts), and Iranian democracy. On the domestic front he cosponsored legislation with civil rights legend Rep. John Lewis (D–Georgia) to create a National Museum of African American History. To Brownback this latter act made sense because he traces his roots to antebellum evangelical abolitionists in Kansas, but his religion is also a central inspiration.[68]

Among Democrats, few representatives reflect the connection between faith and politics as intensely as Tony Hall (D–Ohio), who left Congress in 2003 and went on to serve as ambassador to the United Nations Agencies for Food and Agriculture. A born-again Christian, he is best known as a liberal crusader against world hunger, a cause that he sees as flowing from his Christian calling. He has toured some of the most famine-plagued regions of the world to fight for international relief. In 1993 he even undertook a personal hunger strike to pressure fellow House members to reverse plans to abolish a committee that focused on fighting hunger in the United States and abroad.[69]

Given what we know about the heritage of black churches in the United States, we might expect many African American members of Congress to bring religious influences to their legislative work. Indeed, some black members of Congress, such as former Rep. Floyd Flake (D–New York), have also worked as ministers. But sifting out religious influence from racial concerns is very difficult. Consider the case of

Rep. Donald Payne (D–New Jersey), who is an influential member of the Congressional Black Caucus and chairs the House Subcommittee on Africa. A devout Baptist, he circulates through black congregations to drum up support for his causes, particularly African development aid. But is this work driven by his religious convictions or his sense of solidarity with black Africa? Probably both.[70]

The most celebrated liberal in Congress today may well be the first woman Speaker of the House, Nancy Pelosi (D–California). Strongly supportive of abortion rights, gay rights, funding to combat the spread of HIV/AIDS, and assorted social programs, she is tagged as a "San Francisco liberal" by Republican critics. But Pelosi's religious background and identity seem to set her apart from that label. Pelosi was born Nancy D'Alesandro, the daughter of a legendary politician who essentially ran Baltimore city politics. She still describes herself as a "conservative Catholic," by which she means that her strict Catholic upbringing—observant, respectful of elders—forged aspects of her character. At a time when the old norm of the large Catholic family was becoming rare, Pelosi raised five children as a full-time mother before embarking on her political career. These experiences probably facilitate unusual political alliances. For example, she has championed the cause of persecuted Christians, a cause célèbre of evangelicals, in part out of her concern for the treatment of Catholics in China.[71] Nevertheless, Pelosi has attracted the scorn of Catholic leaders up to and including Pope Benedict XVI for her unyielding pro-choice position on abortion.[72]

These profiles point to the many possibilities for alliances among members of Congress—and other elites, for that matter—who differ ideologically, and that is just what we see. For years Pelosi and Wolf led the fight against granting the People's Republic of China permanent normal trade relations status with the United States and admission to the World Trade Organization without human rights improvement. To promote the broader cause of human rights they have traveled abroad to investigate abuses, cosponsored legislation, and planned strategy together. We see the same kind of collaboration around the ongoing genocide in the Darfur region of Sudan, in which Smith and Payne have joined forces to back legislation that business groups opposed. In the Senate Lieberman and Brownback have teamed up to curb violence and misogyny in movies and rock music, while collaborating on a host of international humanitarian initiatives.[73]

Sorting out religious motives from other factors, of course, is impossible, but probing these alliances suggests that the impact of religion in Congress is far from trivial. Moreover, a testament to the importance of religion, whatever its guise, is the thriving religious culture on Capitol Hill. Full-time chaplains work for the

House and Senate, spending many hours counseling harried politicians. Members of Congress also attend various area churches and religious fellowships, and Capitol Hill Bible studies have proliferated. Often these groups cross party lines and allow members of Congress to ease the frustrations and stresses of political life by praying together, sharing their stories, and offering each other solace. To be sure, such activities blend with lives that also contain plenty of strategic calculation and hardball politics. Religious practice on Capitol Hill is, like so much else, complex and mixed.

RELIGION AND OTHER POLITICAL ELITES

Outside the White House and the halls of Congress are many other political elites who have a keen interest in the interaction of religion and politics. Consider the proliferating think tanks and policy institutes that contribute to the debates between partisans in Washington and elsewhere, as well as organizations that fund efforts to understand religion in public life (Box 6.1). Here, too, we see evidence of a modest religious presence that has made a difference. Important examples include the Ethics and Public Policy Center, the Center for Public Justice, the Center for American

---

BOX 6.1   PATRONS OF RELIGION IN PUBLIC LIFE

Much of the public activity and discussion surrounding religion and politics today would not happen without funding from a small number of large philanthropic organizations. Since the early 1980s, foundations such as Lilly, Templeton, and the Pew Charitable Trusts have provided tens of millions of dollars to the exploration of religion's role in public life. Many of the patrons who created these foundations were themselves deeply committed religious believers. The late J. Howard Pew, for example, head of the Sun Oil Company from 1912 to 1947 and a lifelong Presbyterian, established the Pew Charitable Trusts in 1948 with his siblings to support evangelical parachurch organizations and other religion-based enterprises, including the evangelical magazine *Christianity Today* and Gordon-Conwell Theological Seminary. Today the Pew Charitable Trusts actively supports academic scholarship on religion, especially work focused on evangelicals. The Trusts also supports the Pew Forum on Religion & Public Life, which brings together a wide range of intellectuals "to promote a deeper understanding of how religion shapes the ideas and institutions of American society."

Source: http://www.pewforum.org; Michael S. Hamilton and Johanna G. Yngvason, "Patrons of the Evangelical Mind," *Christianity Today*, July 8, 2002, 42.

Progress, Faith in Public Life, and the Institute on Religion and Democracy in Washington, D.C., as well as the Institute on Religion and Public Life in New York. These institutes conduct policy seminars and produce a flood of publications, including journals. Aware that religion must make its case to skeptics, these groups make a difference by offering an intellectual basis for an active role for religious faith in modern policy debates. They also provide ideas and intellectual support for their political allies.

An arena where religious influence often seems suppressed is in the upper echelons of the executive branch of the U.S. government. Bureaucratic decisions are rarely made in overtly religious contexts, to the extent that the federal bureaucracy has at times been accused of being "anti-religious."[74] Public administration often does not lend itself easily to applying faith to politics and does not often attract employees who are particularly interested in this goal. Moreover, administrative leaders often come from elite educational backgrounds, which we know to be more secular than those of the general population. Still, administrators and managers must address religion in some instances, even if they do not do so willingly.

The courts play an important role in the American policymaking process, far more so than in other nations. Judicial review is a powerful tool, and many judges do not hesitate to use it when they see fit. At the level of the U.S. Supreme Court, we have little evidence about whether—or to what extent—religious convictions influence judicial decisions, partly due to a lack of access to the very private, even reclusive, justices. It is nonetheless remarkable that no fewer than six of the nine current Supreme Court justices (Samuel Alito, Anthony Kennedy, John Roberts, Antonin Scalia, Sonia Sotomayor, and Clarence Thomas) are Catholic, whereas two are Jewish (Stephen Breyer and Ruth Bader Ginsberg) and just one (John Paul Stevens) is Protestant. Although no systematic research has been conducted on the effect of religion on Supreme Court jurisprudence, at least one study of lower courts suggests a modest impact of faith on judicial decision-making, especially among the most religiously committed evangelicals.[75]

Finally, state and local politics, which are arenas of increasing importance, may be influenced by the religious makeup of those holding offices, whether elected or appointed. From school board members to governors, state and local elites make a profound difference on the ordinary lives of citizens—perhaps more so than any official of the federal government. Unfortunately, we do not have much systematic information on the religious affiliations and attitudes of governors, state legislators, or other local officials, much less on whether their religious backgrounds matter in policymaking terms.[76]

At the state level we do see some evidence that religion plays a role, albeit a constrained one, in public policymaking. One example of a religious current in state politics involves abortion, the debate over which intensified after a 1989 U.S. Supreme Court decision gave new latitude to the states to regulate abortion. Accounts of those battles reveal the importance of the attitudes of governors and state legislators. When Catholic and evangelical groups lobbied in various states for more restrictive abortion statutes, success depended in part on the views of elected officials and the political cultures that produced them. Thus restrictive abortion statutes were passed in Idaho and Utah, where Mormons are concentrated; in Pennsylvania, with its sizable traditional Catholic population; and in Louisiana, where traditional Catholics and conservative evangelicals joined forces. Legislators in those states were sympathetic to pro-life religious activists because they shared similar worldviews. On the other hand, legislators in other states that support liberal or libertarian political cultures have largely ignored antiabortion lobbying.

RELIGION AND CULTURAL ELITES

Many more people beyond political elites shape American public life. The elite press plays a highly significant role in shaping American social and political discourses yet are presumed by many to be bastions of secularism. One matter of considerable debate is whether the elite press pays too little attention to religion, perhaps because its reporters and editors might be unaware of or hostile toward religion.[77] Some journalists, at least, are either religious themselves or serious about studying the religious world. This fact is exemplified in the committed membership of the Religion Newswriters Association. *The New York Times*, *The Washington Post*, *Newsweek*, *Time*, and the Associated Press, among many others, all employ skilled and knowledgeable journalists as full-time religion beat writers. PBS features a weekly half-hour television program focused solely on religious issues, *Religion & Ethics NewsWeekly*. Former presidential candidate and ordained Southern Baptist minster Mike Huckabee hosts his own television show on the Fox News Channel (Box 6.2). And there are several top religion news clearinghouses on the Internet, such as BeliefNet.com and ReligionNews.com. The journalists who work for these media outlets typically have good access to religious activists, which can provide activists with a platform from which to articulate their message to a broader public. In addition to religion beat writers, many journalists write about politics for religious publications such as *Christianity Today* and *The National Catholic Reporter*. Moreover, media coverage of some aspects of religion is increasing, especially topics concerning

Islam. Despite this evidence, however, there is still good reason to share Joan Beck's complaint that "religion is the most under-reported story of our time."[78]

Another set of elites who may have substantial influence on the American public, and thus on its religious and political discourses, are those who create popular media, including movies, television, music, books, and magazines. The intersections between religion, politics, and popular culture have not stimulated much research.[79] Nevertheless, we easily can observe the content and reception of popular media in the United States. Some might suggest that the world of mass culture is secular or even hostile to religion, but the real story is much more complicated.

Consider, first, motion pictures. Hollywood has released relatively few major movies in the past two decades that are explicitly religious, and plenty that ridicule

BOX 6.2   MIKE HUCKABEE: A PASTOR RUNS FOR PRESIDENT

Former Arkansas governor Mike Huckabee's 2008 presidential candidacy generated a substantial amount of support among evangelical Protestants, who appreciated his background as an ordained Southern Baptist minister and his frank talk about the relationship of faith to his politics. Politics is Huckabee's second career; he spent twelve years at the pulpit in Texas and Arkansas before entering Arkansas politics in the early 1990s. Some of the first grassroots supporters of his presidential campaign were evangelical homeschoolers in Iowa, who worked tirelessly in 2007 to spread the word about his little-known candidacy to fellow social conservatives. Huckabee gathered substantial momentum and won the Iowa Republican caucuses in convincing fashion despite Mitt Romney's concerted effort to woo the GOP's coveted social conservative constituency. One of Huckabee's campaign ads in Iowa specifically touted him as a "Christian leader," which raised the hackles of many advocates of church-state separation—and led some to accuse him of subtly generating suspicion of Romney's Mormon faith. Had it not been for the relatively strong showing of fellow social conservative Fred Thompson in South Carolina's Republican primary, who drew most of his votes away from Huckabee, he may well have emerged as the GOP's 2008 presidential nominee. After exiting the presidential race, Huckabee moved on to work as a political commentator on the Fox News Channel and ABC Radio. He remains an important figure to watch in Republican politics.

Source: Holly Bailey and Michael Isikoff, "A Pastor's True Calling," *Newsweek*, December 17, 2007, 34; Michael D. Shear and Perry Bacon, "Iowa Chooses Huckabee, Obama; Evangelicals Fuel Win over Romney," *The Washington Post*, January 4, 2008, A1; Peter Slevin and Perry Bacon, "Home-School Ties Aided Huckabee's Iowa Rise: Early Backers Rallied Conservative Network," *The Washington Post*, December 17, 2007, A1.

religion. But there have been notable exceptions, including *Sister Act* (1992), *The Apostle* (1997), *The Green Mile* (1999), *Bruce Almighty* (2003), *The Passion of the Christ* (2004), and *Doubt* (2008). A larger number of Hollywood productions emphasize broader spiritual themes, such as a focus on redemption, as in *The Shawshank Redemption* (1994), or the triumph of basic goodness, as in *Forrest Gump* (1994), and some religious critics, liberal and conservative alike, assess many secular movies as decent, quality entertainment.[80] Still, only a small fraction of Hollywood movies are religious or arguably even spiritual (although in America "spirituality" is a famously elastic term), and critics such as Michael Medved and others insist that Hollywood elites use the movies (not to mention television where evangelical religion especially often takes a beating, for example consistently in HBO and Showtime productions) to undermine traditional religious values.[81]

There is yet another side to the story as well: the growing field of religious media. The marketplace has supported a remarkable demand for Christian-sympathetic popular media through the large network of Christian bookstores around the country. Two popular contemporary examples are film adaptations of the best-selling Left Behind book series and "Veggie Tales," a children's video series that recounts biblical stories with a cast of animated vegetables. There are even Christian video-sharing websites that present themselves as alternatives to YouTube.com, such as Tangle.com. No other medium, however, is more important for religious communication today than radio.[82] One recent survey suggests that in any given month Americans are more likely to use radio, television, and other religious mass media than they are to attend a religious service.[83] Most notably, James Dobson is perhaps better known for his top-rated radio show *Focus on the Family* than he is for the identically named Christian conservative interest group he founded and headed for more than 30 years.

By all accounts, these are also halcyon days for those in the Christian Booksellers Association, not least because of the Left Behind series, which has sold more than 65 million copies since 1995. Besides *The Prayer of Jabez* and *The Purpose Driven Life*, nonfiction bestsellers in 2001 and 2003, respectively, many lines of Christian fiction are now available. So is a vast array of devotional books and many reflections on marriage, family, and children. Scripture-filled tomes, not to mention myriad versions and forms of various Holy Scriptures, continue to sell well. There is also much more to buy in Christian bookstores: diet books for the pious, Last Supper jigsaw puzzles, and biblical action hero figures, among other things.[84] Meanwhile, thousands of religious groups are represented on Facebook, and a wide variety of religious applications are available for the iPhone.

There is also the substantial religious magazine business, not just the "serious" magazines such as *Christianity Today, The Christian Century, Tikkun,* or countless denominational publications, but also such magazines as *Christian Computing* and *Christian MotorSports Illustrated.* All of these magazines, and many more like them, have websites, which comprise just a small part of the vast Internet universe of religious popular media available today.[85]

Religion also figures prominently in the secular world of professional sports. Prayer circles that include members of both teams are a common sight at the conclusion of National Football League games. Some Major League Baseball players choose contemporary Christian songs as their "walk-up" music when they step into the batter's box. The Fellowship of Christian Athletes (FCA) works to bring an evangelical Protestant witness to professional and amateur athletes alike. FCA has relationships with several high-profile professional athletes and coaches who make it a point to incorporate their religious commitments into their public lives. For example, quarterback Kurt Warner is known for his evangelical Christianity, as is pitcher John Smoltz; former NFL head coach Tony Dungy's faith-focused memoir, *Quiet Strength,* topped *The New York Times*'s bestseller list in 2007.

Finally, the music industry also features two large and flourishing religious sectors: gospel music and contemporary Christian music. Gospel is a distinctively American form of music with a long and distinguished history. It informs nearly every American form of music, from blues to jazz to rock and roll and hip hop. Its audience is primarily African American, but its musical and cultural influence reaches across racial and ethnic lines.[86] An even larger, if significantly different, audience exists for contemporary Christian music. In its innumerable forms and fashions, this music mimics every variety of secular rock music, though its lyrics, of course, are different. Some groups are explicitly Christian in their lyrics; others, such as Jars of Clay, are less so. On the whole, the Christian music business is flourishing; for example, the iTunes Store features an extensive Christian and gospel section. The genre of country music has long been filled with religious references and themes as well. Indeed, at one point in 2003, ten of the top sixty country songs expressed religious faith, and Randy Travis's "Three Wooden Crosses" became the first country single from an expressly Christian label to head the charts.

CONCLUSION

The religious views of political and cultural elites do matter. For some, faith clearly shapes worldviews and orientations to politics. But having a religious faith, much less sharing the same faith, does not necessarily engender predictable political views—far from it. Moreover, even those who may belong to the same religious tradition will not always interpret their faith in the same way, whereas people from very different faith backgrounds may share identical positions on public issues. At the same time, religion is not a major part of the calculi of many political and cultural elites. Many other factors—party, constituency, the marketplace, and personal experiences, to name a few—often play a greater role in political priorities and strategies. Nor should we ignore the growing evidence of indifference to religion familiar at elite universities and colleges or the overtly hostile presence of activist groups such as the Freedom from Religion Foundation. In different fashions these realities are also part of the story of elites and religion today in the United States. The picture is complicated, and simplistic assertions about uniform elite hostility to religion hide and distort that complexity and enjoin us to continue to analyze the ways in which elites experience religion or faith in their lives and work.

FURTHER READING

Benson, Peter L., and Dorothy L. Williams. *Religion on Capitol Hill: Myths and Realities*. New York: Oxford University Press, 1982. A pioneering study of how members of Congress experience their faith and connect it with politics.

Espinosa, Gaston. *Religion and the American Presidency: George Washington to George W. Bush*. New York: Columbia University Press, 2009. A fresh new collection of analyses of the role of religion in various presidencies.

Leege, David C., Kenneth D. Wald, Brian S. Krueger, and Paul D. Mueller. *The Politics of Cultural Differences: Social Change and Voter Mobilization in the Post–New Deal Period*. Princeton: Princeton University Press, 2002. An important study by astute scholars of religion in public life.

Lindsay, D. Michael. *Faith in the Halls of Power: How Evangelicals Joined the American Elite*. New York: Oxford University Press, 2007. Massive study of evangelical elites in the United States.

Oldmixon, Elizabeth Anne. *Uncompromising Positions: God, Sex, and the U.S. House of Representatives*. Washington, DC: Georgetown University Press, 2005. An outstanding analysis of the legislative ramifications of religious and cultural conflict.

Rozell, Mark J., and Gleaves Whitney, eds. *Religion and the American Presidency*. New York: Palgrave Macmillan, 2007. A collection of essays that address the role of religion in various presidencies.

Schmalzbauer, John. *People of Faith: Religious Conviction in American Journalism and Higher Education*. Ithaca, NY: Cornell University Press, 2003. An excellent introduction to its subject.

NOTES

1. Allen D. Hertzke, "Faith and Access: Religious Constituencies and the Washington Elites," in *Religion and Political Behavior in the United States*, ed. Ted G. Jelen (New York: Praeger, 1989). On the broad topic of religion and the American presidency, see Gaston Espinosa, ed., *Religion and the American Presidency: George Washington to George W. Bush* (New York: Columbia University Press, 2009); Mark J. Rozell and Gleaves Whitney, eds., *Religion and the American Presidency* (New York: Palgrave Macmillan, 2007).

2. Charles Colson, *Kingdoms in Conflict* (Grand Rapids, MI: Zondervan, 1987).

3. David Kuo, *Tempting Faith: An Inside Story of Political Seduction* (New York: Simon & Schuster, 2006).

4. David C. Leege, Kenneth D. Wald, Brian S. Krueger, and Paul D. Mueller, *The Politics of Cultural Differences: Social Change and Voter Mobilization in the Post–New Deal Period* (Princeton: Princeton University Press, 2002).

5. Vanessa B. Beasley, *You, the People: American National Identity in Presidential Rhetoric* (College Station, TX: Texas A&M Press, 2004); Richard V. Pierard and Robert D. Linder, *Civil Religion and the Presidency* (Grand Rapids, MI: Zondervan, 1988).

6. Thomas J. Carty, "Religion and the Presidency of John F. Kennedy," in *Religion and the American Presidency: George Washington to George W. Bush.*

7. Robert S. Alley, *So Help Me God: Religion and the Presidency, Wilson to Nixon* (Richmond, VA: John Knox Press, 1972).

8. Billy Graham, *Just As I Am: The Autobiography of Billy Graham* (New York: Walker, 1997); Steven P. Miller, *Billy Graham and the Rise of the Republican South* (Philadelphia: University of Pennsylvania Press, 2009).

9. Robert Booth Fowler, *Religion and Politics in America* (Metuchen, NJ: Scarecrow Press, 1985), 113–118.

10. Ibid. See also Graham, *Just As I Am.*

11. D. Jason Berggren and Nicol C. Rae, "Jimmy Carter and George W. Bush: Faith, Foreign Policy, and an Evangelical Presidential Style," *Presidential Studies Quarterly* 36 (2006), 606–632; Jimmy Carter, *Living Faith* (New York: Random House, 1996).

12. See Charles O. Jones, *The Trusteeship Presidency: Jimmy Carter and the United States Congress* (Baton Rouge: Louisiana State University Press, 1988).

13. Carter, *Living Faith*; Kenneth E. Morris, "Religion and the Presidency of Jimmy Carter," in *Religion and the American Presidency: George Washington to George W. Bush*; Jeff Walz, "Jimmy Carter and the Politics of Faith," in *Religion and the American Presidency.*

14. Ibid.

15. See, for example, Frank J. Gaffney, "Tyranny's Enabler," *The Washington Times*, April 15, 2008, A16.

16. Clyde Wilcox and Carin Larson, *Onward Christian Soldiers? The Religious Right in American Politics*, 3rd ed. (Boulder: Westview Press, 2006).

17. Paul Kengor, *God and Ronald Reagan: A Spiritual Life* (New York: HarperCollins, 2004); Wilcox and Larson, *Onward Christian Soldiers?*

18. Kengor, *God and Ronald Reagan*.

19. Robert Booth Fowler, "The Failure of the Religious Right," in *The Religious New Right in American Politics*, ed. Michael Cromartie (Washington, DC: Ethics and Public Policy Center, 1993).

20. Jo Renee Formicola, *John Paul II: Prophetic Politician* (Washington, DC: Georgetown University Press, 2002).

21. Paul Kengor, *The Crusader: Ronald Reagan and the Fall of Communism* (New York: HarperPerennial, 2007); James Mann, *The Rebellion of Ronald Reagan: A History of the End of the Cold War* (New York: Viking, 2009).

22. Kjell O. Lejon, "Religion and the Presidency of George H. W. Bush," in *Religion and the American Presidency: George Washington to George W. Bush*.

23. Geoffrey Layman, *The Great Divide: Religious and Cultural Conflict in American Party Politics* (New York: Columbia University Press, 2001).

24. Wilcox and Larson, *Onward Christian Soldiers?*

25. Paul Kengor, *God and Hillary Clinton: A Spiritual Life* (New York: HarperCollins, 2007).

26. Layman, *The Great Divide*; Laura R. Olson and John C. Green, "The Religion Gap," *PS: Political Science & Politics* 39 (2006), 455–459.

27. David Aikman, *Man of Faith: The Spiritual Journey of George W. Bush* (Nashville: Thomas Nelson, 2004); Paul Kengor, *God and George W. Bush: A Spiritual Life* (New York: HarperCollins, 2004); Stephen Mansfield, *The Faith of George W. Bush* (New York: Tarcher, 2003).

28. Ibid.

29. Berggren and Rae, "Jimmy Carter and George W. Bush."

30. Amy E. Black, Douglas L. Koopman, and David K. Ryden, *Of Little Faith: The Politics of George W. Bush's Faith-Based Initiatives* (Washington, DC: Georgetown University Press, 2004).

31. On the Bush Doctrine and the religious overtones inherent in Bush's foreign policy, see Ivo H. Daalder and James M. Lindsay, *America Unbound: The Bush Revolution in Foreign Policy* (Washington, DC: Brookings Institution, 2003); Kevin R. den Dulk, "Evangelical 'Internationalists' and U.S. Foreign Policy During the Bush Administration," in *Religion*

and the Bush Presidency, ed. Mark J. Rozell and Gleaves Whitney (New York: Palgrave Macmillan, 2007); Michael J. Mazarr, "George W. Bush, Idealist," *International Affairs* 79 (2003), 503–522; Ilan Peleg, *The Legacy of George W. Bush's Foreign Policy: Moving Beyond Neoconservatism* (Boulder: Westview Press, 2009); Bob Woodward, *Bush at War* (New York: Simon & Schuster, 2002). As a small sampling of the criticism aroused by the evangelicalism of Bush's foreign policy, see Jane Lampman, "New Scrutiny of Role of Religion in Bush's Policies," *The Christian Science Monitor*, March 17, 2003; Ewen MacAskill, "George Bush: 'God Told Me to End the Tyranny in Iraq,'" *The Guardian*, October 7, 2005.

32. For personal accounts of Obama's religious journey, see Barack Obama, *The Audacity of Hope: Thoughts on Reclaiming the American Dream* (New York: Three Rivers Press, 2006), chap. 6; Barack Obama, *Dreams from My Father: A Story of Race and Inheritance* (New York: Three Rivers Press, 2004); Barack Obama, "My Spiritual Journey," *Time*, October 16, 2006.

33. Jodi Kantor, "A Candidate, His Minister and the Search for Faith," *The New York Times*, April 30, 2007; Obama, *Dreams from My Father*, chap. 14.

34. On Jeremiah Wright and the dustup during the 2008 presidential campaign, see Steven Gray, "The Unretirement of Reverend Wright," *Time*, June 4, 2008; Jodi Kantor, "Obama Denounces Statements of His Pastor as 'Inflammatory'," *The New York Times*, March 15, 2008. See also Amy Sullivan, "The Obamas Find a Church Home—Away from Home," *Time*, June 29, 2009.

35. Adam Kradel, "Using the Lord's Name: The Use and Impact of Presidential Religious Rhetoric" (PhD dissertation, University of Wisconsin–Madison, 2008); Colleen J. Shogan, *The Moral Rhetoric of American Presidents* (College Station, TX: Texas A&M University Press, 2006).

36. Leege et al., *The Politics of Cultural Differences*.

37. Pew Forum on Religion & Public Life, *Faith on the Hill: The Religious Affiliations of Members of Congress*, http://pewforum.org/docs/?DocID=379 (2008).

38. In January 1960, *Congressional Quarterly Weekly Report* began providing a table reflecting the religious affiliations of members of Congress.

39. Pew Forum, *Faith on the Hill*.

40. Ibid.

41. Ibid.

42. Elizabeth A. Oldmixon and William Hudson, "Catholic Republicans and Conflicting Impulses in the 109th Congress," *Politics & Religion* 1 (2008), 113–136.

43. Pew Forum, *Faith on the Hill*.

44. John C. Green and James L. Guth, "Religion, Representatives, and Roll Calls," *Legislative Studies Quarterly* 16 (November 1991), 571–584; James L. Guth and Lyman A. Kell-

stedt, "Religion and Congress," in *In God We Trust: Religion and American Political Life,* ed. Corwin Smidt (Grand Rapids, MI: Baker Academic, 2001); Elizabeth Anne Oldmixon, *Uncompromising Positions: God, Sex, and the U.S. House of Representatives* (Washington, DC: Georgetown University Press, 2005); Elizabeth A. Oldmixon and Brian Calfano, "The Religious Dynamics of Moral Decision-Making in the U.S. House of Representatives, 1993–2002," *Journal for the Scientific Study of Religion* 46 (2007), 55–70; Lauren Edwards Smith, Laura R. Olson, and Jeffrey A. Fine, "Substantive Religious Representation in the U.S. Senate: Voting Alignment with the Family Research Council," *Political Research Quarterly* 62 (2009), forthcoming.

45. Pew Forum, *Faith on the Hill.*

46. Ibid.

47. Ibid.

48. Ibid.; and Pew Forum on Religion & Public Life, *U.S. Religious Landscape Study,* http://religions.pewforum.org/affiliations (2008).

49. Pew Forum, *Faith on the Hill.*

50. Ibid.

51. John H. Fenton, *The Catholic Vote* (New Orleans, LA: Hauser Press, 1960).

52. Mary Hanna, *Catholics and American Politics* (Cambridge, MA: Harvard University Press, 1979).

53. Oldmixon, *Uncompromising Positions*; David Yamane and Elizabeth A. Oldmixon, "Affiliation, Salience, Advocacy: Three Religious Factors in Public Policy-Making," *Legislative Studies Quarterly* 31 (2006), 433–460.

54. Elizabeth A. Oldmixon, Beth Rosenson, and Kenneth D. Wald, "Conflict over Israel: The Role of Religion, Race, Party and Ideology in the U.S. House of Representatives, 1997–2002," *Terrorism and Political Violence* 17 (2005), 407–426; Beth Rosenson, Elizabeth A. Oldmixon, and Kenneth Wald, "U.S. Senators' Support for Israel Examined Through Sponsorship/Co-Sponsorship Decisions, 1993–2002: The Influence of Elite and Constituent Factors," *Foreign Policy Analysis* 5 (2009), 73–91.

55. Guth and Kellstedt, "Religion and Congress," 229. See also Peter L. Benson and Dorothy L. Williams, *Religion on Capitol Hill: Myths and Realities* (New York: Oxford University Press, 1982); Oldmixon, *Uncompromising Positions.*

56. Leege et al., *The Politics of Cultural Differences.*

57. Benson and Williams, *Religion on Capitol Hill.*

58. See also Oldmixon, *Uncompromising Positions.* Benson and Williams's work presages the literature on the declining relevance of denomination; see Robert Wuthnow, *The Restructuring of American Religion: Society and Faith Since World War Two* (Princeton: Princeton University Press, 1988).

59. Benson and Williams, *Religion on Capitol Hill*; Oldmixon, *Uncompromising Positions*.

60. Michael Barone and Richard E. Cohen, *Almanac of American Politics 2008* (Washington, DC: National Journal, 2007). See also Orrin G. Hatch, "What Kind of Judge?" *National Review*, May 27, 2009.

61. Barone and Cohen, *Almanac of American Politics*; Connie L. McNeely and Susan J. Tolchin, "On the Hill: Jews in the United States Congress," in *Jews in American Politics*, ed. L. Sandy Maisel and Ira N. Forman (Lanham, MD: Rowman and Littlefield, 2001); Kevin Merida, "McCain's Unlikely Standard-Bearer," *The Washington Post*, September 3, 2008.

62. Susan J. Crabtree, "The Chosen Republican," *The Weekly Standard*, January 27, 2003, 14–15.

63. Charles Babington, "S.C. GOP Nominee Regrets Remarks; Gays, Single Moms as Teachers Faulted," *The Washington Post*, October 18, 2004, A6.

64. Adam Nagourney, "Political Shifts on Gay Rights Lag Behind Culture," *The New York Times*, June 27, 2009, A1.

65. Lori Montgomery, "Party Lines Blur for Area Lawmakers," *The Washington Post*, May 24, 2000, A15.

66. Barone and Cohen, *Almanac of American Politics*.

67. Ibid.

68. Allen D. Hertzke, *Freeing God's Children: The Unlikely Alliance for Global Human Rights* (Lanham, MD: Rowman and Littlefield, 2004); Nicholas D. Kristof, "When the Right Is Right," *The New York Times,* December 22, 2004.

69. Tony Hall, *Changing the Face of Hunger* (Nashville: Thomas Nelson, 2007); Allen D. Hertzke, *Freeing God's Children*.

70. Barone and Cohen, *Almanac of American Politics*.

71. Ibid.; and Joe Feuerherd, "Roots in Faith, Family, and Party Guide Pelosi's Move to Power," *National Catholic Reporter*, January 24, 2003.

72. Rachel Donadio, "Visiting Pope, Pelosi Hears a Call to Protect Life," *The New York Times*, February 19, 2009, A17.

73. Hertzke, *Freeing God's Children*.

74. John Aloysius Farrell, "U.S. 'Antireligious Bias' Alleged: Bush Report Decries Faith-Group Hurdles," *The Boston Globe*, August 17, 2001, A2.

75. Donald R. Songer and Susan J. Tabrizi, "The Religious Right in Court: The Decision Making of Christian Evangelicals in State Supreme Courts," *Journal of Politics* 61 (1999), 507–526.

76. But see Melissa M. Deckman, *School Board Battles: The Christian Right in Local Politics* (Washington, DC: Georgetown University Press, 2004); and David Yamane, "Faith

and Access: Personal Religiosity and Religious Group Advocacy in a State Legislature," *Journal for the Scientific Study of Religion* 38 (1999), 543–550.

77. For an optimistic view, see John Dart and Jimmy Allen, *Bridging the Gap: Religion and the News Media* (Nashville, TN: Freedom Forum, 1993); John Schmalzbauer, *People of Faith: Religious Conviction in American Journalism and Higher Education* (Ithaca, NY: Cornell University Press, 2003); Mark Silk, *Unsecular Media: Making News of Religion in America* (Urbana: University of Illinois Press, 1995).

78. The Public Religion Project, *Sightings*, December 6, 1997.

79. But see Kathryn Lofton, *Oprah: The Gospel of an Icon* (Berkeley: University of California Press, forthcoming).

80. Robert K. Johnston, *Reel Spirituality: Theology and Film in Dialogue* (Grand Rapids, MI: Baker Academic, 2000).

81. Michael Medved, *Hollywood v. America* (New York: HarperPerennial, 1993); William D. Romanowski, *Eyes Wide Open: Looking for God in Popular Culture* (Grand Rapids, MI: Brazos Press, 2001).

82. See Paul Apostolidis, *Stations of the Cross: Adorno and Christian Right Radio* (Durham, NC: Duke University Press, 2000).

83. Barna Research Group, "Christian Mass Media Reach More Adults with Christian Message Than Do Churches," *Barna Research Online*, www.barna.org (July 2, 2002).

84. For a fascinating analysis of evangelical diet plans, see R. Marie Griffith, *Born Again Bodies: Flesh and Spirit in American Christianity* (Berkeley: University of California Press, 2004).

85. Stephen Bates, "The Jesus Market," *The Weekly Standard*, December 16, 2002, 24–29.

86. For a history of gospel music see James R. Goff Jr., *Close Harmony: A History of Southern Gospel* (Chapel Hill, NC: University of North Carolina Press, 2002).

7

RELIGION, CIVIL SOCIETY,
AND POLITICAL CULTURE

In previous chapters we have painted a portrait of a religious America that is deeply involved in public life. The combined legacies of religious freedom and democratic government provide the conditions for a robust participation that is unique among Western countries. In complex and dynamic ways, religion in the United States shapes voting patterns, views about policy issues and the role of government, partisan attachments, interest group strategies, and elite-level political choices. The political activism and attitudes of religious people and groups has generated immense interest among political and intellectual observers. Some have approached religious involvement with fear or even antagonism; others have been more welcoming of religious contributions to public affairs. But whatever the motivations that bring people to study the intersections of religion and politics, most have been impressed by religion's vigorous civic engagement, its diverse array of political expressions, and its remarkable ability to adapt to changing political realities.

In this chapter we turn to the role of political culture and civil society in fostering the United States's high levels of religious participation in politics, as well as the effect of religion on political culture itself. By political culture, we mean the widely shared values and attitudes people have about politics and government. Some of these values and attitudes have to do with the appropriate role of government, including how well public policy reflects such core ideals as freedom, equality, or justice. But political culture also encompasses citizens' dispositions toward public life, such as their levels of political interest and knowledge, their embrace of certain civic "virtues," and their perceptions of whether government cares about and responds to their concerns. It is essential in any democracy for the political culture to support widespread political participation by ordinary citizens.[1] We focus on how religion shapes the American political culture—and how that culture in turn shapes religion.

THE TENSION BETWEEN RELIGION AND POLITICAL CULTURE

As we discussed in Chapter 1, some aspects of religion have a deep historical resonance within political culture. The Puritans left a legacy of self-government, a sense of national mission ("the city on a hill"), and the imperative to shape the moral character of citizens for the public good. From the colonial period to today there also has been a steady and remarkable growth of religious pluralism, fueled by waves of immigration and homegrown religious experimentation. That diversity has meant competition, and competition has created incentives for intense religious outreach for new members. This evangelical zeal often has carried over into public life, sometimes in the form of a moral campaign (for example, the Temperance Movement).

That zeal is coupled with an enduring strain of populism that emphasizes grassroots participation in the life of churches and other religious groups. Historically, the direct participation of American laity in the leadership and administration of religious institutions was unusual in comparison to the religious cultures of Europe, where ordinary church members were more accustomed to an experience of religion mediated through clergy and other elites. American-style populism reflected at least two values that on the surface may seem contradictory: on the one hand, the personal freedom of the individual, and on the other, the confidence that individuals working collectively can have enormous impact. Both values—the centrality of the individual and the power of group membership—continue to play powerful roles in American political culture.

Although these historical patterns clearly demonstrate religion's many influences on the political culture, the influence does not move in only one direction. Political culture itself can shape religion. For many religious believers, this is reason enough to approach political culture with considerable ambivalence. On the one hand, they may perceive the broader culture as an important battleground in a conflict over core values or national identity. Religious believers may also insist that they have an obligation to engage in that conflict—and that they expect the political system to respond to their efforts. On the other hand, they may worry that they will meet stiff resistance from a political culture that is already deeply influenced by values they reject. Those with religious beliefs may even be faced with the need to compromise their own values in the political arena. Political engagement, then, seems a quixotic affair at best and downright dangerous at worst.

The contemporary Christian conservative movement illustrates this tension. The political activism of adherents of the movement, often called the Christian Right, grew up primarily among evangelical Protestants in the late 1970s and early 1980s.[2] The movement's main goal has been to take political action in response to what it perceives as an increasingly immoral environment in the United States that is disturbingly hostile to Christianity. Whether their complaint is against secular public schools, vulgar popular culture, interfering government edicts, or collapsing family values, Christian conservatives perceive a systematic assault on traditional standards and Christianity itself in the United States today.

The movement's leaders always have argued that they are not disguised theocrats who wish to establish Christianity as the official religion of the United States. Instead they wish to foster an atmosphere in which committed Christians can practice their religion and see its morality honored in and by the broader culture. They insist that what they see as a fraying of the cultural fabric in the United States can be reversed only through Christian renewal. But the movement also has been an inviting target because its leaders and activists often have attempted to use government to foster cultural change. When the Moral Majority emerged in 1979 as the first major Christian Right organization, its founder, Jerry Falwell, and other leaders saw an opportunity to address conservative discontent with the political direction of the country, as epitomized in U.S. Supreme Court decisions declaring state-sponsored prayer in schools and restrictions on abortion unconstitutional.

Even though the Moral Majority was never as influential as its media coverage would suggest, eventually collapsing in 1988,[3] the Christian conservative movement took stock of the experience and reemerged in the early 1990s with much greater sophistication and organizational acumen. Tapping into those stores of religious populism and evangelical intensity, leaders emphasized channeling the energy of the movement's activists into effective grassroots organizations. This "second coming" of the Christian Right also represented a change in language and tone. Ralph Reed, the executive director of the Christian Coalition from 1989 to 1997, exemplified a new crop of politically savvy movement leaders who reframed issues in terms that would appeal to a broader societal consensus to describe their positions on abortion, education, or same-sex relationships.[4] The Christian Coalition and other movement organizations became a real force in the Republican Party at the state and local level in the 1990s. They were widely hailed as a key force in the Republicans' historic victories in the 1994 midterm elections, when the GOP took majority control of both the U.S. Senate and House of Representatives for the first time in four decades.[5]

By the late 1990s, however, Christian Right leaders were expressing second thoughts about political activism as a means of cultural renewal. Twenty years after the founding of the Moral Majority, some of Falwell's key advisers from that time, including commentator Cal Thomas and preacher Ed Dobson, suggested that Christian conservatives had lost their religious moorings and had become "blinded" by political power.[6] The late Paul Weyrich, a conservative intellectual who coined the term "moral majority," argued that the broader culture had become an "ever-wider sewer" that had "collapsed" so completely that it "simply overwhelms politics." Rather than trying to change that culture, he advised, Christians ought to separate themselves from it.[7]

These elite-level commentaries reflect recent events on the ground. Christian conservatives achieved some electoral and policy victories in the early 2000s, most notably the election of President George W. Bush and the passage of important foreign policy legislation on religious freedom and human rights.[8] These events, combined with the fact that Christian Right organizations remain among the largest and most influential religious interests in Washington, DC, suggest strongly that they are still important political players, especially within the Republican Party. But the movement clearly is losing some steam. By 2009, the Christian Coalition, the Family Research Council, and other Christian conservative groups were experiencing leadership changes, budget shortfalls, and staff reductions, all of which pointed to a waning interest among many rank-and-file members and shifting political fortunes in the era of a Democratic president and majority in Congress.

The experience of the Christian Right underlines both the appeal and the perils of religious interactions with political culture. The Christian conservative movement sought to engage the broader public in a conflict over values but risked losing its own perspective. It is an open question whether the movement's values were actually compromised by its engagement, but this possibility does exist for any religious group that enters the public square.

Moreover, the activism of the Christian Right points to the risk of alienating the very culture that a religious group or movement hopes to transform. For many ordinary citizens who were not part of the movement, Christian Right groups represent key combatants in a "culture war" over values in the United States.[9] Indeed, conservative leaders reinforced the idea of a culture war in their own language, often using the metaphors of battle or war to describe their efforts and to define an enemy. We address the scholarly theory of culture war in Chapter 12, but the point here is that some observers perceived that the Christian Right was fanning the flames of cultural conflict (and perhaps that they even started the conflict), which may have caused a large-scale reaction against the movement's goals. That was an implicit criticism made by Thomas and Dobson, who believed that the Christian Right had hardened much of public opinion against traditionalist Christianity and therefore made the work of changing hearts and minds much more difficult.

This concern about backlash highlights a peculiar aspect of religion's potential to shape political culture that helps explain the cultural ambivalence of some religious groups. Already in the early nineteenth century, Alexis de Tocqueville, the French social theorist, had identified a counterintuitive characteristic of religion's public role in the United States. After comparing the politics of clergy in the United States and Europe, he observed that religion maintained greater influence over political values and attitudes in America precisely when it was perceived as most *detached* from political culture. By remaining aloof from the nitty-gritty of politics, religion was not identified with the self-interest and corrupting influences of political life. This gave religious leaders greater credibility when they decided to speak in broad moral terms about political issues of the day. Detachment also allowed religion to present itself as an appealing refuge from the vagaries of public life, with its unrelenting emphasis on the pursuit of individual self-interest. [10]

Of course, for some religious traditions the entire discussion is irrelevant. They are not ambivalent about cultural engagement; they are indifferent or even hostile to it. The Amish, Jehovah's Witnesses, and numerous other religious sects seek to remain separate from political culture, engaging it only when necessary to protect their own cultural space. But many religious traditions or movements feel a mission to go beyond defense of their own territory. Religionists with very different goals and tactics often share the same desire to use politics and government to embed their values into the political culture. In this broad sense, a liberal Catholic calling for more government spending to ameliorate poverty or a pacifist mainline Protestant marching against the war in Iraq reflect a similar orientation toward political culture as the Christian Right. They, too, are convinced that their values deserve a place in public life, and that through their activism they may be able to redeem political decisions for the good or speak prophetic truth to power. To be sure, the experience of the Christian Right suggests that such engagement risks significant costs. Groups must learn to live with the challenges American political culture can pose to their goals and identity, and their engagement may even lead to withdrawal when it appears political culture is impervious to their efforts. Yet the appeal of the moral campaign can be difficult to resist.

POLITICAL CULTURE AS A CONTEXT
FOR RELIGIOUS PARTICIPATION

To this point, we have examined the potential tension that exists between religion and political culture.[11] But we might also look at the interaction of religion and political culture from a different perspective. Although political scientists often examine religious efforts to shape the values of public life, they also are interested in how political culture in the United States provides opportunities for that religious engagement.

Despite an abstract commitment to the separation of church and state, most Americans also accept the idea that individuals have a right to bring their religious beliefs into the public square. It is one thing to insist that government ought not to support religion through financial support or other resources; it is quite another to argue that private citizens should suppress their religious commitments when they vote, contribute money to political organizations, or advocate their values or policy views before political leaders. American political culture is much more accepting of the political activism of religious individuals and groups than it is of government support for religion.[12] Indeed, the enduring openness to religious participation in public life often is cited as one of those features of American "exceptionalism" that distinguish the United States from its closest political cousins in Western Europe.[13]

On this score, religion and political culture are mutually reinforcing. Religious groups in the colonial era and the early Republic realized that it was in their interest to distinguish the separation of church and *state* from the separation of religion and *politics*. Many groups believed that keeping government out of religious affairs was a way of protecting their religious freedom—a belief we chronicle much more fully in Chapters 8 and 9. Yet that same freedom, which complements the Madisonian emphasis on fostering competing interests in a system of checks and balances, gave religious groups an opportunity to take part in the democratic process itself, thereby adding their voice to the bewildering pluralism of American politics. As we have seen, many religions have welcomed this opportunity to participate.

It is important to keep in mind that American political culture has not always been fully open to all manifestations of religious engagement. The history of the United States is replete with examples of religious minorities losing political access when they are perceived as too far out of the mainstream. As we discuss in Chapter

3, Mormons, Jehovah's Witnesses, and other smaller religious groups have confronted serious challenges to their religious beliefs and practices and in many cases have suffered harsh treatment when seeking redress through political means. Even some larger religious traditions have faced discrimination and violence at the hands of the dominant American political culture. For example, Catholics, Jews, and Muslims alike have faced painful stereotyping and ostracism at different points in U.S. history, and African American churches were burned and bombed during the civil rights movement.

In our contemporary politics, we see the general American preference for religious values in public life quite clearly in mass attitudes about political elites. Opinion surveys consistently reveal that voters are much more likely to cast their ballot for a member of any religious tradition than an atheist. But those surveys also suggest that voters have an implicit hierarchy of preferences in mind when assessing the religious identity of a candidate for office. Hence they are more willing to vote

BOX 7.1   MITT ROMNEY: A MORMON IN THE PRESIDENTIAL PRIMARIES

In most ways, Mitt Romney was the quintessential Republican candidate for the presidency. He previously served as the founder and CEO of a wildly successful business firm, as a governor of a prominent state (Massachusetts), and even as the head of the organizing committee for the 2002 Winter Olympic Games in Salt Lake City. He comes from a rich political lineage (his father was a popular governor of Michigan in the 1960s and later served as secretary of Housing and Urban Development in the Nixon administration; his mother ran unsuccessfully for the U.S. Senate in 1970), and by all accounts he is an articulate family man with few skeletons in his closet.

Yet he is also a devout Mormon, and surveys taken during the 2008 presidential primaries suggested that his faith was a problem for his campaign. Even though Romney generally was seen as the most religious of candidates, his specific faith became a liability. A quarter of voters said that they would be less likely to vote for a Mormon candidate, and the percentage jumped to more than a third among one of the most treasured voting blocs within the modern GOP: evangelical Protestants. Romney recognized the problem and gave a major speech touting his mainstream church-state values, but he was never able to shake fully the lingering doubts of some voters about his faith.

Source: Scott Keeter and Gregory Smith, "How the Public Perceives Romney, Mormons," *Pew Forum on Religion & Public Life*, December 4, 2007.

for a Muslim than an atheist, but less likely to vote for a Muslim than a Mormon, a Mormon than an evangelical, and so on. Perhaps the best recent example of this phenomenon came in the 2008 Republican presidential primary campaign, when Mitt Romney had to address persistent questions about his Mormon faith (see Box 7.1). Even though the religious ordering can shift over time, the hierarchy itself persists as a factor in electoral choices.

Still, even though religious tolerance occasionally has wavered when the majority perceives a group as a threat to the established order, in comparative terms religious liberty has been more widely practiced in the United States than in nearly any other place around the globe. And that liberty speaks to a broader point: American political culture nurtures a set of norms and values that encourage the democratic participation of religious groups and individuals.

RELIGION, CIVIL SOCIETY, AND GOOD CITIZENSHIP

To the extent that elements of an established political culture falter, religion's opportunities within democracy diminish. Hence religious citizens themselves have a vested interest in supporting a political culture that remains open to their participation. A healthy political culture sustains open and democratic institutions and practices. After all, though modern forms of democracy allow ordinary citizens to participate in their own government, those citizens often do not take full advantage of the opportunity. A robust citizenship assumes a set of values (such as trust in political institutions and a belief that one's participation matters) and competencies (such as a basic level of knowledge of how the political system works). Throughout much of American history, these assumptions have shaped public discussion of the contours of a distinctively *democratic* political culture.[14]

In recent decades, however, many observers increasingly have become alarmed at what they perceive as an erosion of the democratic political culture in America. A flood of scholarship has chronicled declining levels of civic engagement in the United States, ranging from voting to grassroots participation in voluntary organizations.[15] These declines are linked to several interrelated factors. For some scholars, the key predictor of decreasing civic engagement is a widespread lack of political knowledge.[16] Others have suggested that American disengagement is the result of lessening "social capital," norms of trust and reciprocity in social interactions that foster collective action.[17] Still other analysts point to underdeveloped civic skills (such as leadership and strategic communication) and other basic citizen capacities.[18]

Despite their different explanations and methods, these scholars agree that the question is not whether the scope and quality of civic engagement has become diminished but rather what can be done to reinvigorate it. In response, numerous associations and individuals have proposed a host of solutions to the problem of declining civic engagement, ranging from beefed up civic education to radical reform of political institutions.[19] These efforts to address perceived civic decline raise a complex and controversial question: Does the role of religion in political culture actually improve the quality of public life? Or has it been one of the sources of decline?

As is often the case, one of the earliest and most prescient observers to ask these questions was Alexis de Tocqueville. In his classic book *Democracy in America*, he expressed his astonishment at the democratic norms developing in the young Republic, to which he traveled in the 1830s. He was especially captivated by a pervasive sense of equality among citizens, which he appreciated in comparison to political culture on the European continent at the time, with its rigid social hierarchies rooted in inherited status. But he also worried about the risks of American-style egalitarianism; left to its own devices, he thought it naturally would lead to individualism and a drift toward a kind of "democratic despotism" as citizens focused on their own self-interests rather than the public good. For Tocqueville, it was a marvel that the United States had not yet succumbed to those tendencies.

What intervened, he observed, was the participation of ordinary Americans in what we might today call "civil society": those myriad associations and institutions that point citizens away from their self-isolation and toward the interests of others. Family, professions, neighborhoods, voluntary associations, and—perhaps most important—religion helped to dampen the powerful appeal of individualism within democratic cultures.

Tocqueville's observations continue to influence thinking about political culture today. Some contemporary commentators have argued, for example, that civil society acts as a set of "mediating structures" between the individual and the state.[20] Not only does civil society act as a powerful source of key political values, but it also places a buffer between the state and the individual citizen who otherwise would be left without much power against the encroachments of government, even to the extreme point of totalitarianism. Indeed, it is often the emergence of a civil society that poses the greatest threat to authoritarian regimes. And religion is distinctive in its ability to maintain its autonomy in such regimes, providing a relatively strong position from which to challenge authoritarianism.[21]

Other scholars tout civil society as a "seedbed" for civic virtues and competence.[22] Most of the nation's founders, for example, suggested that constitutional design would not sustain the American republic by itself. John Adams declared that "pure virtue" is the "only foundation of a free Constitution."[23] Thomas Jefferson touted the importance of individual character and virtue, finding it most fully developed in the yeoman farmer.[24] Even James Madison, who placed great stock in the institutional design of government, nevertheless argued that it could not work without "sufficient virtue" among citizens. But even though one might agree that any government is only as good as its citizens, government cannot necessarily make its citizens good. For many social theorists, instead it is our interactions in our day-to-day networks within civil society that provide opportunities to learn respect for the rights of others, tolerance, interpersonal trust, and a work ethic, among other virtues.[25]

It should not be surprising, then, that religion would be a key component of the discussion about civil society.[26] In the United States, it is no exaggeration to say that religious institutions make up the largest single component of civil society. More than half of all volunteering in the United States happens within religious settings, nearly 60 percent of Americans are members of a house of worship, and well over a third are associated with religious groups other than houses of worship.[27] With such a presence in civil society, religion is bound to have an impact on the thinking and engagement of citizens.

Civic Capacities: Skills, Interest, and Knowledge

One way religious institutions play an important role in helping to sustain a healthy American civic life is by developing civic capacities. In a huge study of civic voluntarism, a team of scholars headed by political scientist Sidney Verba found that churches provide a crucial venue in which people may develop what they term "civic skills."[28] The argument is that people are more likely to participate in politics—and to be more effective participants—when they have experience doing a variety of things that occur frequently in church settings, such as organizing meetings, writing letters, and speaking in public. The basic assumption is that leadership, communication, and other skills are transferable; what is learned in one context can be put to use in another.

People who are deeply involved in their religious institutions, therefore, may be expected to possess relatively high levels of civic skills. Even when controlling for their age or education, the evidence suggests that they do have such skills. Indeed, as central social institutions that host numerous public discussions, self-help groups, and other community activities, houses of worship foster civic skills even among nonmembers.[29] Churches and other religious associations are important for skill-building simply because they provide opportunities that participants would not otherwise have.

To be sure, because religious experiences are not all alike, possibilities for skill development are not equally distributed. Some religious traditions expose their members to a greater range and number of opportunities (in particular, the mainline Protestant and Jewish traditions), whereas others offer fewer possibilities (for example, Roman Catholicism).[30] Regardless of tradition, larger congregations generally have many small groups and other resources available to their members, which heightens the likelihood of skill development compared to smaller congregations that are resource-poor.[31] Even within a specific church, members often cluster in socially homogeneous groups, crowding out others from opportunities for skill development.[32] Nevertheless, whatever a person's specific experience, more committed religionists generally are more likely to be presented with skill-building activities and to take advantage of them.

Another aspect of a citizen's civic capacity is more cognitive than behavioral, focusing on interest in and knowledge about politics. Most democratic theorists insist that an informed and attentive public is a key ingredient to representative government, and empirical scholars have long known that higher levels of political knowledge and interest are strongly associated with more and better civic engagement.[33] Like civic skill development, however, opportunities and motivations for obtaining knowledge or generating interest can vary dramatically. Some factors, including level of education or socioeconomic status, clearly are more important than others.

In their study of civil society and religion, political scientist Corwin Smidt and his colleagues found that though religion does not have a direct effect on levels of political knowledge, it is strongly associated with higher levels of interest in public life—a factor that is itself correlated with political knowledge.[34] Why would religion generate that interest? For one thing, religious institutions are prolific in supplying information to their members. Whether it is an urgent communiqué about human rights abuses from a missionary in a far-flung area of the globe, a flyer about a pro-life rally, or a homily about poverty at Mass, active members of congregations often are inundated with targeted messages. Too much information can confuse and suppress interest as much as it can generate it, but well-crafted communications, especially from trusted cue-givers such as clergy, can carry substantial weight among devout religionists.[35]

Social Capital and the Civic Virtues

In a different vein, a variety of scholars have argued that places of worship facilitate interactions among people that contribute to what political scientist Robert Putnam and others have termed "social capital."[36] Putnam shows that high levels of social capital in society, which develops in networks of trust among citizens, correlates with the effectiveness of that society's government and even its economy. Houses of worship, of course, are a prime area of interest for social capital scholars, who note that churches, synagogues, and other religious institutions have generated immense networks, cohesion, and political mobilization.[37]

Social networks such as religious congregations have become an important area of study because they are thought to be a source of civic dispositions—what theorists have traditionally called virtues—that foster higher-quality interactions among citizens.[38] And recent research does indeed suggest that religion plays a clear role in fostering some of those dispositions. For example, those who attend religious services regularly and engage in private religious practice (prayer or meditation) are more likely than others to place stock in obeying the law, to believe that government is generally trustworthy and responsive (what political scientists call "external political efficacy"), and to cherish a strong work ethic.[39] Each of these virtues can lend stability to the political and economic systems and foster greater democratic participation.

The picture is muddier when looking at dispositions such as trust or tolerance. Putnam has hypothesized that trust will vary depending on the nature of one's associations. Some religious believers, for example, might develop "bonding" trust that results in intense attachments to fellow religionists as well as equally intense skepticism about those outside the group. In those instances, religious involvement may prevent political participation, or it may lead to a kind of participation that is closed off to compromise and deliberation with other groups—precisely the kind of politics that critics identify as undemocratic and at the root of the culture war. But other religious believers might develop "bridging" trust, which means that the attachments they develop in one group make it easier for them to develop attachments outside the group.[40]

Tolerance is an even more complex matter. Although most studies suggest that tolerance is inversely correlated with religiosity (the more devout, the less tolerant, and vice versa), the findings depend on how tolerance is defined, measured, and analyzed.[41] One of the key questions in the literature on tolerance is the difference between political and social tolerance. Whereas religionists (or anyone else) may disapprove intensely of the values and lifestyles represented within a particular group (*social* intolerance), they may still defend the right of members of that group to express themselves in public life (*political* tolerance).[42] Many studies confuse these two forms of tolerance, as well as other dispositions such as prejudice or acceptance. Sometimes, as a result, the most devout religious believers have been perceived as unusually politically intolerant rather than as socially intolerant or prejudiced. The most careful studies suggest that gaps in levels of tolerance among religious traditions are closing and that, on the whole, religious believers are no more politically intolerant than other groups—but more work on the precise relationship of religion and tolerance remains to be done.[43]

The overall picture of religion is that it generally serves as a source for important civic dispositions, though in some instances its role is unclear or problematic. And though religion is one source among many, it is arguably the most prominent part of civil society that fosters these dispositions.

Civic Engagement

Religious commitment also translates frequently into various forms of civic activism. This activism often goes hand-in-hand with evangelism—the effort to win converts or bring new members to one's religion. Recruitment is a must for churches in the competitive environment of American religion, where some churches grow and others decline on a regular basis. For example, the Assemblies of God, a conservative Pentecostal denomination, has grown rapidly in recent times, partly because of its remarkable outreach to Latinos, whose numbers have exploded in the denomination in the last two decades.[44] The thriving LDS Church also illustrates well the importance of active evangelism. Mormons send out an estimated 50,000 young missionaries each year worldwide, and the LDS Church's remarkable growth rates and aggressive missionary activity have led some to predict that it could be one of the major world religions by the middle of the twenty-first century.[45]

Religious commitment to civic activism also often results in joining the full range of civic associations, including secular ones. Those who join churches or other houses of worship are quite likely to belong to *non*religious groups as well—twice as likely, in fact, as those who are not members of a church.[46] Religious Americans epitomize the view that the United States is composed of a people who are joiners.

Religious congregations put their tremendous human resource to a great deal of work in American society. A large share of the charitable giving in the United States is done in and by churches; indeed, citizens who attend church regularly give money to social causes and volunteer to do charitable work at a dramatically higher rate than those who rarely or never attend religious services.[47] People of modest means are particularly likely to donate almost exclusively through religious outlets. This generosity enables churches to operate an impressive array of social organizations, hospitals, schools, universities, charitable agencies, and international relief organizations.[48] Eighty-two percent of American congregations participate in some

BOX 7.2   PARACHURCH GROUPS IN PUBLIC LIFE

Many religious associations are parachurch organizations, groups that are intimately connected with and supported by a religious tradition yet have no formal
ties to a specific religious denomination. For example, with a great deal of support from various Christian churches and individuals, evangelist Charles Colson
has led the most visible movement for prison reform in the 1990s and 2000s. Colson is a former "hatchet man" for President Richard Nixon who went to jail for
his Watergate crimes. After experiencing a religious conversion, Colson created
Prison Fellowship, a worldwide program that not only spreads the Christian
gospel among prisoners but also fights for reform of inhumane prisons. Lauded
by conservatives and liberals alike, Colson's evangelical quest to redeem prisoners and prisons is yet another chapter in a long history of faith-based reformist
campaigns.

Habitat for Humanity is another contemporary example. Through this organization, President Jimmy Carter and many others imbued with religious faith
work to build houses with and for poor people in the United States and abroad.
For them, the need to minister to a suffering world is urgent, and their faith provides the reforming energy to make a difference in people's lives.

Source: *Prison Fellowship*, http://www.pfm.org; *Habitat for Humanity*,
http://www.habitat.org.

form of social service or community development activity designed to assist people
outside the walls of their congregation.[49] One survey suggests that the average
American congregation is more likely to provide its members with basic social outreach opportunities (such as cash or food assistance programs) than with prayer
or theological study groups.[50] Even small denominations make their presence felt.
The Seventh-day Adventists, with about a million members in the United States,
support fifteen colleges and universities, sixty-four healthcare institutions, and numerous K–12 schools and welfare agencies (Box 7.2).[51]

Private education, of course, is a major activity of many religious groups. The
Catholic Church operates the largest religious educational system in the United
States, with roughly 7,500 elementary and secondary schools attended by at least
2.2 million students; evangelical and other religious schools enroll another 2 million
children in more than 20,000 smaller schools.[52] Although many religionists are concerned about the decline in religious school enrollments in the last few decades,[53]

faith-based schooling remains an integral part of many religious traditions' civic outreach. The growing world of homeschooling, which today includes well over a million children, also has relied heavily on networks created by and through religious institutions. Nearly three-quarters of homeschooling parents cite providing "religious or moral instruction" as a reason for their educational choice.[54] In addition, many Christian traditions support their own network of colleges and universities; for example, there are more than 200 Catholic institutions of higher learning, including many prestigious schools such as the University of Notre Dame and Georgetown University.

Social involvement by churches has clear political ramifications. Church-run charities, adoption agencies, educational institutions, and international relief programs operate in a milieu that is heavily influenced by government. Interaction between these institutions and government is inevitable. A large number of religious hospitals and social-service organizations, for example, receive government money to perform their services. Politicians in both major parties clearly understand that no major healthcare policy changes can proceed without the participation of religious hospitals.[55]

In 2001, President George W. Bush established the White House Office of Faith-Based and Community Initiatives as part of his administration's broader efforts to expand public support for religious social services. President Barack Obama has continued this initiative in his administration under the name White House Office of Faith-Based and Neighborhood Partnerships, which is a nod to his background as a faith-based community organizer in Chicago. Although such efforts can be intensely controversial—indeed, Bush's initiatives met stiff resistance in Congress, and Obama's early efforts suggest that similar questions will arise—throughout American history government frequently has partnered with organized religion to shape and implement public policy. Religious institutions fully understand the importance of these inevitable interactions.[56]

CONCLUSION

It should come as little surprise to learn that religion is so intimately tied to American political culture. But the breadth and depth of religion's role is remarkable. Part of its influence lies simply in its immense size: Religion is the most prominent mainstay of civil society in the United States. Yet religion's role in political culture also is marked by the unique goals and intensity of the members of religious associations, for better or worse.

Given religion's powerful influence in political culture, changing patterns in religious belief or affiliation inevitably will impact public life. Some voices in discussions about civil society and political culture already are wondering if recent religious trends, which appear to include a drifting away from traditional religious loyalties among younger citizens, will impoverish the political culture.[57] These are difficult matters to predict, especially in a social sector as dynamic and complex as religion. Perhaps we will see historical faiths repackaged in high-tech forms, or we will see new modes of spirituality organized in ways we cannot yet foresee. To the extent that the social networks of religious life could be lost in these new dynamics, however, we might expect that political culture will suffer as a result.

FURTHER READING

Berger, Peter, and Richard John Neuhaus. *To Empower People: From State to Civil Society*. Washington, DC: American Enterprise Institute, 1995. A discussion of religion (and civil society in general) as "mediating structures."

Cnaan, Ram A., Stephanie Boddie, Charlene McGrew, and Jennifer Kang. *The Other Philadelphia Story: How Local Congregations Support Quality of Life in Urban America*. Philadelphia: University of Pennsylvania Press, 2006. An excellent case study of religion's role in urban life.

Djupe, Paul A., and Christopher P. Gilbert. *The Political Influence of Church*. New York: Cambridge University Press, 2009. An innovative study of the role of churches in shaping civic skills and other aspects of public life.

Fowler, Robert Booth. *Unconventional Partners: Religion and Liberal Culture in the United States*. Grand Rapids, MI: Eerdmans, 1989. Statement of the tension between religion as refuge and the alienating nature of American civil society.

Hunter, James Davidson. *Culture Wars: The Struggle to Define America*. New York: Basic Books, 1991. The leading statement of the culture wars argument.

Monsma, Stephen V., and J. Christopher Soper. *Faith, Hope, and Jobs: Welfare-to-Work in Los Angeles*. Washington, DC: Georgetown University Press, 2006. A detailed study of the effectiveness of faith-based social services in a local setting.

Putnam, Robert. *Bowling Alone: The Collapse and Revival of American Community*. New York: Simon & Schuster, 2001. A landmark study with some attention to the role of religion in generating social capital.

Smidt, Corwin, Kevin R. den Dulk, James M. Penning, Stephen V. Monsma, and Douglas L. Koopman. *Pews, Prayers, and Participation: Religion and Civic Responsibility in*

America. Washington, DC: Georgetown University Press, 2008. An expansive examination of religion, civil society, and civic life.

Verba, Sidney, Kay Scholzman, and Henry E. Brady. *Voice and Equality: Civic Voluntarism in American Politics*. Cambridge, MA: Harvard University Press, 1995. The seminal study of civic skills, including religion's role in developing them.

Wuthnow, Robert. *Saving America? Faith-Based Services and the Future of Civil Society*. Princeton: Princeton University Press, 2004. A broad survey of religious social services and their place in civil society.

NOTES

1. This description of political culture draws from standard discussions in political science. The seminal work is Gabriel Almond and Sidney Verba, *The Civic Culture: Political Attitudes and Democracy in Five Nations* (Princeton: Princeton University Press, 1963).

2. Exactly who belongs to the Christian Right is a matter of dispute, but it is important to bear in mind that the term *Christian Right* does not describe the entire evangelical population of the United States. Moreover, a few non-evangelicals, including some conservative Catholics, have an affinity for the movement (though that affinity is often an uneasy one). There have been many efforts to measure "membership" in the Christian Right; no one has struggled harder with these issues than Clyde Wilcox. See his book, *God's Warriors: The Christian Right in 20th Century America* (Baltimore: Johns Hopkins University Press, 1992); Clyde Wilcox and Carin Larson, *Onward Christian Soldiers? The Religious Right in American Politics*, 3rd ed. (Boulder: Westview Press, 2006).

3. For scholarly assessment of the Christian Right at this stage, see Steve Bruce, *The Rise and Fall of the New Christian Right* (Oxford: Clarendon, 1988); and Robert Booth Fowler, "The Failure of the Religious Right," in *The Religious New Right in American Politics*, ed. Michael Cromartie (Washington, DC: Ethics and Public Policy Center, 1993).

4. Matthew Moen, *The Transformation of the Christian Right* (Tuscaloosa, AL: University of Alabama Press, 1992).

5. Edward L. Cleary and Allen D. Hertzke, eds., *Representing God at the Statehouse: Religion and Politics in the American States* (Lanham, MD: Rowman and Littlefield, 2006); Kimberly H. Conger and John C. Green, "Spreading Out and Digging In," *Campaigns and Elections* 5 (2002), 58–65; Melissa M. Deckman, *School Board Battles: The Christian Right in Local Politics* (Washington, DC: Georgetown University Press, 2004); Mark J. Rozell and Clyde Wilcox, eds., *God at the Grassroots: The Christian Right in the 1994 Elections* (Lanham, MD: Rowman and Littlefield, 1995).

6. Cal Thomas and Ed Dobson, *Blinded by Might: Can the Religious Right Save America?* (Grand Rapids, MI: Zondervan, 1999).

7. Paul Weyrich, "The Moral Minority," [reprint] *Christianity Today*, September 6, 1999.

8. Allen Hertzke, *Freeing God's Children: The Unlikely Alliance for Global Human Rights* (Lanham, MD: Rowman and Littlefield, 2004). For a brief yet wide-ranging discussion of the Christian Right's foreign policy involvement, see Kevin R. den Dulk, "Evangelical 'Internationalists' and U.S. Foreign Policy During the Bush Administration," in *Religion and the Presidency*, eds. Mark J. Rozell and Gleaves Whitney (New York: Palgrave Macmillan, 2007).

9. James Davidson Hunter, *Culture Wars: The Struggle to Define America* (New York: Basic Books, 1991). Political scientists have examined religion's role in the culture wars in various ways, often using the Christian Right as a case study. See, for example, Paul A. Djupe and Laura R. Olson, eds., *Religious Interests in Community Conflict: Beyond the Culture Wars* (Waco, TX: Baylor University Press, 2007); John C. Green, James L. Guth, Corwin E. Smidt, and Lyman A. Kellstedt, *Religion and the Culture Wars: Dispatches from the Front* (Lanham, MD: Rowman and Littlefield, 1996); and Geoffrey C. Layman and John C. Green, "Wars and Rumours of Wars: The Contexts of Cultural Conflict in American Political Behaviour," *British Journal of Political Science* 36 (2006), 61–89.

10. Alexis de Tocqueville, *Democracy in America: And Two Essays on America*, trans. Gerald E. Bevan and Isaac Kramnick (London: Penguin, 2003), 340. For a contemporary discussion, see Robert Booth Fowler, *Unconventional Partners: Religion and Liberal Culture in the United States* (Grand Rapids, MI: Eerdmans, 1989).

11. Stacey Hunter Hecht, "Religion and American Political Culture," in *In God We Trust? Religion and American Political Life*, ed. Corwin Smidt (Grand Rapids, MI: Baker, 2001), 63.

12. See, for example, Corwin E. Smidt, James L. Guth, Lyman Kellstedt, and John C. Green, "Religion in the 2004 American Presidential Election," in *American Politics, Media, and Elections: Contemporary International Perspectives on the U.S. Presidency, Foreign Policy, and Political Communication*, ed. Thomas Pludowski (Turin and Warsaw: Adam Marszalek and Collegium Cicitas Press, 2005).

13. Seymour Martin Lipset, *American Exceptionalism: A Double-Edged Sword* (New York: W.W. Norton, 1997).

14. Michael Schudson, *The Good Citizen: A History of American Civic Life* (New York: Martin Kessler Books, 1998).

15. Thomas E. Patterson, *The Vanishing Voter: Public Involvement in an Age of Uncertainty* (New York: Knopf, 2002); Robert Putnam, *Bowling Alone: The Collapse and Revival of American Community* (New York: Simon Schuster, 2001); Theda Skocpol, *Diminished*

Democracy: From Membership to Management in American Civic Life (Norman, OK: University of Oklahoma Press, 2002); Theda Skocpol and Morris Fiorina, eds., *Civic Engagement in American Democracy* (Washington, DC: Brookings Institution, 1999).

16. Michael X. Delli Carpini, "In Search of the Informed Citizen," *The Communication Review* 4 (2000), 129–164; Michael X. Delli Carpini and Scott Keeter, *What Americans Know About Politics and Why It Matters* (New Haven, CT: Yale University Press, 1996).

17. Putnam, *Bowling Alone.*

18. Sidney Verba, Kay Scholzman, and Henry E. Brady, *Voice and Equality: Civic Voluntarism in American Politics* (Cambridge, MA: Harvard University Press, 1995).

19. See, for example, Bruce A. Ackerman and James S. Fishkin, *Deliberation Day* (New Haven, CT: Yale University Press, 2004); Stephen Macedo, *Democracy at Risk: How Political Choices Undermine Citizen Participation and What We Can Do About It* (Washington, DC: Brookings Institution, 2005); National Commission on Civic Renewal, *A Nation of Spectators: How Civic Disengagement Weakens America* (College Park, MD: University of Maryland, 1998), Elinor Ostrom, "Civic Education for the Next Century: A Task Force to Initiate Professional Activity," *PS: Political Science and Politics* 29 (1996), 755–758.

20. Peter Berger and Richard John Neuhaus, *To Empower People: From State to Civil Society* (Washington, DC: American Enterprise Institute, 1995); Richard John Neuhaus, *The Naked Public Square* (Grand Rapids, MI: Eerdmans, 1984); William A. Galston, "Civil Society and The 'Art of Association,'" *Journal of Democracy* 11 (2000), 64–70.

21. Kenneth D. Wald, Adam L. Silverman, and Kevin S. Fridy, "Making Sense of Religion in Political Life," *Annual Review of Political Science* 8 (2005), 121–143. A good illustration is Poland, which cast off a military government in the late 1980s largely due to the efforts of the Solidarity labor union movement and the support of the Catholic Church.

22. Mary Ann Glendon and David Blankenhorn, eds., *Seedbeds of Virtue: Sources of Competence, Character, and Citizenship in American Society* (Lanham, MD: Rowman and Littlefield, 2005).

23. John Adams, "Letter to Zabdiel Adams, June 21, 1776," in *Letters of Delegates to Congress, 1774–1789*, vol. 4, ed. Paul H. Smith (Washington, DC: Library of Congress, 2000), 279.

24. Thomas Jefferson, "Notes on the State of Virginia," in *The Portable Jefferson*, ed. Merrill D. Peterson (New York: Penguin, 1975), 217.

25. Don E. Eberly, *America's Promise: Civil Society and the Renewal of American Culture* (Lanham, MD: Rowman and Littlefield, 1998); Don E. Eberly and Ryan Streeter, *The Soul of Civil Society: Voluntary Associations and the Public Value of Moral Habits* (Lanham, MD: Rowman and Littlefield, 2002); and Glendon and Blankenhorn, *Seedbeds of Virtue.*

26. Corwin E. Smidt, ed., *Religion as Social Capital: Producing the Common Good* (Waco, TX: Baylor University Press, 2003); Corwin Smidt et al., *Pews, Prayers, and Participation:*

Religion and Civic Responsibility in America (Washington, DC: Georgetown University Press, 2008); Robert Wuthnow, *Saving America? Faith-Based Services and the Future of Civil Society* (Princeton: Princeton University Press, 2004).

27. Smidt et al., *Pews, Prayers, and Participation*, 78.

28. Verba, Scholzman, and Brady, *Voice and Equality*.

29. Ram Cnaan et al., *The Other Philadelphia Story: How Local Congregations Support Quality of Life in Urban America* (Philadelphia: University of Pennsylvania Press, 2006).

30. Smidt et al., *Pews, Prayers, and Participation*, 148–155. See also Robert Wuthnow and John H. Evans, eds., *The Quiet Hand of God: Faith-Based Activism and Mainline Protestantism* (Berkeley: University of California Press, 2002).

31. Wuthnow and Evans, *The Quiet Hand of God,* 171–172. See also Mark Chaves, *Congregations in America* (Cambridge, MA: Harvard University Press, 2004).

32. Paul A. Djupe and Christopher P. Gilbert, *The Political Influence of Church* (New York: Cambridge University Press, 2009); Paul A. Djupe and Christopher P. Gilbert, "The Resourceful Believer: Generating Civic Skills in Church," *The Journal of Politics* 68 (2006), 116–127.

33. Delli Carpini and Keeter, *What Americans Know About Politics*.

34. Smidt et al., *Pews, Prayers, and Participation*, 166–168.

35. Sue E. S. Crawford and Laura R. Olson, eds. *Christian Clergy in American Politics* (Baltimore: Johns Hopkins University Press, 2001); Djupe and Gilbert, *The Political Influence of Church*, chap. 3; James L. Guth, John C. Green, Corwin E. Smidt, Lyman A. Kellstedt, and Margaret M. Poloma, *The Bully Pulpit: The Politics of Protestant Clergy* (Lawrence, KS: University Press of Kansas, 1997); and Corwin E. Smidt, ed., *Pulpit and Politics: Clergy in American Politics at the Advent of the Millennium* (Waco, TX: Baylor University Press, 2004).

36. Robert D. Putnam, *Making Democracy Work: Civic Traditions in Modern Italy* (Princeton: Princeton University Press, 1993).

37. Djupe and Gilbert, *The Political Influence of Church*; Christopher P. Gilbert, *The Impact of Churches on Political Behavior: An Empirical Study* (Westport, CT: Greenwood Press, 1993); Kenneth D. Wald, Dennis E. Owen, and Samuel S. Hill Jr., "Churches as Political Communities," *American Political Science Review* 82 (1988), 531–548; Kenneth D. Wald, Dennis E. Owen, and Samuel S. Hill Jr., "Political Cohesion in Churches," *Journal of Politics* 52 (1990), 197–215. One interesting development is the trend toward small-group ministry (self-help groups, twelve-step programs, and so on) and their role in generating social capital. See Robert Wuthnow, ed., *"I Come Away Stronger": How Small Groups Are Shaping American Religion* (Grand Rapids, MI: Eerdmans, 1994) and Robert Wuthnow, *Sharing the Journey: Support Groups and America's New Quest for Community* (New York: Simon & Schuster, 1996).

38. Jacob R. Neiheisel, Paul A. Djupe, and Anand E. Sokhey, "Veni, Vidi, Disseri: Churches and the Promise of Democratic Deliberation," *American Politics Research* 20 (2006), 1–30.

39. See generally Smidt et al., *Pews, Prayers, and Participation,* chap. 7.

40. Putnam, *Bowling Alone,* chap. 4. See also Diana C. Mutz, "The Consequences of Cross-Cutting Networks for Political Participation," *American Journal of Political Science* 46 (2002), 838–855.

41. The typical approach is to have a survey respondent identify a particularly disliked group, and then to determine how much the respondent would allow a member of that group to engage in public activities (e.g., teach at a school, give a speech).

42. For a discussion of the problems involved in tolerance studies, see James L. Gibson, "Enigmas of Intolerance: Fifty Years After Stouffer's Communism, Conformity, and Civil Liberties," *Perspectives on Politics* 4 (2006), 21–34.

43. Marie A. Eisenstein, *Religion and the Politics of Tolerance: How Christianity Builds Democracy* (Waco, TX: Baylor University Press, 2008); Smidt et al., *Pews, Prayers, and Participation,* 192–201.

44. Data from the Commission on Ethnic Relations, Assemblies of God, USA, http://www.ethnicrelations.ag.org/ethnicrelations/stats.cfm (2008). See also Donald E. Miller and Tetsunao Yamamori, *Global Pentecostalism: The New Face of Christian Social Engagement* (Berkeley: University of California Press, 2007); Arlene Sanchez Walsh, *Latino Pentecostal Identity: Evangelical Faith, Self, and Society* (New York: Columbia University Press, 2004).

45. Rodney Stark, "Modernization and Mormon Growth: The Secularization Thesis Revisited," in *Contemporary Mormonism: Social Science Perspectives,* eds. Marie Cornwall, Tim B. Heaton, and Lawrence A. Young (Urbana: University of Illinois Press, 2001).

46. Smidt et al., *Pews, Prayers, and Participation,* 77–78.

47. Arthur C. Brooks, *Who Really Cares: The Surprising Truth About Compassionate Conservatism* (New York: Basic Books, 2006); and Smidt et al., *Pews, Prayers, and Participation,* chap. 4.

48. Nancy Tatom Ammerman, *Pillars of Faith: American Congregations and Their Partners* (Berkeley: University of California Press, 2005); Ram A. Cnaan, *The Invisible Caring Hand: American Congregations and the Provision of Welfare* (New York: New York University Press, 2001).

49. National Congregations Study, *American Congregations at the Beginning of the 21st Century,* http://www.soc.duke.edu/natcong/Docs/NCSII_report_final.pdf (2009), 11. For a discussion of the data and methods used in this large study of religious congregations, see Mark Chaves et al., "The National Congregations Study: Background, Methods, and Selected Results," *Journal for the Scientific Study of Religion* 38 (1999), 458–476.

50. Carl S. Dudley and David A. Roozen, *Faith Communities Today: A Report on Religion in the United States Today* (Hartford, CT: Hartford Seminary, 2001), 46–47.

51. Office of Archives and Statistics, Seventh-day Adventist Church, *Adventist Online Yearbook 2009,* http://www.adventistyearbook.org (2009).

52. Stephen Broughman, Nancy Swaim, and Patrick Keaton, *Characteristics of Private Schools in the United States: Results from the 2007–08 Private School Universe Survey* (Washington, DC: National Center for Education Statistics, 2009).

53. Chester E. Finn and Andy Smarick, "Our Endangered Catholic Schools," *The Washington Post,* April 21, 2009.

54. U.S. Department of Education, National Center for Education Statistics, *Parent and Family Involvement in Education Survey of the 2003 National Household Education Surveys Program* (NHES), http://nces.ed.gov/.

55. Steve Monsma is one of the best scholars of public-private partnership. See Stephen V. Monsma, *Putting Faith in Partnerships: Welfare-to-Work in Four Cities, Contemporary Political and Social Issues* (Ann Arbor: University of Michigan Press, 2004); Stephen V. Monsma, *When Sacred and Secular Mix: Religious Nonprofit Organizations and Public Money* (Lanham, MD: Rowman and Littlefield, 1996); Stephen V. Monsma and J. Christopher Soper, *Faith, Hope, and Jobs: Welfare-to-Work in Los Angeles* (Washington, DC: Georgetown University Press, 2006).

56. Amy E. Black, Douglas L. Koopman, and David K. Ryden, *Of Little Faith: The Politics of George W. Bush's Faith-Based Initiatives* (Washington, DC: Georgetown University Press, 2004). For a wide-ranging discussion of the values in the debate over faith-based social services, see E. J. Dionne Jr. and Ming Hsu Chen, eds., *Sacred Places, Civic Purposes: Should Government Help Faith-Based Charity?* (Washington, DC: Brookings Institution, 2001).

57. Robert Putnam raises this concern in Daniel Burke, "Congregants Make Better Citizens, New Study Says," *Religious News Service,* May 13, 2009.

8

RELIGIOUS POLITICS AND
THE LEGAL SYSTEM

In this chapter and the next we enter the realm of law and the courts. We also consider policy decisions that are affected by the legal system of the United States. Legal decisions made by state and federal courts have an enormous influence on public policy in areas from government aid to religious social services to prayer in public schools. Groups from all sides have become increasingly involved in legal struggles to promote their points of view. Besides being the arena for struggles over specific policies, American courtrooms are also the setting for the airing of cultural disagreements about the general role of organized religion and the interaction between religion and politics. The stakes are high, and the legal conflicts are often intense.

No one should make the mistake of thinking that the American legal system exists independently of politics. Instead, typical political pushing and shoving are very much a part of the process of settling legal disputes. This is neither shocking nor necessarily lamentable; it is simply reality. This is not to say that politics entirely defines the American legal system. It has its own internal norms, such as the principle of stare decisis (which means standing by previous court decisions) and concern for due process. Moreover, many judges are eminently fair and strive not to allow personal prejudices to color their rulings.

In this chapter we examine the efforts of religio-political forces to affect legal outcomes. We consider some of the reasons for these efforts and the specific resources that help to make groups effective in the legal arena. In the process we introduce some of the most significant organizations involved in the legal struggle over religion and politics. After reflecting on the implications of this struggle, we consider broader theories of how organized religion ought to relate to government, which together form the context of various legal arguments. In Chapter 9, we examine the specific religio-political disputes that have occupied the courts—and how these disputes have been resolved.

JUDICIAL POLITICS

Most religious groups in the United States historically have ignored the courts, but in the past several decades many have become deeply involved with the legal system. It has become routine for such groups to work through the courts in order to try to achieve—or to protect—objectives that they cannot accomplish in any other way. A large variety of religious legal organizations help to shepherd disputes through the courts, often by recruiting aggrieved parties and providing lawyers and funding in a case. Another common approach that religious (and other) groups use in judicial politics today is the filing of amicus curiae (friend of the court) briefs. Amicus briefs are written opinions filed with a court that allow third parties (in this instance religious legal organizations) to register their views on pending cases. Even if the court does not take heed of the views of a particular group filing as amicus curiae, the group's views will nonetheless become a matter of public record, and group leaders can trumpet their efforts to their membership. And there are a host of other tactics too: lobbying about the selection of judges to the federal courts, seeking favorable implementation of court rulings, and influencing elite and mass opinion on the meaning of law.

Why has this turn to the courts taken place? It partly reflects broad-based developments in the American political system as a whole. In the last half of the twentieth century the United States embraced a more centralized national political system. This trend began in the 1930s and 1940s with the emergence and effort of President Franklin Delano Roosevelt, who fought the Great Depression and World War II from the national level. In the process the size and the influence of the federal government began an expansion that has continued to the present day. The increasing focus on the national government was an opportunity for some key advocacy groups, which were already established and poised to nationalize their agendas. Groups such as the National Association for the Advancement of Colored People (NAACP) (founded in 1909) and the American Civil Liberties Union (ACLU) (founded in 1920) fostered a "rights revolution" by actively supporting litigation that tested the boundaries of civil liberties protections.[1] Their efforts went hand in hand with considerable activism on the part of the federal judiciary, most notably the U.S. Supreme Court. Today's interest groups, including religious groups, realize that the federal courts have come to exercise tremendous influence over national policy.

The First Amendment holds that "Congress shall make no law respecting an establishment of religion, or prohibiting the free exercise thereof." Before the 1940s almost all legal disputes over church and state were considered state matters and were resolved in state courts. The religion clauses of the First Amendment were viewed as essentially jurisdictional: Congress had no authority over religious matters, but states did.[2] Because the U.S. Supreme Court had interpreted the First Amendment to apply only to actions of the *national* government for 150 years, states were not forced to comply with the religion clauses of the First Amendment, so state-level church-state disputes were rarely addressed in federal courts. In the 1940s, however, the Court changed its mind about this long-standing interpretation of the First Amendment's meaning and began ruling on a wide range of religious debates from the state and local levels. The Court insisted that national standards were necessary and acceptable—and should supersede state and local norms.

The Court accomplished this goal by interpreting parts of the Fourteenth Amendment, which was passed in the wake of the Civil War, to mean that state and local laws and practices must meet with the standard of the First Amendment. The relevant part of the Fourteenth Amendment holds that: "No State shall . . . deprive any person of life, liberty, or property, without due process of law." According to the Court, this clause means that no *state* should be allowed to abridge religious freedom protected by the First Amendment, despite the fact that the amendment states that "*Congress* shall make no law," not "*Congress and the state legislatures* shall make no law." Since the 1940s, this interpretation has been the Court's standard—and thus the nation's—of determining the proper venue for resolving disputes about the First Amendment's religion clauses. In interpreting the Constitution this way, the Court extended the "doctrine of incorporation," its overall argument that the *states* are bound by the Fourteenth Amendment to guarantee their citizens the civil liberties set forth in the Bill of Rights.

The Court first decided to incorporate the Free Exercise Clause of the First Amendment (" . . . or prohibiting the free exercise thereof") in *Cantwell* v. *Connecticut* (1940). In that case the Court held that the provisions of the First Amendment regarding religious freedom should constrain the actions of state and local governments as well as those of the federal government. The state of Connecticut could not prevent Jehovah's Witnesses from proselytizing because doing so violated their free exercise rights. According to the Court, "The Fourteenth Amendment has rendered the legislatures of the states as incompetent as Congress to enact laws which violate the provisions of the first amendment."[3] With its judgment in *Cantwell*, the Supreme Court claimed for itself great decision-making power over state- and local-level disputes. Imagine the implications of moving from constitutional restrictions on one institution of government (Congress) to more than 90,000 (the combined total of all state and local governments in the United States, which includes towns, cities, counties, independent school districts, and many other regional authorities). One major consequence was that the *Cantwell* precedent sent the message that religious groups, and many others, could turn to the federal courts for the resolution of their problems with any and all governmental institutions and policies.

Other factors were also at work. The simple reality of expanding religious pluralism increased the role of the courts. The influence of minority religions can be exaggerated, but there is no doubt that every year more new religious movements emerge and gather strength in the United States. The growth of this pluralism began in earnest with the expansion of Roman Catholicism in the nineteenth and early twentieth centuries. As religious pluralism broadened in twentieth-century America, an increasing number of religious groups found themselves in conflict with the government or the society around them.

Some of these groups went to the federal courts to seek redress. This was particularly true of small religious groups. Their leaders often believed that Congress and the executive branch would be less likely to be responsive to a small religious minority than would the federal courts.[4] During the 1940s, the Jehovah's Witnesses pioneered this process by seeking relief in the federal courts from assorted local and state regulations limiting their door-to-door proselytizing or requiring salutes to the American flag. Such regulations severely limited Jehovah's Witnesses' freedom to practice their religion, which demands active proselytizing and prohibits the salute of any flag. In many of these instances the Witnesses succeeded in securing their free exercise rights.[5]

The success of the Jehovah's Witnesses encouraged other religious minority groups to believe that the federal courts presented both a possible and proper realm for addressing the unique problems they face. Such groups, in effect, encouraged the federal courts to take an active role in shaping the politics of religion in the United States. Since the 1940s, what was once a trickle of cases has become a flood as the conflict between religion and politics in America is increasingly played out in its courts. The federal courts have been busy since *Cantwell* was decided in 1940, with the Supreme Court alone deciding more than 160 cases dealing with religion.[6] Some of the reason for this broader engagement is the judiciary's own preference for involvement in disputes between organized religion and the political system. Neither the lower federal courts nor the U.S. Supreme Court has shied away from this arena. This extends to the federal courts' willingness to intervene in abortion policy and other issues that concern many religious groups. For better or for worse, the Supreme Court's decision in *Roe* v. *Wade* (1973) that abortion is constitutional has generated an enormous amount of controversy—and legal action.

The nature of the courts' rulings, especially those of the Supreme Court, has magnified legal conflicts that are rooted in church-state disputes and other religious matters. As we note in Chapter 9, the Supreme Court's pronouncements in these areas have too often been unclear—some say contradictory—and thus have resolved little. This uncertainty ensures further litigation and more dispute. Moreover, as the federal courts have taken a more visible role in settling disputes about church-state separation and religious freedom since the 1940s, a wide variety of interest groups have entered the scene. Even religious groups that are successful in legislative and executive arenas realize that they must be participants in *every* major playing field, including the courts, if they are going make their mark on American politics.[7]

KEY PLAYERS

The legal system today bursts with activity as religious associations attempt to influence court rulings. None of these groups represents a majority of the American public. Still, many have had a significant impact on judicial politics at the federal, state, and local levels. Many of the key players are connected with what may be termed the "separationist coalition," which supports an absolute separation between church and state. Recently, however, such groups have been challenged by an emerging set of opposing groups affiliated with evangelical Protestantism.

Separationist organizations come in three varieties. Some trace their roots to a separationist Protestant tradition that goes back to the Puritan leader Roger Williams in colonial Rhode Island.[8] Its members are often quite religious. Their goal is to nurture free exercise rights by keeping religion separate from government. As Roger Williams himself envisioned it in 1744, separationists believe there should be a "wall of Separation between the Garden of the Church and the Wilderness of the World."[9] Williams's legacy lives on in such notable separationist organizations as the Baptist Joint Committee (BJC). Long committed to separation of church and state, the Baptist Joint Committee is one of the most active groups in American judicial politics today. It draws support from a variety of Baptist organizations, though in 1991 it lost the support of the largest Baptist denomination, the Southern Baptist Convention, over disagreements regarding church-state separation and the convention's view that BJC was leaning toward a liberal political agenda.[10]

Another major separationist organization is Americans United for Separation of Church and State, which was founded in 1947 with considerable Protestant support. Its major outlet is *Church and State*, a publication that is distinctly sympathetic to separationist views. Though Americans United has a long history and has enjoyed a great deal of publicity since the 1940s for its zealous opposition to state aid for Catholic schools (if not Catholicism itself), it now is part of the broader separationist coalition that includes other associations that have not historically been aligned with separationist Protestantism (Box 8.1).

Also integral to the separationist coalition are a number of Jewish organizations and their legal arms.[11] The most prominent is the American Jewish Committee, but other groups include the American Jewish Congress and the Anti-Defamation League. Most Jewish groups have been involved in legal battles to promote separation of church and state as a way of protecting Jews (and other religious minorities) from the official establishment of any form of Christianity. Whenever a crèche (manger scene) appears on public property, or Christian prayers are being led by staff at public schools, or other potential violations of the separation of church and state occur, it is common to find the American Jewish Committee and its allies going to court to halt these practices.

BOX 8.1   PEOPLE FOR THE AMERICAN WAY

A separationist group of more recent vintage is People for the American Way (PFAW), created in 1981 by Hollywood producer Norman Lear, who is famous for *All in the Family* and other television comedies. PFAW is not attached to any branch of Christianity or to any religion at all, though it steadfastly maintains that it is sympathetic to religion. It has been extremely active in taking legal action to promote separationism in church-state affairs, especially by trying to defeat or frustrate efforts of the Christian Right. Indeed, PFAW was initially formed to combat the now-defunct Moral Majority. In addition to its continuing role as a "monitor . . . of the Religious and Radical Right," its recent agenda has included vocal support for same-sex marriage and for left-leaning nominees for federal judgeships.

Source: *People for the American Way*, http://www.pfaw.org.

A third, and perhaps more uneasy, partner in the separationist coalition today represents the truly secularist portion of the movement. The American Civil Liberties Union (ACLU) is the most famous and assertive member of this wing. Indeed, the ACLU gets more involved than any other organization in church-state controversies and other legal disputes involving religion. It is committed to full separation of church and state and often to free exercise rights for small religious minorities that have been affected negatively by the state.

Though the ACLU's lack of connection with religion has not prevented it from rallying to help selected religious groups, other secular organizations exist to advance secular values and institutions only. This is a fair description of the objective of the American Atheists and the Freedom from Religion Foundation. American Atheists claims to be "the premier organization laboring for the civil liberties of atheists, and the total, absolute separation of government and religion."[12] This same principle underlies the efforts of the Freedom from Religion Foundation, whose title leaves no doubt about its objectives. Founded in Madison, Wisconsin, by Anne Gaylor and her daughter, Annie Laurie Gaylor, but now operating nationally, the Freedom from Religion Foundation has sought to make a difference in the church-state controversy by fighting in the courts to dismantle all linkages between church and state.[13] These groups have challenged all abridgments of church-state separation, including the printing of "In God We Trust" on U.S. currency, the saying of prayers before public legislative bodies, and more recently efforts to expand state funding of faith-based social services.

Until the late 1970s, separationist groups were largely unopposed by other advocacy groups in the courts.[14] But the activity of the separationist lobby, and public perceptions of its success, has provoked a counterreaction. Regardless of separationist motivations, many worried that the result of strict church-state separation would be a diminished role for religion in public life. Today, religious groups that are determined to fight back in court are a growth industry. Most of these are associated with evangelical Protestantism, but they often have contributors who are sympathetic with their efforts regardless of religious background. [15]

Some religious legal organizations have existed for decades. The Christian Legal Society was founded in 1962, for example. Most, however, were born in the 1980s and 1990s when conservative groups discovered that whatever one's influence on legislatures, executives, or the people in general, the courts matter too. This sense has heightened religious groups' concern about the judicial selection process and strengthened their resolve to be involved in the politics of court decisions. In some instances, mass membership groups such as the Moral Majority or Concerned

Women for America created legal departments within their own organizations. But more often leaders realized a need to establish stand-alone groups to focus specifically on law and courts.

Perhaps the most prominent religious legal organization with Christian conservative roots is the American Center for Law and Justice (ACLJ), a creation of Rev. Pat Robertson and his associates. Under the leadership of Jay Sekulow, an effective litigator with media savvy, the ACLJ quickly became a major evangelical player in legal politics after its founding in 1990. The ACLJ has entered many legal disputes in various capacities and has been remarkably active in the Supreme Court itself, with Sekulow arguing several religious freedom and free speech cases before the justices.[16] The group has been quite adept at reaching out to the evangelical community through Robertson's media outlets and a radio show hosted by Sekulow. This exposure has helped ACLJ to secure a great deal of financial support from ordinary religious conservatives, as well as from other sources.

One important group providing that support is the Alliance Defense Fund (ADF). James Dobson, D. James Kennedy, Bill Bright, and other prominent evangelicals founded the ADF in 1994 to empower allies such as the ACLJ through financial and other forms of support. By providing grants to other organizations, ADF seeks to help coordinate the efforts of social conservatives at legal advocacy and to channel the flow of church-state and "family values" cases on court dockets.

BOX 8.2   HOME SCHOOL LEGAL DEFENSE ASSOCIATION

Some legal advocacy groups have a very specialized role. A good example is the Home School Legal Defense Association (HSLDA), a Christian conservative group that defends homeschooling families against government oversight and control. Homeschooling is increasingly popular as an educational choice, which gives HSLDA a great deal of work to do. Since its founding by Michael Farris and Mike Smith in 1983, HSLDA has been focused largely on state-level policy because states promulgate and administer most of the rules governing education in the United States. The HSLDA's tactics run the gamut from litigation to legislative lobbying. Farris and the HSLDA have even spun off a Christian institution of higher education, Patrick Henry College in Purcellville, Virginia, which began operations in 2000 and primarily serves homeschoolers with interests in government and other forms of public service.

Source: *Home School Legal Defense Association*, http://www.hslda.org.

The group has funded many notable cases, including *Rosenberger* v. *University of Virginia* (1995), in which several Christian college students won their challenge to a state university policy of denying certain funds to religious groups. Today, the ADF has branched out to take cases directly into litigation, rather than merely funding other organizations to do so. It also operates a training program for like-minded attorneys through its National Litigation Academy (Box 8.2).

But not all non-separatist legal groups represent evangelical Protestants and their interests. The Office of the General Counsel of the United States Conference of Catholic Bishops (USCCB) plays a significant role in church-state disputes. It provides the bishops and various ecclesial departments with legal advice and represents the American Church in litigation both directly as a party and indirectly by filing amicus curiae briefs.[17] Given the Catholic Church's many interests, from immigration to abortion to clergy abuse allegations, the Church's lawyers are kept very busy. Many specific denominations also undertake their own legal efforts, particularly as amicus curiae. The pro-life Lutheran Church–Missouri Synod, for example, frequently files amicus briefs with the Supreme Court in abortion cases.

FACTORS FOR SUCCESS

What contributes to the success or failure of advocacy organizations as they enter the courts over church-state matters? Of course, sympathetic judges and propitious times always help, but what else matters? What are the dynamics that contribute to legal success? One crucial factor is money; litigation and other forms of legal advocacy are expensive. This painful but real fact is often an awkward matter, especially for mass membership groups that rely on their constituents for direct donations of time and money. There can be substantial competition among various legal action organizations for limited donors and dollars. Moreover, fundraising efforts require both time and money and leave less of both for the legal causes at hand.

Equally important, of course, are experience and expertise, both of which take time to develop. We have already noted that in building effective lobbying organizations, people who know their way around Congress or the statehouses are indispensable. So are those who understand the concerns of the religious groups they represent, how their members think, and how they want their story told. The same applies to religious associations in the legal arena. After all, they are really just interest groups involved in legal advocacy, lobbying the courts for their self-defined interests. The lawyers who spearhead these efforts must know both the legal and religious terrain. Indeed, it helps to have lawyers with the passion that comes with being personally committed to a group's cause, especially because groups often must rely on the volunteer labor of those attorneys.[18] New groups, including those from the evangelical perspective, have sometimes neglected these resources, but they have slowly come to nurture savvy legal activists.

A third factor for success is support for legal activism among group members and donors. If a group's members do not want their contributions to fund legal efforts, the group will find itself seriously stifled. Government support has also been of great assistance at times. This was true for many conservative Christian legal organizations during Republican presidencies, when they found themselves in the favorable position of working with Republican-appointed Justice Department lawyers on the same cases, toward the same ends. Finally, support from the larger public can help too. Public support generates funds and favorable publicity, both of which may affect legal contests in myriad ways.

The embrace of legal strategizing by religious groups appears to be growing. This makes sense in light of the increasing religious pluralism of American society. Today less than 60 percent of the U.S. population claim to be Protestants.[19] Moreover, the fault lines within Protestantism over moral and political issues have now become as deep as any between Protestants and members of other religious traditions. In short, American society now faces an expanding religious pluralism that is accompanied by moral pluralism. Such a context is hardly a congenial one for any religious group that tries to affect politics by working only through legislatures or presidents.

This reality is sharpened in light of the fact that American religious traditions are increasingly politically organized and face organized opposition themselves. In religion, as elsewhere, the truth today is as James Madison suggested it should be in *Federalist No. 51*: Interest checks interest, and ambition checks ambition. Such a situation almost compels those who seek social change into the courts, for it is often the case that judges alone make authoritative decisions breaking the organized pluralist stalemate that so often holds sway. The courts can render clear decisions; they can break impasses; and they can side with even the smallest religious interest if they feel that the law or the Constitution directs such a decision.

It often makes sense for religious organizations to take legal action in the current political arena. Yet we need to be clear that such a step, especially for many religious minority groups, is usually a defensive move designed to protect against domination by more powerful groups and perspectives. Indeed, in an increasingly pluralistic society, there is little else that small religious groups can do when they perceive themselves to be threatened. In times of crisis, they have only one serious recourse: the law through the courts.

Religious groups are increasingly using the courts to publicize themselves for their members and the broader society as well. When a group is involved in litigation, its members learn it is actively pursuing the group's goals. And even if the group has little actual influence over the judges' decision, it can still claim credit from its members if the case is decided in line with the group's stated agenda. Litigation can also attract the attention of people outside of the group, which attracts new members and lays the foundation for coalition-building with other groups. Coalition-building is particularly valuable because it can facilitate a division of labor. The ACLJ, for example, hires some of its lawyers from the evangelical Regent University School of Law. In its earlier years, it also received financial and research support from the Christian Coalition. None of this would have been possible if the ACLJ were shy about its engagement in judicial politics. Coalition-building can also allow religious legal organizations to pursue a wider variety of goals. Some groups may focus on education, others on abortion, and still others on pornography, but they offer mutual support at the same time.

For many religious groups, the politics of legal action offers distinct advantages. Taking politics to the courts requires neither a large membership nor elite access in the powerful worlds of official Washington and the national media nor vast financial resources. Thus legal strategies make sense for small, otherwise powerless groups. For better-endowed and well-connected interests that would usually lose if popularly elected legislatures had the last word on their concerns, going to court also makes sense.

For some religions, legal strategies present an additional advantage of fostering the illusion that they avoid politics, a world that many groups (such as the Jehovah's Witnesses and the Amish) dislike, fear, or oppose. They trade on the conventional wisdom that the courts are a pure, nonpolitical realm, uninvolved in the grubby world of clashing interest groups. This sometimes treasured—but inaccurate—belief attracts many religious groups to the courts to accomplish what are ultimately political ends.

For the United States as a whole, the strategy of fighting battles between religion and politics in the legal system presents mixed blessings. There is much dispute about whether religio-political controversies ought to be resolved in a democratic arena or a federal courtroom. Should religious freedom be subject to definition by the majority? Should the limits of government establishment of religion be outlined by the majority? Indeed, some participants in the church-state debates of today wonder whether democracy is an important value to begin with. Those who point out that democracy is not enshrined in the Bible or any other sacred text refuse to worry about whether the courts contribute to or hinder democracy.

For such individuals, the real issue is the need to protect rights, whether they are the rights of the Amish, strict separationists, or Mormons. By this view, if the courts serve as a setting where such questions may be addressed—and addressed without inflaming biases that often accompany religious diversity, free exercise, and official establishment—then they contribute immeasurably to a healthy society. And, one may argue, sometimes the result is a flowering of democracy because freedom and democracy go hand in hand.

THE POLITICS OF CHURCH AND STATE

In the midst of the legal struggle for advantage in debates about religion and politics today lie various approaches to the relationship between church and state. There is much at stake: not simply how government relates to religious institutions, but also fundamental beliefs about the normative role of religious values in politics and society. How should the courts and those who appeal to them for recourse establish relationships between church and state, and between religion and politics?

The Supreme Court has framed the answer in terms of *neutrality*—broadly speaking, the idea that government ought not to play favorites when it comes to religion. The Supreme Court's most prominent version of the neutrality doctrine was formulated in the classic case *Lemon* v. *Kurtzman* (1971). It held that if a law has a secular purpose and a secular effect (i.e., the "primary effect" of government's actions must "neither advance nor inhibit religion"), and does not result in excessive entanglement between religion and government, then it is constitutional. By this view, it is acceptable for there to be incidental government support for religion, but only as a byproduct of some law that is secular both in intent and primary effect. Similarly, it is acceptable to impair religious freedom, but only as a byproduct of a law with a secular purpose and a secular effect.

Nearly all groups involved in church-state debates invoke the value of neutrality; very few would suggest that government should be able to prefer a specific religious faith or set of faiths over all others, at least in an intentional way. But groups that accept the general idea of neutrality often take opposite positions—and vehemently so—about how neutrality ought to be put into practice. There is also widespread frustration with the Court's way of handling neutrality, though for different reasons. Chapter 9 will examine some of the specific church-state matters that the courts have adjudicated. Here, however, we introduce two classic perspectives on neutrality in church-state relations and the extent to which the courts have embraced each in recent decades.

The Separatist Approach

For a separatist, the First Amendment's religion clauses—"Congress shall make no law respecting an establishment of religion, or prohibiting the free exercise thereof"—mean that government cannot be involved with religion *in any way*.[20] Separatists look with pride to those chapters in colonial history that were part of the journey toward separation of church and state. They honor Roger Williams, founder of Rhode Island, for his determination to separate church and state, and William Penn, founder of Pennsylvania, for his commitment to Quaker tolerance of other religious faiths. They respect the histories of such colonies as New York and Pennsylvania that pioneered the tradition of separatism. Such colonies were sure that true free exercise was possible only when the state and the law were kept apart from organized religion.

Though church-state relations during the colonial era were complicated, there is no doubt that the separationist point of view united many people. Separatism formed an umbrella under which those who feared state religions and those who were skeptical of religion in any form could gather. It also accommodated those whose ardent commitment to minority and dissenting religions made them worry about how they—and thus true religion—would fare if the government were to become involved in religious matters. From these diffuse roots, ranging from the skeptical Thomas Jefferson to the earnest New England Baptists, the separatist tradition grew.[21] Sophisticated separatists, however, were and are well aware that even after the adoption of the Constitution and the Bill of Rights, the American record was hardly separationist. Religion (especially Christianity) has always been deeply connected with, and often supported by, the state.

Thus there has been much for separatists to litigate. Separatists have been concerned about the saying of prayers and other religious references at the opening of sessions of state legislatures and Congress, the president's inauguration, and even the opening session of the U.S. Supreme Court itself. They worry about the employment of government-sponsored chaplains in the military and government aid for religious hospitals, religious social service agencies, and religious colleges. They note with displeasure the references to God on American currency and in the Pledge of Allegiance. They dislike seeing crèches on public land in December and hearing government officials invoke the name of God on Thanksgiving. In short, separatists argue that American culture is schizophrenic in that it is theoretically committed to the principle of separatism—yet far from separatist in practice.

Public attitudes are equally mixed. Studies consistently demonstrate that people in the United States reflexively endorse "separation of church and state" and oppose the mixing of religion and politics in the abstract. But there is often considerable support for specific actions that hardly fit with such a view. Consider opinion on the role of religion in public schools: Two-thirds of the American people support a moment of silence for meditation or prayer in public schools (and a quarter support an actual spoken prayer),[22] and two-thirds also agree that religious accounts of the origin of the human species should be taught alongside evolution in public schools.[23]

Separatists hold that the absence of official sanctioning of religion by government and religious free exercise are inseparable. They believe that the more government remains separate from religion, the more citizens will be able to enjoy religious freedom. Separatists argue that this belief was held by many of the framers of the American Constitution, including James Madison, who wrote the Bill of Rights. The idea is that an activist government presents a real threat when it becomes involved with religious institutions.

Hence the Supreme Court's efforts to address church-state relations through the *Lemon* test (the constitutionality of laws with a secular intent and effect, despite potential outcomes for religious groups) and other legal approaches often anger separatists. Separatists appreciate that these approaches eliminate flagrant, overt aid to organized religion and forbid any formal establishment of religion. But they want the Court to take religion into account in order to ensure that no matter what a law's main purpose or principal effect, religion does not obtain any government benefits. For separatists, what the Supreme Court calls "neutrality" can be (and has been) used by the courts as a way to turn a blind eye toward the clever ways government hides laws that aid and support religious purposes under seemingly secular objectives and language. For radical separatists, state laws that allow nonprofit groups freedom from taxation would constitute a prime example. Under the Court's predominant approach, such laws would be constitutional because they have a secular purpose and mainly secular effects (because they are for nonprofit groups of all types). But in practice such rules grant an enormous privilege to religious nonprofit organizations. They meet the nonprofit test and may thus receive substantial state benefits. To be fully neutral, separatists say, government ought not to support religion in any shape or form, even if that support is secondary to a secular purpose.

Accommodationist Perspectives

In contrast to strict separatists, others have advocated for an accommodating stance of the state toward religion. This position on church-state relationships comes in many forms. Some members of the Supreme Court, for example, have offered a modified version of the Court's *Lemon* doctrine that one justice termed "benevolent neutrality."[24] Supporters of this approach approve of neutrality as the proper stance for the courts because they are confident that it will prevent religion and churches from becoming a more prominent factor in government decisions. At the same time, however, benevolent neutrality tries to have it both ways. Its advocates argue that there should be sympathetic acceptance from time to time of the religious effects of secular government actions and laws.

Supporters of the benevolent neutrality position maintain that application of the secular purpose and secular effect test avoids government sponsorship of religion, but at the same time they insist that this test must not be followed in such a rigid fashion that religious freedom is lost. Government must not sponsor religion, but it must not destroy it either. Though government should generally stay neutral, it must do so in a benevolent mood, and no fixed formula can make that happen. Judgment is therefore needed on a case-by-case basis, according to the benevolent neutrality view.

A stronger statement of church-state accommodation is known as "equal treatment." Its supporters maintain that the courts should sanction government assistance to churches and other religious groups *as long as this is done for all of them equally* (equal treatment) and *if it would encourage free exercise of religion*. Those in favor of equal treatment declare that religion sometimes needs the state to help free exercise become a reality. Thus separationists may not necessarily be correct when they assert that free exercise expands when the separation between church and state grows.[25]

In American history this was, in effect, part of the case made by those (primarily Roman Catholics) who felt that state aid for religious schools was a good idea. From time to time they succeeded. For example, in the years after the Civil War, President Ulysses S. Grant undertook an effort to promote peace between whites and Native Americans by encouraging the assimilation of Native Americans through education. To provide such education, he turned to churches and granted them the privilege of establishing schools on reservations. For the last three decades of the nineteenth century, Congress funded a number of religious groups as part of this effort, including the Catholic Church. In 1899, however, the entire program came to an end, in part because Protestant groups objected to the funding of Catholic schools.

This education program was very much the exception rather than the rule. A portion of the traditional argument in favor of state aid for Catholic schools was practical: Catholics wanted and needed the money to keep their schools going. Another part, though, is the argument some Catholics make that access to religious school education is vital for real free exercise of religion. The only way to achieve this goal for many Catholics is through government assistance. This view has come to be shared in the present time by some evangelical Protestant "Christian school" supporters, including many proponents of state-funded educational vouchers. But it has yet to garner broader levels of public support.[26]

In other areas, equal treatment garners much support, such as widespread support for tax deductions for all nonprofit religious organizations. There is no doubt that such policies help organized religion in a material sense and may therefore encourage its existence. Recent efforts to expand public funding for faith-based social services have also been based explicitly on the equal treatment view. Proponents of broader funding argue that government support of religious agencies is constitutionally permissible as long as money is available to all groups, religious and nonreligious alike.

Opponents of equal treatment contend that nontraditional forms of equal treatment (such as substantial state aid for religious schools) and in some cases all forms (including property tax forgiveness) are unconstitutional threats to religious freedom. According to such critics, having the state involved with religion, and certainly with religious schools, raises the very real specter of state control. That, they believe, would be a disaster.

The argument goes back and forth (see Box 8.3). Those who favor positive accommodation, as they might put it, sometimes suggest a case-by-case approach. They often turn back to history to make part of their case. As they read it, the historical record reveals a complex and diverse pattern in which there was once a great deal of official establishment and accommodation of religion that did not involve the sacrifice of free exercise or the establishment of a single church.

For proponents of equal treatment, sweeping historical claims about separationism and the framers simply do not work. They point out that when the First Amendment was adopted, a number of states continued to maintain official religions. Massachusetts, the last to give up its established church, did not do so until 1833. Moreover, whereas Congress operated in the early years as though the First Amendment prohibited all government connection with religion or churches, at other times it gave a contrary signal. The very year Congress approved the First

Amendment, for example, it also reenacted the Northwest Ordinance, the document governing much of the western U.S. territory (now the Midwest). Section III of the Northwest Ordinance observed that "religion, morality, and knowledge being necessary to good government and the happiness of mankind, schools and the means of learning shall forever be encouraged."[27]

BOX 8.3   RELIGIOUS NONPROFIT ORGANIZATIONS AND PUBLIC MONEY

A paradox of American politics is that, although fierce legal battles are fought over state aid to parochial schools, billions of dollars of government funds flow annually through other religiously based nonprofit organizations. Normally this occurs without fanfare or legal challenge.

Since colonial days, all levels of American government have sought to achieve public policy goals by working through nonprofit charities, hospitals, educational institutions, and relief agencies. Many of these nonprofits are faith-based and receive a substantial portion of their budgets from government contracts, grants, or patron vouchers. This system works well from the standpoints of government because nonprofit organizations are closer to the communities they serve, less bureaucratic, more flexible, and perhaps more effective. In turn, religious communities are left relatively free to provide faith-inspired services, such as assistance for the needy, adoption services, refugee settlement, and healthcare.

Public support for faith-based nonprofits, however, recently has come under greater scrutiny. Since the welfare reforms of 1996, a greater range of religious social services than in the past has been competing for public money. Unlike Catholic Charities, Lutheran Social Services, and other regular recipients of public funds, many religious social service organizations are now more upfront about their religious identity, integrating religious practices such as prayer and worship into their provision of social services. This practice has begun to raise questions about the constitutionality of public funding of religious nonprofits. Those questions have been at the forefront as President Barack Obama considers whether to extend efforts started by the George W. Bush administration to expand public financing of faith-based social services.

Source: Amy E. Black, Douglas L. Koopman, and David K. Ryden, *Of Little Faith: The Politics of George W. Bush's Faith-Based Initiatives* (Washington, DC: Georgetown University Press, 2004); John J. DiIulio Jr., *Godly Republic: A Centrist Blueprint for America's Faith-Based Future* (Berkeley: University of California Press, 2007); and Stephen V. Monsma, *When Sacred and Secular Mix: Religious Nonprofit Organizations and Public Money* (Lanham, MD: Rowman and Littlefield, 1996).

Advocates of further state aid to religion also take issue with the image of such crucial constitutional framers as Thomas Jefferson and James Madison as radical separationists. They argue that neither Jefferson nor Madison believed that there needed to be dogmatic lines separating church and state, and that normatively speaking, such lines should not be drawn in a complex, diverse political order. It is no simple matter; free exercise has sometimes been harmed by the state's assistance to religious groups, but it also sometimes has required such aid.[28]

Some proponents of equal treatment openly declare that what they favor amounts to multiple establishment—the official (or semiofficial) establishment of all faiths in the United States—because of the country's enormous religious pluralism. Advocates of this approach embrace as reality exactly what their opponents believe—and fear—is the essential truth about equal treatment. For advocates of multiple establishment, the logic of equal treatment can derive from a postmodern world in which there are no shared truths, and where the necessity of pluralist tolerance is absolutely essential.[29]

CONCLUSION

More than 150 years ago Alexis de Tocqueville discussed the inclination of Americans to try to resolve policy disputes in the courts. He saw the legal system as a way for people in the United States to avoid messy and contentious political fights. Instead, they used "neutral" judges and courtrooms to work out resolutions. Today there are many more factors compelling people to turn to the legal system to address policy conflicts, including the presence in the United States of more than a million lawyers.

In any case, Tocqueville would probably be astounded today at how often policy conflicts are met and sometimes resolved in the courts. This is certainly true in the area of religion and politics and church and state. The legal system is, in fact, perhaps the favorite avenue for religious politics, and its terrain is contested with all the resources and political skills that can be mustered by the interested parties. Thus it is essential for any religious group entering the political realm in the United States to know how judicial politics works.

Courts are political institutions and must be so in matters of church and state and religion and politics. They can help achieve compromises that respect the past and yet acknowledge the more diverse present. The results may often be messy and short on neat logic, but few things in politics are neat and logical, and given the nature of the human being, perhaps that is just as well.

FURTHER READING

den Dulk, Kevin R. "Purpose-Driven Lawyers: Evangelical Cause Lawyering and the Culture War." In *The Cultural Lives of Cause Lawyers*, eds. Austin Sarat and Stuart Scheingold. New York: Cambridge University Press, 2008. A study of key leaders in evangelical legal groups.

Fisher, Louis. *Religious Liberty in America: Political Safeguards*. Lawrence, KS: University Press of Kansas, 2002. A provocative study that suggests courts do no better than the legislative process in protecting religious liberty.

Hamburger, Philip. *Separation of Church and State*. Cambridge, MA: Harvard University Press, 2002. A stimulating argument that church-state separatism has no historical foundations.

Ivers, Gregg. *To Build a Wall: American Jews and the Separation of Church and State*. Charlottesville, VA: University of Virginia Press, 1995. An examination of the role of Jewish groups in church-state relations.

Kramnick, Isaac, and R. Laurence Moore. *The Godless Constitution: A Moral Defense of the Secular State*. 2nd ed. New York: W. W. Norton, 2005. A probing separatist interpretation of the founding period.

Monsma, Stephen V., and J. Christopher Soper. *The Challenge of Pluralism: Church and State in Five Democracies*. 2nd ed. Lanham, MD: Rowman and Littlefield, 2009. A superb cross-national analysis of church-state relations in the United States and abroad.

Pfeffer, Leo. *Religion, State, and the Burger Court*. Buffalo, NY: Prometheus, 1984. The classic defense of separatism.

Waldman, Steven. *Founding Faith: Providence, Politics, and the Birth of Religious Freedom in America*. New York: Random House, 2008. A balanced treatment of the founders' own religion and their views of church and state.

NOTES

1. Charles R. Epp, *The Rights Revolution: Lawyers, Activists, and Supreme Courts in Comparative Perspective* (Chicago: University of Chicago Press, 1998).

2. Steven D. Smith, *Foreordained Failure: The Quest for a Constitutional Principle of Religious Freedom* (Princeton: Princeton University Press, 1999).

3. *Cantwell v. Connecticut*, 310 US 296 (1940).

4. In many instances these beliefs may have been mistaken. See Louis Fisher, *Religious Liberty in America: Political Safeguards* (Lawrence, KS: University Press of Kansas, 2002).

5. See Shawn Francis Peters, *Judging Jehovah's Witnesses: Religious Persecution and the Dawn of the Rights Revolution* (Lawrence, KS: University Press of Kansas, 2000).

6. John Witte Jr. provides an exhaustive listing of religion clause cases through 2004 in his *Religion and the American Constitutional Experiment: Essential Rights and Liberties*, 2nd ed. (Boulder: Westview Press, 2005), appendix 3. We have added some cases that have been decided since the publication of Witte's book or that address religion using a clause of the Constitution other than the Free Exercise or Establishment Clauses. We discuss those cases more fully in the next chapter.

7. Kevin R. den Dulk and J. Mitchell Pickerill, "Bridging the Lawmaking Process: Organized Interests, Court-Congress Interaction, and Church-State Relations," *Polity* 35 (2003), 419–440.

8. For an interesting separationist interpretation of the founding, see Isaac Kramnick and R. Laurence Moore, *The Godless Constitution: The Case Against Religious Correctness* (New York: W. W. Norton, 1996).

9. Roger Williams, "Mr. Cotton's Letter Lately Printed, Examined and Answered," in *Religion and Constitutional Government in the United States*, ed. John E. Semonche (Carrboro, NC: Signal Books, 1985), 77.

10. Laura Sessions Stepp, "Conservative Reelected to Lead Baptists," *The Washington Post*, June 5, 1991, A4.

11. On this topic, see Gregg Ivers, *To Build a Wall: American Jews and the Separation of Church and State* (Charlottesville, VA: University of Virginia Press, 1995).

12. http://www.atheists.org/.

13. http://www.ffrf.org/.

14. Frank Sorauf, *The Wall of Separation: Constitutional Politics of Church and State* (Princeton: Princeton University Press, 1976).

15. See Kevin R. den Dulk, "In Legal Culture, but Not of It: The Role of Cause Lawyers in Evangelical Legal Mobilization," in *Cause Lawyering and Social Movements*, eds. Austin Sarat and Stuart Scheingold (Palo Alto, CA: Stanford University Press, 2006); and Kevin R. den Dulk, "Purpose-Driven Lawyers: Evangelical Cause Lawyering and the Culture War," in *The Cultural Lives of Cause Lawyers*, eds. Austin Sarat and Stuart Scheingold (New York: Cambridge University Press, 2008). See also Steven P. Brown, *Trumping Religion: The New Christian Right, The Free Speech Clause, and the Courts* (Tuscaloosa, AL: University of Alabama Press, 2002).

16. See, for example, *McConnell v. FEC*, 540 U.S. 93 (2003); *Locke v. Davey*, 540 U.S. 712 (2004); and *Pleasant Grove City v. Summum*, 125 S. Ct.1125 (2009).

17. http://www.nccbuscc.org/ogc.

18. Austin Sarat and Stuart Scheingold, *Cause Lawyers and Social Movements* (Palo Alto, CA: Stanford University Press, 2006).

19. See Pew Forum on Religion & Public Life, U.S. Religious Landscape Study, http://religions.pewforum.org/reports (2008), which is based on an immense survey of 35,000 Americans in the summer of 2007.

20. Perhaps the leading writer in support of separationism has been Leo Pfeffer, former chief attorney for the American Jewish Congress. See Leo Pfeffer, *Religion, State, and the Burger Court* (Buffalo, NY: Prometheus, 1984).

21. Several interesting books on religious freedom in the founding period include Leonard Levy, *The Establishment Clause: Religion and the First Amendment*, 2nd ed. (Raleigh, NC: University of North Carolina Press, 1994); Jon Meacham, *American Gospel: God, the Founding Fathers, and the Making of a Nation* (New York: Random House, 2006); William L. Miller, *The First Liberty and the American Republic* (New York: Knopf, 1986); and Steven Waldman, *Founding Faith: Providence, Politics, and the Birth of Religious Freedom in America* (New York: Random House, 2008).

22. Alec Gallup, George Gallup, and Frank Newport, *The Gallup Poll: Public Opinion 2005* (Lanham, MD: Rowman and Littlefield, 2006), 318.

23. Andrew Kohut et al., "Religion a Strength and Weakness for Both Parties," (Washington, DC: Pew Research Center/Pew Forum, 2006), 10.

24. Chief Justice Warren Burger explicitly argued for this position for the first time in *Walz* v. *Tax Commission*, 397 U.S. 664 (1970). For approaches somewhat sympathetic to "benevolent neutrality," see Robert T. Miller and Ronald B. Flowers, eds., *Toward Benevolent Neutrality: Church, State, and the Supreme Court* (Waco, TX: Baylor University Press, 1987); and A. James Reichley, *Faith in Politics* (Washington, DC: Brookings Institution, 2002), chap. 3.

25. For a collection of essays arguing several sides of the equal treatment approach, see Stephen V. Monsma and J. Christopher Soper, *Equal Treatment of Religion in a Pluralistic Society* (Grand Rapids, MI: Eerdmans, 1997). See also the excellent comparative study in Monsma and Soper, *The Challenge of Pluralism: Church and State in Five Democracies*, 2nd ed. (Lanham, MD: Rowman and Littlefield, 2009).

26. Hubert Morken and Jo Renee Formicola, *The Politics of School Choice* (Lanham, MD: Rowman and Littlefield, 1999).

27. 1 Statute 50, 52, Article III.

28. On the historical record, several interesting discussions are Robert L. Cord, *Separation of Church and State: Historical Fact and Current Fiction* (New York: Lambeth, 1982); Thomas J. Curry, *The First Freedoms* (New York: Oxford University Press, 1986); Michael

Malbin, *Religion and Politics: The Intentions of the Authors of the First Amendment* (Washington, DC: American Enterprise Institute, 1978); Meacham, *American Gospel*; Waldman, *Founding Faith*; and Witte, *Religion and the American Constitutional Experiment.*

29. See Robert Booth Fowler, "A Postmodern Defense of Government Aid to Religious Schools," in *Everson Revisited: Religion, Education, and Law at the Crossroads*, eds. Jo Renee Formicola and Hubert Morken (Lanham, MD: Rowman and Littlefield, 1997).

9

CHURCH AND STATE IN THE COURTS

Religious liberty has been called America's "first freedom," and rightly so. The enduring religious pluralism in the United States would be impossible without wide latitude for various religious beliefs and expressions. Much of this freedom flows from the Constitution itself. The framers put religious freedom in the forefront, as embodied in the first sixteen words of the Bill of Rights' First Amendment: "Congress shall make no law respecting an establishment of religion, or prohibiting the free exercise thereof." But securing religious freedom has often been a struggle, in part because the issues that arise under the First Amendment are rarely clear-cut. Political institutions, and especially courts, have been thrust into the unenviable role of defining the limits of religious freedom and the proper interaction of church and state.

The First Amendment and its religion clauses were adopted by the first Congress of the United States, under the leadership of James Madison. Congress began its work on this task in the spring of 1789 because of agitation during the debates about ratification for the inclusion of a list of guaranteed civil liberties in the Constitution. Chief among the agitators for the Bill of Rights were the Antifederalists, who feared that the expansion of the federal government under the new Constitution would curtail personal liberty. Records of the congressional debate indicate that bargaining and compromise were vital to the eventual agreement on the content and wording of the First Amendment. James Madison introduced the proposed amendment in its first form in June 1789. It subsequently went through several revisions before a conference committee agreed on a bill that passed Congress in September 1789 and was later sent to the states, all of which duly ratified it.

Madison knew he had to fashion an amendment that would satisfy critics who feared that the Constitution was hostile to religion (and suspected the same of him). Madison wanted to include what he called "rights of conscience" in the First Amendment, but some critics thought that the provision of such rights might result in government neutrality between religion and atheism, so it was dropped. Madison also failed in his attempt to eliminate the official establishment of religion at the state level. The final version of the First Amendment applied only to the federal government ("*Congress* shall make no law . . .").

From the beginning, the issues of church-state policy that have arisen from disagreements over the meaning of the First Amendment have included (1) how to balance free exercise of religion with otherwise constitutional laws that interfere with it, and (2) how to decide when government activities that somehow involve or even benefit religion amount to an unconstitutional establishment of religion. In most of this chapter we explore these two concerns separately, following the Supreme Court's own practice of fashioning precedents and complex tests that address "free exercise" of religion and "establishment" of religion as separate and independent concepts. We conclude the chapter, however, by discussing a "free speech" alternative to the religion clauses, as well as the many ways free exercise and establishment interact and at times conflict.

RELIGIOUS FREE EXERCISE

The framers of the Constitution thought governments posed a constant threat to the free exercise of religion, especially for religious minorities and dissenters. They based this view on their sometimes negative experiences with the British government and even with their own colonial governments. Thus the framers were eager to protect the free exercise of religion from government interference. For them, protecting free exercise meant curtailing or eliminating government establishment of, and interference with, religion.

Thomas Jefferson, who wrote the Declaration of Independence, and James Madison, the principal author of the Constitution and the First Amendment, were among the strongest proponents of religious free exercise. Both had been active in opposing the establishment of religion in colonial Virginia. They also helped to bring about the disestablishment of the Anglican (now Episcopal) Church there. Neither Jefferson nor Madison advocated complete separation of church and state during their subsequent presidencies, but both tried to move in that direction. Political reality, however, forced them to accept some compromises to accommodate organized religion at the federal level. And as presidents they did nothing to interfere with the states, where there was sometimes very little separation between church and state. Still, both men made important contributions to the development of American free exercise rights.[1]

Historically, Americans have enjoyed broad free exercise rights. The majority of early Americans were Protestant, and free exercise rights abounded for most of them. Though Protestantism was dominant, free exercise rights were gradually extended to Catholics, Jews, and others. Of course such groups could not constitutionally be denied free exercise rights. Still, they faced varying degrees of discrimination, which in time gave way to a broad-based acceptance of the pluralist reality of American religious life. Plenty of constitutional argument and political conflict occurred along the way, but free exercise has steadily expanded in the United States.

Today, Americans may justifiably be proud of the existence of an enormous degree of religious freedom—encompassing many religious persuasions, groups, and practices. This does not deny the history of conflict that paved the road to free exercise, nor does it deny that religions still struggle for their free exercise rights. There will always be religious groups that push against the margins of American political culture and its written and unwritten rules about the limits of acceptable religious practices.

In attempting to interpret the Framers' mandate that citizens should have the freedom to practice whatever religion they choose, the Supreme Court has distinguished between religious beliefs themselves and actions taken as a result of those beliefs. Beliefs are absolutely protected, but religiously motivated action, such as drug use as part of a religious ceremony, that the Court decides contravenes established law may be restricted. It should be noted, however, that the Court has avoided addressing religious freedom under some circumstances. Indeed, until the 1940s federal courts often ducked religious issues altogether. They also tried to make sure that the other branches of government followed suit. For example, courts have been loath to adjudicate arguments among members of disbanded religious groups. They have understood that to get involved in these often-bitter fights may be to interfere improperly with a religion and by extension deter free exercise. This standard remains today. Religious groups are allowed to resolve their own disputes, under their own rules, as much as possible. This is especially so when the basic doctrines of a religion itself are at issue.[2]

If the courts have generally avoided becoming involved in arguments within religious organizations, they have also steered away from attempting to settle disagreements over what constitutes a religion. Judges realize that this is treacherous ground, but their policy of avoidance has, in fact, proven to be supportive of free exercise. After all, if the definition of religion were left to the government rather than to believers themselves, free exercise could be threatened.

It is not easy to resolve disputes involving religion, but the courts' standard policy has been to avoid deciding whether the claims of a given religion are true. For example, in *United States* v. *Ballard* (1944), the Supreme Court was asked to decide whether a man who was using the U.S. mail to solicit funds for his "I Am Movement" was guilty of mail fraud. Ballard, who said he was a divine messenger who could communicate with Jesus Christ, had his conviction overturned. The Court stated that "Men may believe what they cannot prove. Religious experiences which are as real as life to some may be incomprehensible to others. . . . If one could be sent to jail because a jury in a hostile environment found his or her religious teachings false, little indeed would be left of religious freedom."[3]

Even so, the Court has not been wholly successful in staying out of the business of defining religion, especially when fundamental roles of government are at stake. Consider the government's policies on taxation. In *Hernandez* v. *Commissioner* (1989), which involved the Church of Scientology, the Supreme Court ruled that fees for specific services such as training in Scientology could not be counted as nontaxable gifts. Critics of the Court's decision in this case complained that it implied Scientology was not a serious religion, thereby setting a dangerous precedent. If Scientology is not a religion, then what are the parameters of the religious and the secular—and who sets them?

The Hernandez case points to the continuing controversy over what exactly constitutes a religion—and what services an organized religion may provide. The nonprofit activities of organized religions are free from taxation, a policy that has long been in place. But just what is a "religion," and what is a "nonprofit activity"? The traditional approach has been that minimizing government interference in such matters maximizes religious freedom, but it also leaves room for abuse.

Some controversial religious practices make headlines. Often the courts have decided cases in ways that affirm religious freedom. One example has to do with the issue of clergy malpractice. Clergy often provide advice to members of their congregations, but what happens if that advice is potentially harmful? Courts' usual response have been to avoid addressing such an issue when it arises.[4] Another issue concerns the level of confidentiality clergy should be allowed to maintain. This is especially difficult when clergy learn, through pastoral counseling, that a member of the congregation has committed a serious crime, such as child abuse or even murder. State policies differ, but the current trend is toward requiring clergy to report violations of the law when they learn of them, though some clergy argue that this represents an erosion of their pastor-penitent privilege. Information gleaned through the seal of private confession in Roman Catholicism, however, remains sacrosanct. The confidentiality of pastoral counseling is far more controversial, all the more so in the wake of revelations of sexual abuse by some Catholic priests.[5]

Another sensitive question is the extent to which personal risk-taking should be allowed within a church. The issues almost always arise as a result of health risks incurred because of religious practices. Examples include Jehovah's Witnesses' refusal to accept blood transfusions, Christian Scientists' belief in faith healing (and their consequent rejection of modern medicine), and the practice of serpent handling in a handful of Pentecostal churches. Such issues may be approached from many directions, and of course it matters whether church groups are honest with their members about the possible consequences of any risky behaviors they practice and encourage. The limits of religious freedom become especially important when the lives and fundamental health of children are at stake.[6]

Disputes also swirl around the question of whether there should be limits to some religious groups' perpetual search for converts. Almost all religions assert that they seek only followers who knowingly choose their faith, so they renounce the use of fraud or manipulation to trick people into embracing their faith. But what constitutes a trick or a fraud? For many atheists, to use the extreme example, every religion is in the business of fraud. How much can government regulate what it—or society— determines to be fraudulent behavior without infringing on free exercise?

Some exceptions to allowing free exercise have occurred, such as the Court's decision to allow a congressional ban on the Mormon practice of polygamy in *Reynolds* v. *United States* (1879). This decision was long ago, however, and in more recent times the Courts have supported broad free exercise rights in the United States. The law is often murky, and even contradictory, but many rulings testify to the American commitment to free exercise, especially for mainstream religions.

Cantwell v. *Connecticut* (1940) is a classic case in which the Supreme Court affirmed a generous range of free exercise rights. In *Cantwell*, the Court invoked both religion clauses and other parts of the First Amendment to strike down local ordinances that interfered with Jehovah's Witnesses' desire to distribute literature to and request contributions from the general public. The Court's decision in *Cantwell* to allow religious groups the right to proselytize pursuant to their freedom of religion has been repeatedly reaffirmed, subject to restrictions on the setting.[7] Likewise, state attempts to penalize fund-raising by unpopular religions have been rejected.[8] The Court has also ruled that neither clergy nor religious organizations may be prevented from becoming involved in politics.[9] Similarly, the Court has granted some religious freedom in federal institutions (prisons are the most controversial), but only so long as religious practices do not disrupt standard operating procedures.[10]

In public schools, the courts have created a rather narrow zone of free exercise. Still, in *Pierce* v. *Society of Sisters* (1928) the Supreme Court supported the right of Roman Catholic schools (and thus other private schools) to exist alongside public ones. In *West Virginia State Board of Education* v. *Barnette* (1944) the Court held that Jehovah's Witnesses have the right to refuse to say the Pledge of Allegiance in school, as their religion forbids commitment to any nation-state. And in *Wisconsin* v. *Yoder* (1972), the Court upheld the refusal of Amish people to allow their teen-agers to attend high school, accepting Amish religious doctrine that does not require or respect such schooling. All these decisions, especially taken together, are important. They demonstrate that public education must be aware that it operates in an environment of modest protected religious free exercise and must take this reality into account.

THE LIMITS OF FREE EXERCISE

In principle, however, there is no debate about the government's and the Constitution's ultimate authority, including the authority to restrict the free exercise of religion. Even rights granted in the Constitution and the Bill of Rights are not absolute because any given right must be balanced by others' provided rights and government and constitutional goals and provisions. It is a complicated business that is rarely about absolutes.

Many of the Supreme Court's most controversial free exercise decisions in recent years have addressed disputes in which the state's authority and need for security are at stake. In *Goldman* v. *Weinberger* (1986) it decided to uphold military regulations providing that no Jewish person could wear a yarmulke (skullcap) while on duty in the U.S. military. At issue was not the wisdom of the regulation but whether or not the Court should defer to military rules and the reasons behind them, namely the need to maintain military order and regularity. The Court concluded that it should defer to the military. Congress later passed a law allowing Jews to wear yarmulkes in the military, but it did so without challenging the authority of the federal government to decide such matters. A similar issue arose in a New Jersey case, *O'Lone* v. *Estate of Shabazz* (1987), in which Muslims in state prisons claimed that prison work rules interfered with their practice of Islam. The Court held that deference to prison rules and the administrators who make them (that is, the government) must take precedence over free exercise.

Other cases have considered challenges to public health regulations or other matters that touch on community values or the common good. The view that some government provisions designed to protect the general welfare have priority over the First Amendment's guarantee of free exercise has been endorsed in the courts for some time. A long line of cases has held that such things as required vaccinations to protect public health or laws forbidding child labor supersede free exercise rights, even though some groups' religious freedoms may thereby be violated. For example, in *Braunfeld v. Brown* (1981), the Court ruled against a group of Orthodox Jews who felt that their ability to earn a living was being compromised by Pennsylvania's Sunday closing laws. Their religion forbade them to work on Saturday, and the state forbade them to work on Sunday. The Court recognized that the Pennsylvania law made Orthodox Judaism "more expensive" than Christianity, but because the law did not prevent anyone from the actual *practice* of religion—"the Sunday law simply regulates a secular activity"—it did not violate the Free Exercise Clause.[11]

In areas such as these the crucial question centers on where to draw the line between the pursuit of government goals and the protection of religious free exercise. The fact is, the U.S. Supreme Court has never sent a clear message about where that line ought to be drawn. It has usually appeared to be more impressed with upholding government policy than with protecting some small, dissenting religious group. But no obvious and consistent pattern has emerged. From the late 1930s until the 1960s, however, it was a safe bet that most free exercise appeals would meet with defeat in court. The Supreme Court usually sided with the federal and state governments and their laws in such conflicts. After the 1960s, however, these matters became less clear, as the pendulum began to swing toward the expansion of free exercise rights.

In the landmark free exercise case of *Sherbert v. Verner* (1963), the Court stated that the standard of "strict scrutiny" (the most exacting level of judicial review) must apply to any law that conflicts with the free exercise of religion. By imposing this standard the justices meant to underline the importance of free exercise, though they did not mean that any laws clashing with free exercise would automatically fail the strict scrutiny test. In *Sherbert*, a Seventh-day Adventist won her claim against South Carolina for denying her unemployment benefits after she was fired from her job for refusing to work on Saturday (the Adventist Sabbath). The Court stated clearly that "the burden on the free exercise of appellant's religion must be justified by *a compelling state interest*."[12] Thus the *Sherbert* case set a high standard, which the Court continued to use for many years in deciding a variety of free exercise disputes.

The Rehnquist Court, however, was less congenial to free exercise claims—which usually involve the practices of minority religions. In the much-discussed 1990 case of *Employment Division* v. *Smith*, the Court specifically reversed the strict scrutiny doctrine that it had set forth in *Sherbert*. No longer would states be forced to demonstrate a compelling interest if their laws had the effect of restricting free exercise rights. Though the picture is complicated and the results mixed, the Court has been increasingly willing to uphold "common good" legislation despite protests of particular religious groups and individuals who have contended that such laws infringe upon their religious practices.

In the *Smith* case, the Supreme Court affirmed Oregon's drug policy. In that state, two Native American drug counselors had been fired and prevented from collecting unemployment compensation. They had been fired for violating terms of their employment that prohibited the use of peyote, an illegal hallucinogenic drug that plays a significant spiritual role in their religion as members of the Native American Church. The Court essentially held that laws that do not target religion directly, such as Oregon's generally applicable drug laws, are constitutionally valid, even if they incidentally restrict religious practice. Though the Court's ruling in *Smith* came as something of a surprise to legal observers and advocates, it was the legal doctrine upon which the ruling was based that caused a real uproar. The Court declared that it was no longer committed to automatic "strict scrutiny" of laws that restrict free exercise of religion, thereby undoing the decades-old *Sherbert* precedent. In *Sherbert*, of course, the Court had not said that laws restricting free exercise were inherently unconstitutional, but it did suggest they would find the going tough. The reversal of this precedent seemed to bring to a close an era in which the Court provided an especially protected role for religious exercise in the United States.

Thus the Supreme Court's 1993 decision in *Church of the Lukumi Babalu Aye* v. *City of Hialeah* came as a relief to free exercise critics. In this case the Court struck down an ordinance passed by the city of Hialeah, Florida, that prohibited the ritual sacrifice of animals. The court ruled that this ordinance had been designed specifically to forbid animal-killing rituals that are practiced as part of Santeria, an Afro-Caribbean religion. The Court agreed with the Santerian Church of the Lukumi that the ordinance in question was extremely selective because it did not forbid other forms of animal killing, such as hunting or Jewish ritual preparation of kosher food. It was aimed instead at one group alone: practitioners of Santeria. What distinguishes the *Smith* case from the *Lukumi* case is that laws interfering with the free exercise of particular faiths that do not further a major state policy may be ruled unconstitutional. Laws pursuant to the common good that are not intended to oppress a particular religious group, however, are likely to be upheld under the *Smith* precedent.

Some critics complain that Court rulings that uphold common-good legislation actually do promote particular moral positions at the expense of pure religious free exercise. They are correct, of course, but the reverse is just as true when free exercise claims do win out. In each instance moral choices are at issue. The question becomes one of where religious free exercise ought to rank in comparison with other values. In the American legal system free exercise is not always at the top of the list (see Box 9.1).

Though today the Supreme Court would no longer defend decisions in the language of Christian morality, as was the case in *Reynolds*, it often accedes to the decisions of Congress and state legislatures, even at the expense of religious free exercise. Much of the Court's recent energy for such decisions has not come from sympathy with such laws themselves but instead from a commitment to the proposition that courts ought not to interfere with the decisions of democratically elected legislatures.

In response to the Court's decision in *Smith*, religious groups united to push the Religious Freedom Restoration Act (RFRA) through Congress. This law, which President Clinton signed in 1994, required the federal courts to return to the doctrine of strict scrutiny when reviewing any law that abridges religious free exercise

---

BOX 9.1 THE "CONSCIENCE RULE" AND FREE EXERCISE OF RELIGION

Sometimes conflicts over competing values come to a head because government actively seeks to foster religious freedom. Consider the George W. Bush administration's issuance of a "conscience rule" in late 2008, which protected government employees who refused to provide abortion services or referrals because of their beliefs about the issue. Although pro-life groups hailed the rule as a victory for religious freedom, pro-choice organizations worked hard to overturn it, seeing it as an attack on women's reproductive rights. President Barack Obama began the process to rescind the rule soon after taking office, but the question of certain conscience-based exemptions from public policy is far from settled. Another area where there is increasing dispute is the question of whether private citizens such as photographers, caterers, or even clergy ought to be exempt from antidiscrimination laws if they refuse to provide their services at same-sex marriage ceremonies.

Source: Rob Stein, "Health Workers' 'Conscience' Rule Set to Be Voided," *The Washington Post*, February 28, 2009.

rights. In essence, Congress forced the Court to return to the *Sherbert* precedent, which effectively undercut the Court's logic in the *Smith* case. In 1997, however, the Supreme Court retaliated and struck down the portion of RFRA that the Court perceived as meddling in its power of constitutional interpretation. Congress's initial passage of RFRA actually constituted an example of the influence American religious groups can exercise when they unite. But its days were numbered.

The Supreme Court declared RFRA unconstitutional in *City of Boerne* v. *Flores* (1997). A Catholic parish in Boerne, Texas, wished to expand the size of its church sanctuary but was denied a building permit. The city's policies on the protection of the historic district in which the church was located prevented any further development. Buoyed by RFRA, the parish argued that the city did not have a compelling interest in preventing it from expanding. The Court supported the city's counterargument, simultaneously striking down the provision of RFRA that called for the existence of a compelling state interest for state and local laws to restrict free exercise rights.

Despite the *Boerne* decision, the legacy of RFRA lives on. The Supreme Court had rejected only Congress's attempt to impose, via the Court's decisions, the old *Sherbert* standard on the actions of state and local governments. Those governments, however, could place restrictions on themselves—and many did in the wake of *Boerne*, passing their own state-level versions of RFRA by requiring that their own actions burdening religion have a compelling state interest. By the same token, the U.S. Congress could also impose on itself the *Sherbert* standard. In fact, the U.S. Supreme Court, in a case that must have provided the justices a sense of sweet irony, did apply RFRA against the Congress in a dispute over the importation of hoasca, a banned hallucinogen under *federal* drug law, that was used by a Christian spiritist movement in the Southwest.[13] The Court held that Congress and the executive branch had not shown a compelling reason under RFRA for refusing to grant a faith-based exemption for use of the drug.

The debate between the Court and Congress continues in other ways over the proper limits of free exercise. In August 1997, the Clinton administration outlined a plan to protect religious expression in federal government offices. The guidelines allow bureaucrats to wear religious jewelry, hold prayer meetings during lunch breaks, distribute religious literature to coworkers, and keep scriptures on their desks. In formulating the plan, the administration was assisted by a wide array of interest groups, from the conservative Christian Legal Society, to the liberal National Council of Churches, to the separationist People for the American Way.[14] A similar coalition of groups supported the Religious Land Use and Institutionalized

Persons Act, which was passed in 2000. The law places limits on the ability of local governments to restrict religious groups from developing property and seeks to secure greater protection for the religious practice of people in prisons, mental hospitals, and other institutions. The law already has been invoked in several disputes over church development, and the Supreme Court has held that it is an appropriate means for prisoners to challenge state restrictions on their religious worship while incarcerated.[15]

THE POLITICS OF RELIGIOUS ESTABLISHMENT

Whether church and state in the United States are entwined in various forms of connection that amount to the establishment of religion by government or are separate, in theory or in practice, is a controversial matter. Perhaps the best strategy is to say that everything depends on what we mean by the term *establishment*. Without doubt plenty of official religious establishment has occurred throughout American history. Most of the colonies officially established one Protestant church or another and required all taxpayers to help finance that single church. Though the First Amendment of the U.S. Constitution outlawed the establishment of any single religion at *the national level*, some states continued to support their own established churches. This practice came to an end when in 1833 Massachusetts became the last state to do away with officially established religion. That marked the end of *legal* establishment, but it was hardly the end of the notion of establishment. After all, throughout much of the nineteenth century, the United States had established Christianity in an implicit way—and Protestantism in particular. This was most obvious in the widespread reading of the Protestant King James Bible in nineteenth-century public schools.

Separationist and antireligion lobbies have had only mixed success in attempting to dismantle these more subtle forms of establishment. For example, atheist leader Madalyn Murray O'Hair failed in her 1979 attempt to persuade the United States Court of Appeals (Fifth Circuit) to banish "In God We Trust" from the currency (*O'Hair* v. *Blumenthal*). Efforts in 1983 to get the Supreme Court to eliminate prayer at the beginning of legislative sessions also proved unsuccessful (*Marsh* v. *Chambers*). The weight of the traditional establishment of what may be called *religion in general* has been substantial throughout American history (see Box 9.2). Nonetheless, pressures against the symbolic establishment of *Christianity* have grown stronger over the years—and have been increasingly successful. The coalition against official endorsements of Christianity is often broad and frequently includes the American Civil Liberties Union, Americans United for Separation of Church and State, and the legal arms of prominent Jewish groups.

On the other hand, the technique most often used by those who wish to defend symbolic establishment has been to repackage establishment and present it—for the benefit of the courts—as something that is not religious at all. In instances when these efforts succeed, courts appear to wink and go on to what they judge to be more important matters. This has been evident in arguments over public crèches (manger scenes depicting Jesus' birth). In both *Lynch* v. *Donnelly* (1984) and *Allegheny County* v. *Greater Pittsburgh ACLU* (1989), the Supreme Court allowed crèches to stand on public land or in connection with public buildings only if they are merely one element of what the Court describes as a "winter display." When crèches exist alone as a Christian symbol, however, as was the case in a Pittsburgh courthouse in *Allegheny County* v. *Greater Pittsburgh ACLU*, the Court has deemed them unconstitutional. In *Van Orden* v. *Perry* (2006), a similar line of reasoning led the Court to accept the display of the Ten Commandments at the Texas State Capitol.

BOX 9.2 "UNDER GOD" IN THE PLEDGE OF ALLEGIANCE

In 2000, Michael Newdow, a doctor, lawyer, and vocal atheist from Sacramento, California, sued the Elk Grove Unified School District, in which his daughter was a student. He alleged that the daily recitation of the Pledge of Allegiance, which includes the phrase "under God," amounted to an unconstitutional imposition of religion on his daughter. In 2002, the Ninth Circuit Court of Appeals issued a controversial ruling agreeing with Newdow's position, arguing that even though the reference to God did not require fealty to a particular faith, it was not neutral between religion and nonreligion. In effect the decision prohibited the use of the offending phrase within the Ninth Circuit's jurisdiction (which roughly covers all of the western United States). Given the awkward circumstance of "under God" being unconstitutional in some states and constitutional in others, the U.S. Supreme Court stepped in to settle the dispute in 2004. However, the Court tossed the case on a legal technicality: Newdow, who was divorced, did not have custodial rights of his daughter and therefore did not have the right to sue on her behalf. The fate of "under God" in the Pledge is still unclear, however, because another group of parents, with Newdow's help, recently filed a similar suit that is making its way through the court system.

Source: *Newdow* v. *Elk Grove Unified School District*, 542 U.S. 1 (9th cir. 2004).

A plurality of justices argued the display had a historical significance that was not merely religious.[16]

The courts have also allowed governments in the United States—local, state, and federal— to funnel tremendous amounts of financial aid to various religions. These practices, of course, establish religions and religion in general and certainly do not affirm the principle of separation of church and state. Government aid to nonprofit organizations (including religious groups) is vast. Examples of this practice, affirmed by the courts since 1899 in *Bradfield* v. *Roberts*, include assistance to religious hospitals and clinics, orphanages, halfway houses, retirement homes, refugee resettlement projects, and other social service endeavors and programs. The exact amounts of aid and the specific rules governing its use vary from federal to state governments, from state to state, and from one policy area to another, but the practice itself is widespread.

As we noted in Chapter 8, one of the Court's efforts to fashion a governing principle for establishment cases is the so-called *Lemon* test. Formulated in *Lemon* v. *Kurtzman* (1971), the *Lemon* test holds that laws are constitutional when they serve a secular legislative purpose, neither advance nor inhibit religion, and do not foster an "excessive entanglement" between government and religion.[17] In establishment cases the *Lemon* test has been used in a variety of ways, and its implementation has been a controversial undertaking even within the Supreme Court. Justice Antonin Scalia, for example, has bemoaned "the strange Establishment Clause geometry of crooked lines and wavering shapes [the *Lemon* test's] intermittent use has produced."[18]

The *Lemon* test allows the constitutional provision of substantial government aid to religious organizations of all sorts. Thus if governments decide that aid to nonprofit hospitals is in the public interest, then it is constitutional because the legislation from which the hospitals would benefit may be said to have a secular purpose, neither to advance nor to inhibit religion, and to fail to foster any excessive entanglements between church and state. It is still true, however, that in such a situation government is undeniably aiding religious groups and thus promoting some form of religious establishment. Granted, this sort of implicit establishment is by no means the same as the official establishments of the colonial era. In that age, government support was enjoyed exclusively by one church. Instead, the modern arrangement normally takes the form of "multiple establishment." Government provides aid in a particular policy area to all qualified applicants. For example, both secular and religious hospitals (of many denominations) may receive government funds.

Contemporary establishment also occurs in the common practice of granting all nonprofit groups (again, including religious institutions) freedom from property taxes. Because churches, synagogues, and mosques often occupy extensive and highly valuable properties, this arrangement is a tremendous financial boon for them. This has been defended not as a grant to religious groups per se but rather as a neutral law with the secular purpose of helping nonprofit (and only nonprofit) groups that benefit society. Though some separationists have argued strenuously against this arrangement as a flagrant form of establishment, they have not succeeded in the courts. Establishment in the United States is often legal if it is indirect and accomplished through neutral laws that stand up to the *Lemon* test.

Education policy is another arena in which many conflicts have emerged over religious establishment. The battle over religion in schools has been waged throughout American history, and it continues unabated today. The American culture's faith in schooling ensures that struggles over education policy will continue, for Americans believe that a great deal is at stake.

All sorts of religious practices in schools, some of which have reflected the beliefs of a particular religious group, have been common throughout the history of American public education. Public prayers and Bible reading in class have been the most widespread of these practices. However, such policies began to face serious criticism after World War II when religious "release-time" education became a widespread fashion. Such programs allowed religious teachers to come into public schools during regular hours and teach religious lessons to students who had the permission of a parent or guardian. In the late 1940s and early 1950s, the Supreme Court was indecisive about the constitutionality of this practice. In *McCollum* v. *Board of Education* (1948), release-time classes held on school grounds were ruled unconstitutional. In 1952, the Court seemed to reverse itself in *Zorach* v. *Clauson*, but the release-time classes at stake in that case took place off of school property.

Even though release-time programs are no longer popular in most places, the disputes surrounding them were an early sign of the courts' willingness to tackle establishment issues that related to public education. Steadily since the 1960s, courts have brought about a sweeping disestablishment of conventional religion in public schools. This is seen as a great victory by separationist and antireligious groups that argue religion has no place in the classroom.

The Court's first step was to remove state-sponsored prayer from the schools in the monumental 1962 case of *Engel* v. *Vitale*. One year later, the Court also put a stop to Bible reading in public schools in *Abington School District* v. *Schempp* (1963). In 1980, the posting of the Ten Commandments in classrooms was ruled unconstitutional (*Stone* v. *Graham*). For some critics the last straw came in *Wallace* v. *Jaffree* (1985), in which the Court struck down an Alabama law requiring public school teachers to open each day with a moment of silence. The Court interpreted the law as Alabama's "effort to return voluntary prayer to our public schools."[19] The Court did not accept Alabama's argument that the moment of silence served the secular purpose of encouraging good student behavior. The latest issue of this nature to come before the Court has involved the constitutionality of prayer at public school graduation ceremonies and other public events. The Supreme Court rejected clergy-led graduation prayers in *Lee* v. *Weisman* (1992) and student-led prayers at high school sporting events in *Santa Fe Independent School District* v. *Doe* (2000).

Critics often note that the exit of familiar religion(s) from public schools has only meant its replacement by a "religion" of secularism or secular humanism, a kind of antireligion that celebrates humans or nature and implicitly or explicitly ridicules traditional religion(s). But in the 1987 case of *Smith* v. *Board of Commissioners*, the United States Court of Appeals (Eleventh Circuit) disagreed, apparently believing instead that it is possible to foster neutrality and that is where the matter rests in the courts at this point.

Some religious groups have welcomed judicial efforts to force religion out of the public schools. They believe religion belongs at home and in church; they often have no use for vague nondenominational religion in the first place. Other observers, however, are uneasy about the need for many public schools to go to great lengths to avoid the presentation or teaching of anything traditionally religious.

Despite a long history of religious establishment in American public schools, the teaching of overtly religious lessons has now ceased in most school districts. This fact is reflected in the failure of efforts by conservative Protestants to force school districts in several southern states to provide instruction in creationism or intelligent design. Courts have invariably deemed such efforts a manifest establishment of religion. Instead, the Supreme Court has protected the teaching of evolution. In 1968, the Court struck down an Arkansas law forbidding the teaching of evolutionary theory in *Epperson* v. *Arkansas*. It is also unconstitutional for a state to require the teaching of both creationism and Darwinism, according to the Court's ruling in *Edwards* v. *Aguillard* (1987). In both instances the Court felt that the states in question were specifically attempting to establish Christianity (see Box 9.3).

Disputes over the judiciary's view of establishment have also raged in the context of financial aid to religious schools. Historically this meant that aid to Roman Catholic schools was denied on establishment grounds because to give such aid would

---

BOX 9.3   THE CONSTITUTIONALITY OF "INTELLIGENT DESIGN"

The courts are only beginning to weigh in on the constitutionality of recent efforts in several states to require the teaching of "intelligent design," the theory that an intelligence of some kind guided evolution rather than a random process. Proponents of intelligent design note that the theory does not assume the existence of a divinity from any particular religious faith and therefore avoids Establishment Clause problems; critics counter that the idea is simply a veiled effort to smuggle in specific religious understandings of human origins and therefore deserves the same fate as the "creation-science" at issue in *Edwards* v. *Aguillard*.

Source: *Kitzmiller* v. *Dover Area School District*, 400 F. Supp. 2d 707 (2005).

---

be to establish a branch of Christianity, Roman Catholicism. Because public schools once were permeated by practices such as group readings from the Protestant King James Bible, skeptics have suggested that the real problem was not with establishment per se; it was rather a question of which religion would be given preference in most public schools. Though modern courts have removed much of the old Protestant establishment from public schools, their record is complicated on the matter of financial aid to religious schools. Aid for teacher salaries, which is by far the greatest portion of school budgets, repeatedly has failed on establishment grounds, as was the case in *Lemon* v. *Kurtzman* (1971).

At the same time, the Supreme Court has upheld state laws allowing several significant forms of assistance to religious schools. According to the Court's 1947 decision in *Everson* v. *Board of Education*, public school buses may be used to transport children to and from religious schools. The Court argued that the aid primarily benefitted children, not schools, so transportation to religious schools was not perceived as a substantial violation of the Establishment Clause. A similar logic drove the Court's 1968 decision in *Board of Education* v. *Allen*, in which it upheld New York's policy of allowing religious schools to borrow secular textbooks from public school districts. In *Meek* v. *Pittenger* (1975), however, the Court ruled that neither state-paid staff nor instructional materials other than books could be loaned to religious schools. In *Wolman* v. *Walter* (1977), the Court affirmed *Meek* and further rejected state aid by declaring that public school buses could not be used to transport children from religious schools on field trips. Finally, in *Aguilar* v. *Felton*

(1985), the Court struck down a New York law providing state-financed remedial courses and guidance services in religious schools. But just over a decade later, the Court specifically overturned *Aguilar* in *Agostini* v. *Felton* (1997), holding that public school teachers may provide state-mandated special services in religious schools. And following *Agostini* came the Court's decision in *Mitchell* v. *Helms* (2000), in which the Court upheld state aid to parochial schools in the form of computers and other instructional materials and equipment. The logic of the *Mitchell* case effectively overturned the Court's decisions in *Meek*.

In other cases the Court has ruled that government funds could be used to pay an interpreter to accompany a deaf student attending a religious school, as it did in *Zobrest* v. *Catalina Foothills School District* (1993). Proponents could see no problem with this because insignificant establishment, at most, was at issue. Opponents, however, said the policy was a serious breach of the no-establishment principle because taxpayers would be financing translation by the interpreter of such sectarian events as mass in the school. In *Kiryas Joel Village School District* v. *Grumet* (1994), however, the Court held that New York could not set up a special school district for disabled children in an Orthodox Jewish town in suburban New York City. Whereas only one student was being assisted in *Zobrest*, the Court saw the creation of an entire school district for disabled Orthodox Jewish children as another matter altogether.

Taken as a whole, Establishment Clause jurisprudence in the twentieth century amounted to nothing more than a confusing mess to many observers. As one remarks:

> Bus trips from home to religious schools are constitutional, but bus trips from religious schools to local museums are unconstitutional. . . . Standardized tests are o.k., but teacher-prepared tests are not. Government can provide parochial schools with books but not maps, provoking Senator Daniel Moynihan's quip: "What about atlases?" The Court has invoked *Lemon* to strike down a nativity scene surrounded by poinsettias and to uphold a nativity scene surrounded by elephants, teddy bears, Santa's workshop, and a talking wishing well.[20]

The Court's logic has been based on its attempt to balance two goals: ensuring no establishment and benefiting children. On the one hand, the Court's reasoning has been that establishment is especially dangerous in the schools because children are much more vulnerable to inculcation than are adults; on the other hand, that very vulnerability has led the Court to avoid disadvantaging children in any fundamental way if they happen to attend religious schools. Thus the Court has been understanding if states decide that all children need textbooks and transportation to school. State-paid religious school teachers, however, would move too far toward establishment.

Obviously there is room for argument on every point. Some contend that if religious schools can receive only a certain amount of aid for specific government services, then families of religious school students ought also to receive some compensation for the costs they incur in sending their children to these schools. Families that send children to religious schools commonly complain that they are forced to pay twice to educate their children—once through taxes to support public schools they do not use and again in tuition to the religious school. Opponents reply that no one is forced to send their children to a religious school and that public schools enhance the common good. They question why taxpayers should have to pay for the choices of one small portion of the population, especially when those choices may involve an establishment of religion.

However, some Catholics, evangelical Protestants, Muslims, and Orthodox Jews believe today that they must send their children to religious schools in order to practice their religion freely—especially in light of what they perceive to be growing secularism in public schools. For them, state support for religious schools, if it is made available to all, does not involve much establishment. Nor, they insist, does it hinder free exercise. Critics reply that such support does constitute unacceptable religious establishment because it makes all citizens contribute to the education of children in religious schools. Such critics find allies among some supporters of religious schools who fear that the heavy hand of government regulation might come along with aid.

In the past, the courts have sided with citizens who oppose any form of financial relief for families sending children to private schools. State tuition grants, for example, have been held unconstitutional. The governing rule now, however, is not quite the same. In 1983, the Supreme Court decided in *Mueller* v. *Allen* that Minnesota's policy of allowing tax deductions for tuition, textbooks, and transportation to private schools—including religious ones—was permissible. The Court cast aside charges of establishment because Minnesota made such expenses deductible only if they were provided to all state-approved private schools. Minnesota has now expanded its program to allow tax deductions for *any* expense (within prescribed financial limits) for private education and has introduced a $1,000 tax credit for lower-income citizens who incur expenses other than tuition costs in sending their children to private schools.

The courts have addressed the efforts of many states and localities to adopt "school choice" plans, which permit families and students to choose between public and private schools at state expense. Still, it is not obvious what the Supreme Court's reaction would be if these plans become widespread. Several cities, including Milwaukee, Wisconsin, and Cleveland, Ohio, now have school choice plans in operation that provide grants of money (sometimes called vouchers) to low-income families that may be used at certain private schools, including religious ones.

In 2002, the U.S. Supreme Court upheld Cleveland's plan in *Zelman* v. *Simmons-Harris*. Though nearly all of the students participating in the program used their grants to attend religious schools, the Court decided that the program was designed to enable a purely private choice. Parents, not government, choose to send their children to religious schools under the program, and so the program did not involve unconstitutional government support for religion. The decision was clearly a victory for school choice advocates, including those who desire greater governmental accommodation of religion in public life. But the decision is unlikely to be the last word on broader-based voucher programs, which have been proposed with great controversy in Washington, DC, Florida, California, and Michigan, among other states.

The courts have consistently ruled that aid directed to religious colleges and universities raises considerably less concern about establishment. The assumption is that college students, as adults, are a good deal less vulnerable to religious propaganda than are children and young adults in K–12 schools. Thus aid may be provided to religious colleges for buildings as long as they are not used for worship or sectarian education, according to the Court's decisions in *Tilton* v. *Richardson* (1971) and *Roemer* v. *Board of Public Works* (1976).

EQUAL ACCESS: AN ALTERNATIVE
APPROACH TO CHURCH AND STATE

As we have noted, many legal observers and practitioners have become frustrated by the Supreme Court's approach to church-state relations, which they see as unpredictable and even threatening to religious freedom. Conservative evangelicals especially came to realize that they needed to turn to legal doctrine that benefited from clearer judicial vision.[21] Beginning in the early 1980s, they found it by moving away from a sole reliance on the Religion Clauses and focusing on the constitutional protection of speech and expression. By interpreting religious practices as a form of expression, they were able to put a well-developed and relatively predictable body of case law to work on their behalf. The basic free speech principle is that government cannot limit expression—including religious expression—merely because it dislikes or fears the content of what is expressed. By defining religion as just another form of expression, religion does not claim special constitutional status, thereby avoiding many constitutional problems, including establishment concerns regarding religion-based exemptions from state law or certain forms of state-aid to religious schools.

Some of the earliest efforts along these lines dealt with student-led religious groups in public schools. The Supreme Court upheld such a policy for college campuses in 1981 by arguing that if a university offers the use of facilities to one extracurricular group, it must do so for all (*Widmar* v. *Vincent*). In 1984, Congress passed the Equal Access Act, which applied the same principle to public high schools. It provided that high schools had to allow student-led religious groups to meet after school if other extracurricular clubs were also permitted to do so. Many schools have resisted, but the Supreme Court affirmed the law in *Board of Education* v. *Mergens* (1990) by contending that granting space to an after-school Bible club did not amount to an unconstitutional establishment of religion—as long as a teacher, as a government employee, did not lead club meetings. To do otherwise would mean that the state was unreasonably discriminating against a particular

BOX 9.4   RELIGIOUS MONUMENTS AND "GOVERNMENT SPEECH"

A recent case involving a small religious sect in Utah illustrates another way that free speech principles can shape church-state relations. In 1978, Claude "Corky" Nowell of Utah, founder of the Summum Church, claimed to encounter highly intelligent beings who revealed seven key principles or "aphorisms" of nature. In the mid-2000s, the Summum sought to erect a monument to the "Seven Aphorisms" in a public park in Pleasant Grove, Utah. Even though the park already included several monuments, including one honoring the Ten Commandments, the city of Pleasant Grove denied the Summum's request. The Summum sued, claiming that Pleasant Grove had established religion by preferring one religious display over another. In 2009, the U.S. Supreme Court settled the matter by upholding Pleasant Grove's decision to prevent the Summum monument from being erected. The Court found that Pleasant Grove's acceptance of permanent monuments for display in the park amounted to government speech and that that government need not be neutral—including religiously neutral—when it speaks on its own behalf.

Source: *Pleasant Grove City* v. *Summum*, 129 S. Ct. 1125 (2009).

form of expression—in this case, religious expression—and therefore violating the bedrock principles of free speech.

The impact of the Court's decision to allow high school Bible clubs to form already has been felt, as an increasing number of schools have developed such clubs. Close to 20 percent of all American high schools now have at least one extracurricular religious club. High school ministries such as Young Life, the Fellowship of Christian Athletes, Youth for Christ, First Priority, and Student Venture (the high school ministry of Campus Crusade for Christ) have been active on campuses across the country, in some cases for many decades.[22]

Battles over such clubs and organizations continue, however. In 1993, the Court ruled that if a school district allows other community groups to use its buildings when classes are not in session, then religious groups must also be offered the same privilege (*Lamb's Chapel* v. *Center Moriches Union Free School District*). The Court also held in *Rosenberger* v. *Rector* (1995) that because the University of Virginia provides support to a wide variety of student publications, it must as a matter of equal access do the same for a campus Christian publication. The university at first had not assisted the Christian publication for fear of violating the Establishment Clause, but it was ultimately compelled to do so partly as the result of violating the Free Speech Clause (see Box 9.4).

It is, however, quite possible to disagree with the Court and insist that the principle of equal access simply uses the pretext of free speech to establish religion. Though school teachers may not run Bible clubs and other religious groups that meet after school, meetings do take place on public school grounds. Nevertheless, advocates respond that neutrality under the Free Speech Clause, coupled with the Religion Clauses and principles of equal protection, requires that the state allow all forms of expression access to a generally available public good.

CONCLUSION

One of the most interesting questions in modern church-state politics is the relationship between free exercise and establishment. The framers of the Constitution took for granted that establishment of religion by definition meant restriction of free exercise rights. And they were correct in instances when establishment means state sponsorship of a single religion. At least for practitioners of minority religions, free exercise was bound to be burdened (at best) in the face of a single established religion. At worst, they would face drastic curtailment of their free exercise rights.

Much current church-state jurisprudence proceeds under the same assumption, namely that no official establishment can possibly enhance the free exercise of religion. But this assumption is not always self-evidently true; sometimes, in fact, establishment may bolster the free exercise rights of many citizens. The classic illustration is provided by the benefits that flow from state aid to religious schools. If state aid is given to all religious schools, religious free exercise may be expanded for families that desire a religious education for their children but cannot afford it—a key contention of many groups and commentators who supported the *Zelman* decision. Some critics point out that implicit in this view is the idea that somehow government has an obligation to promote the free exercise of religion, an assumption at which they insist the First Amendment does not even hint. They read the First Amendment to mean that government should not interfere with religious free exercise, which is far different from providing active support for religion.

Such an interpretation of the First Amendment is only one possible understanding of its protection of free exercise rights. But even if one concludes that the First Amendment requires government to *promote* free exercise, it does not follow that it should also offer state aid to religious schools. The point is that it is not always obvious that an increase in establishment (of all religions) leads necessarily to a decrease in free exercise rights. In some instances, the opposite may be true. Some argue that, as a result, sweeping formulas should be replaced by more case-by-case analysis and discussion. The courts have argued for decades that some forms of religious expression in public schools constitute unacceptable establishment. To say the least, these decisions have offended many critics who contend that the resulting absence of religious expression in the public schools amounts to an establishment of secularism.

It is also crucial to ask whether the political issues of the day should be fought out in the courts in the first place.[23] And the issue is not only one of how elitist or democratic the courts may be, though that is certainly a subject that deserves reflection. Nor is the question as straightforward as deciding on the wisdom of removing controversial religio-political issues from the public arena. The fact is that the legal remedy, given its focus on adversarial conflict, often exacerbates tensions and thus frequently fails to encourage the compromise that is essential for the increasingly multicultural and multireligious character of American society.

Certainly there is a need for a perspective on church-state politics that is much more sophisticated than that which often dominates the headlines. There are more than just two positions. There are many kinds of establishment and separationism, many degrees of free exercise and limits on free exercise. Everything is dependent upon specific circumstances. The concrete issues that shape the politics of church and state are complicated, fascinating, and always evolving.

FURTHER READING

Greenawalt, Kent. *Religion and the Constitution: Free Exercise and Fairness*. Princeton: Princeton University Press, 2006. A nuanced and closely reasoned perspective in favor of strong religious liberty protections.

Hamilton, Marci. *God vs. the Gavel: Religion and the Rule of Law*. New York: Cambridge University Press, 2005. An impassioned argument that the public good should often trump religious liberty claims.

Nussbaum, Martha. *Liberty of Conscience: In Defense of America's Tradition of Religious Equality*. New York: Basic Books, 2008. A probing historical and legal analysis of the American tradition of religious freedom.

Wilson, John F., and Donald L. Drakeman. *Church and State in American History*. Boulder: Westview Press, 2003. A wide-ranging compilation of key cases and commentaries on its subject.

Witte, John. *Religion and the American Constitutional Experiment: Essential Rights and Liberties*. 2nd ed. Boulder: Westview Press, 2005. A valuable introduction to the context for religious liberty in America.

NOTES

1. See, for example, Thomas J. Curry, *The First Freedoms* (New York: Oxford University Press, 1986); Michael Malbin, *Religion and Politics: The Intentions of the Authors of the First Amendment* (Washington, DC: American Enterprise Institute, 1978); William L. Miller, *The First Liberty and the American Republic* (New York: Knopf, 1986); and Vincent Phillip Muñoz, "James Madison's Principle of Religious Liberty," *American Political Science Review* 97 (2003), 17–32.

2. See, for example, *Watson* v. *Jones*, 80 U.S. 679 (1871); and *Jones* v. *Wolf*, 443 U.S. 595 (1979).

3. *United States* v. *Ballard*, 322 U.S. 78 (1944).

4. We draw much of the following discussion on clergy malpractice from Margaret P. Battin, *Ethics in the Sanctuary: Examining the Practices of Organized Religion* (New Haven, CT: Yale University Press, 1990); and Mark Weitz, *Clergy Malpractice in America: Nally v. Grace Community Church of the Valley* (Lawrence, KS: University Press of Kansas, 2001).

5. For a discussion of the legal ramifications of the scandals, see Marc D. Stern, "Masses of Torts," *Religion in the News* 6 (Summer 2003), 2–3, 26.

6. A particularly strong voice on these matters is constitutional lawyer Marci Hamilton. See Marci Hamilton, *God vs. The Gavel: Religion and the Rule of Law* (New York: Cambridge University Press, 2005); and Marci Hamilton, *Justice Denied: What America Must Do to Protect Its Children* (New York: Cambridge University Press, 2008).

7. See *Airport Commissioners v. Jews for Jesus*, 482 U.S. 569 (1987).

8. See *Larsen v. Valente*, 456 U.S. 228 (1982).

9. See *McDaniel v. Paty*, 435 U.S. 618 (1978); *Catholic Conference v. Abortion Rights Mobilization*, 487 U.S. 72 (1988).

10. See *Cruz v. Beto*, 405 U.S. 319 (1972); *O'Lone v. Estate of Shabazz*, 482 U.S. 342 (1987); and *Cutter v. Wilkinson*, 544 U.S. 709 (2005). On the general question of the legal issues surrounding religious practice in prison, see Winnifred Fallers Sullivan, *Prison Religion: Faith-Based Reform and the Constitution* (Princeton: Princeton University Press, 2009).

11. *Braunfeld v. Brown*, 366 U.S. 599 (1961). Also see *Jacobson v. Massachusetts*, 197 U.S. 11 (1905); *Prince v. Massachusetts*, 321 U.S. 158 (1944).

12. *Sherbert v. Verner*, 374 U.S. 398 (1963).

13. *Gonzales v. O Centro Espirita Beneficiente Uniao Do Vegetal*, 546 U.S. 418 (2006).

14. Peter Baker, "Workplace Religion Policy Due," *The Washington Post*, August 14, 1997, 1A.

15. See *Cutter v. Wilkinson*, 544 U.S. 709 (2005); Sullivan, *Prison Religion*.

16. *Van Orden* was decided at the same time as *McCreary County v. ACLU of Kentucky*, 545 U.S. 844 (2006), which held that the context surrounding Ten Commandments displays in some county courthouses suggested that counties had no secular purpose and therefore violated the Establishment Clause.

17. On the matter of excessive entanglement, also see *Walz v. Tax Commission*, 397 U.S. 664 (1970).

18. Justice Scalia made this comment in his opinion in *Lamb's Chapel v. Center Moriches Union Free School District*, 508 U.S. 385 (1993).

19. *Wallace v. Jaffree*, 105 S. Ct. 2479 (1985).

20. Jeffrey Rosen, "Lemon Law," *New Republic* 208 (March 29, 1993), 17.

21. Steven P. Brown, *Trumping Religion: The New Christian Right, the Free Speech Clause, and the Courts* (Tuscaloosa, AL: University of Alabama Press, 2002).

22. On Young Life, see http://www.younglife.org; on Fellowship of Christian Athletes, http://www.fca.org; on Youth for Christ, http://www.yfc.net; on Student Venture, http://www.studentventure.com.

23. Margaret Battin first got us to take this subject seriously.

10

LATINO AND AFRICAN AMERICAN RELIGION AND POLITICS

Throughout this book, we often have distinguished Americans not simply by the diversity of their religious traditions and behaviors but also by their race. Thus we have focused not only on evangelicals as a group but have divided evangelicals into white and African American categories when explaining political beliefs and behaviors; similarly, we have placed Latino and non-Latino Catholics into separate groups. This is an acknowledgement that racial and ethnic identity is inextricably linked with religion in the United States, and that fact has political significance. In this chapter we take a step back to consider the complex interaction of race, religion, and politics in America.

We focus on two crucial, prominent racial and ethnic groups in the United States: Latinos and African Americans. Religion has always been a highly significant force in the African American and Latino communities. In few other racial or ethnic groups, in fact, does religion play a more central role. But the two groups have distinctive histories and diverse cultures that make them a useful comparison as we consider the impact of religion on politics within these two communities. We begin with Latinos, a community that is growing rapidly in the United States and catching the attention of the political establishment as a result—a fact on full display in the past several presidential election campaigns. We then consider the rich traditions of religion and politics within the African American community.

THE CHANGING STATUS OF LATINO RELIGION

There is no better place to begin a discussion of Latino religion than with the role of Roman Catholicism in Hispanic culture and history.[1] Hispanic Catholicism has remarkably deep roots in North America, predating even the immigration of Puritans to the United States in the early 1600s. The Spanish brought Roman Catholicism with them during their conquests in the continent in the sixteenth century. Fueled by the efforts of Catholic missionaries, who were intimately connected with Spanish colonization, Catholicism spread through the native populations of the American Southwest—a region that now includes Texas, New Mexico, Arizona, California, and the fringes of bordering states. Simply looking at a map of the region, with its hundreds of cities, streets, and public spaces named in Spanish after saints and other symbols of the Catholic faith (consider the names of California's three most prominent cities—Los Angeles, San Francisco, and San Diego—as just one illustration), we sense the unmistakable legacy of both Catholicism and Spanish colonization in the American Southwest.

Roman Catholicism continues to play a central role in the lives of Latino Americans. Today about two-thirds claim an affiliation with Catholicism, and many are intensely committed to the beliefs and practices of the institutional Church.[2] Slightly more Latino than non-Latino whites attend religious services regularly and claim that religion is very important to them.[3] Certain aspects of Catholicism resonate particularly well with Hispanics, including a strong attachment to Mary as mother of God, reflecting the Latino emphasis on family.[4]

Although many Latinos share the Spanish language and other aspects of culture, worship styles and religious practices among Latino Catholics vary widely. Much of the diversity is tied to different countries of origin; Mexicans, Cubans, Puerto Ricans, Dominicans, and Latinos with other national roots often take somewhat different approaches in their practice of the Catholic faith. The differences are especially pronounced among foreign-born Hispanics who have had relatively little exposure to the enormous pressure of assimilation into the broader American culture.[5]

Although expressions of Catholicism among Latino Americans are both vibrant and diverse, the relationship between the Latino community and the Catholic religious tradition sometimes has been an uneasy and ambivalent one. During the Spanish colonial period, for example, Latino converts often were suspicious that Catholic missions were complicit in the brutalities of conquest. Many others over the decades have felt an alienation from the immigrant groups that dominated Catholic leadership, most notably those with roots in Ireland, Germany, Poland,

and other European countries. And today Latino connections to the Catholic Church are diminishing, with some Latinos now converting to other faiths or maintaining a spiritual life outside the institutional Church. This is a matter of increasing concern for the Catholic hierarchy.[6]

This uneasy relationship with the organized Church today is partly the result of secular cultural and economic pressures beyond the Church's control. As second- and third-generation Latinos assimilate into American culture and join the middle class, they often lose parts of cultural identity, including their Catholicism, that their parents or grandparents brought from their countries of origin. But many Latinos also perceive that throughout its history the Church itself often has been inattentive to the unique culture and concerns of Hispanic Catholics.[7] For example, a common complaint is a chronic shortage of Spanish-language masses or Latino-oriented youth ministries.[8] Or consider Latino participation in the Catholic hierarchy, a key feature of church life. Until the 1940s, Spaniards remained the largest group of Spanish-speaking priests in the American Catholic Church, and the first Mexican American bishop, Patricio Flores, was not installed until 1970. Although the number of Latino bishops has grown since the 1970s, the historical lack of integration into church government simply reinforces the belief of some Latinos that they have been "second-class citizens" within the Church.

It is in this milieu that a familiar, and very intense, competition has emerged between the Catholic Church and non-Catholic religious traditions for Latino members. Many Protestant denominations now have departments that focus entirely on Hispanic outreach, and they often offer Spanish-speaking worship services and various forms of social and economic aid to Latino communities. A strong majority of Latino Americans remain Catholic (some 68 percent), and their absolute numbers have steadily expanded as a result of continuing immigration from Mexico and other Latin and South American Catholic countries.

At the same time a substantial Protestant minority has grown among Latinos in the United States. Some 15 percent of Latinos are Protestants, some from Central American countries where a spirited Protestantism is now flourishing but many who have converted from Catholicism in the United States. Other Latinos in the United States are not involved in religion at all.[9]

Within Latino Catholicism itself there is a strong strain of Pentecostal or charismatic faith, one that stresses a religion that is vibrantly experiential and spirit-filled, something that is routine in many Protestant Latino churches. Fully half of all Catholic Latinos use words such as "Pentecostal" and "charismatic" to describe their faith, compared to just 10 percent of non-Hispanic Catholics.[10] These "renewalist" Latino

Catholics remain loyal to the Catholic Church, but they are much more likely than other Catholics to report experiencing or observing divine revelations, miraculous healings, or even speaking in tongues.[11]

Pentecostal and charismatic Protestant churches have emerged as a real alternative to the Catholic Church for Latinos. But we must be careful to paint an accurate picture of Latino Pentecostals. Latino Pentecostalism in America is a century-old movement that has attracted many Mexicans and other immigrants with its emphasis on gifts of the Holy Spirit; Pentecostalism is open to all and intentionally subordinates racial and social differences. Some Latino Pentecostals are former Catholics, but many others have been lifelong adherents of Pentecostal faiths, often within established denominations such as Assemblies of God and the Vineyard. Indeed, it is not uncommon for Pentecostalism in Latino American families to run generations deep.[12]

Nor should anyone think that Latino Protestantism has grown only because the Catholic Church has wholly ignored or always taken for granted its Latino membership. Far from it. A quarter to a third of all Catholics in the United States are Latino, a fact not lost on Catholic Church leaders.[13] Some bishops and archbishops have been keenly attentive to both the special character and diversity of Latino spiritual expressions within American Catholicism. For example, Robert Emmett Lucey, archbishop of San Antonio from 1941 to 1969, was particularly instrumental in raising social justice concerns on behalf of his Hispanic parishioners, who as immigrants frequently faced poverty and a lack of job skills. Lucey's efforts culminated in the formation of the bishop's Committee for the Spanish Speaking in 1945. Since the 1970s, the U.S. Conference of Catholic Bishops has sponsored several gatherings (called *Encuentros*) of pastoral leaders to discuss plans for ministering to Latino Catholics. The USCCB also recently issued a major study that addresses the need for focus on the Latino membership.[14] And, in light of the legacy of Latino Catholic immigration, the American Church has taken up major fundraising for Catholic churches in Latin American countries since at least the 1960s. At the same time few Catholic churches can match the intimacy and community of many Protestant Latino churches. Nor do many have a Latino minister as is standard in Protestant Latino congregations. These limitations have damaged the appeal of the Catholic Church for more than a few Latinos, but they have also stimulated the Catholic Church to move aggressively to address these problems.[15]

In short, the religious divisions within the Latino community are real and momentous for various religious traditions in America. These divisions also are developing at precisely the same time that political elites are becoming more aware that Latinos constitute a tremendous political resource.

LATINOS IN PUBLIC LIFE

The Hispanic population, which includes more than 44 million Americans and has grown more than 150 percent since 1980, has surpassed African Americans as the largest racial or ethnic minority in the United States.[16] This fact alone has enormous political implications. It is no wonder that elected officials and political parties have embarked on an intense competition for the Latino electorate, even though low voter turnout in past elections has diminished some of its potential influence. The Latino presence in American politics also has generated myriad policy debates, from the status of undocumented workers to affirmative action in education to English-only requirements. The high profile of these political and policy issues will only increase over time as the number of Latino Americans continues to grow.

The Hispanic population is undergoing rapid cultural change as well. To be sure, many Latinos, particularly the foreign born, maintain strong ties to the cultures of Cuba, Mexico, Puerto Rico, the Dominican Republic, and other countries in Latin America and the Caribbean. But others, especially those who are native-born Americans, have assimilated into American culture. Many now count English as their primary language, although a larger proportion is bilingual.[17] In fact, language acquisition gives us a clue as to how assimilation might affect religion because Latinos who claim to be primarily English speakers are also more likely to be members of Protestant churches. [18]

This range of dynamics accounts for the significant differences between foreign- and native-born Latinos on a variety of issues, including opinion on matters of politics and culture. When the foreign- versus native-born division is combined with the diversity of religious traditions and areas of origin, it becomes difficult to identify strong cohesion in Latino perspectives on public life. There is certainly no monolithic Latino opinion, and that fact has political implications too.

We can say, however, that Latinos as a group are somewhat more conservative than non-Hispanic whites on issues such as gender roles, abortion, homosexuality, and other matters that touch on family life. The role of family is a key factor in the political thinking of Latinos, with foreign-born and Spanish-dominant speakers most likely to espouse traditionalist views of family, including opposition to abortion rights and same-sex marriage. Even when controlling for these factors, however, high attendance rates in Catholic or evangelical churches tends to remain a key predictor of conservatism on socio-moral issues.[19] Latinos as a group also are generally conservative on matters of church and state, as illustrated in their support of organized prayer in public schools (70 percent) and providing parents with state-funded educational vouchers (60 percent).[20]

On many issues related to economics and immigration, however, Latinos move to the left of the ideological spectrum. Although they favor the role of churches in providing social services, Hispanics are more likely than non-Hispanic whites to accept the possibility of higher taxes in exchange for more government services. This view, which is correlated with the generally lower socioeconomic standing of Hispanic Americans, also reflects the liberationist religious teachings on social justice and "the option for the poor," especially within Catholicism.[21] Moreover, Latinos are much more likely than other demographic groups to support providing welfare benefits to illegal immigrants.[22] The lesson here is that ethnic identity and immigrant history shape how Latinos from across religious traditions think about public policy issues.

It may be tempting to see in these issue positions the makings of another group of quintessential swing voters, not unlike the Catholic voting population as a whole. There may be some evidence of the emergence of a new swing electorate, but it is difficult to point to religion as a source of such an alignment.[23] To be sure, the distinction between Protestant and Catholic Latinos appears to explain some differences in partisan voting and identification. Thirty-six percent of Latino evangelicals, for example, identify with the Democratic Party, in contrast to 55 percent of Latino Catholics; Republican Party affiliation reflects the gap in reverse, with 36 percent of Latino evangelicals identifying with the GOP in comparison to only 18 percent of Latino Catholics.[24] Yet despite these differences, about half of all Latinos identify with the Democratic Party, compared to about one-in-five for the Republicans.[25] What is more, recent voting patterns suggest that stated partisanship does not necessarily predict vote choice—and may portend changes in party identification in the future. At least one postelection survey in 2008 suggested that even Latino evangelicals flipped the partisan direction of their vote from the previous election. Whereas 58 percent of Latino evangelicals voted for George W. Bush in 2004, 57 percent voted for Barack Obama in 2008.[26] In addition, to the extent that Latinos do constitute a swing electorate, a host of factors other than religion, including class, generation, and country of origin, shape their voting patterns.

Are there other indicators of religion-based political behavior among Latinos? The conventional wisdom is that, aside from myriad religious social service agencies that serve Latino populations, few distinctively religious groups engage in political advocacy on behalf of Latinos. It is certainly true that many of the most prominent Latino groups—the League of United Latin American Citizens, the Mexican American Legal Defense and Educational Fund, and the National Council of La Raza, to name a few—are not explicitly religious in character or focus. Some emerging research, however, suggests that the extent of faith-based Latino activism has been underestimated. [27] Moreover, even with prominent secular groups leading the way, the very existence of those groups points to the real possibilities for mobilization among Latinos—mobilization that religious institutions could foster. The example of César Chávez, the legendary farmworkers organizer, is instructive. Spurred by a deep liberationist understanding of his own Roman Catholicism, Chávez helped unionize thousands of Hispanic farmworkers in California from the 1950s until his death in 1993.[28] His work with farmworkers caught the eye of many Catholic priests and other religious leaders, who provided vocal support; he even ended one of his several hunger strikes with a special Catholic mass attended by religious elites from across traditions.[29]

Nevertheless, significant challenges stand in the way of religion-based mobilization of Latinos as a group. For example, the rapid assimilation of many second- and third-generation Latinos may decrease the likelihood that the Latino community as a whole will emerge as a distinctive political group.[30] After all, if most Latinos become deeply acculturated into mainstream American society, there may be nothing particularly "Latino" about their political attitudes or behaviors after a few more generations. To the extent that religion plays a role in politics, then, Latinos in the future may appear like anyone else within the religious traditions into which they assimilate.

Moreover, the very description of a group of Americans as "Latino" or "Hispanic" belies the many ways nonwhite Hispanics perceive their own ethnic identity. Many prefer to think of themselves as Cuban American, Mexican American, or Puerto Rican (for example) rather than Latino, and these categories matter both for religion and politics. Cuban Americans in South Florida have a very different political focus from, say, Mexican Americans in California or Puerto Ricans in New York City.[31] The nuances and syncretism of religious practices across these countries of origin reinforce differences among Latino Americans, making broad-based political mobilization less likely than if a homogeneous group could be defined clearly.[32]

In any event, there is no doubt that Latinos are becoming more visible players in American politics. As an important part of Barack Obama's winning coalition, they were a much-discussed voting bloc in the 2008 presidential election.[33] As their voting turnout rates and other forms of political participation increase—and with every election the trend continues in that direction—Hispanic Americans will grow ever more important politically. It remains to be seen whether religion will play a significant role in defining the nature and scope of Latino political mobilization, but the rich history of Catholicism and other faiths within the Latino community gives religion strong potential as a political resource.

AFRICAN AMERICAN RELIGION AND POLITICS: TOWARD A BROADER VIEW

In his fascinating and sometimes eccentric *American Religion*, Harold Bloom argues convincingly that to understand African American expressions of Christianity in the United States, one must appreciate both their evangelical side and their distinctly African American side.[34] Whereas Roman Catholicism has had a profound influence on Latino Americans, black Christianity is rooted in American evangelicalism. Like the influence of colonization and assimilation in Hispanic history, black evangelicalism also has been shaped profoundly by the historical experience of race in the United States. It is important to remember that African American religion is overwhelmingly Protestant—and evangelical—in character. African American Christians are keenly focused on scripture, and many affirm the Bible as literally true. In fact, nearly two-thirds of African Americans (62 percent) claim that it is true in all aspects or nearly so. Moreover, 80 percent of all African Americans report praying daily, compared to the national average of 58 percent.[35]

Another indication of the evangelicalism of African American Christianity involves worship style. African American services emphasize preaching and music and often considerable expressiveness, as is also the case in white and interracial Pentecostal worship services. There is little of the liturgy or firm traditionalism that characterizes most Roman Catholic and many mainline Protestant worship services. This is not to say that the typical African American worship service is indistinguishable from a white evangelical service. In African American churches, there is significantly more interaction between the congregation and the pastor during worship. Music plays a central role; there is a clear connection between the call and response musical motif and the typical flow of an African American service. African American church music is significant both within and outside of the religious context. In worship, musical expression is a central element of emotional religious experience. In the broader culture, African American spirituals gave rise to a myriad of other musical forms, from gospel to blues to jazz and rock and roll.

A third similarity between white and black evangelicalism involves church organization. Both African American and white evangelical denominations favor a loose organizational structure that tends to uphold the autonomy of the individual congregation. Such conventions (as in the white Southern Baptist Convention and the black National Baptist Convention, USA, Inc.) bring together many individual congregations under one umbrella, but unlike hierarchical denominations such as the Episcopal Church, they usually do not supply much direction from the top.

Christianity in the black community, as in the white community, has experienced numerous and sometimes contentious conflicts that have produced permanent schisms, sometimes over doctrine and sometimes over personalities. Many African American Baptists, who comprise more than a third of the black population, are affiliated with several different denominations, including the National Baptist Convention, USA, Inc., and the Progressive National Baptist Convention Incorporated.[36] The second largest black Protestant sub-tradition is Pentecostalism, which has been growing rapidly in the African American community. It is organized in several major denominations, especially the Church of God in Christ (COGIC)—which is one of the fastest-growing denominations in the United States—and numerous independent churches.[37] Another historically prominent sub-tradition is the black Methodist tradition, exemplified by the African Methodist Episcopal (AME) Church (which is the oldest African American denomination), the African Methodist Episcopal Zion (AMEZ) Church, and the Christian Methodist Episcopal (CME) Church.

In evangelical churches, whether they have white, black, or multiracial congregations, the laity normally hire their pastor directly without involvement by the denomination. In most black churches the pastor (who is almost always a man by tradition) is a powerful and generally dominant figure. The pastor is almost always the center of his church, and he makes the important decisions about community and political activities. His church often rises and falls with him. Recruiting a good pastor is therefore essential for every African American church.[38]

A recent study of African American clergy found that many have not completed college or advanced theological training, although some black pastors are highly educated. For financial reasons, a significant number of African American clergy find employment outside of their congregations. There are plenty of exceptions, but often black pastors must confront economic struggles in their personal and family lives as well as in their churches, especially when they serve small or rural congregations. The situation often is complicated by a wide range of challenging circumstances facing black Americans. African American clergy who serve in urban areas must contend with issues of drug abuse, violence, and abject poverty on a regular basis. Sometimes black pastors have to take personal action just to keep members of their congregations and residents of their church neighborhoods alive.[39] Samuel G. Freedman's powerful *Upon This Rock: The Miracle of a Black*

Church describes some of these challenges in unmistakable terms.[40] At the same time, a large number of black churches serve the ever-expanding African American middle and upper classes.

Attracting young people is a universal challenge faced by all American religious groups. Black clergy routinely worry that they have a particularly hard time attracting young black men to church. Many African American congregations have a large majority of female members,[41] and there is a feeling in some African American circles that church, if not religion, is for women, except for the key position of minister. Moreover, some religious alternatives seem to appeal more to men than to women in the African American community. Among these alternatives is Islam; a vast majority of African American Muslims are men.[42]

It is crucial to remember that African American Christianity is inseparable from the history and shared experiences of black people in the United States. To know the history of African American Christianity is to understand its traditions of both resistance and accommodation; to appreciate its communal side and its individualism; and to recognize its prophetic dimension and its priestly focus.[43] Religion has served as a crucial refuge for African Americans for several hundred years. During slavery and beyond, the church was the one place where African Americans usually could be safe and free. The church remains today as the central institution of the black community and is integral to the identities of many African American citizens, as well as a crucial resource in their civic activism.[44]

But the distinctly African American side of Christianity has significance that transcends the black community. African American spirituals, such as "Were You There?" or "Swing Low, Sweet Chariot," are now widely sung by Christians of all racial and ethnic backgrounds.[45] This fact is both ironic and inspiring because these spirituals emerged from the dim days of slavery. African slaves, stripped of freedom, invented the spirituals to bring themselves hope during long, difficult, and boring days of forced labor. One spiritual, for example, contains the lyric "Before I'll be a slave, I'll be buried in my grave, and go home to my Father and be free." Slavery ended, but among its legacies is the black spiritual, with its emphasis on Christianity and the theme of liberation. The black spiritual is but one of the many essential contributions made by African Americans to the broader culture of the United States.

From the beginning African American Christianity has emphasized an image of God as a consoler as well as a liberator of the oppressed. In this sense religion can be a vehicle of hope for the weary and the downtrodden, a function that continues to be important for African Americans today as it was in the days of slavery.

To this day many religious African Americans find some comfort in the assurance of heavenly peace and salvation through a fervent and celebratory belief in a benevolent God. At the same time, religion also has served as a powerful justification and mobilizing force for civil rights activism among African Americans.[46] There is also a long-standing effort within some theological circles to maintain a strong black liberation ideology. James Cone and Cornel West have been the leading black liberation theologians. Cone played a crucial role in the late 1960s as elements of the civil rights movement turned toward more radical expressions of discontent. His seminal work, *Black Theology and Black Power*, justified the black power movement in religious terms.[47] West, a public intellectual and religion professor at Princeton University, has written extensively on the subjugation of African Americans, most notably in his now-classic book, *Race Matters*.[48]

HISTORY AND BLACK POLITICAL ATTITUDES

What is most striking about religion and politics in the African American community is the close connection between the two. Politics is centrally important in black Christianity, and African American churches often are openly involved in politics in a variety of ways. There is simply no sharp division between religion and politics in the black community today; in a sense, African Americans embrace the Old Testament model in which the paths of religion and politics often crossed.

Before the civil rights revolution in the South, however, involvement in politics could be dangerous and sometimes deadly for African Americans. To be sure, African American churches long have held that the Gospels emphasize social justice and equity. Even before the civil rights movement began in the 1950s, plenty of African American citizens were fighting for change, albeit behind the scenes. By and large, however, before the 1950s most African Americans, especially in the South, justifiably saw the public arena as a dangerous place that ought to be avoided.[49] Thus, politics was relevant in the early years of black Christianity only in a theological sense; the image of Jesus Christ as an avenging liberator of the downtrodden spoke poignantly to the early African American experience.

During the more than two centuries of slavery in North America, many black people converted to Christianity, although American Christianity remained a distinctly white religion. Few allowances were made for black adaptations of white Christianity, but distinctly African-inspired versions of Christianity developed nonetheless. The first black Baptist congregations were organized in the South at the end of the eighteenth century, but many slaves were not allowed to attend any services at these or other churches. Therefore clandestine worship groups formed on plantations, coming to be known collectively as "the invisible institution."[50] At night, slaves taught themselves to read the Bible, which provided both spiritual and intellectual refuge from the drudgery and pain of the forced labor they endured during the day.

The early African American Methodist churches were organized not by slaves but by free people living in the North who saw white churches as complicit in the perpetuation of the institution of slavery. Segregation was enforced in white churches even in the North. Northern black Christians felt that by creating their own, separate churches, they would be able to assert their collective power more forcefully. The beginnings of organized, separate black Protestant expression date to 1787, when several African Americans withdrew from St. George's Methodist Episcopal Church in Philadelphia. They met and prayed together informally for years with other African Americans. Finally in 1794 the white Methodist Bishop Francis Asbury dedicated Bethel Church of Philadelphia, the first African Methodist Episcopal church, which survives to this day and is known as Mother Bethel.[51]

African American religion entered a new era after the Civil War. Black Christianity became more formally organized, and it no longer operated under any form of white tutelage. This period saw major expansion of black Baptist and Methodist denominations. Later in this era, the African American Pentecostal movement was born in California. African American Pentecostal leaders today are proud of the fact that their religious movement does not trace its roots explicitly to European Protestantism. Thus black religion thrived and diversified in the wake of emancipation, but after Reconstruction African Americans shied away from open political engagement. The vast majority of African Americans lived in the South in the late nineteenth and early twentieth centuries, and the political freedom of Reconstruction proved fleeting.

During World War I, African Americans began moving north in search of jobs and a better life outside of the segregated South. This process accelerated during World War II and in the years afterward, when the mechanization of southern agriculture spurred even more northward migration. Eventually about half of all African Americans settled outside the South. Large northern cities soon developed sizable African American communities, which bred a comfort level that moved many African Americans to express their opinions freely and without substantial fear both in and outside of church. These changes did not, however, give rise to much political mobilization in the African American religious community. Old suspicions remained, and evangelical theology continued to teach what previous black experience had underlined: that politics was corrupt and dangerous. African American churches continued to shun official political involvement and urged their members to follow suit.[52]

Despite this legacy, everything began to change in the 1950s and the 1960s. African American churches shifted dramatically toward political engagement, and this shift changed history. The civil rights movement that began in the 1950s was led in its earliest, and arguably most productive, years by black Baptist pastors and congregations. Rev. Martin Luther King Jr. was certainly the most visible pastor in the movement's leadership, but he worked in coalition with other prominent African American clergy, such as Rev. Ralph Abernathy and Rev. Fred Shuttlesworth, through the Southern Christian Leadership Conference.

For these pastors, the time had come to claim civil rights for all African Americans. They had few doubts that God supported this prophetic decision, and by the 1960s African American churches—particularly Baptist churches—throughout the South were transformed into organizational centers for the civil rights movement. Although African American clergy did not constitute the only force arrayed on behalf of the civil rights revolution, without the crucial support of black churches, it would never have happened.[53] It was in church that African Americans heard the message that called them into the politics of protest and found the moral inspiration to risk a great deal individually for the collective benefit of all. It was also in church that they planned strategy and developed the skills they would need to take up the cause of civil rights.

The movement for civil rights, however, did not win quick support from all African American churches. Such involvement—and confrontation—with the world did not sit well with the dominant black evangelical theology, nor did it square with the painful—and sometimes fatal—experiences of African Americans who previously had dared to assert themselves politically. Thus a strong and active resistance to the civil rights movement emerged from within organized black Christianity. Perhaps the most visible opponent was Rev. Joseph H. Jackson, longtime head of the National Baptist Convention, USA, Inc., and a major figure in the African American Christian community. In his retrospective account, he portrays himself and others like him as deeply committed to traditional "Christian activism" on behalf of African Americans. But he—and many other voices of African American religion—opposed Dr. King's particular form of religious politics.[54]

One of the civil rights movement's most obvious victories actually happened within African American religion. The movement changed long-standing attitudes regarding political involvement. This sea change produced the political church that is common—though not universal—in the African American community today. To be sure, a certain ambivalence remains. African Americans accept and often welcome political involvement by their churches and especially by their pastors. Many, but by no means all, African American pastors are deeply involved in politics. Some preach regularly about political issues. Some invite candidates for public office to address their congregations from the pulpit. Some run local political organizations and lead marches. Some speak out frequently about politics in the local media. And some even wear two hats by serving simultaneously as clergy and as elected or appointed public officials.[55]

At the same time, like all laity, members of African American congregations expect that political activity by their clergy will not come at the expense of visiting sick members, preaching effectively, or being available to counsel those with personal crises.[56] And there are some African American pastors and traditions that are skeptical of political activism. This is particularly the case among the many African American Pentecostals.[57]

The civil rights movement put black churches squarely on the liberal side of American politics.[58] In the process, civil rights liberalism strengthened economic liberalism among African Americans. At that time, both forms of liberalism were firmly and increasingly becoming associated with allegiance to the Democratic Party. Indeed, by the end of the 1960s, the Democratic presidential nominee could count on receiving about 85 percent of the vote of the expanding African American electorate. The political attitudes of African Americans today are closely linked to perceptions of their collective treatment in American society and the continuing need to work toward equality and economic opportunity. This has led many African Americans to embrace a strongly favorable view of government and what it might do for them. Such attitudes reinforce support for the Democratic party, which is more sympathetic to government action than is the GOP.[59]

CONNECTIONS BETWEEN RELIGION AND POLITICS

As we have already suggested, the most visible connections between black religion and American politics have come through the actions of various African American clergy. Especially since the 1960s, many black pastors have been deeply involved in politics. Rev. Martin Luther King Jr. became the most famous model of "black pastor as political activist" during his leadership in the civil rights movement in the 1950s and 1960s. King's activism attracted a host of other African American pastors to politics. After his historic presidential candidacies in 1984 and 1988 and numerous involvements since, Rev. Jesse Jackson remains one symbol of African American clerical activism. Another is Rev. Al Sharpton, who has been a powerful voice in New York City electoral politics and who mounted a campaign for the 2004 Democratic presidential nomination. Today black clergy are engaged at all levels of politics, addressing local issues, lobbying government, and serving as elected officials themselves.[60] By no means have all African Americans rallied around highly visible clergy such as Jackson. And Jackson in particular has a host of critics in the African American community—especially in Chicago—who complain that he always seeks the limelight but rarely carries a project through to completion. Yet few critics object to him on the basis of his religious focus and there remains affection and support for Jackson among many African Americans in the United States.[61]

Jackson's presidential campaigns, especially his 1988 run, have been studied at length, and scholars have confirmed that Jackson won massive support from African American Christians. Although racial pride was the single most important factor in rallying support to Jackson, the religious dimension also was significant. This was particularly true among African American women, who are statistically more likely than men to be religious. Women were absolutely central to both Jackson campaigns, from his campaign organization to the voting booth. Jackson's support network also included such established African American religious figures as Rev. T. J. Jemison, the former leader of the National Baptist Convention, USA, Inc. Much of Jackson's campaign rhetoric was distinctly Christian in its overtones and orientation. He emphasized empathy for the downtrodden and determination to build community despite the terrible wounds caused by poverty, drugs, and crime.[62]

The Jackson campaigns also illustrated another dimension of black religious politics that was reflected once again in the historic 2008 election of Barack Obama as the first African American president: the tremendous importance of local churches. Jackson's campaigns demonstrated the potential of African American churches as electoral precincts where rallies could be held, publicity produced, and organizations formed to ensure significant support from the black community.[63] Like Jackson's campaign, Obama's team relied heavily on the get-out-the-vote efforts of local black churches, which supported him enthusiastically and in unprecedented numbers.[64] As a longtime member of an African American church in Chicago and as a former faith-based neighborhood organizer, Obama clearly understood the crucial political importance of mobilizing through churches.

African American pastors and churches are convinced that political activity is a legitimate and necessary means of improving the African American lot on Earth. Ninety percent of African American clergy approve of political action, according to one study.[65] African American Christianity in the United States today is self-consciously political and increasingly comfortable with that fact. In this way it is unlike most of the rest of religion in the United States. Although organized American religion in general has become more openly political today than it was thirty years ago, many people have not made peace with this development. Politics has only one comfortable home in American religion, and that is in African American churches.

In many cases, there is a tight congruence between what black leaders and churches propose politically and what the African American community will support. This is definitely the case with regard to the key issue of improving economic opportunities for African American citizens. Yet there are other issues around which many religious African Americans hold views that diverge somewhat from those of their more secular counterparts. Many African American Christians espouse conservative attitudes on such issues as abortion and women's roles in the church. At the same time, African Americans as a group are more sympathetic to gay rights and economic parity for women than are white evangelicals.[66] The picture is mixed and complicated, but noneconomic issues have not affected African American politics greatly because economic justice and civil rights have remained the political priorities of most black religious leaders.[67] Whether these priorities might change or expand in the Obama era remains to be seen.[68]

Most major African American interest groups, such as the National Association for the Advancement of Colored People (NAACP) and the Urban League, are secular organizations. The lack of a religious orientation on the part of these groups is an artifact of their creation in the early twentieth century. Groups such as the NAACP often were intended to be an alternative to black churches, which activists sometimes perceived as being overly concerned with the next world—and thus not sufficiently devoted to assisting African Americans in this world. Yet today there is regular contact between African American pastors and churches and branches of the NAACP and the Urban League. This is inevitable because these organizations are just as intertwined with the black middle class as are the large African American denominations.

ISLAM IN THE AFRICAN AMERICAN COMMUNITY

Today a modest but growing number of African Americans are Muslims, many of whom are rather recent converts.[69] The story of the Muslim dimension of the African American experience illustrates clearly the fluid nature of American religious culture and the unpredictable political consequences that arise from religious movements (see Box 10.1).

Although a number of Africans were followers of Islam before they were enslaved in America, only traces of that heritage survived. Modest interest in Islam
existed among some nineteenth-century African Americans; certain black intellectuals saw it as an authentic African legacy that had been erased by the slave master.
By the early part of the twentieth century, however, unorthodox, "proto-Islamic"
movements emerged among growing African American populations in some
northern cities.[70] These were tiny, isolated groups with teachings that diverged considerably from mainstream Islam.

Most notable among these groups was Elijah Mohammed's Nation of Islam. Cen-
tered in Detroit, the Nation of Islam initially was a religion of the urban dispossessed,
and it remained small and largely unrecognized until its most gifted disciple, Malcolm X, burst onto the scene in the 1960s. In the 1990s, Malcolm became a cultural
icon, with the ubiquitous merchandising of "X" hats and sweatshirts, after the 1992
release of filmmaker Spike Lee's movie about his life, *Malcolm X*. Even those with
only a vague understanding of Malcolm's legacy have come to admire his reputation

---

BOX 10.1   ELIJAH MOHAMMED

Born Robert Poole, Elijah Mohammed claimed to have received a fantastic theological revelation from his predecessor as head of the Nation of Islam, a myste-
rious Detroit silk merchant named Mr. Farad. At the heart of his revelation was
the idea that whites were a race of devils and an aberration. Blacks, on the other
hand, were descendants of an ancient master race whose wizards had ruled for
millions of years over an empire that even included Mars. Whites were genetically
created by a malcontented mad scientist. They gained ancestry through "Trick-
nology" and enslaved the remnant of the "Original People," the "Tribe of
Shabazz."

Elijah Mohammed was quite critical of African American Christians, particularly
clergy. He called black Christian clergy fools for encouraging and spreading the
religion of slave masters. During the 1960s, Mohammed made inroads among
African Americans, and the Nation of Islam grew. However, a rift between Mohammed and Malcolm X halted the movement's growth. After his death in 1975,
Elijah Mohammed's son, Warith Deen Mohammed, became the most prominent
African American leader in mainstream Islam. The Nation of Islam ultimately
was taken over by the controversial Louis Farrakhan, who continues to preach
Mohammed's message of racial separation.

Source: Gayraud S. Wilmore, *Black Religion and Black Radicalism: An Interpretation of the
Religious History of Afro-American People*, 3rd ed. (Maryknoll, NY: Orbis, 1998).

for uncompromising militancy in the face of white American racism. A popular speaker, he offered an early challenge to Dr. King's nonviolent resistance campaign, which helped to inspire the black power movement. In many respects King and Malcolm represented opposite poles of the African American experience. King was born to middle-class respectability; his highly educated father was a prominent pastor. On the other hand, Malcolm was a street hustler and former convict turned leader of outcast black Muslims. Whereas King preached nonviolent action, Malcolm threatened violence, although he was moving away from this stance at the time of his death.[71]

The Nation of Islam appealed to African Americans in the 1950s and 1960s for two distinct reasons. First, its unique spin on mainstream Islam preached an attractive message to alienated urban blacks—particularly men and incarcerated people—that placed their plight on the shoulders of a race of "white devils" destined by Allah to be eradicated. The Nation of Islam also emphasized education, sexual discipline, hard work, cleanliness, conservative dress, economic self-sufficiency, and rejection of the white man's welfare. This aspect of the faith was especially appealing to leaders such as Malcolm X, who expressed deep concern over the growing number of young African Americans who lived the kind of self-destructive street life from which Islam had freed him.

Second, Islam's patriarchal aspect appealed to black men emasculated by racist society; as a result, the membership of the Nation of Islam remained heavily male. In contrast to the matriarchal culture that characterizes the broader African American community, the Nation of Islam taught that the man was the head of the family and the woman was to be his helpmate and homemaker. Black Muslims attained a certain stature in many cities—even among some non-Muslims—for being proud, disciplined, and militantly separatist.

By 1960, the Nation of Islam still had a small membership but was making a serious effort to create a separate society of schools, businesses, and radio stations, as well as a well-armed militia (the Fruit of Islam) that operated in a number of cities.[72] The political significance of the movement was magnified by Malcolm's high level of visibility. He combined Elijah Mohammed's interpretation of Muslim theology with a call for black consciousness, assertion, and pride. Malcolm told angry African Americans that they had every right to use whatever it took to defend themselves against violence by whites, and he challenged the very premises of Dr. King's nonviolent push for integration and civil rights. Like black Christian liberation theologians, Malcolm proposed separation from whites instead of integration. He declared: "We, the black man of the world, created the white man and we will also kill him." This rhetoric, of course, was explosive in the atmosphere of the mid-1960s.[73]

The most remarkable part of Malcolm's story, however, came toward the end of his life. Disciplined and puritanical in his behavior, Malcolm X was shocked to learn that Elijah Mohammed was living a lavish and lascivious life. A rift quickly developed between them, as did political divisions. When Malcolm remarked that John F. Kennedy's assassination marked "the chickens coming home to roost," Mohammed ostracized him. Malcolm had become too visible, too controversial, and too much of a threat to Mohammed's leadership.

One of Malcolm's responses was to embark on his hajj, the traditional Muslim pilgrimage to Mecca, in 1964. The hajj experience transformed Malcolm's understanding of Islam and led him to reject the divergent teachings of the Nation of Islam. Upon returning to America he renounced the "white devil" theology and announced that he had taken a new name, El-Hajj Malik El-Shabazz, an indication of his embrace of mainstream Islam.[74] Cut off from the Nation of Islam, he founded his own Sunni mosque and created the Organization of Afro-American Unity. His broadened vision of Islam was still incomplete when he was gunned down by Nation of Islam assassins in 1965.

Malcolm's legacy is a complex one. To the end he remained pessimistic about the possibility of eradicating white racism in America. He was suspicious of white liberals who wanted to "help" the cause, and he continued to preach a kind of separatist doctrine that emphasized African American self-sufficiency. Thus he symbolized black pride and assertion for those for whom integration proved less than salutary. Many decades after his death, the challenges faced by the urban underclass continue to reflect the glaring failure of integration among a segment of the African American population.[75]

The Nation of Islam has a separate, and somewhat ironic, legacy that is less well appreciated. When Elijah Mohammed died in 1975, his son Wallace (who took the name Warith Deen Mohammed) assumed the leadership of the Nation of Islam. Quietly but assiduously he began to lead the movement toward a merger with mainstream Islam, which was the very direction Malcolm X had envisioned. Like Malcolm, Warith Deen Mohammed rejected the racist teachings of his father. He dismantled some existing black Muslim institutions and integrated them into mosques, which were growing thanks to the immigration of Muslims from Asia and Africa. Today, the vast majority of African American Muslims worship alongside Muslims of all ethnic backgrounds in Sunni (and a few Shi'a) mosques around the United States.[76]

This movement into mainstream Islam probably facilitated the conversion of more African Americans to Islam by providing them with the grounding of a prominent world religion as an alternative to the "white man's" Christianity. African Americans now make up approximately 20 percent of the nation's Muslim population. However, neither the precise size of the Muslim population nor the proportion of African Americans within it is known with great accuracy, in part because of the measurement problems discussed in Chapter 3.[77]

A tiny minority of African Americans remains loyal to the Nation of Islam and Elijah Mohammed's separatist vision.[78] The Nation of Islam today is led by the fiery Louis Farrakhan, who continues to preach black superiority and separation. Farrakhan has achieved an influence well beyond his core religious following (which numbers no more than 10,000) because he articulates the same rage as did the young Malcolm X. Critics are uneasy, however, about what they see as Farrakhan's anti-Semitism. Farrakhan gained prominence in 1984 when his association with Jesse Jackson (to whom he provided bodyguards) became an issue in the presidential campaign. At that time Farrakhan referred to Jews as members of a "gutter religion," and Jackson was chastised for not renouncing such talk and severing his ties with Farrakhan. The issue dogged Jackson's presidential quest in both 1984 and 1988.[79]

Farrakhan's politics represents a mixture of militant racial separatism, self-reliance, and traditional moral values. On abortion, gay rights, and welfare his message is pointedly conservative. His actual political impact, however, is difficult to measure. His organization has gotten nowhere when it has fielded candidates for local and national offices, but it has attracted broad support for its antidrug activities.[80] Farrakhan also organized the widely publicized Million Man March in 1995. There is no doubt that Farrakhan has some followers, particularly in urban areas, but his influence is relatively circumscribed.

CONCLUSION

The growing Muslim presence in the United States likely will make an increasingly important mark on American culture and politics, following in the long-established tradition of African American Christianity. The connections between religion and politics among Latinos, in contrast, are not as clear. In many respects, Hispanic American religious traditions are still searching for their political voice. That search is shaped profoundly by the historical narratives of colonization, immigration, and assimilation, as well as by the existence of diverse subcultures within the Latino community itself. The religious pluralism we observe among Hispanic Americans reflects this history. It remains to be seen whether religion can provide some unity among the many voices that speak to Latino perspectives on American public life.

FURTHER READING

Chappell, David. *A Stone of Hope: Prophetic Religion and the Death of Jim Crow*. Chapel Hill, NC: University of North Carolina Press, 2004. An account of the crucial role of churches and pastors in civil rights activism in the segregationist South.

Cone, James. *A Black Theology of Liberation*. Philadelphia: Lippincott, 1970. The classic text on black liberation theology.

Espinosa, Gaston, Virgilio Elizondo, and Jesse Miranda, eds. *Latino Religions and Civic Activism in the United States*. New York: Oxford University Press, 2005. A challenge to conventional wisdom that religion has had little influence on Latino civic activism.

Garrow, David J. *Bearing the Cross: Martin Luther King Jr. and the Southern Leadership Conference*. New York: William Morrow, 1986. The story of King's political and religious activism.

Harris, Fredrick C. *Something Within: Religion in African-American Political Activism*. New York: Oxford University Press, 1999. An excellent examination of the role of religion in African American political mobilization.

Hertzke, Allen D. *Echoes of Discontent: Jesse Jackson, Pat Robertson, and the Resurgence of Populism*. Washington, DC: CQ Press, 1993. Discussion of the 1988 Jesse Jackson campaign.

Lincoln, C. Eric, and Lawrence H. Mamiya. *The Black Church in the African American Experience*. Durham, NC: Duke University Press, 1990. Superb work on African American religion.

Malcolm X, with Alex Haley. *The Autobiography of Malcolm X*. New York: Grove Press, 1965. Malcolm X's account of his life.

Sanchez Walsh, Arlene M. *Latino Pentecostal Identity: Evangelical Faith, Self, and Society*. New York: Columbia University Press, 2003. A fascinating study of diverse expressions of Latino Pentecostalism.

Suro, Roberto, et al. "Changing Faiths: Latinos and the Transformation of American Religion." Washington, DC: Pew Hispanic Center/Pew Forum, 2007. Quality data on the dynamic role of religion in the Latino experience.

Wood, Richard L. *Faith in Action: Religion, Race, and Democratic Organizing in America*. Chicago: University of Chicago Press, 2002. Examines the intersection of race, political organizing, and religion, especially in urban areas.

NOTES

1. In this chapter we use the terms "Latino" and "Hispanic" interchangeably, though the latter term is often used to denote a broader category of people with origins in Spain as well as Latin America and the Caribbean.

2. Roberto Suro et al., "Changing Faiths: Latinos and the Transformation of American Religion" (Washington, DC: Pew Hispanic Center/Pew Forum, 2007), 5.

3. Ibid., 16.

4. Ibid., 18; William V. D'Antonio, "Latino Catholics: How Different?" *National Catholic Reporter*, October 29, 1999.

5. George E. Schultze, *Strangers in a Foreign Land: The Organizing of Catholic Latinos in the United States* (Lanham, MD: Lexington, 2006); Catherine Wilson, *The Politics of Latino Faith: Religion, Identity, and Urban Community* (New York: New York University Press, 2008).

6. Schultze, *Strangers in a Foreign Land*; United States Conference of Catholic Bishops, Committee on Hispanic Affairs, *Hispanic Ministry at the Turn of the Millennium* (Washington, DC: USCCB, 1999).

7. Janet Kornblum, "More Hispanic Catholics Losing Their Religion," *USA Today*, December 12, 2002, A1; Lisa Makson, "Latinos Call U.S. Culture Hostile Climate for Faith," *National Catholic Register*, March 9–15, 2003, 1, 12.

8. Jeff Guntzel, "Between Two Cultures," *National Catholic Reporter*, January 30, 2004.

9. "Separated Brothers," *The Economist*, July 18, 2009, 31; Suro, "Changing Faiths," 39–42; Gaston Espinosa, Virgilio Elizondo, and Jesse Miranda, "Hispanic Churches in American Public Life: Summary of Findings," *Interim Reports* 2 (January 2002); Chris L. Jenkins, "Islam Luring More Latinos," *The Washington Post*, January 7, 2001, C1.

10. Suro, "Changing Faiths," 27.

11. See also Schultze, *Strangers in a Foreign Land*.

12. Arlene M. Sanchez Walsh, *Latino Pentecostal Identity: Evangelical Faith, Self, and Society* (New York: Columbia University Press, 2003).

13. Pew Forum on Religion & Public Life, *U.S. Religious Landscape Study*, http://religions .pewforum.org/portraits (2008); Schultze, *Strangers in a Foreign Land*.

14. Committee on Hispanic Affairs, *Hispanic Ministry at the Turn of the Millennium*.

15. United States Conference of Catholic Bishops, "Collection for the Church in Latin America: 2007 Annual Report" (Washington, DC: USCCB, 2008); "Separated Brothers," 31.

16. U.S Census Bureau, "2005–07 American Community Survey," http://factfinder .census.gov/ (2007).

17. Pew Hispanic Center/Kaiser Family Foundation, *2002 National Survey of Latinos: Summary of Findings*, http://latinostudies.nd.edu/cslr/research/pubs/HispChurchesEnglish WEB.pdf, 2002, 16.

18. Suro, "Changing Faiths," 9.

19. Ibid., 70.

20. Espinosa et al., "Hispanic Churches in American Public Life: Summary of Findings," 21.

21. For data on these issues, see Suro, "Changing Faiths," 73–75. For a history of Latino religion from a liberationist perspective, see Moises Sandoval, *On the Move: A History of the Hispanic Church in the United States* (Maryknoll, NY: Orbis Books, 1990).

22. Espinosa et al., "Hispanic Churches in American Public Life," 21.

23. Louis DeSipio and Rudolfo O. de la Garza, eds. *Awash in the Mainstream: Latino Politics in the 1996 Election* (Boulder: Westview Press, 1999).

24. Suro, "Changing Faiths," 79.

25. Ibid.

26. Gaston Espinosa, "Obama Threaded the Moral Needle of Latino Evangelicals in '08," *Religion Dispatches*, June 28, 2009.

27. Gaston Espinosa, Virgilio Elizondo, and Jesse Miranda, eds., *Latino Religions and Civic Activism in the United States* (New York: Oxford University Press, 2005); Wilson, *The Politics of Latino Faith*.

28. For a discussion of Chávez's religiosity, see Frederick John Dalton, *The Moral Vision of Cesar Chavez* (Maryknoll, NY: Orbis Books, 2003); and Luis D. Leon, "Cesar Chavez and Mexican American Civil Religion," in *Latino Religions and Civic Activism in the United States*, eds. Gaston Espinosa, Virgilio Elizondo, and Jesse Miranda (New York: Oxford University Press, 2005).

29. Marco G. Prouty, *Cesar Chavez, the Catholic Bishops, and the Farmworkers' Struggle for Social Justice* (Tucson: University of Arizona Press, 2008).

30. Louis DeSipio, *Counting on the Latino Vote: Latinos as a New Electorate* (Charlottesville, VA: University of Virginia, 1996).

31. Rudolfo O. de la Garza, *Latino Voices: Mexican, Puerto Rican, and Cuban Perspectives on American Politics* (Boulder: Westview Press, 1993).

32. For a broad discussion of Latino politics, see John A. Garcia, *Latino Politics in America: Community, Culture, and Interests* (Lanham, MD: Rowman and Littlefield, 2003).

33. Julia Preston, "In Big Shift, Latino Vote Was Heavily for Obama," *The New York Times*, November 7, 2008, A24; Larry Rohter, "McCain Is Faltering Among Hispanic Voters," *The New York Times*, October 23, 2008, A23.

34. Harold Bloom, *The American Religion* (New York: Simon & Schuster, 1992), chap. 5.

35. Pew Forum, *U.S. Religious Landscape Study*.

36. For more information about size of the specific denominations listed here, see Pew Forum, *U.S. Religious Landscape Study*, 12.

37. See Arthur Paris, *Black Pentecostalism: Southern Religion in an Urban World* (Amherst, MA: University of Massachusetts Press, 1982).

38. The classic work is Charles Hamilton, *The Black Preacher in America* (New York: Morrow, 1972).

39. Laura R. Olson, *Filled with Spirit and Power: Protestant Clergy in Politics* (Albany: State University of New York Press, 2000).

40. Samuel G. Freedman, *Upon This Rock: The Miracle of a Black Church* (New York: HarperCollins, 1993).

41. Pew Forum, *U.S. Religious Landscape Study*.

42. On this discussion and the entire subject of this chapter, see the wonderfully informative C. Eric Lincoln and Lawrence Mamiya, *The Black Church in the African American Experience* (Durham, NC: Duke University Press, 1990).

43. Ibid.

44. See David L. Chappell, *A Stone of Hope: Prophetic Religion and the Death of Jim Crow* (Chapel Hill, NC: University of North Carolina Press, 2003); Harwood K. McClerking and Eric L. McDaniel, "Belonging and Doing: Political Churches and Black Political Participation," *Political Psychology* 26 (2005), 721–733; and Clyde Wilcox and Leopoldo Gomez, "Religion, Group Identification, and Politics Among American Blacks," *Sociological Analysis* 51 (1990), 271–285.

45. See J. Wendell Mapson Jr., *The Ministry of Music in the Black Church* (Valley Forge, PA: Judson, 1984).

46. Lincoln and Mamiya, *The Black Church*.

47. James Cone, *Black Theology and Black Power* (New York: Seabury, 1969).

48. Cornel West, *Race Matters* (Boston: Beacon, 1993).

49. See Peter J. Paris, *The Social Teaching of the Black Churches* (Philadelphia: Fortress Press, 1985); Barbara Dianne Savage, *Your Spirits Walk Beside Us: The Politics of Black Religion* (Cambridge, MA: Belknap Press of Harvard University Press, 2008); James Melvin Washington, *Frustrated Fellowship: The Black Baptist Quest for Social Power* (Macon, GA: Mercer University Press, 1982).

50. Lincoln and Mamiya, *The Black Church*, chap. 2; Albert J. Raboteau, *Slave Religion: The "Invisible Institution" in the Antebellum South* (New York: Oxford University Press, 1978).

51. Lincoln and Mamiya, *The Black Church*, chap. 3.

52. Savage, *Your Spirits Walk Beside Us.*

53. See Chappell, *A Stone of Hope*; David J. Garrow, *Bearing the Cross: Martin Luther King, Jr. and the Southern Christian Leadership Conference* (New York: Morrow, 1986); Martin Luther King Jr., *Why We Can't Wait* (New York: Mentor, 1964); Aldon D. Morris, *The Origins of the Civil Rights Movement* (New York: Free Press, 1984); and Hart M. Nelsen and Anne Kusener Nelsen, *The Black Church in the Sixties* (Lexington: University of Kentucky Press, 1975).

54. Joseph H. Jackson, *A Story of Christian Activism: The History of the National Baptist Convention USA, Inc.* (Nashville, TN: Townsend, 1980).

55. Fredrick C. Harris, *Something Within: Religion in African-American Political Activism* (New York: Oxford University Press, 1999); R. Drew Smith and Fredrick C. Harris, eds., *Black Churches and Local Politics: Clergy Influence, Organizational Partnerships, and Civic Empowerment* (Lanham, MD: Rowman and Littlefield, 2005); Richard L. Wood, *Faith in Action: Religion, Race, and Democratic Organizing in America* (Chicago: University of Chicago Press, 2002).

56. James H. Harris, *Black Ministers and Laity in the Urban Church* (Lanham, MD: University Press of America, 1987); Smith and Harris, *Black Churches and Local Politics.*

57. Allison Calhoun-Brown, "The Politics of African American Churches: The Psychological Impact of Organizational Resources," *Journal of Politics* 58 (1996), 935–953.

58. Harris, *Something Within*; Smith and Harris, *Black Churches and Local Politics.*

59. Hanes Walton and Robert C. Smith, *American Politics and the African American Quest for Universal Freedom*, 5th ed. (New York: Longman, 2007), chap. 10.

60. Smith and Harris, *Black Churches and Local Politics.*

61. For example, see Adolph L. Reed Jr., *The Jesse Jackson Phenomenon* (New Haven, CT: Yale University Press, 1986); for a critical view of Jackson in conflict with other African American activists in Chicago, see Gary Rivlin, *Fire on the Prairie: Chicago's Harold Washington and the Politics of Race* (New York: Henry Holt, 1992), 80–95 and 163–167.

62. Allen D. Hertzke, *Echoes of Discontent: Jesse Jackson, Pat Robertson, and the Resurgence of Populism* (Washington, DC: CQ Press, 1993), chaps. 3, 4, and 6; Charles P. Henry, *Culture and African-American Politics* (Bloomington, IN: Indiana University Press, 1990).

63. Hertzke, *Echoes of Discontent.*

64. Corwin Smidt et al., *The Disappearing God Gap? Religion in the 2008 Presidential Election* (New York: Oxford University Press, forthcoming).

65. Lincoln and Mamiya, *The Black Church.*

66. Pew Forum on Religion & Public Life, *U.S. Religious Landscape Study.*

67. Harris, *Something Within*; Michael Leo Owens, *God and Government in the Ghetto: The Politics of Church-State Collaboration in Black America* (Chicago: University of Chicago Press, 2007).

68. Samuel G. Freedman, "After Obama Victory, Test for the Black Clergy," *The New York Times*, November 15, 2008, A19.

69. The "challenge of Islam" is how one of the major studies of the black church depicts the growth of the Muslim population. See Lincoln and Mamiya, *The Black Church*, 388–391.

70. Ibid.

71. For an excellent analysis of the life and times of Malcolm X, see Marshall Frady, "The Children of Malcolm," *The New Yorker*, October 12, 1992. See also David Mills, "Malcolm X: The Messenger and His Message," *The Washington Post Weekly Edition*, March 26–April 1, 1990.

72. An indication of how difficult it is to get a handle on small religious groups is the widely varying estimates of the black Muslim membership in the early 1960s. Frady suggests its membership was as small as 10,000; Lincoln and Mamiya suggest it was as sizable as 100,000. Even the higher figure, however, is tiny compared to the black Christian population, which numbered in the millions.

73. See Frady, "The Children of Malcolm."

74. Malcolm X, with Alex Haley, *The Autobiography of Malcolm X* (New York: Grove, 1964).

75. Douglas Massey and Nancy Denton, *American Apartheid: Segregation and the Making of the Underclass* (Cambridge, MA: Harvard University Press, 1998); William Julius Wilson, *The Truly Disadvantaged: The Inner City, the Underclass, and Public Policy* (Chicago: University of Chicago Press, 1990).

76. For an excellent look at American Muslims, see Steven Barboza, *American Jihad: Islam After Malcolm X* (New York: Doubleday, 1993).

77. Andrew Kohut et al, *Muslim Americans: Middle Class and Mostly Mainstream*, http://pewforum.org/surveys/muslim-american/ (2007), 17.

78. Don Terry, "Minister Far Shrona Foreman, Muslims' Tentative Electoral Venture," *National Journal*, September 1, 1990.

79. See Hertzke, *Echoes of Discontent*.

80. Shrona Foreman, "Muslims' Tentative Electoral Venture," *National Journal*, September 1, 1990.

11

GENDER, RELIGION, AND POLITICS

In any consideration of religion and politics in the United States today, women merit special attention. Of course, by no means do all American women share the same religion or politics, but at present gender is a strong predictor of religious participation. In this chapter we first consider the facts about women's involvement in religion in the United States. Next we discuss some of the ways in which female religious activists involve themselves in political life. Third, we explore the religious and political attitudes of women in the pews.

GENDER AND RELIGION IN AMERICAN LIFE

There is no doubt that American women as a group are more religiously observant than men. Public opinion polls have noted this discrepancy for years. Consider the following findings from a massive survey conducted in 2008 by the Pew Forum on Religion & Public Life: Women are more likely to be affiliated with a religion than men (86 to 79 percent), to have an absolutely certain belief in God or a universal spirit (77 to 65 percent), to pray daily (66 to 49 percent), to say religion is very important in their lives (63 to 49 percent), and to attend worship services at least weekly (44 to 34 percent).[1]

These attitudes extend even to women who came to adulthood in the 1960s and early 1970s, the so-called baby boom generation, which sometimes is characterized as the least religious age cohort in American history. In fact, boomer women have not brought about a break in the long tradition of religiosity among American women. Even in this generation of "rebels," a sizable majority of women rate religion as very important in their lives. Most of the rest say it is fairly important in their lives. About two-thirds expect that religion will become even more important to them in the future.[2]

African American women tend to be even more religious than white women. Black churches in the United States attract and retain the support of the vast majority of black women, and they tend to be filled largely by women and children and much less by men, which has caused some concern in the black community.[3] African American women often are quite sympathetic to certain aspects of feminism, including greater economic and professional opportunities for women; however, as we noted in Chapter 10, African American clergy are almost exclusively male. This is not to say that women are not respected in African American churches; they are, and in some historically black denominations elder women bear the formal honorary title of "Mother." Still, traditional gender roles predominate in African American religious circles, even though the bulk of black laity are women. How long this tradition of female parishioners and male clergy will endure, however, is one of the most intriguing questions facing black Christianity in the United States.

Women also play a central role in the operation of most white churches and synagogues in the United States. In the Catholic Church, women—both laity and more than 65,000 women religious (nuns)—do a significant amount of the day-to-day work of parish life. Some even serve as lay ecclesial ministers in parishes that lack priests, a fact that is said to trouble the Vatican.[4] A growing proportion of mainline Protestant ministers and Jewish rabbis are female, though they still remain below 50 percent of the total and considerably less than that in the larger and more prominent churches and temples where, if they are present, they often serve under a male head minister or rabbi. However, given current trends in Protestant seminaries at least it is likely that women will comprise a majority of mainline Protestant clergy by 2050.[5] Many Jewish women of the baby boom generation have displayed renewed interest in their faith tradition. Despite fierce debate and concern within the Jewish community about the continued vitality of Judaism—and the Jewish people themselves—in the United States, there are clear signs that many Jewish women (in particular) have chosen to preserve Jewish traditions, sometimes religious, sometimes cultural, that their parents often did not emphasize.[6]

Gender dynamics in American church life are not restricted to the central place of women. In recent times we have seen highly publicized religious events geared specifically toward men, such as the 1995 Million Man March and the Promise Keepers rallies of the past two decades. The Million Man March was organized and led by controversial Nation of Islam leader Louis Farrakhan; the Promise Keepers purvey a distinctly evangelical Protestant message.[7] Today there is an abundance of male-only prayer groups, reading clubs, and religious retreats throughout organized religion in the United States. These trends among men may be a conscious effort to reverse the decline of male interest in religion, a reaction to the dominance of women, or simply a recognition that in spiritual matters, as in other dimensions of life, men and women do not always have the same needs.[8] But the fact is clear: Men from a variety of walks of life—black and white, Protestant and Muslim—are reasserting their place in organized religion, the family, and society precisely at the time when women are becoming more prominent in these realms.

RELIGIOUS WOMEN'S DIVERGING PERSPECTIVES ON AMERICAN POLITICS

A great many connections exist between religious women and politics in the United States today. As is the case for American women in general, the *political* orientations of religious women today defy easy characterization. For example, women are organized for social change in groups that range from the liberal Women-Church Convergence to the conservative Concerned Women for America.

Another significant trend in the relationships among religion, politics, and gender in the United States is the "gender gap" in voting behavior that has been evident for several decades. The gender gap in presidential voting first appeared in 1964, when women lent the vast bulk of their support to Lyndon Johnson in his contest with the hawkish Barry Goldwater. By 1996, women were 14 percentage points more Democratic than men.[9] The gender gap narrowed a bit around the 2000 and 2004 elections of George W. Bush, however, with southern women actually preferring Bush over either Al Gore or John Kerry.[10] Because evangelical Protestantism is the dominant religion of the American South, it would appear that conservative evangelical women today are bucking the broader "gender gap" trend. To wit: In 2008, John McCain earned an astonishing 71 percent of evangelical women's votes despite receiving just 43 percent of women's votes in the electorate at large.[11]

Women also lead the way theologically; they are active within Christianity and Judaism both in challenging and defending existing beliefs, practices, and structures. More and more women are finding ways to bring their viewpoints to bear upon traditionally male-dominated religious traditions. More radical women have been involved in developing new (or reborn) spiritualities such as ecofeminism, witchcraft, and goddess religions that are designed to transform not only religion

but every aspect of social and political life. Other women inevitably organize in opposition to such new religions and their social agendas.

Conservative Intersections

Today it is not uncommon to find religious women committed to conservative political causes. When John McCain selected former Alaska governor Sarah Palin as
his running mate in the 2008 presidential election, he rallied many evangelical Protestant women to his—or perhaps more accurately, Palin's—cause. Survey data
strongly suggest that Palin's most dedicated supporters are evangelical women,
which almost certainly is a reflection of her own evangelical Protestantism and her
vocally pro-life stance on abortion.[12]

A longer-standing manifestation of conservative religious women's political
clout is the prominent interest group Concerned Women for America (CWA),
which has been in existence since 1979. It is a decidedly right-wing political group
with a large national membership of evangelical Protestant women who believe
in the literal truth of the Bible, hold conservative political beliefs, and vote Republican.[13] Beverly LaHaye founded CWA in 1979 and remained as its leader until
1998. LaHaye has written many books, including *I Am a Woman by God's Design*,
in which she addresses a wide range of political issues and endorses the view that
women should submit to male headship in marriage.[14] Her writings tightly inter-
weave political conservatism and Christianity. LaHaye and CWA have been particularly interested and involved in "family" issues and lobbying on behalf of the
pro-life cause. CWA operates largely through state and local chapters connected
to the national headquarters.[15]

Eagle Forum is another women-led political organization involved in fighting
for conservative political and moral concerns. It was founded in 1979 by Phyllis
Schlafly, a conservative Catholic, following her successful leadership of a movement
comprised largely of women that defeated the Equal Rights Amendment.[16] Eagle
Forum is explicitly Christian, although it is interdenominational within that context,
and its agenda is less focused than CWA's is on issues of family and personal morality. It addresses economic and foreign policy issues at least as often as it does socio-
moral ones.[17]

Organizations such as Concerned Women for America and Eagle Forum are
important, but they do not begin to tell the entire story of religious women's involvement in conservative politics. Everywhere one looks in conservative politics
today, in fact, religious women seem to be involved. For example, women often
spearhead struggles at the local level over school curricula, library books, public
religious ceremonies, and similar issues. Such local disputes lie at the center of re-

ligious politics in the United States. It is there that conservative women are both the generals and foot soldiers in religio-political battles.[18]

One significant challenge facing conservative religious women today is that in both local and national conflicts, they may lack elite access in comparison with more liberal religious women. There are relatively few formal leadership opportunities available to women within evangelical Protestantism or the Catholic Church. The women who do have access to the ministry or rabbinate are almost universally liberal, in part because the traditions that allow them to become religious leaders are themselves progressive.[19] Conservative religious women face greater challenges simply because their religious traditions tend to be more formally male-dominated.

Nevertheless, some studies suggest a softening of opinion around the issue of women's ordination. Many evangelical Protestants today favor women's ordination, and even among self-described fundamentalists, a majority of men and women are no longer strongly opposed. On the other hand, the majority of theologically conservative Protestants—men and women alike—continue to hold that the male should be the head of the household and make all major family decisions. Even this view is slowly losing some strength, however. The decline is especially sharp among evangelical college students, among whom a majority no longer agree that a husband should have the final say.[20]

There are even competing evangelical organizations addressing the proper role for the Christian woman. The Council on Biblical Manhood and Womanhood developed a mediating position between patriarchy and feminism, which it calls the "complementarian" view. Its advocates insist that the Bible holds that men and women are fully equal in God's eyes, but God calls them to different and complementary roles. Women are called to serve in the home as wives and mothers, not to enter realms traditionally reserved for men, such as the ministry or head of the household. On the other hand, Christians for Biblical Equality argues that the Bible teaches equality among men and women, which includes opening roles in the church, the home, and elsewhere equally to both genders. Christians for Biblical Equality asserts that God puts no barriers on the possibilities for humans of either gender. This struggle within conservative Protestantism illustrates the mixed views that exist today among sincere women and men seeking to follow God's written word.[21]

Liberal Intersections

By no means should anyone assume that religious women are necessarily conservative. Indeed this is far from the case, as exemplified by the religious commitment Hillary Rodham Clinton has brought to her long and distinguished political career (see Box 11.1). Nor is the connection between religious women and progressive politics a new phenomenon. For example, Dorothy Day cofounded the Catholic Worker Movement in 1933 to address the needs of the disadvantaged in cities across the United States; Day is now under consideration for sainthood by the Roman Catholic Church.[22] Feminism and faith go hand in hand for many women, and this connection often manifests itself in political progressivism. Indeed, tremendous diversity characterizes the many liberal organizations that connect religious women to politics. Such groups ordinarily concentrate on the status of women in society, religion, and politics.

Two of the more visible liberal organizations linking religious women to progressive politics today are Catholics for Choice and Church Women United (whose

---

BOX 11.1   HILLARY RODHAM CLINTON: LIBERAL METHODIST

Secretary of State Hillary Rodham Clinton was born into a Methodist family with lineal roots back to England, where Methodism was born. She attended First United Methodist Church in Park Ridge, Illinois. A pious young woman, she volunteered in the 1964 campaign of Republican presidential candidate Barry Goldwater. Like many of her generation, however, she was swept up in the movement against the war in Vietnam in college and became a liberal Democrat. Still, she remained active in religious circles.

As a student at Wellesley College, Hillary Rodham attended church, joined an interdenominational chapel society, and read widely among the liberal theologians of the time. She took naturally to the intensifying social justice activism in the United Methodist Church, which epitomized the mainline Protestant emphasis on using government to promote economic and social justice for the disadvantaged.

Throughout her adult life Hillary Rodham Clinton has remained a United Methodist. When Bill Clinton was governor of Arkansas, Hillary often attended services at his Baptist church first and then worshiped in her own Methodist congregation, where she also taught Sunday school. When Bill Clinton was president, the family attended Foundry United Methodist Church. Its pastor at the time, Rev. J. Phillip Wogaman, is a noted progressive theologian and ethicist. Sometimes castigated as left-wing and "New Age" for her advocacy of the "politics of meaning," Secretary Clinton contends that she is actually an old-fashioned Methodist striving to build the Kingdom of God on Earth.

Source: Paul Kengor, *God and Hillary Clinton: A Spiritual Life* (New York: HarperCollins, 2007).

members are mainline Protestants). Founded in 1973, Catholics for Choice works to "shape and advance sexual and reproductive ethics that are based on justice, reflect a commitment to women's well-being and respect and affirm the capacity of women and men to make moral decisions about their lives."[23] Church Women United was founded in 1941 and became active politically in the 1950s and 1960s on behalf of civil rights causes. It moved on in the later 1960s to focus on issues of special concern to women, particularly their rights and their development as individuals. Yet the organization has seen better days. Fewer middle-class women who have the time to devote to such organizations are available today than was the case thirty years ago.[24]

In recent years another prominent liberal group has been Women-Church Convergence, a loosely structured organization founded by Catholic women and strongly promoted by Rosemary Radford Ruether, an activist feminist Catholic theologian. Women-Church Convergence has been at the forefront of the attempt to develop a feminist religion with a suitable political agenda. Its theology emphasizes a vaguely Christian God, creed, and church, all of which must be strongly egalitarian and communitarian. The group is committed to encouraging society at large to embrace its vision and goals.[25]

Ruether in particular has encouraged women to form feminist communities of egalitarian worship outside of the Catholic Church and the rest of Christianity, which she deems too hierarchical and male-oriented. Supporters of Women-Church Convergence share the premise of women's equality with men and affirming human equality with God as their friend rather than a looming authoritarian presence—as well as the belief that political action must be taken to reorient society to these ends.[26]

To this point, Women-Church Convergence is but one expression of the feminist movement within American religion. It has been most active, especially within the Catholic Church, around issues such as abortion rights and the ordination of women. Its larger effort, however, has been aimed toward changing consciousness among the faithful to advance an egalitarian and communal social and religious order. As the Church has moved toward a more traditional stance in many areas, however, Women-Church has declined in prominence and impact.[27]

Another illustration is provided by the considerable number of African American women who provide most of the time and energy fueling local African American political causes. Again and again, religious black women provide the muscle for many day-to-day political efforts. But one must be careful in generalizing about

African American women and politics. Black women have been at the forefront of efforts to create school choice in Cleveland and Milwaukee, among other places, and to permit state aid to religiously connected social services, causes that are not fashionable among white liberal women activists.[28]

Many Jewish women also are active in liberal politics. This is especially note-worthy within the Democratic Party, but also in a host of public actions and lob-bying associations, including various feminist, reproductive choice, and peace groups.[29] For example, the National Council of Jewish Women (NCJW), which traces its roots to 1893, is a Jewish women's liberal grassroots political organization. As its website states: "Inspired by Jewish values, NCJW strives for social justice by improving the quality of life for women, children, and families and by safeguarding individual rights and freedoms," which translates into a political agenda that em-phasizes civil liberties, civil rights and economic justice, women's issues, reproduc-tive choice, and church-state separation.[30] NCJW also has a substantial interest in international issues, particularly those that affect Israel and its welfare.

Another example of liberal politics among religious women is evident in the emergence of explicitly feminist theologies. It is a bad idea to make generalizations about the complex subject of Christian or Jewish feminist theology, but the rise of feminist theology represents both an intellectual and a political movement of tremendous significance. The principal goal of feminist theologians is to attack past and present male domination within religion. In advancing this goal, they raise fun-damental questions about images of God as Father and the all-male hierarchies of some faiths and religious institutions. Some feminist theologians seek to undermine and then abolish male (and all other) hierarchies in every part of society, including the political order.[31]

In this context, some feminist thinkers view traditional Western religions (pri-marily Christianity) as redeemable, whereas others have concluded that feminism requires a complete break with the Judeo-Christian tradition and the Western so-cieties with which it is associated. This is not the only dividing line among religious feminists, but it is an essential and illuminating one.[32]

Feminism and the Redeemability of Religion

There is no doubt that tremendous intellectual energy has gone into the devel-opment of feminist theology, nor that it has taken a number of different direc-tions beyond a shared attack on patriarchy. A great deal of feminist theology is seen through a historical lens and involves close investigation of the Bible and the early history of Christianity. Feminist theologians indict the patriarchal aspects of the Bible and early Christianity, or, in a more optimistic mindset, they seek to recast the record in the light of a lost, nonpatriarchal, early Christianity. Despite its challenges to organized religion, many strains of feminist thought uphold faith as a positive force in human life. Feminists who hold this view argue that religion is redeemable when it takes gender-egalitarian and feminist perspectives into account.

Anne Carr, a Catholic nun, was a leading feminist theologian and the first permanent female faculty member at the prestigious University of Chicago Divinity School. For Carr, Christianity and feminism can and should go together; by no means did she feel that all of Christianity should be discarded as hopelessly antifeminist. In Carr's estimation, God is not essentially male but rather a deeply relational being who exists in association with all humans. People of God must insist that women be welcomed in all roles in church and society. Women must be allowed to be active participants in lives of choice, human growth, and vigorous participation in relationships with God and all of God's people.[33]

Sallie McFague has developed a somewhat more radical view. McFague has been a leader in developing new models of God to replace what she terms "God-he." McFague and other theorists do not deny the Christian tradition; they simply wish to offer reconceptualized images of who and what God is. Some theorists propose viewing God as an androgynous being. Others portray God as mother, friend, or lover. Their objective is to reimagine God, which may pave the way to systemic political and social change.[34]

Feminist currents have had a powerful impact within Judaism as well. Many Jewish feminists have concluded that Judaism as they understand it is redeemable as a religion, or at least as a spiritual tradition. The effects of feminism in Judaism are most obvious in the dramatic breakthroughs of the past twenty years for women who wish to serve as rabbis. Although no woman was ordained a rabbi until 1972, that now seems ancient history within Judaism. At first only the liberal, nontraditional, and small Reconstructionist branch of Judaism allowed women rabbis, but then Reform Judaism and now Conservative Judaism abolished age-old prohibitions against women rabbis. On the whole, research clearly demonstrates that Jewish women as a group are more liberal—often far more liberal—than other Americans on so-called "women's issues" and on almost all other political questions.[35]

Feminism and the Irredeemability of Religion

Many feminist religious thinkers have given up entirely on the Christian and Jewish religions. To these women, Western faiths may have a few positive qualities, but they are at root sexist and supportive of the repression of women. Such theorists insist that Americans must rethink religion and society in a radical way. They believe that if religion is altered drastically, male images of God will fade, as will any sense of hierarchy or division in the universe. Radical feminist theologians prize the ideals of equality, community, and holism and believe that these ideals may be realized by developing entirely new religious, political, and societal arrangements.

Mary Daly is perhaps the most important advocate of the argument that Western religions are irredeemable and that radical shifts in both religion and politics are necessary. In 1973, she published the first of her many books, *Beyond God the Father*. In the 1970s, Daly was still accepting of some aspects of the Christian tradition, though she was already arguing that Christianity was too male-dominated in both theory and practice. Eventually she left Christianity altogether. Today she continues to write and speak from her self-described "radical elemental feminist" perspective.[36]

Goddess religion is an example of a spiritual direction taken by some women who repudiate Christianity and Judaism altogether. The position of goddess worshippers is that in ancient times, goddesses were the most common form of deity. In such societies, life was better for women—and for men as well—because society was more egalitarian, communal, and peaceful. In the eyes of goddess worshippers, such societies sadly fell under the repression of male-dominated social orders. Defenders of goddess religion insist that old goddess models need to be rediscovered to replace the antifemale, hierarchical, and dualistic forms of religion that have oppressed women for centuries.[37] Some critics are skeptical of claims about the extent of past civilizations' allegiance to goddesses. Others protest casual generalizations about past goddess religions across cultures and millennia. Still others note that ancient goddesses were fertility deities, a rather dubious model for modern feminists.

Rosemary Radford Ruether approaches these dilemmas from a radical feminist perspective that is somewhat more sympathetic to Christianity. She appreciates the idea of a female deity; for her it provides an alternative conception of God that many women find attractive, even as she points to problems inherent in goddess religion. Ruether also argues that for adherents of Western religious traditions, interest in goddess religion can only create fissures. As radical as Ruether is, she is not prepared to give up Christianity for goddess worship.[38]

Another current direction in feminist spirituality is the Wiccan religion, or witchcraft. Its adherents consider mainstream Western religions hopeless because of their historic oppression of women. Although witchcraft has had an underground life throughout American society, in recent times it has emerged more openly. It is no longer unusual to find an advertisement for Wicca services alongside those of more mainstream faith traditions. Nor is it unusual to encounter voices of the Wiccan religion such as Starhawk or Margot Adler in public forums or on television talk shows; Starhawk contributes to *The Washington Post*, and Adler is a correspondent on National Public Radio. Witchcraft has entered mainstream popular culture as well, as exemplified by J. K. Rowling's best-selling Harry Potter book series.

People are divided over what witchcraft involves. Practitioners themselves do not agree, except in their view that human consciousness can be altered through rituals and practices and that the power of the natural and spiritual worlds have concrete effects on people and events. According to this view, there are spiritual powers and forces in the universe to which people can connect if they know how. Many practitioners of witchcraft use various rituals from the past, but some also embrace newer traditions. Witchcraft is a relatively open, pluralistic, and malleable form of spirituality. Some forms of witchcraft are exclusively lesbian; others are self-consciously feminist; still others have no such boundaries. The lines between one version and another may be significant at times, but overall the movement has been highly inclusive.

Ecofeminism

Ecofeminist spirituality is a third feminist approach that views Western religion as largely irredeemable. While the term "ecofeminism" dates from 1974, the ecofeminist movement has ancient roots. Many devotees of ecofeminist spirituality explicitly repudiate the Judeo-Christian religious tradition as male-centered. In both Judaism and Christianity, ecofeminists argue, both nature and women have been mistreated. For ecofeminists, reforms within the Judeo-Christian tradition can never go far enough to eliminate the patriarchal structures of thought and organization that have facilitated this oppression. Thus ecofeminism involves a widespread search for alternative means of spiritual sustenance. Above all, ecofeminists search for holistic spiritualities. Sometimes they direct favorable attention to goddess and nature religions, witchcraft, Native American faiths, and Buddhism, among others. Ecofeminists who are unwilling to abandon Christianity strive to recast its traditional vocabularies and conceptions.[39]

Ecofeminism's basic premise is that both nature and women have been oppressed throughout Western history by men, male hierarchies (men over women, men over nature), male dualisms (mind over body, men over nature and women), and male-centered religions (especially Christianity and Judaism). This domination has proceeded in direct disregard for the holism that ecofeminists maintain is characteristic of both women and nature. Ecofeminists say it is obvious that both nature and women have suffered terribly under male domination. They note that women who have not cooperated with the male-dominated society have paid a high price (as did practitioners of Wicca, for example, in the early years of American history).[40]

The political side of ecofeminism treasures the goal of liberation—both of nature and women. In working toward such liberation, ecofeminists advocate transcending hierarchy and dualism (that is, male rule in all areas of life), particularly in the realms of religion and politics. They believe that women must lead the way to a revolution to create an egalitarian community where holism, care, and healing will flourish among human beings.

The ecofeminist expectation is that in this ideal community, spiritualism also will be nourished. Many, perhaps most, ecofeminists are self-consciously spiritual in their outlook; nature provides the common source of grounding and moral standards. Although ecofeminism emphasizes unity and community, its proponents often celebrate women as being especially close to nature thanks to the experiences of menstruation and childbirth. More than a few hints of female triumphalism are inherent in this view that do not mix well with the ecofeminist ideal of terminating male domination. Equally debatable has been the ecofeminist invocation of nature as the standard of value, as well as the claim that past societies worked better because they were closer to nature. Women critics of ecofeminism in particular have challenged the ecofeminist contention that in nature one can discover the proper moral foundation for society.[41]

THE POLITICS OF WOMEN IN THE PEWS

Political debates about feminist theology and the redeemability of the Judeo-Christian tradition dominate a good deal of the intellectual discourse surrounding women, religion, and politics. However, these matters do not appear to have engaged many rank-and-file women in the pews of churches and synagogues. Indeed, the fact is that except for women clergy (who are markedly liberal in their political attitudes[42]), the more a woman is involved in organized religion, the more likely she is to be relatively conservative on political and religious questions. Studies of the baby boom generation of women illustrate that the more a woman socialized in the 1960s and early 1970s is connected to a congregation, the more conservative she will be on such issues as women's ordination. On the other hand, women who are attracted to less conventional spiritual journeys—often those falling outside the bounds of organized religion—are much more likely to have liberal religious and political attitudes, including a strong attachment to feminism.[43]

It is instructive to consider the specific case of Catholic women. They display a strong preference for women's equality, and as a group they are considerably more feminist on a wide range of issues than are Protestant women. Age constitutes a sharp dividing line among Catholic women, with the generation of women who reached adulthood in the 1960s and early 1970s forming the sharpest line of demarcation. Younger Catholic women are much more liberal on matters involving the priesthood, and they express a greater overall degree of discomfort with the Church. Some Catholic women also express conflicted feelings about the Catholic Church as an institution. Many feel that the Church needs to be more respectful of women in general.[44]

At the same time, however, there are others who are concerned about the major role women do in fact play in the Catholic Church. After all, approximately 90 percent of all lay employees of the Church are women, and the majority of regular mass attendees are women. Critics raise the specter of what they call the "feminization of the church," expressing their fears that fewer men will be interested in Roman Catholicism if the Church becomes perceived as too much of a female institution, much less actually becomes "feminized."[45] Such concerns, however, are softening as the Church in the United States has turned in a more traditional direction and younger priests begin to take over churches, welcoming women and men but not interested in changing the traditional male-led arrangement of the Church.

It is noteworthy in this context that Pope John Paul II and now Pope Benedict XVI have both treasured the contributions made by women to the life and work of the Catholic Church—and both have had a profound, lifelong reverence for Mary, the mother of Jesus Christ. At the same time, however, they have been clear that women priests conflict with the model of the original Apostles and with Catholic tradition and are not going to be part of the Catholic Church.[46]

The variety of attitudes espoused by Catholic women in the pews is exemplified by opinions about abortion. As we know, much of the movement against abortion is fought by combatants based in organized religion.[47] The split among women on abortion along religious lines is palpable. The more a woman is involved in religion, and the more traditional her religious views, the more likely she is to oppose abortion. This does not mean that all active Catholic or Protestant women are pro-life. This is far from the case. But it is true that the intensity of one's religious commitment is one of the best predictors of conservative abortion attitudes.[48] Religious

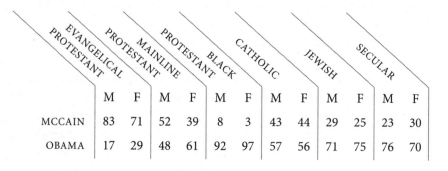

	EVANGELICAL PROTESTANT		MAINLINE PROTESTANT		BLACK PROTESTANT		CATHOLIC		JEWISH		SECULAR	
	M	F	M	F	M	F	M	F	M	F	M	F
MCCAIN	83	71	52	39	8	3	43	44	29	25	23	30
OBAMA	17	29	48	61	92	97	57	56	71	75	76	70

Table 11.1   Presidential Vote by Religious Tradition and Gender, 2008
Source: Paul B. Henry Institute, *National Survey on Religion and Public Life*, 2008.

(and secular) women on both sides of the abortion debate often have more in common with each other than is often assumed. Women on both sides often share a strong belief in the intrinsic value of women—and of motherhood. They frequently share a certain suspicion of men and a sense that women ultimately must rely on themselves.[49]

As noted above, gender also has been a major dividing point in voting behavior in recent years. Women of all faiths—with the noteworthy exception of evangelical Protestants—were substantially more likely than their male counterparts to have voted for Barack Obama in 2008 (see Table 11.1). Often gender has a more significant effect on partisanship and voting behavior than religion itself; mainline Protestant women were more likely than mainline men to vote for Obama in 2008, for example. Even among evangelical Protestants, who heavily favored John McCain in 2008, we see a mild gender divide: 83 percent of evangelical men voted for McCain compared to 71 percent of evangelical women. In short, political differences between the genders within most American religious groups are profound and may grow even more pronounced in the years to come.

THE POLITICS OF WOMEN CLERGY

The final significant dynamic connecting gender, religion, and politics in the twenty-first century is the increasing presence of women in the American ministry and rabbinate. It took generations of struggle before women were allowed to become clergy, but women now constitute about 10 percent of all American religious leaders, and their ranks continue to expand; women now comprise the majority of the student bodies of some major seminaries.[50] In fact, in some mainline Protestant denominations, such as the United Church of Christ and the Presbyterian Church (U.S.A.), women now account for close to one-quarter of all clergy.[51]

As we noted above, women also play essential roles in the Roman Catholic Church. The vast majority of parish leaders and church employees who are women often have significant influence and in practice frequently run many parishes and other Catholic institutions. For example, women religious (nuns) have served the Church, and its schools and hospitals, for centuries. One analyst labels them "America's first feminists."[52] Their numbers are in steep decline today, but nuns are nevertheless indispensable to the Church's day-to-day operations. Some orders of American nuns also are known for their political liberalism. In fact, the Leadership Conference of Women Religious, which comprises 95 percent of all American nuns, is deeply engaged in political action around a range of social justice issues consistent with the long tradition of Catholic social teaching.[53] Likewise, nuns founded NETWORK, a Catholic interest group, in 1971 to "act for justice" by lobbying government on issues of poverty, racism, and violence.[54] The declining number of priests promises to increase the importance of women's informal leadership roles within American Catholicism despite some active opposition from the Church's hierarchy.[55]

Very few white evangelical or black pastors are women. In most evangelical circles, traditional gender roles and the idea of male headship preclude women from serving as clergy. However, some moderate evangelical congregations—and more than a few Pentecostal churches—do allow women to serve in limited pastoral roles. Most black clergywomen actually serve in largely white denominations or churches, although there are some women preachers in Pentecostal African American churches.[56] Nonetheless, women have made some inroads toward the evangelical pulpit in both white and black churches. The most visible of these advances came when the African Methodist Episcopal (AME) Church installed its first female bishop, Vashti Murphy McKenzie, in 2000.

There is no consensus in American religious circles about whether the Bible allows or prohibits women's ordination. The passages most often cited come from the epistles of St. Paul. Christian opponents of women's ordination point to scriptural passages including 1 Timothy 2:11–12, which says: "Let a woman learn in silence with all submissiveness. I permit no woman to teach or to have authority over men; she is to keep silent." However, some proponents point to passages such as Galatians 3:28: "There is neither Jew nor Greek, there is neither slave nor free, there is neither male nor female; for you are all one in Christ Jesus."[57] Others wonder whether biblical passages not directly connected with the Gospels of Jesus should govern American church practices more than 2000 years after they were composed. Such controversy, and the ensuing skepticism that some still have toward clergy-women today, has the potential either to stifle—or spur—political activity among women of the cloth.

The simple fact of being a female religious leader carries political connotations. Today's clergywomen have cause to feel feminist bonds of sisterhood with the early pioneers of the political struggle for women's equality in the United States. In 1848, Seneca Falls, New York, played host to one of the first organized public discussions of women's rights. One of the many resolutions debated at Seneca Falls during the drafting of the *Declaration of Sentiments and Resolutions* proposed "that the speedy success of our course depends upon the zealous and untiring efforts of both men and women, for the overthrow of the monopoly of the pulpit, and for the securing to women an equal participation with men in the various trades, professions, and commerce."[58] A generation after Seneca Falls, Frances Willard, founder of the Woman's Christian Temperance Union, saw fit to publish a book titled *Woman in the Pulpit*.[59] It is telling that women's acceptance into the male-dominated clergy profession has been seen from the outset as an important prong of women's equality.

James Davison Hunter and Kimon Howland Sargeant have argued that as more women enter the ministry, the religious traditions that ordain them might move to the left politically.[60] There is good reason to believe that this may be a correct assessment. Recent research shows that Protestant and Jewish clergywomen are consistently liberal in their political attitudes, particularly around rights issues such as gender equality and gay rights.[61] And many clergywomen are not afraid to let their political voices be heard, both in their congregations and in their broader communities. Whether the influx of women into the ministry will profoundly transform the relationship between religion and politics in the United States, however, remains to be seen.

CONCLUSION

In spite of the many crosscurrents, women play a central role in American religion, and their importance is growing. The future of women, religion, and politics is not obvious, but the politics of religion will continue to involve women's voices. Indeed, organized religion ultimately may be led by women. One area to watch most closely in the future is the place of feminist movements within American religion and reactions to the presence of feminist influences. Feminists will challenge some of the theologies and practices of American religion, including ordination issues, the proper role of religious hierarchies, and much more. Women will not just affect politics within churches and religions; they will affect the stance and involvement of organized religion on issues of gender and family in American politics broadly construed.

Also important to observe will be the continuing conflict over abortion and developments regarding other moral issues, such as gay rights, in the United States. The role of conservative religious women in promoting and defending a traditional "family agenda" may turn out to be as influential as the more progressive voices of feminist religious elites. We have noted that religious women often are divided in their orientations toward feminism, as is the case in the population at large. Although a majority of female religious leaders are liberal, women in the pews reflect a full range of political attitudes. Whether this gap closes or becomes wider in the years ahead, particularly as more and more women are ordained as clergy, will have major implications for the effectiveness of religious women in politics.

Finally, it will be fascinating to observe national political developments, including presidential campaigns, to see what connections they make—or attempt to make—with religious women. As the election of the first female president draws nearer, it will be essential to analyze the ways in which female candidates attempt to use religious appeals to win over women in the electorate. The more American politics focuses on issues that are important to religious women, or on candidates' positions on such issues, the more likely religious women are to be mobilized. Religious women were mobilized during the 1988 presidential campaigns of Jesse Jackson and Pat Robertson. Evangelical Protestant women played a significant role in electing and reelecting George W. Bush and some galvanized around Sarah Palin's vice-presidential candidacy in 2008. In the same election cycle, women from a wide range of other religious perspectives joined together to support both Hillary Rodham Clinton and Barack Obama. It remains to be seen exactly how gender will continue to intersect with religion in ways that are politically significant, but we can rest assured that studying women, religion, and politics will be an important enterprise for decades to come.

FURTHER READING

Chaves, Mark. *Ordaining Women: Culture and Conflict in Religious Organizations.* Cambridge, MA: Harvard University Press, 1997. An excellent study of conflict over women's ordination in religious groups.

Daly, Mary. *Beyond God the Father: Toward a Philosophy of Women's Liberation*. Boston: Beacon, 1973. Radical feminist attack on traditional religion.

Davidman, Lynn. *Tradition in a Rootless World: Women Turn to Orthodox Judaism*. Berkeley: University of California Press, 1991. Detailed analysis of women and traditional Judaism.

Diamond, Irene, and Gloria Feman Orenstein, eds. *Reweaving the World: The Emergence of Ecofeminism*. San Francisco: Sierra Club, 1990. Thorough considerations of ecofeminism.

Griffith, R. Marie. *God's Daughters: Evangelical Women and the Power of Submission*. Berkeley: University of California Press, 1997. An examination of women and feminism within evangelical (particularly Pentecostal) Protestantism.

McFague, Sallie. *Models of God: Theology for an Ecological, Nuclear Age*. Philadelphia: Fortress, 1987. Reflections of an influential feminist liberal Protestant theologian.

Olson, Laura R., Sue E. S. Crawford, and Melissa M. Deckman. *Women with a Mission: Religion, Gender, and the Politics of Women Clergy*. Tuscaloosa, AL: University of Alabama Press, 2005. Analysis of the political orientations of women clergy.

Ruether, Rosemary Radford. *Gaia and God: An Ecofeminist Theology of Earth Healing*. San Francisco: HarperCollins, 1992. The perspective of a leading feminist theologian.

Streichen, Donna. *Ungodly Rage: The Hidden Face of Catholic Feminism*. San Francisco: St. Ignatius, 1991. Sharp criticism of religious feminists in action.

NOTES

1. Pew Forum on Religion & Public Life, *The Stronger Sex—Spiritually Speaking*, http://pewforum.org/docs/?DocID=403 (2009).

2. Wade Clark Roof, *A Generation of Seekers: The Spiritual Journeys of the Baby Boom Generation* (San Francisco: HarperSanFrancisco, 1993); Wade Clark Roof, *Spiritual Marketplace: Baby Boomers and the Remaking of American Religion* (Princeton: Princeton University Press, 1999).

3. An excellent discussion of the gender divide in black churches is found in C. Eric Lincoln and Lawrence H. Mamiya, *The Black Church in the African American Experience* (Durham, NC: Duke University Press, 1990), chap. 10; an illuminating approach from another direction is Samuel G. Freedman, *Upon This Rock: The Miracles of a Black Church* (New York: HarperCollins, 1993).

4. John L. Allen Jr., "Lay Ecclesial Ministry and the Feminization of the Church," *National Catholic Reporter*, June 29, 2007.

5. Barbara Brown Zikmund, Adair T. Lummis, and Patricia Mei Yin Chang, *Clergy Women: An Uphill Calling* (Louisville, KY: Westminster John Knox, 1998).

6. Lynn Davidman, *Tradition in a Rootless World: Women Turn to Orthodox Judaism* (Berkeley: University of California Press, 1991).

7. On the Promise Keepers, see John P. Bartkowski, *The Promise Keepers: Servants, Soldiers, and Godly Men* (New Brunswick, NJ: Rutgers University Press, 2004).

8. Rodney Stark, "Physiology and Faith: Addressing the 'Universal' Gender Difference in Religious Commitment," *Journal for the Scientific Study of Religion* 41 (2002), 495–507. See also W. Bradford Wilcox, *Soft Patriarchs, New Men: How Christianity Shapes Fathers and Husbands* (Chicago: University of Chicago Press, 2004).

9. Karen M. Kaufmann, "The Gender Gap," in *Beyond Red State, Blue State: Electoral Gaps in the Twenty-First Century American Electorate*, eds. Laura R. Olson and John C. Green (Upper Saddle River, NJ: Prentice Hall, 2008).

10. Ibid.

11. Calvin College, Paul B. Henry Institute, *National Survey on Religion and Public Life*, www.calvin.edu/henry/civic/CivicRespGrant/surveyfind.htm, 2008.

12. Jodi Kantor and Rachel L. Swarns, "A New Twist in the Debate over Mothers," *The New York Times*, September 2, 2008; Ann Rodgers, "Evangelical Women View Palin as Role Model, Stereotype Breaker," *The Pittsburgh Post-Gazette*, October 26, 2008; Kim Severson, "They Raise Children, Pray and Rally Around a Running Mate," *The New York Times*, September 5, 2008.

13. Concerned Women for America, http://www.cwfa.org, 2009.

14. Beverly LaHaye, *I Am a Woman by God's Design* (Old Tappan, NJ: Revell, 1980). For a general analysis of evangelical views on male headship and submissiveness, see Brenda E. Brasher, *Godly Women: Fundamentalism and Female Power* (New Brunswick, NJ: Rutgers University Press, 1998); R. Marie Griffith, *God's Daughters: Evangelical Women and the Power of Submission* (Berkeley: University of California Press, 1997).

15. Concerned Women for America, http://www.cwfa.org/about.asp.

16. On Schlafly's STOP ERA movement, see Jane J. Mansbridge, *Why We Lost the ERA* (Chicago: University of Chicago Press, 1986).

17. See Eagle Forum, http://www.eagleforum.org; Phyllis Schlafly, *The Power of the Christian Woman* (Cincinnati: Standard, 1981).

18. Stephen Bates, *Battleground: One Mother's Crusade, the Religious Right, and the Struggle for Control of Our Classrooms* (New York: Poseidon Press, 1993); Melissa M. Deckman, *School Board Battles: The Christian Right in Local Politics* (Washington, DC: Georgetown University Press, 2004).

19. Laura R. Olson, Sue E. S. Crawford, and Melissa M. Deckman, *Women with a Mission: Religion, Gender, and the Politics of Women Clergy* (Tuscaloosa, AL: University of Alabama Press, 2005).

20. Debra Bendel Daniels, "Evangelical Feminism: The Equalitarian-Complementarian Debate" (PhD dissertation, University of Wisconsin–Madison, 2003); Griffith, *God's Daughters*; James M. Penning and Corwin E. Smidt, *Evangelicalism: The Next Generation* (Grand Rapids, MI: Baker Books, 2002), 81; Agnieszka Tennant, "Adam and Eve in the 21st Century," *Christianity Today*, March 11, 2002.

21. Daniels, "Evangelical Feminism"; Julie Ingersoll, *Evangelical Christian Women: War Stories in the Gender Battles* (New York: New York University Press, 2003), especially chap. 1; Christel Manning, *God Gave Us the Right: Conservative Catholic, Evangelical Protestant, and Orthodox Jewish Women Grapple with Feminism* (New Brunswick, NJ: Rutgers University Press, 1999).

22. Dorothy Day, *The Long Loneliness: The Autobiography of the Legendary Catholic Social Activist* (New York: Harper & Row, 1952).

23. Catholics for Choice, http://www.catholicsforchoice.org/about/ourwork/default.asp.

24. R. Marie Griffith, "The Generous Side of Christian Faith: The Successes and Challenges of Mainline Women's Groups," in *The Quiet Hand of God: Faith-Based Activism and the Public Role of Mainline Protestantism*, eds. Robert Wuthnow and John H. Evans (Berkeley: University of California Press, 2002); Barbara Brown Zikmund, "Women's Organizations: Centers of Denominational Loyalty and Expressions of Christian Unity," in *Beyond Establishment: Protestant Identity in a Post-Protestant Age*, eds. Jackson Carroll and Wade Clark Roof (Louisville, KY: Westminster, 1993).

25. See Rosemary Radford Ruether, *Women-Church: Theology and Practice of Feminist Liturgical Communities* (San Francisco: Harper & Row, 1985); Mary Jo Weaver, *New Catholic Women: A Contemporary Challenge to Traditional Religious Authority* (Bloomington, IN: Indiana University Press, 1985).

26. Rosemary Radford Ruether, *Gaia and God: An Ecofeminist Theology of Earth Healing* (San Francisco: HarperCollins, 1992); Peter Steinfels, "Catholic Feminists Ask, Can We Remain Catholic?" *New York Times*, April 16, 1993, A9.

27. See Women-Church Convergence, http://www. women-churchconvergence.org/home.htm.

28. See Cheryl Townsend Gilkes, *If It Wasn't for the Women . . . : Black Women's Experience and Womanist Culture in Church and Community* (Maryknoll, NY: Orbis, 2001).

29. Joyce Antler, "Activists and Organizers: Jewish Women and American Politics," in *Jews in American Politics*, eds. L. Sandy Maisel and Ira N. Forman (Lanham, MD: Rowman and Littlefield, 2001).

30. National Council of Jewish Women, http://www.ncjw.org.

31. The classic work here is Mary Daly, *Beyond God the Father: Toward a Philosophy of Women's Liberation* (Boston: Beacon, 1973); see also Beverly Wildung Harrison, "The Power of Anger in the World of Love," in *Feminist Theology*, ed. Ann Loades (Louisville, KY: Westminster, 1990); and Letty M. Russell, "Good Housekeeping," in *Feminist Theology*.

32. For example, see Elaine Pagels, *Adam, Eve, and the Serpent* (New York: Random House, 1988). Also, exploration of many of the essays in Loades, ed., *Feminist Theology*, or Rosemary Radford Ruether, *Feminist Theologies: Legacy and Prospect* (Minneapolis: Augsburg Fortress, 2007), would be a good way to get an idea of the diversity of feminist theology and of where one might want to go to pursue it; see also Sallie McFague, *Models of God: Theology for an Ecological, Nuclear Age* (Philadelphia: Fortress, 1987).

33. Anne E. Carr, *Transforming Grace: Christian Tradition and Women's Experience* (New York: Continuum, 1996).

34. McFague, *Models of God*.

35. See Antler, "Activists and Organizers"; Davidman, *Tradition in a Rootless World*; Olson, Crawford, and Deckman, *Women with a Mission*; Rita J. Simon, Angela J. Scanlan, and Pamela S. Nadell, "Rabbis and Ministers: Women of the Book and the Cloth," *Sociology of Religion*, 54 (1993), 115–122.

36. Daly, *Beyond God the Father*, is essential reading, and Daly's personal website is illuminating as well: http://www.marydaly.net/.

37. Some relevant works, supportive, ambivalent, and hostile: Janet Biehl, *Rethinking Ecofeminist Politics* (Boston: South End Press, 1991); Carol Christ, *Laughter of Aphrodite: Reflections on a Journey to the Goddess* (San Francisco: HarperSanFrancisco, 1987); Susanne Heine, *Matriarchs, Goddesses and Images of God* (Minneapolis: Augsburg, 1988); Mary A. Kassian, *The Feminist Gospel: The Movement to Unite Feminism with the Church* (New York: Crossway, 1992); Ruether, *Gaia and God*; and Roof, *A Generation of Seekers*, 142–143.

38. For example, see Rosemary Radford Ruether, *Sexism and God-Talk: Toward a Feminist Theology* (Boston: Beacon, 1983).

39. See Charlene Spretnak, *The Politics of Women's Spirituality: Essays on the Rise of Spiritual Power Within the Feminist Movement* (Garden City, NY: Doubleday, 1982); Ruether, *Gaia and God*.

40. Key sources include Irene Diamond and Gloria Feman Orenstein, eds., *Reweaving the World: The Emergence of Ecofeminism* (San Francisco: Sierra Club, 1990); Carol Merchant, *The Death of Nature* (San Francisco: HarperSanFrancisco, 1980); Judith Plant, ed., *Healing the Words: The Promise of Ecofeminism* (Philadelphia: New Society, 1989); and Rosemary Radford Ruether, *Integrating Ecofeminism, Globalization, and World Religions* (Lanham, MD: Rowman and Littlefield, 2005).

41. See such critics as Biehl, *Rethinking Ecofeminist Politics*; Heine, *Matriarchs, Goddesses and Images of God*; Kassian, *The Feminist Gospel*.

42. Olson, Crawford, and Deckman, *Women with a Mission*.

43. Roof, *A Generation of Seekers*, 222–223.

44. Elaine Howard Ecklund, "Catholic Women Negotiate Feminism: A Research Note," *Sociology of Religion* 64 (2003), 515–524; Mary Fainsod Katzenstein, *Faithful and Fearless: Moving Feminist Protest Inside the Church and Military* (Princeton: Princeton University Press, 1998); Jane Redmont, *Generous Lives: American Catholic Women Today* (New York: William Morrow, 1992); Roof, *A Generation of Seekers*, 231–232; Weaver, *New Catholic Women*.

45. See Leon J. Podles, *The Church Impotent: The Feminization of Christianity* (Dallas: Spence, 1999).

46. John Paul II, *Man and Woman He Created Them: A Theology of the Body*, trans. Michael M. Waldstein (Boston: Pauline Books, 2006); Pope John Paul II, Apostolic Letter *Mulieris Dignitatem* (1988); John Paul II, Apostolic Letter *Ordinatio Sacerdotalis* (1994).

47. Kristin Luker, *Abortion and the Politics of Motherhood* (Berkeley: University of California Press, 1984).

48. Elizabeth Adell Cook, Ted. G. Jelen, and Clyde Wilcox, *Between Two Absolutes: Public Opinion and the Politics of Abortion* (Boulder: Westview Press, 1992), chap. 7.

49. Faye D. Ginsburg, *Contested Lives: The Abortion Debate in an American Community* (Berkeley: University of California Press, 1989).

50. Mark Chaves, *Ordaining Women: Culture and Conflict in Religious Organizations* (Cambridge, MA: Harvard University Press, 1997); Zikmund, Lummis, and Chang, *Clergy Women*.

51. Patricia M. Y. Chang, "Female Clergy in the Contemporary Protestant Church: A Current Assessment," *Journal for the Scientific Study of Religion* 36 (1997), 565–573; Zikmund, Lummis, and Chang, *Clergy Women*.

52. John Fialka, *Sisters: Catholic Nuns and the Making of America* (New York: St. Martin's Press, 2003). See also Carol K. Coburn, *Spirited Lives: How Nuns Shaped Catholic Culture and American Life, 1836–1920* (Chapel Hill, NC: University of North Carolina Press, 1999).

53. Katzenstein, *Faithful and Fearless*; Leadership Conference of Women Religious, http://www.lcwr.org/lcwrsocialjustice/socialjusticeoverview.htm, 2009.

54. NETWORK: A National Catholic Social Justice Lobby, http://www.networklobby.org.

55. Thomas C. Fox, "Vatican Investigates U.S. Women Religious Leadership," *National Catholic Reporter*, April 14, 2009; Laurie Goodstein, "U.S. Nuns Facing Vatican Scrutiny,"

The New York Times, July 1, 2009; Ruth Wallace, *They Call Her Pastor: A New Role for Catholic Women* (Albany: State University of New York Press, 1992).

56. Melissa M. Deckman, Sue E. S. Crawford, Laura R. Olson, and John C. Green, "Clergy and the Politics of Gender: Women and Political Opportunity in Mainline Protestant Churches," *Journal for the Scientific Study of Religion* 42 (2003), 621–631; Olson, Crawford, and Deckman, *Women with a Mission.*

57. Chaves, *Ordaining Women.*

58. The *Declaration of Sentiments and Resolutions* was a bold assertion of women's equality modeled on the Declaration of Independence: www.fordham.edu/halsell/mod/Senecafalls.html, 1998.

59. Frances E. Willard, *Woman in the Pulpit* (Chicago: Woman's Christian Temperance Publication Association, 1889).

60. James Davison Hunter and Kimon Howland Sargeant, "Religion and the Transformation of Public Culture," *Social Research* 60 (1993), 545–570. See also Olson, Crawford, and Deckman, *Women with a Mission.*

61. Sue E. S. Crawford, Melissa M. Deckman, and Christi J. Braun, "Gender and the Political Choices of Women Clergy," in *Christian Clergy in American Politics*, eds. Sue E. S. Crawford and Laura R. Olson (Baltimore: Johns Hopkins University Press, 2001); Deckman et al., "Clergy and the Politics of Gender"; Olson, Crawford, and Deckman, *Women with a Mission*; Laura R. Olson, Sue E. S. Crawford, and James L. Guth, "Changing Issue Agendas of Women Clergy," *Journal for the Scientific Study of Religion* 39 (2000), 140–153.

12

THEORIES OF RELIGION, CULTURE, AND AMERICAN POLITICS

Now that we have studied religion in American politics in its wide variety of forms, we need to step back to appreciate the bigger picture. In this concluding chapter we explore several broad theoretical interpretations of the relationships among religion, politics, and culture. These broader theories should help us put much of the previous discussion into a more meaningful context. Each of these theories helps us comprehend the sometimes bewildering complexity of religion's relevance to American politics. Some of the theories emphasize worldwide forces, whereas others restrict themselves to the United States. Each has its own emphases, makes its own case, and offers distinctive illumination in the quest to understand the place of religion in the political culture of the United States.

CULTURE WARS

No theory of religion, politics, and culture in the United States today has gotten more attention than the "culture wars" thesis.[1] This theory asserts that the contours of religion and politics in America today are best understood by recognizing the existence of deep social divisions over values and lifestyles. This thesis separates Americans, particularly elites, into two categories: conservatives and progressives. Conservatives, on the one hand, adhere to and emphasize traditional values: religion, marriage and family, discipline, and opposition to abortion and homosexuality. On the other hand, progressives stress the importance of choice and diversity in every area of life, including religion, family, and sexuality. The culture wars thesis holds that supporters of each perspective are sharply critical of—and feel threatened by—the other point of view. Each is struggling for dominance in American culture.

This division cuts across all sorts of lines in American life, including traditional religious lines.[2] Thus some traditional Catholics today find themselves aligned with conservative evangelicals on many social and political issues. Both groups oppose abortion, support public expressions of faith, criticize secularism in public schools, and decry the lingering effects of the sexual revolution. Theological and cultural differences remain between traditional Catholics and evangelical Protestants, to be sure, but many in each group unite in rejecting what they see as a secular assault on time-honored traditions and values. Thus a kind of cultural alliance now exists among conservative evangelicals, traditional Catholics, and some Orthodox and Ultraorthodox Jews. Activists call this alliance an ecumenism of orthodoxy.[3]

On the other side are liberal Protestants, progressive Catholics, most Jews, and secular Americans, who together constitute the progressive coalition. Liberal Protestants often find that they have more in common with liberal Catholics, Jews, and secular elites than they do with conservatives within their own denominations.[4] They speak a common language of peace and justice, and they prioritize civil rights issues (around race, gender, and sexuality), economic inequality, and skepticism of military action, rather than the socio-moral matters that tend to resonate most on the right.

African American denominations often join the liberal alliance, but the fit is not always snug. For example, some leaders of African American Christian denominations helped block the gay-majority Fellowship of Metropolitan Community Churches from obtaining membership in the National Council of Churches. Similarly, black Muslims join with progressives on U.S. policy toward Israel, but on abortion, drugs, alcohol, and gay rights they agree with evangelicals and traditional Catholics.

A similar fault line also separates the genders. Conservative evangelical and traditional Catholic women often see themselves deeply at odds with their more liberal sisters in mainline churches, Jewish synagogues, and even many Catholic parishes. Many female pro-life activists judge feminists as adversaries, despite sharing with them a confrontational style of political engagement that feminists generally applaud. In churches and outside them, progressive women believe just as strongly that their conservative sisters are a negative force at best and a group of traitors at worst.

Several scholars advance evidence of a culture war. James Guth and his colleagues have found strong evidence that something akin to a culture war split does, in fact, divide Protestant clergy into two groups.[5] Robert Wuthnow concludes that a massive restructuring of American religion occurred in the wake of World War II, which had the effect of polarizing Americans within their religious traditions. Not too long ago, he argues, denominations meant something distinctive. To be a Methodist, Presbyterian, Catholic, Lutheran, or Baptist implied a shared religious and ethnic heritage with distinctive customs and beliefs. Today, however, a theological and cultural divide cuts across Christian church bodies. Politically speaking, it matters more whether one is a liberal Catholic or a conservative Catholic, or a liberal Methodist or an evangelical Methodist, than whether one is a Methodist or a Catholic. Thus a liberal Methodist might feel more comfortable with secular liberals than with fellow Christians who call themselves evangelicals.[6] We see clear evidence of these intradenominational tensions in the recent debates about homosexuality in mainline Protestant denominations.[7]

An even stronger case is made by James Davison Hunter. In his classic book titled *Culture Wars*, Hunter articulates the culture wars thesis clearly and then explains how it plays out in a number of areas of American life, including religion and politics.[8] Hunter notes various divisions as they manifest themselves in specific skirmishes over school curricula, gay rights ordinances, state-level abortion battles, and similar issues.

Imagine two women who have certain things in common. Both are married, both are college graduates, both are church members, and both are economically comfortable. One woman attends an independent evangelical church, views abortion as anathema, and is an avid reader of the conservative religious and political literature found in many Christian bookstores. Deeply alienated from the public schools, which she sees as having low academic standards and as promoting secular and hedonistic values, she has chosen to homeschool her children. She is an active member of a homeschool association, which provides her with information about Christian curricula and ways to avoid being harassed by state education authorities. She sees that she is engaged in a conflict with the "dominant" culture, which includes the movie and television industries, public education, "antifamily" feminists, gay activists, and the government. She is a conservative Republican.

The other woman sees the defining experience of her life as her participation in the civil rights movement and Vietnam war protests. She is now an active member of a United Methodist congregation known for its peace and justice activism. A strong feminist and a supporter of abortion rights, she belongs to several progressive political organizations and donates to political action committees that support women candidates. She dislikes television preachers and fears fundamentalist influence in school board elections. She deplores what she sees as religious attempts to censor books and the arts. She has gay and lesbian friends and supports their struggle for equal rights. To her, the idea of a "dominant culture" equals white male businessmen who belong to country clubs. She is a liberal Democrat.

Even though the example of these two women illustrates the sometime reality of polarization within the world of religion, the truth is that scholars have found that relatively few people are comfortable with either side of the culture war. Many are in fact unaware of any culture war. To be sure, many parents—from moderate Catholics to conservative Protestants—view television as unhealthy and get angry when public schools uncritically embrace the latest curriculum fad. They take their children to church and otherwise attempt to counteract the messages purveyed by the pop culture. But they do not necessarily view these actions as battles in some cosmic conflict over the very soul of America. Whether more Americans will embrace the culture wars perspective in the future remains to be seen.[9]

There is also a self-fulfilling quality inherent in discussion of the culture wars. Mutual stereotyping, polarization, and inflamed passions actually may help create culture wars where none previously existed. Moreover, talk of culture wars undermines the possibility that adversaries may discover common ground. Compromise, that staple of American politics, is hard if one's opponents are, or are perceived as being, enemies bent on destroying one's very way of life. The two hypothetical women described above might in fact share the views that television is largely trash, that public schools are too lax, or that pornography has an unhealthy influence, but they miss the chance to work together to address such feelings because of the blinding rhetoric of cultural conflict.

Yet there are unmistakable signs of culture wars in the United States, particularly among political elites. The core question at stake in the culture wars is one of the appropriate character of American society. And there is no longer just one culture war in American society. In a society characterized by ever-increasing religious pluralism, many newer groups wrestle with how to preserve their traditional values, which often are deeply intertwined with their religion, in the diverse and often hostile strands of American culture. This has been notably true for many Muslims as they struggle to reconcile their faith with American popular culture. For example, some interpretations of Islam demand that women's heads be covered, but most U.S. state laws require that they remove those coverings for pictures on driver's licenses.[10] Traditional Muslim values also insist that women not touch or have any romantic relationships with men until marriage, whereas ordinary American customs are quite different. In fact, in some places in the U.S., all-female Muslim high school proms are held.[11]

The examples are numerous, as are the varieties and intensities of skirmishes in the culture wars as religion clashes with American culture. This is why the culture wars theory remains essential to any understanding of religion and politics in the United States today. By itself it is not a sufficient guide, but without it we would be at a loss.

THE SECULARIZATION THESIS

Whereas the culture wars thesis focuses on today's struggles, the "secularization" thesis takes a longer view of religion in America. It suggests that we look away from the events directly before us to analyze broader historical developments that have served to condition culture, religion, and politics.

Proponents of the secularization thesis argue that religion has declined as secularism has advanced. They contend that this development is an inescapable result of modernity, which has already greatly influenced Western Europe and, to a lesser degree, the United States. As modernity advances, secularism spreads in its wake, eroding the social and cultural significance of religion. With religion's gradual decline, secularization theorists conclude, we can expect to see religious involvement with politics decrease in the long run, both in the United States and elsewhere.[12]

However, the short-run picture can be different, and we sometimes see temporary surges in religio-political involvement. Losing out to secularism, some religious groups might turn to politics in an attempt to stem the tide. Such efforts represent a sort of dying gasp on the part of religious forces. For some secularization theorists, this perspective describes the current situation in the United States. Assorted religious groups with different—even opposing—agendas hurl themselves into American political life, trying desperately to halt a perceived decline that threatens traditional American religion, values, and culture.[13]

Some classic advocates of the secularization thesis were giants of nineteenth-century European thought. Karl Marx (1818–1883) was among them. He was certain that class struggle resulting in the triumph of socialism would be the story of modern life—a tale in which religion would be relegated to "the dustbin of history." Max Weber (1864–1920), the great German sociologist, was another classic secularization theorist. He believed that with modernity would come forces of rationalism and bureaucratization that would defeat organized religion, if not entirely eliminate religious people. Sigmund Freud (1856–1939), the founder of psychoanalysis, also addressed secularization. Freud was quite interested in religion and religious traditions, especially those of his fellow Jews. Though Freud knew that there was no guarantee religion would fade, he hoped that "the future of an illusion" would prove poor as people came to see that the modern world gave them a chance to be free of religion.[14]

Because secularization theorists take modernization to be the key to the decline of religion, we need to have some sense of what they mean by the term "modernization." Among the factors analysts usually include in defining this concept are an embrace of scientific ways of thinking, modern technological advances, complex economic life, contemporary forms of mass communication and entertainment, and the growth of government bureaucracies and public education. Secularization theorists note that in modern societies rational, scientific approaches dominate, while in traditional societies, religious worldviews take precedence. In modern societies public policy is dominated by clashes of self-interested individuals and groups pursuing their rational interests. Education becomes an engine of secularization as it teaches scientific explanations of earthly phenomena. The capitalist marketplace also mutes religious enthusiasm as it directs people to a consumer culture and the workaday corporate world.

There is ample support for the secularization thesis. Religion governs the United States today much less than it does, say, a traditional African tribe, or than it did in earlier eras of American history. There is no doubt even that many religious Americans compartmentalize their faith today and do not manifest it in many areas of their lives.[15] Moreover, many of the major institutions of the United States—giant corporations, public schools and universities, government bureaucracies, television networks—now operate on the basis of secular concerns and logic.[16] Often these institutions ignore the religious and spiritual dimensions of life; a few are positively hostile toward them.

Yet in recent years the secularization thesis has come under fire. It has lost a bit of its luster, in large part because of the continuing resilience of religious faith in the face of secular forces. In recent decades there has been a notable growth of evangelical commitment in the United States, a resurgence of religious practice in Russia and Eastern Europe, and a major increase in religious energy in many Islamic countries. Religion's demise, once predicted so confidently, has just not taken place in most parts of the world, nor is there evidence that religion is going to vanish anytime soon.[17]

Moreover, in recent years religion has not always been content to remain in a narrow, compartmentalized realm. Religion has been busy in the larger, public world, challenging secular authorities in the United States, many African countries, all over the Muslim world, and elsewhere. Although religion may not be as tightly interwoven into most people's lives as it once was, it clearly has not disintegrated.

Indeed, it may be that the secularization thesis somehow reverses reality. Perhaps the "unsecularization"—or even sacralization—of the world is one of the characteristics of our modern age.[18]

The response of those who have been impressed with the secularization view is that religion's current health may be temporary. To them, religious vitality today is further proof of secularization's progress through the world—no more than a temporary reaction to the inevitable. Perhaps they are right; perhaps secularization will succeed in the long run. But as of now there are many reasons for doubt, including the fact that the death of religion now seems very much overdue. Modernity has infused many corners of the world, but billions of people often have chosen to retain their religious faith.

The secularization thesis has several variants that are as intriguing as the main theory itself. One such variant is the "elite secularization thesis." In this view, even though religion continues to speak to most human beings, elites and elite institutions have become highly secular. The idea is that the larger secularization thesis applies to one (crucial) sector of the population only: elites. In the United States a number of theorists advance this analysis. The late Richard John Neuhaus, for example, used the metaphor of a "naked public square" to describe how elites largely banished faith-based, moral arguments from American politics. According to Neuhaus, the language of rights, efficiency, and practicality crowded out considerations of moral obligation and timeless spiritual truths.[19] This view is echoed by Stephen Carter in *The Culture of Disbelief*, in which he takes elites in American media, law, and education to task for trivializing faith.[20]

As we saw in our chapter on elites and religion and politics (Chapter 6), there is evidence that some American elites, such as media elites, are more secular than the population at large. Some academics, reporters, media elites, political leaders, and government bureaucrats profess a religious faith, but relatively few are comfortable with born-again evangelicalism, traditional Catholicism, Orthodox Judaism, or revivalist Islam.[21] A serious problem with the elite secularization thesis, however, is the unevenness of the phenomenon. To be sure, many national news media elites are highly secular. So are a fair number of the people who dominate the entertainment media, such as television, movies, and popular music. But elected officials—members of Congress and state legislators, not to mention presidents—better reflect the religious diversity of the population at large.[22] Moreover, the remarkable growth of scholarship and intellectual discourse on religion and society belies the notion of totally hostile elites. There are now several widely cited elite journals publishing criticism of other elites for their hostility to faith.

Another variant on secularization is sociologist David Yamane's neosecularization thesis. Yamane pointedly argues that it is erroneous to claim that religion is disappearing from American life and that the secularization thesis is simply incorrect as a description of the contemporary United States. Yet Yamane insists that secularization is occurring nonetheless in individual American lives, institutions, and the culture as a whole. The key is to understand that religion, even as it continues to be very much alive, is receding steadily into private realms of American life and culture. For Yamane, the true test of secularization is not whether religion is disappearing but whether its role is diminishing in ordinary lives and institutions, as well as in the broader culture. And Yamane argues that it is clear when one observes the United States and its culture from a historical perspective that religion's influence has declined.[23]

THE CULTURE SHIFT THESIS

Ronald Inglehart has pioneered another approach to understanding secularization today that has gained substantial notice among scholars. His "culture shift" thesis dovetails with the secularization thesis in holding that the influence of old-time religion is dying. Inglehart explains this death by arguing that cultures, especially in the Western world, are changing in response to modernization. Old institutions, the old politics of class and economics, and old modes of thinking are receding (despite occasional revivals).[24] The result, however, is not what the standard secularization thesis would predict. Spiritual concerns have not disappeared, nor will they disappear. If anything, spiritual concerns are growing, but this concern is made manifest less through formal institutions than through individual journeys of the spirit. It follows for the culture shift analysis that formal religious involvement in politics will decline over time, but that does not mean that the spiritual concerns of individual citizens will decline in their impact on politics and elsewhere. Thus, according to this view, what looks like secularization around us actually may be a shift in the nature of spiritual life from the organized and public to the individual and private. It is not the end of the influence of spiritual concerns but rather a change in how they work.[25]

There is plenty of evidence that something like a culture shift has taken place in the United States. Wade Clark Roof has portrayed a resulting baby boom "generation of seekers" who look in a wide variety of places—some of them unconventional—for spiritual fulfillment; subsequent studies have demonstrated that the same phenomenon applies to Generations X and Y.[26] Similarly, Robert Fuller describes a huge portion of the United States as "spiritual, but not religious," reflecting this seeker movement. He contends that as many as 20 percent of the American public has spiritual concerns, sometimes very serious ones, which they do not pursue in traditional religious institutions or forms. All sorts of mystical, healing, holistic, feminist, Eastern, and other spiritualities are very much part of the American landscape now, as culture shift analysts would predict. For Fuller, everywhere we look we see the prevalence of this "seeker spirituality."[27]

Sociologist Phillip Hammond argues that American religion is actually undergoing a major "disestablishment" that demonstrates how widespread the culture shift has been. As Hammond describes it, American culture now honors choice, expressivism, and individualism in religion just as it does in other sectors. Traditional religions in the United States that focus on duty, institutions, and collective practices face a tremendous challenge and are slowly losing out. Mainline Protestantism in particular is suffering, though it is far from alone in its predicament. All established churches and synagogues are threatened by the movement toward individualistic spirituality.[28]

To be sure, many seekers remain within the realm of traditional organized religions, where they are bringing about major change. For example, one excellent recent study of evangelical Protestant churches that reflect this "new paradigm" (and are booming as a result) notes that members of such churches insist on expressive and contemporary music and other means of worship that allow them to move beyond what they see as rather staid, traditional experiences in order to achieve a deeply felt, individualistic spirituality.[29] Such religious practitioners also emphasize the importance of a personal relationship with Jesus Christ, support the institution of the nuclear family, encourage participation in small groups at church, and radiate a decidedly unstuffy aura. The overall result is something very different from traditional Catholic and mainline Protestant worship experiences. For their part, many Catholic and mainline Protestant congregations have been implementing aspects of evangelical worship in special "seeker" services designed for those who desire a more emotional, expressive religious experience.[30]

It remains to be seen what the long-term consequences of the experiences of the seeker phenomenon will be for religion and politics. If American religion is transformed further into individualistic spirituality, its impact on political life might be less focused, organized, and unified. Thus the politics of religion may become less important over time, just as the secularization thesis suggests (albeit for quite different reasons). On the other hand, this is not self-evident. After all, if spirituality becomes more important and more deeply valued among more Americans, it is bound to affect their political outlooks and behavior, possibly more intensely—and more widely—than ever before.

CIVIL RELIGION

Another theoretical perspective that seeks to illuminate the relationship between religion and politics in America is the "civil religion" thesis. This view contends that the most important religion in the United States actually has nothing to do with specific denominations or religious traditions. Instead, the predominant American religious dimension is a shared but vague political religion—a religion that broadly celebrates America and its culture—the civil religion. Civil religion in the United States emphasizes America's unique, "blessed" status among the nations of the world and inspires in its followers a sense of American patriotism. The quick appearance of American flags and signs reading "God Bless America" in the days and weeks immediately following the terrorist attacks of September 11, 2001, provides clear evidence of the civil religion.

Those attracted to this perspective agree that the civil religion exists right alongside sectarian religions in the United States without challenging them. Civil religion is nonsectarian in its assumption that God has blessed the United States, endowed it with special opportunities, and assigned it responsibilities to do good in the world. Civil religion is important, analysts suggest, because it enhances national stability, governmental legitimacy, and a feeling of shared purpose among citizens. Every nation has a vague "faith" of sorts, a belief in itself, a civil religion—and in the United States this civil religion is infused profoundly with a sense that God has provided Americans with special blessings.

The civil religion thesis downplays the importance of various (perhaps passing) events such as culture wars or evidence of secularization. Instead, it points toward enduring connections between government and religion (despite the constitutional separation of church and state) and warns that the "religion" that matters most in political terms may not be practiced in conventional houses of worship. The idea of the civil religion first received extensive attention in a 1967 essay by prominent sociologist Robert Bellah. In a comparison of the inaugural addresses of Abraham Lincoln and John F. Kennedy, Bellah notes that these two seminal American leaders from different eras both asserted that the nation had a divine purpose and called upon God to bless the country.[31] Other scholars since have observed that presidential inauguration ceremonies are steeped in religious imagery; incoming presidents almost always make reference to God. Moreover, it is now de rigueur for an American president to end all major speeches with some variant of the phrase "God bless you, and God bless the United States of America."

Historian Sidney Mead approaches the idea of civil religion by documenting how a "national religion" grew steadily during the early years of the Republic and had established itself firmly by the time of the Civil War. As Mead observes, there are really two forms of faith in the United States—first, the faiths of specific religious groups and denominations, and second, what he terms "the American faith," or the civil religion. Both religious forms, he realizes, are intertwined and mutually supportive. Patriotism in some churches and synagogues is palpable, as anyone who has seen the American flag in houses of worship or heard a spirited singing of "God Bless America" can attest. In turn, religious Americans gain affirmation of the importance of their faith when they hear political leaders publicly call on God, when they use currency that reads "In God We Trust," and when they repeat the Pledge of Allegiance, which proclaims the existence of one nation "under God."[32]

In the end, the ultimate question is how to evaluate the civil religion thesis. Does the United States have a civil religion? Some evidence does support the assertion. From Abraham Lincoln's sublime vision of the nation as the "last, best hope of earth" to Ronald Reagan's invocation of the Puritan "city on a hill" metaphor, civil religious images abound of America as an agent of the divine with special duties on Earth. And this is a view that many religious leaders like to echo; for decades evangelist Billy Graham has invoked God's blessing on the nation's leaders, institutions, and purposes.

And everywhere are signs of civil religious rituals, such as Fourth of July ceremonies, Memorial Day observances, and everything surrounding that most distinctly civil religious holiday, Thanksgiving. Each yearly ritual marks the calendar with its own blend of religion and patriotism, faith and political history. American civil religion has its own sacred places too, such as the majestic Lincoln Memorial in Washington, DC, and the hallowed battleground of Gettysburg, Pennsylvania. Some documents have symbolic sacred status as well, such as the original Declaration of Independence and the Constitution. At the National Archives in Washington, visitors wishing to view these two documents encounter a reverent atmosphere not unlike that of a grand house of worship. The area is softly lit and so quiet that people start whispering upon entering. They walk up a narrow, semicircular corridor until they enter the room containing glass cases, impervious even to nuclear war, that hold these documents for the faithful to venerate. Guards prevent visitors from getting too close to the glass, and the cases descend below the ground for safekeeping every night.

Finally, there are the symbolic prophets and saviors of the American civil religion. In Washington, DC, one can read prophetic words carved in stone at the Jefferson Memorial or stare in awe at the soaring monument to George Washington. At the very center of the civil religion is Lincoln, "the martyred Christ of Democracy's passion play."[33] The story of his presidency, remarkable maturation, single-minded sense of purpose, and tragic assassination invokes religious images of Christlike sacrifice and death for the nation's rebirth.

In short, we feel that the United States does embrace something of a civil religion, but this conclusion is far from universally shared.[34] There is evidence of it in the culture, however thinly it may be worn in these increasingly multicultural and fractious times. Perhaps the larger question is whether the civil religion thesis helps us understand religion and politics in the United States. Civil religion does tell us something about what still binds many Americans together politically. Even though it may appear to some scholars that civil religion is declining in the face of cultural pluralism and political cynicism, expressions of national unity after the September 11, 2001, attacks raise doubts about this assumption. In any case, the civil religion thesis does not help us understand much about how specific religious *traditions* interact with politics. It tells us nothing about how individual citizens' religious beliefs affect voting behavior, or the agendas of religious interest groups, or church-state conflicts in the boiling pot of religion and politics in America.

THE UNCONVENTIONAL PARTNERS THESIS

Another perspective on the relationships among culture, religion, and politics is the "unconventional partners" thesis. Though this theoretical perspective takes some inspiration from the civil religion thesis, the unconventional partners framework is broader, looking beyond the periodic rituals of civil religion to deeper, day-to-day manifestations of religion's relationship to American culture. The unconventional partners thesis posits that religion plays a significant political role because it helps to sustain America's individualistic political culture and its governmental institutions. Religion accomplishes this task not through active engagement in politics but by offering a source of meaning, morality, and community that neither the culture nor the government can provide. In doing so, it relieves pressure on—and strengthens—both the culture and the government. In turn, the government and the culture promote broad religious freedom, allowing the religious sector to thrive. But this symbiotic relationship is largely unintentional—hence the "unconventional partners" label.[35]

An early variant of this theory was put forward by the French statesman-author Alexis de Tocqueville. Observing conditions in America in the early nineteenth century, Tocqueville noted that in his native France the "spirits of religion and of freedom" marched in opposite directions. Not so in America, where he found that the spirit of liberty and the spirit of religion marched together, supporting and reinforcing each other. Tocqueville was impressed with the extent of political freedom enjoyed by American citizens (then defined as white males). But his European experience taught him that such freedom easily could degenerate into anarchy and then despotism. Moreover, even if such perils were avoided, maximum individual freedom, when left to itself, could promote a materialistic society of individual strivers isolated from their fellow citizens. To his amazement, this was not what Tocqueville discovered to be the case in the United States.

He concluded that the explanation for the symbiotic relationship between religion and politics in America was the crucial role that religion played in instilling moral self-restraint, combined with the way congregational life helped people overcome their isolation. When political freedom implied that a nineteenth-century man could do as he pleased, religion taught him he should not do things that were destructive to his family or the community. Thus religion made liberal democracy possible by instilling the inner mores that prevented American society from plunging into chaos. In turn, religion (in general) and congregations (in particular) thrived in the United States because they were left relatively free from persecution and unencumbered by the debilitating government paternalism found in Europe.[36] Thus an unintentional symbiosis developed between government and religion, each sustaining the other.

Of course, the contemporary United States is a far cry from the still-developing country Tocqueville observed in the 1830s. In many ways American culture today is far more materialistic, skeptical, and focused on individuals than was the case in the early years of the Republic. However, the intensification of American individualism has served only to strengthen the continuing partnership between religion and culture. In its present form, organized religion helps to sustain an individualistic society in a paradoxical way: by offering people a temporary refuge from the more isolating aspects of the culture. Indeed, evidence abounds that people who turn to organized religion do so because they seek something different than the reality in which they live and work. They want a refuge from the enormous burden of living in a society where meaning, morality, and community often are confusing or missing altogether.

However, it is crucial to understand that the unconventional partners thesis sees people getting involved in organized religion for temporary refuge only, not as a permanent or radical alternative to the broader society. Most people want religion to give them just enough communal sharing and spiritual sustenance to enable them to persist in the broader culture. Without this kind of refuge, the unconventional partners thesis argues, society might find itself wracked by radical challenges from both the right and the left. Thus religion sustains the social order by providing what that very order lacks.

The unconventional partners thesis identifies a number of ways in which religion aids American culture. First, for many citizens, religion provides meaning—a grounding for values in a culture in which such meaning is far from automatically available. Second, it helps provide moral values for a culture in which skepticism and cynicism are pervasive. Finally, it encourages community in a culture wracked by anomie. Study after study demonstrates the extent to which people understand religion in precisely these ways: as a place to go in search of meaning, morality, or community. When a religion or a congregation can offer people these things, it flourishes; when it cannot, people drift away.[37] Community and meaning may come in a variety of forms within the capacious realm of American religion. There is no single voice, to say the least, but this very fact is an immense plus for the culture. It means that American religion can and does serve many more people in this pluralistic age than it would were there only one religion in the land.

The other side of the unconventional partnership is, of course, the ironic fact that American culture and government serve to assist religion. There are many ways in which they do so, despite illusions of a high wall of separation between church and state in America. Perhaps the most important form of assistance comes in the generous protection of religious free exercise. The First Amendment is alive and well. The fact that both government and culture have some sympathy for religion is essential to the viability of organized religious life in the United States.

Moreover, the American legal system sometimes has shown a proclivity to extend the government's protective role to minority religions, even when their beliefs or practices are controversial. Though the courts' attitudes vary from case to case and from time to time, they have been forced to respond to the reality of religious pluralism in the United States. This is a tremendous gift not only to specific religions but to religion in general throughout the nation. It confirms that religion is important, no matter what form it takes.

At another level, organized religion has reaped extraordinary financial advantages from both government and the culture on which government rests. As we discussed in Chapter 8, the United States demonstrates a great deal of "multiple establishment," which results in all sorts of concrete financial benefits, from aid to church hospitals to freedom from property taxes for houses of worship. No precise figures are available for how much direct or indirect aid religious institutions receive, but it is certainly many billions of dollars. This sort of assistance matters, but so too does the climate of broad religious freedom. It constitutes the other side of the partnership from which both religion and culture benefit.

The unconventional partnership between religion and culture has existed for a long time in the United States. Government may provide more aid today, but that is mainly a reflection of the overall growth of government through American history. Religious freedom today has a broader range than was the case in previous eras, but it is an extension of more than two centuries of determination, initially expressed in the First Amendment, to guarantee religious freedom.

The unconventional partners thesis also offers some perspective on legal conflicts between church and state and on the activities of religious interest groups. The occasional sound and fury of conflict should not drown out the reality of a continuing partnership between religion and American culture. This is not to say that the ordinary aspects of religion and politics—interest groups, voting, reform efforts, and court cases—are meaningless; far from it. They are an important part of the religion and politics story. But the unconventional partners thesis reminds us that their significance must be tempered in light of the deep affinity between religion and culture in the United States. That relationship will remain secure, for better or for worse, as long as organized religion does not transform itself from a temporary refuge into a permanent enemy of American culture, and as long as those who seek a total separation of religion and government do not fully succeed.

What remains to be seen is what the effect of the rising number of citizens in the United States who are either not interested in religion or are hostile to it will have. There is little doubt, as we have seen, that these numbers, though encompassing well less than a quarter of the population, nevertheless are increasing. For them, religion and the government do not necessarily work together in ways that are beneficial, however they may be intended. For the larger group, those with no religion and in many cases no interest in religion, the intertwinings of religion and government are likely to be of scant importance and therefore the maintenance of this partnership of equally modest value. For those who are determinedly against religion the traditional partnership is a pernicious reality that should come to an end. As the numbers of the indifferent and antireligious grow, if they do, perhaps the "unconventional partnership" between religion and government in our culture will fade with unknown and at present unknowable consequences.

POPULISM

The unconventional partners thesis tends to discount the importance of direct religious participation in politics, but this view is not shared by those who are impressed with the frequency and power of religiously based populist movements in American politics. American politics has seen a great deal of religious energy throughout its history. Some observers stress the role of populist movements in generating much of the resulting political activism.[38]

The link between populism and religion flows in part from the nature of religious life in America. Because congregations operate in a highly competitive religious marketplace, they live or die on the basis of popular support. Only churches that tap into the deepest needs, frustrations, and anxieties of their members will thrive. Moreover, unlike the elite membership of most interest groups, congregational membership is extremely broad and diverse. There is no other institution or activity in which Americans of all socioeconomic strata participate in such large numbers. Especially in a highly individualistic and mobile society, religious institutions represent one of the few settings in which many people meet—and sometimes discover common political grievances.[39] In spite of some skittishness about political engagement, church-based political movements have allowed segments of the population that otherwise are unable to find a political voice to register their discontent. Local churches, synagogues, and mosques become the focal point of community responses to threats of all sorts. They are places in which to organize, develop leadership, and call upon members for sacrifice.[40]

At the national level, the church-based political mobilization of African Americans and the political emergence of evangelical Protestants are the most prominent recent examples of this populist-religious intersection. Both movements are undeniably expressions of populism that have achieved a far-reaching impact on political party platforms, voter alignment, and presidential politics. That the same theory can accommodate such different movements illuminates its broad utility.

From the civil rights movement of the 1950s and 1960s to the two presidential campaigns of Jesse Jackson in 1984 and 1988, black churches have provided most of the organizational base, leadership, money, and moral support for African American political mobilization. In doing so, black congregations channeled aspirations for equal rights in the 1950s, continued the struggle in the 1960s, and voiced discontent with lingering economic disparities in the 1990s and beyond.[41] Similarly, since the late 1970s, evangelical churches have captured the growing discontent of their members with the "decaying" state of American culture, family breakup, loss of discipline in schools, legal abortion, and similar issues, turning many of their members toward political activism as a result.

By 1988 these two populist movements had gained enough steam to propel the presidential candidacies of Jesse Jackson and Pat Robertson, two ministers who had never held elective office but who each enjoyed a strong church base and a loyal following. Despite their ideological differences, both candidates shared much of the traditional populist view of the world. Jackson expressed prophetic outrage at what he viewed as the economic abandonment of working-class and impoverished Americans; Robertson vented his anger against cultural elites, who in his view were undermining traditional values. Both candidates used their religious charisma to champion "the people" and to castigate elites. Moreover, both emphasized to some degree the historic populist blend of economic progressivism and social conservatism.

Jackson's economic and civil rights platform drew on a strong dose of religious fervor and moral traditionalism. He admonished his followers to heed the Ten Commandments and to shun illegal drugs, sexual promiscuity, and laziness. Robertson's moral conservatism, on the other hand, was mixed with a populist distrust of large banks, economic conglomerates, and elite foreign policymakers. Jackson and Robertson both evoked a populist style in their politics and a characteristic populist mix of ideological perspectives.[42] This populist style continues to appear, albeit in somewhat different forms, in the appeal of contemporary politicians from Barack Obama to Mike Huckabee to Sarah Palin.

As we can see, the populist thesis emphasizes not only the ways in which religious traditions can vent their discontent but also how they can infuse the political system with a politics that may not fit neatly into the left-right political spectrum. Moreover, events in other countries—from Afghanistan to Northern Ireland to Sudan to the Philippines—suggest that this link between religion and populist uprisings may be a global phenomenon. As such, the populist thesis helps us to understand the ways in which religion sometimes taps sentiments that elites do not notice or acknowledge.

Two cautions are in order. First, given the importance of charismatic leadership in mobilizing populist discontent, one must question whether such leaders reflect—or in fact create—popular concerns. Critics assert that both Jackson and Robertson exhibited a tendency to conflate their personal aspirations with the concerns of the communities they claimed to represent, a tendency that limited their ability to work within the existing political system. Perhaps the populist style in general expresses discontent better than it fashions realistic remedies.

Second, one must resist taking the populist thesis too far. Most congregations are neither positioned nor inclined to sustain major political efforts. Even if individual Americans experience frustration with current politics, they may not be able to vent that frustration through their congregations. Finally, and perhaps most important, it is not clear how often the populist thesis helps us define the link between religion and politics in American life.

THE MARKET THESIS, RELIGIOUS PLURALISM, AND POLITICS

The most controversial theoretical approach to the study of religion and politics in the United States is the "market" thesis. Its proponents argue that religion's relative strength in every society is largely a function of how much competition is present between and among religious traditions, and the degree to which that competition is unfettered. According to the market thesis, which draws heavily on economic theory, religion in the United States is and should remain very strong, which has obvious implications for the continuing political relevance of American religion.[43]

First, we know that there is intense competition in the American religious marketplace. This competition draws people in and provides them with an almost unbelievable variety of religious niches from which to choose. And congregations advertise their services just like secular businesses do, via billboards, advertisements, the Internet—and even with free gifts. Some congregations market themselves as friendly places where it is not necessary to dress up on Sunday morning. Others promote themselves as offering a distinctive theological, social, or political outlook. Still others attempt to meet members' every need, offering everything from a range of worship experiences to small-group friendship networks to sports leagues to healthcare clinics. This diversity suits Americans' pluralist tastes. Market theorists believe that congregations that fare poorly are simply not competing hard enough.

Second, although plenty of traditional "establishment" religion exists in the United States, the fact is that there is no single official American religion. This means that religious freedom is broadly extended to all groups. The implication for us, of course, is that because American religion is like this—strong, competitive, and free—it is able to exert political force.

Market theorists compare and contrast the enduring strength of religion in the United States with its relevance in other countries to illustrate their thesis more fully. For example, market theorists note that the intense religious competition that exists today in Latin America and much of Africa is resulting in tremendous growth among a variety of religious groups. They observe, however, that this growth has been possible only when governments have abandoned old alliances with particular religious groups; such arrangements inevitably restricted or even forbade competition.[44]

Market theorists note that in much of Western Europe, religion is weak and in serious decline; consequently, its political impact has also diminished. They explain these developments partly as the result of limited competition fostered by the existence of long-standing state-established churches. The Church of England, for example, is the United Kingdom's official state church. One of Queen Elizabeth II's official roles as monarch is her constitutional position as "Defender of the Faith": Supreme Governor of the Church of England. Yet many of England's majestic churches sit virtually empty most Sundays, and most research shows that Britons are no longer a particularly religious people.[45]

Whenever religious groups that lack the fire to compete aggressively for souls dominate, all religions pay a steep and inevitable price. Competitive evangelicalism appears to be an essential ingredient for the success of any religious group, according to market theorists. Tired, insular religions that in some countries are propped up by government face serious decline and an attending loss of political influence.[46]

TOWARD THE FUTURE

Which of these theories, alone or in combination with others, will best serve to illuminate the relationship between religion and politics in the United States in our twenty-first century remains to be seen. Perhaps none of them will prove especially useful. None of them can explain everything, even though each offers a useful perspective. Moreover, what the future will produce in terms of the theory and practice of religion and politics in the United States may surprise all of us. After all, who predicted the rise of the Christian Right in the 1980s? Who expected that an African American minister named Martin Luther King would emerge in the 1950s to change fundamentally how we view race and civil rights in America? Who could have known in 1960 that Catholics and evangelical Protestants one day would be forming political alliances? And who thought that Mormons, Muslims, and a host of other small religious groups would have begun to emerge as important political players today? The subject of religion and politics in America, because it is so dynamic, defies any single theory with which to capture its essence. But that should not deter us from trying to understand its contribution to the life and culture of the United States.

FURTHER READING

Bruce, Steve. *God Is Dead: Secularization in the West*. Oxford: Blackwell, 2002. A contemporary application of secularization theory.

Finke, Roger, and Rodney Stark. *The Churching of America, 1776–2005: Winners and Losers in Our Religious Economy*. New Brunswick, NJ: Rutgers University Press, 2005. A recent restatement of the market model from its two leading proponents.

Fowler, Robert Booth. *Unconventional Partners: Religion and Liberal Culture in the United States*. Grand Rapids, MI: Eerdmans, 1989. A contemporary account of the unconventional partners thesis.

Hertzke, Allen. *Echoes of Discontent: Jesse Jackson, Pat Robertson, and the Resurgence of Populism*. Washington, DC: CQ Press, 1993. Leading statement of the populist thesis.

Hunter, James Davison. *Culture Wars: The Struggle to Define America*. New York: Basic Books, 1991. Classic articulation of the culture wars argument.

Inglehart, Ronald. *Culture Shift in Advanced Industrial Society*. Princeton: Princeton University Press, 1990. Best statement of the culture shift theory.

Richey, Russell, and Donald Jones, eds. *American Civil Religion*. New York: Harper and Row, 1974. Interesting views on civil religion theory.

Smith, Christian, ed. *The Secular Revolution: Power, Interests, and Conflict in the Secularization of American Life*. Berkeley: University of California Press, 2003. A set of provocative arguments about the reasons for American secularization.

Wuthnow, Robert. *The Restructuring of American Religion: Society and Faith Since World War Two*. Princeton: Princeton University Press, 1988. Essential theorization on religion in the United States.

NOTES

1. James Davison Hunter, *Culture Wars: The Struggle to Define America* (New York: Basic Books, 1991).

2. Robert Wuthnow, *The Restructuring of American Religion: Society and Faith Since World War Two* (Princeton: Princeton University Press, 1988).

3. On the growing political affinity between evangelical Protestants and traditional Catholics, see Carin Robinson, "Doctrine, Discussion, and Disagreement: Evangelical Protestant Interaction with Catholics in American Politics" (PhD dissertation, Georgetown University, 2008).

4. Wuthnow, *The Restructuring of American Religion*.

5. James L. Guth, John C. Green, Corwin E. Smidt, Lyman A. Kellstedt, and Margaret M. Poloma, *The Bully Pulpit: The Politics of Protestant Clergy* (Lawrence, KS: University

Press of Kansas, 1997). See also John C. Green, James Guth, Corwin Smidt, and Lyman Kellstedt, eds., *Religion and the Culture Wars: Dispatches from the Front* (Lanham, MD: Rowman and Littlefield, 1996).

6. Wuthnow, *The Restructuring of American Religion.*

7. Wendy Cadge, "Vital Conflicts: The Mainline Protestant Denominations Debate Homosexuality," in *The Quiet Hand of God: Faith-Based Activism and the Public Role of Mainline Protestantism*, eds. Robert Wuthnow and John H. Evans (Berkeley: University of California Press, 2003).

8. Hunter, *Culture Wars.* See also James Davison Hunter, *Before the Shooting Begins: Searching for Democracy in America's Culture War* (New York: Free Press, 1994).

9. Paul DiMaggio, John H. Evans, and Bethany Bryson, "Have Americans' Social Attitudes Become More Polarized?" *American Journal of Sociology* 102 (1996), 690–755; John H. Evans, "'Culture War' or Status Group Ideology as the Basis of U.S. Moral Politics," *International Journal of Sociology and Social Policy* 16 (1996), 15–34; John H. Evans, "Have Americans' Attitudes Become More Polarized?—An Update," *Social Science Quarterly* 84 (2003), 71–90; Morris P. Fiorina, *Culture Wars? The Myth of Polarized America* (New York: Longman, 2006); Alan Wolfe, *One Nation, After All* (New York: Penguin, 1998); Robert Wuthnow, "Divided We Fall: America's Two Civil Religions," *Christian Century*, April 20, 1988, 395–399.

10. Susan Martin Taylor, "A Fight for Religion or Something More?" *The St. Petersburg Times*, June 15, 2003, 2A.

11. Patricia Leigh Brown, "For the Muslim Prom Queen, There Are No Kings Allowed," *The New York Times*, June 7, 2003, A1.

12. For a general discussion of secularization theory, see Steve Bruce, *God Is Dead: Secularization in the West* (Oxford: Blackwell, 2002), chap. 1; and Steve Bruce, *Religion and Modernization* (New York: Oxford University Press, 1992). See also Pippa Norris and Ronald Inglehart, *Sacred and Secular: Religion and Politics Worldwide* (New York: Cambridge University Press, 2004).

13. See Andrew R. Murphy, *Prodigal Nation: Moral Decline and Divine Punishment from New England to 9/11* (New York: Oxford University Press, 2009).

14. See Karl Marx's "Economic and Philosophic Manuscripts," "Critique of Hegel's Philosophy of Right," and "Critique of the Gotha Program," in *The Marx-Engels Readers*, 2nd ed., ed. Robert C. Tucker (New York: W. W. Norton, 1978); Max Weber, *The Protestant Ethic and the Spirit of Capitalism* (New York: Scribner's, 1958); Sigmund Freud, *The Future of an Illusion* (Garden City, NY: Doubleday, 1964).

15. For a rich analysis of the ramifications of how young people experience faith today, see Robert Wuthnow, *After the Baby Boomers: How Twenty- and Thirty-Somethings Are Shaping the Future of American Religion* (Princeton: Princeton University Press, 2007).

16. See, for example, George Marsden, *The Soul of the American University: From Protestant Establishment to Established Nonbelief* (New York: Oxford University Press, 1996); and Christian Smith, ed., *The Secular Revolution: Power, Interests, and Conflict in the Secularization of American Life* (Berkeley: University of California Press, 2003).

17. See Norris and Inglehart, *Sacred and Secular*.

18. See, for example, Peter Berger et al., *The Desecularization of the World: Resurgent Religion and World Politics* (Grand Rapids, MI: Eerdmans, 1999); and Samuel P. Huntington Jr., *The Clash of Civilizations and the Remaking of World Order* (New York: Simon & Schuster, 1998).

19. Richard John Neuhaus, *The Naked Public Square: Religion and Democracy in America* (Grand Rapids, MI: Eerdmans, 1984).

20. Stephen Carter, *The Culture of Disbelief: How American Law and Politics Trivialize Religious Devotion* (New York: Basic Books, 1993).

21. For a fascinating look at the religious orientations of one elite sector of American society, see Elaine Howard Ecklund and Christopher Scheitle, "Religion Among Academic Scientists: Distinctions, Disciplines, and Demographics," *Social Problems* 54 (2007), 289–307.

22. A description of the nature of religion among members of Congress is found in Peter L. Benson and Dorothy L. Williams, *Religion on Capitol Hill: Myths and Realities* (New York: Oxford University Press, 1982).

23. David Yamane, "Secularization on Trial: In Defense of a Neosecularization Paradigm," *Journal for the Scientific Study of Religion* 36 (January 1997), 109–122. See also Mark Chaves, "Secularization as Declining Religious Authority," *Social Forces* 72 (1994), 749–774.

24. See Geoffrey C. Layman and Edward G. Carmines, "Cultural Conflict in American Politics: Religious Traditionalism, Postmaterialism, and U.S. Political Behavior," *Journal of Politics* 59 (August 1997), 751–777.

25. Ronald Inglehart, *Culture Shift in Advanced Industrial Society* (Princeton: Princeton University Press, 1990). See also Norris and Inglehart, *Sacred and Secular*; Robert Wuthnow, *After Heaven: Spirituality in America Since the 1950s* (Berkeley: University of California Press, 1998).

26. On the baby boom generation, see Wade Clark Roof, *A Generation of Seekers: The Spiritual Journeys of the Baby Boom Generation* (San Francisco: HarperSanFrancisco, 1993); and Wade Clark Roof, *Spiritual Marketplace: Baby Boomers and the Remaking of American Religion* (Princeton: Princeton University Press, 1999). On Generations X and Y, see Richard Flory and Donald E. Miller, *Finding Faith: The Spiritual Quest of the Post-Boomer Generation* (New Brunswick, NJ: Rutgers University Press, 2008); Christian Smith, *Soul Searching: The Religious and Spiritual Lives of American Teenagers* (New York: Oxford University Press, 2005); Wuthnow, *After the Baby Boomers*. See also Robert N. Bellah,

Richard Madsen, William M. Sullivan, Ann Swidler, and Steven M. Tipton, *Habits of the Heart: Individualism and Commitment in American Life* (Berkeley: University of California Press, 1985).

27. Robert C. Fuller, *Spiritual But Not Religious: Understanding Unchurched America* (New York: Oxford University Press, 2001). See also Bellah et al., *Habits of the Heart.*

28. Phillip Hammond, *Religion and Personal Autonomy: The Third Disestablishment* (Columbia, SC: University of South Carolina Press, 1992).

29. Donald E. Miller, *Reinventing Protestantism: Christianity in the New Millennium* (Berkeley: University of California Press, 1997); Kimon Howland Sargeant, *Seeker Churches: Promoting Traditional Religion in a Nontraditional Way* (New Brunswick, NJ: Rutgers University Press, 2000).

30. See Roof, *Spiritual Marketplace*; Sargeant, *Seeker Churches.*

31. Robert N. Bellah, "Civil Religion in America," *Daedalus* 96 (1967), 1–21.

32. Sidney Mead, *The Lively Experiment* (New York: Harper and Row, 1975).

33. Clinton L. Rossiter, *The American Presidency*, rev. ed. (Baltimore, MD: Johns Hopkins University Press, 1960), 102.

34. For example, see John Wilson, *Public Religion in American Culture* (Philadelphia: Temple University Press, 1979).

35. For this thesis, see Robert Booth Fowler, *Unconventional Partners: Religion and Liberal Culture in the United States* (Grand Rapids, MI: Eerdmans, 1989).

36. Alexis de Tocqueville, *Democracy in America* (Garden City, NY: Doubleday/Anchor, 1969).

37. On these points, see also Roger Finke and Rodney Stark, *The Churching of America, 1776–2005: Winners and Losers in Our Religious Economy* (New Brunswick, NJ: Rutgers University Press, 2005).

38. Allen D. Hertzke, *Echoes of Discontent: Jesse Jackson, Pat Robertson, and the Resurgence of Populism* (Washington, DC: CQ Press, 1993).

39. See Paul A. Djupe and Christopher P. Gilbert, *The Political Influence of Church* (New York: Cambridge University Press, 2009).

40. Ibid. See also Paul A. Djupe and Laura R. Olson, eds., *Religious Interests in Community Conflict* (Waco, TX: Baylor University Press, 2007); Aldon D. Morris, *The Origins of the Civil Rights Movement: Black Communities Organizing for Change* (New York: Free Press, 1984).

41. Fredrick C. Harris, *Something Within: Religion in African-American Political Activism* (New York: Oxford University Press, 1999); R. Drew Smith and Fredrick C. Harris, eds., *Black Churches and Local Politics: Clergy Influence, Organizational Partnerships, and Civic Empowerment* (Lanham, MD: Rowman and Littlefield, 2005).

42. Hertzke, *Echoes of Discontent.*

43. Finke and Stark, *The Churching of America*; Laurence Iannaccone, "Why Strict Churches Are Strong," *American Journal of Sociology* 99 (1994), 1180–1211; Lawrence A. Young, ed., *Rational Choice Theory and Religion: Summary and Assessment* (New York: Routledge, 1997).

44. Steve Bruce, *God Is Dead: Secularization in the West* (Oxford: Blackwell, 2002).

45. Norris and Inglehart, *Sacred and Secular*.

46. See Finke and Stark, *The Churching of America*.

APPENDIX: INTERNET RESOURCES

RELIGIOUS TRADITIONS

Roman Catholic

- U.S. Conference of Catholic Bishops, www.nccbuscc.org/.

Evangelical Protestant

- Assemblies of God, www.ag.org/top/.
- Lutheran Church—Missouri Synod, www.lcms.org/.
- Presbyterian Church in America, www.pcanet.org/.
- Seventh-day Adventists, www.sda.org/.
- Southern Baptist Convention, www.sbc.net/.

Mainline Protestant

- American Baptist Churches USA, www.abc-usa.org/.
- Episcopal Church, iamepiscopalian.org/.
- Evangelical Lutheran Church in America, www.elca.org/.
- Presbyterian Church (U.S.A.), www.pcusa.org/.
- United Church of Christ, www.ucc.org/.
- United Methodist Church, www.umc.org/.

Jewish

- Orthodox Judaism, www.ou.org/.
- Union for Reform Judaism, urj.org/.
- United Synagogue of Conservative Judaism, www.uscj.org/.

African American Protestant

- African Methodist Episcopal (AME), www.ame-today.com/.
- Church of God in Christ, www.cogic.org/.
- National Baptist Convention, USA, www.nationalbaptist.com/.

Other

- Ahmadiyya Muslim Community, www.alislam.org/.
- Baha'i, www.bahai.us/.
- Buddhism, www.buddhanet.net/.
- Church of Jesus Christ of Latter-day Saints, www.lds.org/.
- Coptic Christians, www.copts.com/english.
- Hinduism, www.iskcon.com/.
- Islamic Society of North America, www.isna.net/.
- Jehovah's Witnesses, www.watchtower.org/.
- Unitarian Universalist Association, www.uua.org/.
- Uyghur American Association, www.uyghuramerican.org

ADVOCACY GROUPS

- Adventist Development and Relief Agency International, www.adra.org/.
- American Center for Law and Justice, www.aclj.org/.
- American Friends Service Committee, www.afsc.org/.
- American Humanist Association, www.americanhumanist.org/.
- American Islamic Congress, www.aicongress.org/.
- American Israel Public Affairs Committee, www.aipac.org/.
- American Jewish Committee, www.ajc.org/.
- American Jewish Congress, www.ajcongress.org/.
- American Jewish World Service, www.ajws.org/.
- Americans United for the Separation of Church and State, au.org/.
- Anti-Defamation League, www.adl.org/.
- Baptist Joint Committee for Religious Liberty, www.bjcpa.org/.
- Becket Fund for Religious Liberty, www.becketfund.org/.
- B'nai B'rith International, www.bnaibrith.org/.
- Bread for the World, www.bread.org/.
- Catholic Conferences at the State Level, www.nasccd.org/.
- Catholic Family and Human Rights Institute, www.c-fam.org/.
- Catholic League for Religious and Civil Rights, www.catholicleague.org/.
- Catholic Mobilizing Network to End the Use of the Death Penalty, www.catholicsmobilizing.org/.
- Catholic Relief Services, www.crs.org/.
- Catholics for Choice, www.catholicsforchoice.org/.
- Catholics United, www.catholics-united.org/.

- Center of Concern, www.coc.org/.
- China Aid, www.chinaaid.org/.
- Christian Coalition of America, www.cc.org/.
- Christian Freedom International, www.christianfreedom.org/.
- Christian Legal Society, www.clsnet.org/.
- Church World Service, , www.churchworldservice.org/.
- Concerned Women for America, www.cwfa.org/.
- Culture of Life Foundation, www.culture-of-life.org/.
- Eagle Forum, www.eagleforum.org/.
- Episcopal Public Policy Network, www.episcopalchurch.org/eppn.
- Ethics and Religious Liberty Commission, www.erlc.com/.
- Evangelicals for Social Action, www.esa-online.org/.
- Faith & Reason Institute for the Study of Religion & Culture, www.frinstitute.org/.
- Faith in Public Life, faithinpubliclife.org/.
- Family Research Council, www.frc.org/.
- Focus on the Family, www.fotf.org/.
- Free Muslims Coalition, www.freemuslims.org/.
- Freedom from Religion Foundation, www.ffrf.org/.
- Habitat for Humanity, , www.habitat.org/.
- Industrial Areas Foundation, www.industrialareasfoundation.org/.
- Institute on Religion and Democracy, www.ird.org/.
- Interfaith Alliance, interfaithalliance.org/.
- Jewish Council for Public Affairs, www.jewishpublicaffairs.org/.
- Lutheran Social Services in America, , www.lutheranservices.org/.
- Maryknoll Fathers and Brothers, society.maryknoll.org/.
- Mennonite Central Committee, mcc.org/us.
- National Association of Evangelicals, www.nae.net/.
- National Council of Churches USA, www.ncccusa.org/.
- National Jewish Democratic Council, www.njdc.org/.
- National Religious Campaign Against Torture, www.nrcat.org/.
- National Right to Life Committee, www.nrlc.org/.
- People for the American Way, www.pfaw.org/.
- PICO (People Improving Communities through Organizing) National Network, www.piconetwork.org/.
- Religious Coalition for Reproductive Choice , www.rcrc.org/.
- Republican Jewish Coalition, www.rjchq.org/.
- Rutherford Institute, www.rutherford.org/.
- Secular Coalition for America, www.secular.org/.
- Sikh Council on Religion and Education, www.sikhcouncilusa.org/.
- Sojourners, www.sojo.org/.
- Traditional Values Coalition, www.traditionalvalues.org/.
- United Methodist Church General Board of Church and Society, www.umc-gbcs.org/.

INFORMATION SOURCES

- American National Election Studies, www.umich.edu/~nes/.
- Association of Religion Data Archives, www.thearda.com/.
- Barna Group, www.barna.org/.
- BeliefNet, www.beliefnet.com/.
- Hartford Institute for Religion Research, hirr.hartsem.edu/.
- Paul B. Henry Institute, www.calvin.edu/henry.
- Pew Forum on Religion & Public Life, pewforum.org/.
- *Religion & Ethics NewsWeekly*
- Religion Dispatches, www.religiondispatches.org/.
- *The Washington Post*'s "On Faith" Project, newsweek.washingtonpost.com/onfaith/.

INDEX

and Christianity, 297
clergy, 296, 308–310, 311
and conservatism, 298–299, 311
and ecofeminism, 305–306
and evangelical Protestantism, 298
and Islam, 60
Jewish, 296, 302
and Judaism, 297
and liberalism, 299–302, 311
and moral issues, 311
and new spiritualities, 297–298
ordination of, 299
in organized religion, 295–296,
    306–307
and presidential election, 2008, 297
religious (nuns), 309

voting patterns of, 297, 308, 308 (table)
    See also Feminism; Gender
Women-Church Convergence, 297, 301
World Bank, 152
World Vision, 152, 153
Wright, Wendy, 142

Yamane, David, 326
Young, Brigham, 8
Young Life, 265
Youth for Christ, 265

Zelman v. *Simmons-Harris*, 263, 266
Zobrest v. *Catalina Foothills School District*,
    261
Zorach v. *Clauson*, 258